Sustainable Consumption and the Good Life

What does it mean to live a good life in a time when the planet is overheating, the human population continues to steadily reach new peaks, oceans are turning more acidic, and fertile soils the world over are eroding at unprecedented rates? These and other simultaneous harms and threats demand creative responses at several levels of consideration and action.

Written by an international team of contributors, this book examines in-depth the relationship between sustainability and the good life. Drawing on a wealth of theories, from social practice theory to architecture and design theory, and disciplines, such as anthropology and environmental philosophy, this book promotes participatory action-research-based approaches to encourage sustainability and wellbeing at local levels. It covers topical issues such as the politics of prosperity, globalization, and indigenous notions of "the good life" and "happiness". Finally, it places a strong emphasis on food at the heart of the sustainability and good life debate, for instance binding the global south to the north through import and exports, or linking everyday lives to ideals within the dream of the good life, with cookbooks and shows.

This interdisciplinary book provides invaluable insights for researchers and postgraduate students interested in the contribution of the environmental humanities to the sustainability debate.

Karen Lykke Syse is Associate Professor at the Centre for Development and the Environment, University of Oslo, Norway.

Martin Lee Mueller is a Research Fellow at the Centre for Development and the Environment, University of Oslo, Norway.

Routledge Environmental Humanities

Series editors: Iain McCalman and Libby Robin

The *Routledge Environmental Humanities* series is an original and inspiring venture recognising that today's world agricultural and water crises, ocean pollution and resource depletion, global warming from greenhouse gases, urban sprawl, over-population, food insecurity and environmental justice are all *crises of culture*.

The reality of understanding and finding adaptive solutions to our present and future environmental challenges has shifted the epicentre of environmental studies away from an exclusively scientific and technological framework to one that depends on the human-focused disciplines and ideas of the humanities and allied social sciences.

We thus welcome book proposals from all humanities and social sciences disciplines for an inclusive and interdisciplinary series. We favour manuscripts aimed at an international readership and written in a lively and accessible style. The readership comprises scholars and students from the humanities and social sciences and thoughtful readers concerned about the human dimensions of environmental change.

Rethinking Invasion Ecologies from the Environmental Humanities
Jodi Frawley and Iain McCalman

The Broken Promise of Agricultural Progress
An environmental history
Cameron Muir

The Biosphere and the Bioregion
Essential writings of Peter Berg
Cheryll Glotfelty and Eve Quesnel

Sustainable Consumption and the Good Life
Interdisciplinary perspectives
Edited by Karen Lykke Syse and Martin Lee Mueller

'Unlimited growth has not only damaged the biosphere, but also disrupted solidarity and cohesion within and between human groups. *Sustainable Consumption and the Good Life* presents and questions various adaptations to the environmental crises. The book is timely as it challenges and reframes issues of consumption and well-being to meet the demands of an overheating planet.'

Peder Anker, New York University, USA

'Living well is an aspiration freighted with environmental, economic and ethical import. It pulses through contemporary society, just as it did the ancient world. In this book, affirmative responses are found to critical questions about new designs for life, always mindful of twenty-first century challenges. It gives us insights into how consumptive habits can become more just and wise, as well as answerable to needs and relations scaled from the personal to the planetary. In these pages, our own reckoning is identified as the means for a powerful reawakening.'

Hayden Lorimer, University of Glasgow, UK

Sustainable Consumption and the Good Life

Interdisciplinary perspectives

Edited by
Karen Lykke Syse and
Martin Lee Mueller

Taylor & Francis Group

LONDON AND NEW YORK

from Routledge

First published 2015 by Routledge

2 Park Square, Milton Park, Abingdon, Oxon OX14 4RN
711 Third Avenue, New York, NY 10017, USA

Routledge is an imprint of the Taylor & Francis Group, an informa business

First issued in paperback 2016

British Library Cataloguing-in-Publication Data
A catalogue record for this book is available from the British Library

Library of Congress Cataloging-in-Publication Data
A catalog record for this book has been requested

ISBN: 978-1-138-01300-1 (hbk)
ISBN: 978-1-138-21246-6 (pbk)

Typeset in Goudy
by Keystroke, Station Road, Codsall, Wolverhampton

Contents

List of figures and tables

Figures

Tables

List of contributors

Kristian Bjørkdahl, Rokkan Centre for Social Studies, Uni Research, Bergen

Bengt Brülde, University of Gothenburg

Lawrence Buell, Harvard University/Centre for Development and the Environment, University of Oslo

Thorunn Gullaksen Endreson, Centre for Development and the Environment, University of Oslo

Thomas Hylland Eriksen, University of Oslo

Mònica Guillen-Royo, Centre for Development and the Environment, University of Oslo

Ottar Hellevik, University of Oslo

Martin Lee Mueller, Centre for Development and the Environment, University of Oslo

Ines Omann, Helmholtz Centre for Environmental Research, Leipzig

Jesper Pagh, Department of Environmental, Social and Spatial Change, Roskilde University, Copenhagen

Felix Rauschmayer, Helmholtz Centre for Environmental Research, Leipzig

Kate Soper, London Metropolitan University

Karen Lykke Syse, Centre for Development and the Environment, University of Oslo

Harold Wilhite, Centre for Development and the Environment, University of Oslo

Tanja Winther, Centre for Development and the Environment, University of Oslo

Introduction

Karen Lykke Syse and Martin Lee Mueller

What does it mean to live a good life in a time when the planet is overheating, the human population continues to steadily reach new peaks, oceans are turning more acidic, and fertile soils the world over are eroding at unprecedented rates? These and other simultaneous harms and threats demand creative responses at several levels of consideration and action. Drawing on the expertise from an inter-disciplinary pool of contributors from the United States, the United Kingdom, Germany, Catalonia/Spain, Denmark, Sweden, and Norway, this book explores the convergence between sustainability issues, consumption practice and ideas of the good life in both the global north and south. While the number of people suffering from hunger or malnutrition has stagnated at around 1 billion, as many as 3 billion people in the world today suffer from overweight and obesity (Ng et al., 2014). Although worldwide hunger, malnutrition, and famine have not yet been fully overcome, people in both the north and south now enjoy unpre-cedented levels of wealth. An increasing number of people all over the world are enjoying higher life expectancy, and according to an OECD working paper, by 2030 the global middle class is expected to grow from under 2 billion consumers today to nearly 5 billion (Kharas, 2010). In what has traditionally been called the West, large numbers of people have lived in material affluence for many decades. This affluence has led to consumption practices which – if maintained by the global middle classes – will far exceed the limits of our planet. But are Western levels of consumption the necessary means to happiness? Discontent lingers even while growth accelerates, and this discontent expresses itself in the revitalisation of an ancient notion – namely that the good life is lived in proximity to nature, and is not dependent on material wealth above a certain level of necessity and comfort. Happiness is closely correlated with possibilities to reconnect the sphere of humans, somehow, with the larger living world. This sense to reconnect finds practical and creative expressions in a multitude of ways – from farmers' markets, transition towns, the slow food movement, to nature writing, urban gardening, the rural renaissance, décroissance, the growth of green movements, and a general focus on ecological issues throughout society. All of these can be interpreted as signs that many find the promises of modernity – the trinity of progress, growth, and happiness through material wealth – unfulfilling. Unlimited progress and growth have turned out to ravage the biosphere, but also to disrupt solidarity and cohesion within and between human groups, leaving either in various states of fragmentation and disruption.

Research on happiness determinants, for instance, has shown that the promotion and use of local orchards, community gardens, allotments, and guerrilla gardening have a positive effect on people's physical and psychological well-being (Abraham et al., 2010). This supports well-established findings that money plays a marginal role for people's well-being above a certain threshold, and that personal and social relationships, employment, and relative status are more significant determinants for good living than wealth (see the contributions of Ottar Hellevik and Thomas Hylland Eriksen in this collection). Moreover, human-needs research indicates that sustainability and human flourishing are interlinked, and that aspects of a society, its people, and spaces that satisfy needs also need to foster sustainability.

According to Epicurus, 'philosophy is an activity, which, through discourse and reasoning, procures for us a happy life' (Comte-Sponville, 2011:xvii). Philosophers from Aristotle to Martha Nussbaum have striven to answer what a good life ought to entail. According to Nussbaum, 'certain functions are particularly central in human life, in the sense that their presence or absence is typically understood to be a mark of the presence or absence of human life' (Nussbaum, 2011:18). Nussbaum has compiled a list of such central functions: life, bodily health, bodily integrity, senses, imagination and thought, emotions, practical reason, affiliation, relationship with other species (animals, plants, and nature), play, and finally control over one's environment. A number of contributors to this volume are affiliated with the Centre for Development and the Environment at the University of Oslo, formerly the academic home of the renowned ecophilosopher and mountaineer Arne Næss. Having himself spent many years on his beloved mountain, Hallingskarvet, Næss summed up the benefits of simple, good living in proximity to the wild outdoors in his memorable catchphrase 'simple in means, rich in ends'. It is a notion which Kate Soper takes up for further discussion in her contribution to this collection. In this book, we step beyond the disciplinary boundaries of philosophy to also encompass the humanities and social sciences, so as to explore ways in which less, or qualitatively different, consumption can be a path to both sustainability and the good life. We draw on contributions from a variety of disciplinary approaches to explore various inter-related aspects of the phenomenon and the recent recurrence of the motif of living well. Although both sustainability and consumption issues have been thoroughly studied by social sciences and to a certain degree by the humanities, the triple helix of sustainability, consumption, and the good life has yet to be explored.

Why do we entertain a wish to bring the three concepts into conversation with one another? Arguably, in doing so, a certain amount of tension arises. Unsustainable consumption can in some cases be the means to an end which is a materialistic interpretation of the good life, while other ways of exploring the concept show that leading a good life can be both ends and means to less consumption and more awareness of sustainability issues. A way of solving the dilemma might have been to ask all the authors to use the term 'well-being' rather than 'the good life', as 'well-being' is relatively easier to define and limit. However, we have chosen the more overarching and inclusive term, which has allowed us to broaden the scope of our inquiry. 'The good life' calls forth associations, next to many others, with glossy magazines, TV-shows, growing one's own vegetables, wining and dining, and staying healthy, happy, and energetic. As such, the term has an air of lightness and playfulness, unlike the more technical 'well-being'. But as Yi-Fu Tuan remarks, 'if life is to be truly good the playful thrust must be anchored in respect for truth and in a reflexive awareness in one's own mortality' (1986:11). When we cross-pollinate 'sustainability' with 'the good life', the question of the good life becomes thoroughly anchored not only in our own mortality, but in the mortality of the Earth itself.

That the good life entails a certain retreat to or reconnection with nature is well established in the humanities. When Livy tells the classical story of the Rise of Rome, he also describes a theme which still runs thick in Western thought: the concept of the good life in the country. Horatius the warrior has become a war hero and has done his duty to Rome. He then leaves the town and public life, and retires to his house in the country in pursuit of a simpler, more meaningful life (Livius and Luce, 1998). Livy not only describes a tradition of retiring to the country, he also starts a literary tradition of describing a life close to nature as intrinsically good. In present-day literary studies, ecocriticism has been the main avenue within which the motif of the sustainable good life has been investigated at some depth. Since Leo Marx's *The Machine in the Garden* (1964), ecocritics have been engaged with sustainability issues. There are two ecocritical contributions in this volume: Lawrence Buell, in Chapter 1, argues that the fruits of a thriving literary and ethical imagination spanning the past two centuries are crucial to diagnosing and solving the challenges of sustainability and the good life. He develops a layered argument spanning the individual level (discussing the practice of voluntary simplicity), the community level (concerning bioregional citizenship), and the national and international levels (being the arenas for distributive justice). Thorunn Gullaksen Endreson, in Chapter 2, also looks at the role of literature and sustainability. As ecological crises are often met with dystopian narratives of gloom and doom, she explores whether utopian narratives might prove to speak more compellingly and persuasively than narratives of looming disasters. Utopian narratives may, under the right historic, cultural, and personal conditions, turn out to be transforming reading experiences. Only by actually envisioning that we have a future can we start mobilising towards that future, and the path to this sustainable future does not need to be frugal in every sense. In fact, the philosopher Kate Soper argues, in Chapter 3, that alternative hedonism can open up a post-consumerist approach to human flourishing, one which avoids both the simplistic assessments of need and the authoritarian tendencies of earlier critiques of commodification. She also discusses how thinking about pleasure and human well-being offers a way through the tensions between the more subjective and utilitarian, and the more objective Aristotelian philosophies of happiness and the 'politics of prosperity'.

Moving from qualitative philosophy to quantitative sociology, Ottar Hellevik analyses, in Chapter 4, the relationship between values, subjective quality of life, and sustainability, using data spanning the period between 1985 and 2011, gathered through broad biannual surveys carried out in Norway. He shows how a value dimension opposing materialistic and idealistic values is strongly correlated with happiness and satisfaction with life, as well as with attitudes towards ecological protection, redistribution of wealth, and support for the welfare state. His work implies that an idealistic idea of the good life is superior to a materialistic one, both with regard to subjective quality of life and with regard to support for sustainable policies and practices. Hellevik's chapter provides a thorough empirical foundation which supports the claim that money can't buy happiness, and that whatever we mean when we speak of 'the good life', we cannot have a full understanding of it unless we transcend the narrow bounds of materialistic concerns. Yet moving back to philosophy, Bengt Brülde argues, in Chapter 5, that our happiness actually would be affected if we adopted a more sustainable lifestyle, and concludes that most people would probably be somewhat *less* happy if they lived more sustainably – at least in the short run. Brülde suggests that we should not appeal to people's self-interest if we want them to make more ecologically responsible choices, but to moral considerations. Juxtaposing these two chapters is interesting, as they approach the question of the good life from two different angles and disciplines. Is making a moral choice about acting in an ecologically responsible way simply an individual choice? This takes us to reductionist assumptions about consumers and the socio-material contexts of choice. The anthropologist Harold Wilhite asks us, in Chapter 6, to consider how energy-intensive habits have been shaped in the West, and further to consider the way such habits have shown themselves to be starkly resistant to rapid change. Cultural learning, repetitive actions, and purposive training all help shape, and harden, habits. In order to reduce consumption footprints to levels necessary to halt further meddling with the already changing climate, the deeply seated links between consumption, economic progress, and well-being will need to be broken and reformed.

In Chapter 7, Felix Rauschmayer and Ines Omann also explore issues of everyday life. They show how the strategies we implement neither necessarily realise all our needs nor concord with our values, and that tensions occur in our daily life and even more in sustainability transitions. They propose a four-step process, suggesting that working with these tensions may lead to a more sustainable and high-quality life. The topic of well-being and sustainability is also the concern of Mònica Guillen-Royo in Chapter 8. Using a framework called Human Scale Development and action-research design, she discusses the processes and outcomes of a sustainable development project undertaken in a municipality in the Peruvian Andes. Guillen-Royo shows how communities can improve both the well-being of their members and the conditions of their bioregions in which they dwell, thus contradicting traditional arguments which suggest that there is a conflict between the interests of present and future generations when defining sustainable development interventions.

Staying within the global south in Chapter 9, Tanja Winther provides an anthropological account of the rising electricity consumption in rural Zanzibar and discusses electricity's uses – and non-uses – in the light of people's perceptions and experiences of the good life. How do people who have not had access to unlimited amounts of energy and consumer items respond when such items are introduced to their community? Winther's study contrasts two areas of consumption – television and food. In an early phase, television sets were exclusive objects of desire and considered socially dangerous, but they soon became normalised. After a while, the shared consumption of television programmes formed part of good living, signifying 'development' and 'progress'. In contrast, Zanzibaris kept their food at a distance from electricity. Food nonetheless continued to be associated with the good life, underscoring rural Zanzibaris' sense of belonging.

Food touches on fundamental and metaphysical questions of how we relate to each other and the world – there is a good reason why Jack Goody's book summing up his lifelong research in the field of development and anthropology is called *Food and Love* (1998). Food is a cross-cutting topic that glues the global south to the north through global food systems, and it cements everyday lives to ideals and concepts within the dream of the good life, as Karen Lykke Syse explores in Chapter 10. Here she casts a look at celebrity chefs encouraging people to reconnect to nature by re-establishing the links between animals and meat, or vegetable plots and ratatouille. New venues for consumption both of food and food culture have evolved, and the creative force that drives such alternative consumption – or, to use Kate Soper's term, such alternative hedonism – is the urge to craft ways of consuming that are less damaging to, or even beneficial for, the planet.

But clearly, bridging concerns of sustainability successfully with those of consumption is a great theoretical and practical challenge, as we see illustrated in Chapter 11. Food halls and market places have become part of city planning, and notions about sustainable places and spaces do not always materialise in the way they were intended to at the idea stage. Jesper Pagh presents the newly opened Torvehallerne market in Copenhagen as a central case in this respect, and discusses how a performative turn within food consumption, a longing for the good life, and the need to belong to a community have created new political-economic situations for urban design and development. This has in turn led to an increased privatisation of public space under the cover of urban regeneration and thoughtful planning for the common good. With an outset in architecture and design theory and history, Pagh discusses the commodification of architecture in recent decades, and the ways in which architects – though envisioning the good life in sustainable cities – in this respect serve to propagate, rather than undermine, a neoliberal agenda in contemporary urban planning.

In Chapter 12, Kristian Bjørkdahl explores another physical space. When the battery cage was first introduced, ideas of industrialised egg production went against the grain of all established wisdom about hens and their welfare. Previously it was held that a happy hen was a hen living out its natural inclinations, but with the arrival of the battery cage, the industry shifted focus towards productivity and absence of disease – as if hens were 'animal machines'. When the

EU's ban on battery cages went into effect, the industry thus enacted a new evasion strategy: instead of talking about hens' productivity, they now started talking about the cages – replacing 'bare' cages with 'enriched' ones. Bjørkdahl's contribution unveils newspeak used to cover up the fact that issues of welfare and well-being for both animals and humans is not something to be taken for granted.

In Chapter 13, Martin Lee Mueller casts a light on another case of industrial animal husbandry: the salmon farming industry. Mueller brings out its anthropocentric bias and its die-hard fixation with Cartesian thought. Taking up a critique begun in Bjørkdahl's piece, this biophilic chapter makes a case against seeing animals as 'mere machines', and for recognising life's innate interconnectedness, diversity, and co-dependence. Our particularly human lives, Mueller writes, unfold within the larger, richly diverse more-than-human community that is the living Earth itself. The implication is that only by acting in ways that respect this larger context of our own lives can we secure a good life – or indeed any life at all – both for those currently dwelling on the Earth, and for those not yet born.

Finally, Thomas Hylland Eriksen provides us with an Afterword, wryly comparing members of affluent societies with the big bad wolf, suffering from a hangover: overfed and woozy, we lounge around wondering what to do next. Eriksen provides provocative comments, a few questions, and thankfully, some direction. He claims that the good life, and the good society, is not the same as affluence and longevity, and that a global collective project is needed to meet the demands of an overheating planet. This book may provide a modest contribution to such a collective project. It gives a glimpse both of the vastness of the undertaking, the height of the stakes, but also of the creative energy already being applied – across disciplines, across the academia-public divide – to asking, with sustained zeal, what it means to imagine and indeed create a good life, given the realities of a plundered planet.

References

Abraham, A., Sommerhalder, K. and Abel, T. (2010) 'Landscape and well-being: a scoping study on the health-promoting impact of outdoor environments' in *International Journal of Public Health*, 55. pp. 59–69.
Comte-Sponville, A. (2011) *The Little Book Of Philosophy*. London: Random House.
Goody, J. (1998) *Food and Love: A Cultural History of East and West*. London – New York: Verso.
Kharas, H. (2010) *The Emerging Middle Class in Developing Countries*. Paris: OECD Development Centre.
Livius, T. and Luce, T.J. (1998) *Ab urbe condita, Liber 1-5*. Oxford: Oxford University Press.
Marx, L. (1964) *The Machine in the Garden. Technology and the Pastoral Ideal in America*. New York: Oxford University Press.
Ng, M. et al. (2014) 'Global, regional, and national prevalence of overweight and obesity in children and adults during 1980–2013: a systematic analysis for the Global Burden of Disease Study 2013' in *The Lancet*.
Nussbaum, M.C. (2011) *Creating Capabilities*. Cambridge, MA: Harvard University Press.
Tuan, Y.-F. (1986) *The Good Life*. Madison, WI: University of Wisconsin Press.

1 Enough is enough?

Re-imagining an ethics and aesthetics of sustainability for the twenty-first century

Lawrence Buell

'Sustainability' and 'the good life' are both very elastic terms – *so* elastic as to raise suspicions of bad faith.[1] On one hand, what many consider the 'good life' is ecologically unsustainable. On the other hand, 'sustainability' has a bad history of being co-opted as a euphemism in order to justify a degree of economic development only a little less bad than worst-case exploitation. Such has been the ambiguous legacy of the landmark 1987 Brundtland report, *Our Common Future*, as the eminent Norwegian environmental philosopher and activist Arne Næss (2008:294–297) was one of the first to foresee. If we hope to be good earth citizens, then we must narrow down what counts as the good life to practices that would enable and further ecological sustainability and narrow down 'sustainability' to mean an order of existence better than the *status quo*: one that would conduce to and insofar as possible optimize the flourishing of human beings together with that of nonhuman life and planetary health generally. Næss's admonition could not be more telling: 'a *development* is ecologically sustainable if and only if there is a long-term trend that ensures, or that may justifiably be considered to ensure, ecological sustainability' (2008:298).

Within these normative bounds I shall venture some reflections about 'enoughness', both at the level of personal ethics and at various social levels. Given the nature of the subject, this discussion will perforce be more exploratory than prescriptive and more idealistic than pragmatic, suggesting pathways far easier to commend in principle than to realize in practice. As I do, readers will quickly perceive my disciplinary bias as an environmental humanist, a bias that I seek to turn to advantage here, however. For I maintain that literature and other expressive arts – by reason of their power to rivet attention and to motivate through narrative, image and symbol – have a much more significant role to play in identifying and combatting today's environmental crises than is usually recognized.

The impediments to bridging the gap between notional value and behavioural practice begin with the divergences in understanding of 'enoughness' among persons and across societies and historical epochs. These differences in turn are influenced by judgement calls about many specific ethico-environmental factors such as proper standard of living, proper balance of work and leisure, level of resource consumption possible without exhausting supply, and so on.

It is hardly surprising, therefore, to find philosophers drawing the line very differently when defining the standard of material enoughness necessary to the good life. In Aristotle's *Nicomachean Ethics*, the good life – for male citizens, that is – presupposes a certain affluence, a certain surplus of assets: because, he writes, 'it is impossible or at least not easy to perform noble actions if one lacks the wherewithal' (1962:21; I.1099a). Whereas for the Stoic Epictetus the proper 'measure of possession' is minimum bodily need: 'If you go beyond its fitness to the foot', he warns, the shoe 'comes first to be gilded, then purple, then studded with jewels. For to that which once exceeds the fit measure there is no limit' (1944:347).

In modernity, the dominant tendency has of course not only been more Aristotelian than Stoic but also to go far beyond the moderation Aristotle elsewhere counsels. 'What is "enough"?' asks E. F. Schumacher in *Small is Beautiful*:

> Who can tell us? Certainly not the economist who pursues "economic growth" as the highest of all values, and therefore has no concept of "enough." There are poor societies which have too little; but where is the rich country that says: "Halt! We have enough?" There is none.
>
> (1973:25)

Schumacher wrote those words 40 years ago, and they are even truer today. No rich country, indeed only one country worldwide, meets the UN Human Development Index's criteria for both sufficient human well-being and sufficiently light 'ecological footprint': Cuba.[2]

Not that the wealthy countries of the world should rush to imitate the Cubans. The point is simply that the world at large has a grave ethics of sustainability problem. In a thoughtful assessment of the ethics of enoughness at the personal level, Robert and Edward Sidalsky – a British father–son team of economist and philosopher – make the same claim about intrinsic human nature that Schumacher makes about societies. Human 'material wants know no natural bounds'; 'they will expand without end unless we consciously restrain them' (2012:69).

The Sidalskys are too anthropocentric to say anything very useful about environmental ethics *per se*. But that does not lessen the relevance for our purposes of their historical diagnosis that the inherent human susceptibility to immoderation has been aggravated in modernity. As they see it, a crucial unintended consequence of scientific and industrial revolution was an ethical paradigm shift. During the nineteenth century, they argue, this led to a fetishization of economic growth that still persists as the key measure of social well-being and, concomitantly, to the displacement of traditional sufficiency-based models of the good life by an ethos of ceaseless striving after progress and improvement.

Against this, the Sidalskys offer a counter-model to the bad ethics of progress-first: seven basic requisites of the good life, in the following order of importance: health, security, respect, personality (that is, a sense of inward freedom), 'harmony with nature', 'friendship' and 'leisure' (ibid.:165). This recipe of ingredients is certainly worth consideration. My chief interest here, however, is not in such 'bottom-line' seven-step solutions, but in frameworks and fundamentals. For an environmental humanist, the importance of *Small is Beautiful* and *How Much is Enough?* lies especially in the failure of modern ethical imagination, individual and collective, that they both describe. This failure requires value transformations on three interlocking levels, which if seriously undertaken by a critical mass of people might bring about all else. These are: voluntary simplicity at the individual level, bioregional mindfulness at the subnational level and ecosocial equity at the national and international levels. In what follows, I shall take up each in turn.

Voluntary simplicity

The question of enoughness arguably starts with individual persons, especially those with the freedom and means to make discretionary choices. If a large number of well-off people, in the rich world especially, made a concerted effort to consume less and manage with less stuff, planetary health would surely benefit.

Voluntary simplicity (VS) is an ethos towards which many more are attracted than can justly boast of having achieved, however. I cannot deny living in a single-family home in a prosperous suburb, notwithstanding the distinct remembrance of passionately agreeing with my best friend in youth that the curse of life was superfluous property. But I take consolation knowing I am not alone. The prominent American poet-essayist and agricultural reformer, Wendell Berry, rightly insists that: 'A protest meeting on the issue of environmental abuse is . . . a convocation of the guilty'. (1972:74). The protesters themselves are inevitably more or less complicit in the wrongs they decry. So too with a forum on VS at a Western research university. Many, if not most, of the participants who are sympathetic to the VS as an ideal are likely to prove reluctant, when put to the test, to adjust their lifestyles more than a limited degree in accordance with it. In a late 1990s poll of American attitudes towards materialism, 83 per cent of those responding agreed that the US consumes too much and a still higher percentage agreed that 'protecting the environment will require "major changes in the way we live"', but only 28 per cent claimed they themselves had voluntarily made lifestyle changes in accordance within the past five years (UNEP). I suspect that the same poll would yield quite similar results today. Such has long been the nature of what might be called 'environmental doublethink'.

A certain slippage between professed values and behaviour is only to be expected. Such has no doubt been the case universally and for all time. The prophets of the great world religions stood for a degree of self-restraint that institutionalized Confucianism, Christianity and Buddhism have never matched. In the secular arena, US history offers perhaps a particularly egregious case insofar as American promise has for centuries been linked both to striking it rich and to the dream of a purified social order. As the American historian David Shi writes, the dream of the simple life – Puritan, Quaker, Shaker, Transcendentalist, etc. – took hold in early colonial times and remains deeply embedded in national culture, but it also has a way of 'becoming enmeshed in its opposite' even while serving 'as the nation's conscience', and 'thereby providing a vivifying counter-point to the excesses of materialist individualism'. 'The simple life', he predicts, 'will persist both as an enduring myth and as an actual way of living' (1985: 277–279), but with no guarantee that any one movement will endure for long.

Indeed, there is good reason to worry about worsening trend lines in the contemporary US, of accelerated techno-social change depleting planetary natural resources and a widening gap between haves and have-nots.[3] These have been aggravated by the entrenchment of the conjoined assumptions that economic growth is the key to well-being and that mass consumption is crucial to that growth process. The 'Consumer Republic', as historian Lizbeth Cohen aptly calls the American variant of that persuasion, seems actually to have been born during the Great Depression, although it did not really take off until the broad-based boom in national prosperity after World War II, which devastated the economies of all other major world powers and put the US in a uniquely advantageous competitive position for the next several decades. The consumer republic 'promised the socially progressive end of economic equality' (Cohen 2003:118) – unfortunately without establishing adequate 'means of redistributing existing wealth' (ibid.:129), the temporizing argument among policy-makers and legislators being that 'an ever growing economy built around the dynamics of increased productivity and mass purchasing power would expand the overall pie without reducing the size of any of the portions' (ibid.:401). Although this grand vision looks less credible today, Cohen rightly points out that 'patriotic shopping' continues to get held up in the twenty-first century as a distraction from foreign wars and as a remedy for recessions, despite recurring worry that the US and many European countries are spending beyond their means.[4]

Meanwhile, however, the valuation of economic prosperity itself as a measure of well-being has been increasingly questioned by economists and psychologists as well as ethicists. Does more money really make people happier? The unsur-prising answer seems to be that although every society's haves are happier than its have-nots, 'extra income increases happiness less and less as people get richer' (Layard 2005:230).[5] On a 2005 life-satisfaction poll, the cohort of 'Forbes richest Americans' rated only slightly above groups of 'Traditional Masai' tribesmen and of Pennsylvania Amish farming communities (cf. Biswas-Diener 2008:314). That the Masai and the Amish, whose ecological footprints are so much smaller than the billionaires, claim to feel so good – relatively speaking – seems a strong *prima facie* argument for simplicity as a corrective to the prodigalities of affluence.

VS as a self-conscious persuasion by that name, arose in the US as a counter-weight to the Consumer Republic idea. Social philosopher Richard Gregg, a Gandhi admirer and nonviolence advocate, coined the term in a 1936 pamphlet written, he wrote, against 'Henry Ford's idea that civilization progresses by the increase in the number of people's desires and their satisfaction'. (1936:4–5). Gregg would keep consumption within bounds by propagating an ethic of 'singleness of purpose, sincerity and honesty within [and] avoidance of exterior clutter, of many possessions irrelevant to the chief purpose of life' (ibid.:25).

Gregg knew that he did not invent the ethic he describes. He cites many precedents ancient and modern – Moses, Buddha and Gandhi among them. Of the *American* precursor whom Gandhi himself would have cited, however, Gregg curiously makes no mention: Henry David Thoreau. That Thoreau could matter much more to Gandhi than to Gandhi's disciple Gregg can ironically be traced to Thoreau's own mentor Ralph Waldo Emerson. In late Victorian Britain, admiration for Thoreau as a progressive thinker in matters of politics, diet and general lifestyle was nurtured by the radical intelligentsia whom the young Gandhi met there, whereas the stateside vision of Thoreau that dominated until the mid-twentieth century was the image made famous by Emerson's remembrance of him as a standoffish person who could be admired only with a shudder, because 'the severity of his ideal interfered to deprive him of a healthy sufficiency of human society' (1903–4:479).

What this image blocks out is restored by sociologist Robert Wuthnow's enlistment of Thoreau in a perceptive book about traditions of moral restraint embedded in the American version of the Protestant work ethic. Wuthnow distinguishes two such strands, which he calls 'ascetic moralism' and 'expressive moralism' (1996:340). Both, he rightly claims, still persist, although in attenuated form. The first operates according to a 'fixed set of morally prescribed rules of behavior' (ibid.:72) that regulate it. The second operates from the quest for modes of work fulfilling to the spirit. Wuthnow classifies Thoreau as a type-two expressive moralist.

Emerson of course knew Thoreau intimately and Wuthnow only through his writings. But Wuthnow is the better guide to the spirit of Thoreau's *Walden* (1971[1854]) – his most influential book, and today a classic of American literature well-known worldwide. This philosophical reminiscence of the author's two-year homesteading experiment sets forth its programme of simplifying the terms of existence to the bare essentials, not as austerity for its own sake but to optimize the possibility of human flourishing. Thoreau seeks to persuade us that 'to sustain one's self on this earth is not a hardship but a pastime, if we will live simply and wisely' (1971[1854]:70). Even more fundamental than his dictum 'simplify, simplify, simplify' is what he calls living 'deliberately'. By this Thoreau means a slowing-down of the tempo of life to the point that mind and senses become attuned to extract the maximum of aesthetic pleasure and heightened consciousness from each moment, from sunrise to sunset and beyond, so that even 'the faint hum of a mosquito making its invisible and unimaginable tour through my apartment at earliest dawn when I was sitting with doors and windows open' (ibid.:89–90) finds its place in a ritual of awakening experienced as intensely meaningful. Countless touches of this kind make *Walden* a testament to the pleasures of what today American gurus and bloggers on VS call 'downshifting'.

A better example from Thoreau's day of 'ascetic moralism', Wuthnow's type-one, is a book about to go into its 33rd printing as *Walden* went to press: a tract called *The American Frugal Housewife*, by Lydia Maria Child (1835). It too is much admired today in American VS circles, rivalling even *Walden*. The two books resemble each other in their vigilant attachment to small things and overlooked moments in daily life. But Child prizes frugality as an ethical goal in itself rather than as a pathway to intellectual or aesthetic refinement, declaring at the outset:

> Nothing should be thrown away so long as it is possible to make any use of it, however trifling that use may be; and whatever the size of a family, every member should be employed either in earning or saving money.
>
> (1835:3)

The justification of thrift, efficiency and living simply is that it's the right way to be.

But is VS of either kind still possible in the urbanized, high-tech world of today? Yes it is. Here are two examples, one ascetic and the other expressive. In 1977, former professor Charles Gray decided at the age of 52 that the 'crisis of late Twentieth century humanity' demanded that he live within what he considered the 'World Equity Budget' – that is, his proportional share of 'the world's total [dollar] income' – which he reckoned to be $142 per month (Gray 1995:98–100). That demanded a far more drastic lifestyle change than anything Thoreau or Child underwent. It immediately cost him his marriage and plunged him into loneliness and depression until he found ways to adjust. But he kept to it at least until the time of his writing nearly 20 years later.

A less drastic but equally suggestive case is written up in Colin Beavan's book *No Impact Man* (2009; see also his blog, Beavan n.d.). A couple in their early forties with an infant daughter commit to a one-year experiment in incremental downscaling from their NYC apartment base: first take the stairs, not the elevator, and walk everywhere rather than drive or ride; then reduce trash to zero including no more Styrofoam and disposable diapers; then eat only food as local as possible, grown within 250 miles at most; then reduce electricity use to the bare minimum and depend as much as possible on a rooftop solar energy device. Although sometimes annoyingly self-promotional, Beavan delivers in the long run a persuasive account of eco-responsible negotiation of metropolitan living – and how his family of three found new and unexpected satisfactions from that experience.

More questionable about VS initiatives of whatever kind than feasibility is how far they go towards addressing large-scale problems of overconsumption and maldistribution of the resources.[6] The personal-integrity-first approach more or less endemic to VS ethics is a particularly problematic roadblock. Thoreau's great political essay 'Civil Disobedience' praises heroic individual acts of conscience in disentangling the self from the state; but it took Gandhi and Martin Luther King to convert that vision into a movement. To be sure, some personal initiatives do have potential for immediate broader social impact – like Austrian millionaire Karl Rabeder's 2010 commitment to donate his whole fortune to a microcredit nonprofit for small entrepreneurs in Latin America and 'move into a small wooden hut in the mountains or a studio in Innsbruck' (Neilan 2010). Far less dramatic but potentially even more important if practiced on a large scale would be some version of the kind of voluntary transference of wealth proposed by philosopher Peter Singer:

that anyone who has enough money to spend on the luxuries and frivolities so common in affluent societies should give at least 1 cent in every dollar of their income to those who have trouble getting enough to eat, clean water to drink, shelter from the elements, and basic health care.

(2002:194)

Indeed, Singer's proposed voluntarism (uncharacteristically for that notoriously pugnacious advocate of animal rights) is arguably much more modest than it needs or deserves to be. I suspect that few, if any, in the top 5–10 per cent income bracket of household income worldwide would find it much of a sacrifice to donate to the purposes Singer itemizes an amount at least equal to that which they spend on all forms of entertainment annually – recreational travel, artistic and sports events, restaurant meals, etc.

Still, it remains a serious question whether philanthropy or even significant personal economic sacrifice at the individual level stands a chance of making a more than modest contribution towards remediation of today's crises of global inequity and environmental sustainability. As the French philosopher Michel Serres observes in another context, generally if not invariably individual action 'has as much effect on the world as a butterfly in the Australian desert' – that is, 'except for the rarest of exceptions – nil' (1995:19).

Altogether, then, VS seems a necessary but insufficient constituent of a robust enoughness ethics, especially given the social pressures exerted upon the lone individual anywhere. Differential of socialization doubtless goes a long way towards explaining not only first-world habits of overconsumption but also why the Masai and the Amish are so content. We also need feasible alternative models for *collective* sustainable living above and beyond individually chosen redirections of lifestyle.

Place-based communities, utopian or otherwise, that attempt to subsist within the ecological constraints of the spaces they occupy are perhaps the most obvious place to look. One example of a fairly large and growing initiative of this kind in contemporary times is the movement known in North America as bioregionalism.

Bioregionalism

Bioregionalism potentially corrects against VS's person-first emphasis by conceiving individuals as embedded within mutually cooperating communities that hope to sustain themselves through time insofar as possible in deference to the ecological limits of their physical environments.[7] 'A fully developed bioregionalism', as one representative assessment puts it, 'favours a planetary diversity of place-based bioregional economics conservatively and carefully producing and consuming primarily for their own populations' needs', with 'local communities of place . . . networked at broader geographical scales from the local watershed and larger regional watersheds to the continental scale' (Carr 2004:3, 49). As this latter stipulation suggests, the geographical dimensions of a bioregion are seen as being set on the one hand ecosystemically by 'natural' boundaries like watersheds or drainage basins and on the other hand by the collective memory of the inhabitants, rather than by cartographic or jurisdictional fiat. In principle, then, they are defined more from the ground up than the top down. As such, bioregions are both natural and cultural constructs, inasmuch as place-attachment presupposes a fusion of physiographic givens and communal experience.

The term bioregionalism dates only from the 1970s. Ernest Callenbach's *Ecotopia* (1975), a futuristic novel that presupposes the secession of the Pacific region north of San Francisco to Washington from the rest of the US, was perhaps the most attention-getting expression of its spirit at the time. But as with VS, bioregionalism's underlying vision has much older and more eclectic roots. To a considerable extent it boils down to an updated, more environmental sustainability conscious attempt to recuperate selected now-endangered traits of preindustrial society and economy – e.g. continuity of life in place, local self-sufficiency, and communal interdependence – such that one finds a considerable degree of resonance between North American-style formulations of bioregionalism and semi-idealized recollection of the dispensation of premodern land-based solidarity in urbanized and urbanizing societies everywhere, from Norway to China. The writings of the two most prominent advocates among senior American bioregional literati bear this out: sustainable agriculture advocate Wendell Berry and poet-critic Gary Snyder.

Berry's many books trace bioregional ethics back through cultural history from the grasp of local knowledge shown by the self-sufficient religiocentric agrarian communities scattered throughout his part of the American Midwest, to nineteenth-century Anglo-European provincial writers like Thomas Hardy (whose country of the imagination was the author's home district of southwest England), to Thomas Jefferson's vision of the US as a nation of self-sufficient small farmers, to the georgic tradition that dates to classical antiquity. For Snyder, the compelling precedents are *non*-Western: classical Chinese and Japanese sages of Taoism and Zen, and Native American placed-based culture-ways. Roughly speaking, Snyder leans towards Wuthnow's 'expressive' pole, celebrating the cultural/aesthetic richness of multi-ethnic citizenship within the watershed, whereas Berry leans towards the 'ascetic' pole, piously reminding his audiences of the need for the 'little economy' of secular human life to conform itself to the 'Great' economy, meaning for him the principles of ecological sustainability that to him are nothing less than the outward and visible manifestation of the law of God (1987:54–75).[8]

In all versions of bioregionalism, personhood is conceived socially rather than atomistically; the claims of collective life in place take precedence over individual desires. And in most versions, productive labour that involves intimate inter-action with the material environment – farming, subsistence hunting, building – is accorded higher intrinsic value than for VS ethics. For some, specifically ecological labour is *the* core vision, as with Wes Jackson's Land Institute in Salina, Kansas, which seeks 'to develop an agricultural system with the ecological stability of the prairie and a grain yield comparable to [conventionally-grown] annual crops' (Land Institute n.d.).

Where bioregionalism and VS converge is their shared understanding of sustenance worthy of the name as furthered rather than compromized by conscienceful restraint. As Berry puts it, communitarian, place-based stewardship asks us 'to . . . need less, to care more for the needs of others. We must understand what the health of the earth requires, and we must put that before all other needs' (1977:65–66). The result, he insists, will be 'poorer in luxuries . . . but . . . richer in meaning and more abundant in real pleasure' (1972:81).

Without doubt, as he argues, committed communities of more or less equal small-scale stakeholders with eco-savvy local knowledge leading prudent, temperate lives are likely to do less environmental damage, raise more healthier locally grown food at lower per capita cost, and deliver more forms of social sustenance too than the national average at less than average cost.

For reasons easy to surmise, the aspect of bioregional thinking that has had by far the greatest appeal to date is its vision of foodway reform, in particular the value it sets on producing and consuming nutritious food grown locally and insofar as possible without agro-chemicals. The majority of urbanites and suburbanites, who are probably also the principal consumers of bioregional writing, do not seriously want to relocate to small self-contained communities beyond convenient reach of metropolitan areas. Nor do they want to practise economic self-sufficiency beyond a limited degree when push comes to shove. But everyone must eat; and almost everyone is attracted to the idea of a healthy, nutritious diet; and many enjoy growing at least some of what they eat. Hence, for example, the enormous popularity of the novelist Barbara Kingsolver's *Animal, Vegetable, Miracle* (2007), a lively and genially contentious bioregional memoir of the author's and her family's first 'locavore year' of living in a small rural community near the part of Appalachia where she grew up. The book chronicles – with many tasty-sounding recipes along the way – their conscienceful effort to avoid all kitchen-table *and* restaurant food grown by CAFOs (Concentrated Animal Feeding Operations) and chemical-intensive methods of fertilization, and to subsist on produce grown or raised nearby, depending insofar as possible on their own garden and livestock.

In these ways, *Animal, Vegetable, Miracle* fuses the most appealing features of bioregional and VS thinking into an eminently readable, aesthetically engaging narrative manifesto. Whatever the book's actual influence upon the hearts and minds of its readers, furthermore, it's unquestionably a barometer of an auspicious broader trend-line in national culture and behaviour during the last quarter-century. As the author puts it towards the close, 'when our family gave up meat from CAFOs' in the 1990s, 'that choice was synonymous with becoming a vegetarian. No real alternatives existed. Now they do' (2007:228), – in supermarkets as well as country-town farmer's markets. In other words, even though bioregional ethics and aesthetics have clearly not (yet) succeeded in transforming North American residential patterns or even in bringing about a major resurgence of small-scale earth-friendly agricultural practices, the increasing number of available consumer options and the increasing consumer demand for fresher, more locally grown food bespeaks a significant resonance between bioregionalist thinking and public sentiment at large – in this particular sector at least. Beavan's *No Impact Man*, discussed earlier, attests to this as well.

The fact that bioregionalism's greatest success to date lies in its point of greatest appeal to middle-class consumerism also points to inherent vulnerabilities that threaten to limit, if not altogether disenable, its efficacy as a programme for a more environmentally sustainable society. These include nostalgia for organic communities of bygone days that may never actually have existed in the form imagined and downplaying the systemic hazards of provincialism, xenophobia and hierarchicalism that can overtake place-based communities in practice. With such thoughts in mind, my fellow ecocritic Ursula Heise, in her important *Sense of Place and Sense of Planet*, critiques what she sees as the overprivileging of place-attachment in earlier-stage ecocritical work as inadequate for today's world, in which local communities are increasingly networked globally and the defining environmental crises – pollution, global warming and species extinction – are planetary in reach (2008:28–62 and *passim*). My gentler concurring judgement is that bioregionalism potentially serves important purposes, both social and ecological, but that enoughness ethics most definitely needs to be conceived and implemented on a much larger social scale in order to stand a chance of making a difference outside scattered pocket cultures or companies of the faithful.

Relatedly, and no less seriously, as one of its advocates candidly admits, 'the bioregional movement does not have a worked-out strategy on what to do about the corporate sector' (Carr 2004:301). Although VS and bioregionalism both run counter to the institutions and culture of global capitalism – the primary threat to environmental sustainability – their proclivity is rather to opt out of the socio-economic mainstream than to urge a comprehensive dismantling or, when they do, to propose a counter-model that would seem workable for an increasingly networked world only at the social margins. For VS this is only to be expected, given its micro-scale commitment to begin with, the preeminent importance it attaches to individual choice. As for bioregionalism, although its commitment to *social* as against purely individual reform makes it more dispositionally hostile to systemic capitalism, its commitment to restoring local autonomy inhibits it from advocating 'radical restructuring of current social arrangements', such as a centrally mandated 'redistribution of wealth' (Evanoff 2011:149).

Any such project of course poses a far more formidable challenge than for-mation of communal solidarity at the comparatively small-scale levels envisaged by Berry, Snyder and Kingsolver. Political theorist Robyn Eckersley, hopeful as she strives to be in articulating a better pathway for sustainability for national and world governance than the best model currently on offer – namely, sustainable development or 'ecological modernization' ushered in by the Brundtland report – feels obliged to concede that 'the project of building the green state of the kind I have defended can never be finalized' (2004:169).[9] That too, I suppose, is why Arne Næss declared himself an optimist for the twenty-*second* century, not the twenty-first (2008:308).

Ecosocial equity

Earlier I mentioned studies of reported well-being by income level across cultures. Of special interest for its conspectus of such work is Richard Wilkinson's and Kate Pickett's *The Spirit Level* (2010), a synthesis by two epidemiologists of research in many disciplines and numerous governmental and NGO reports. These studies demonstrate, the authors argue, that nations in the developed world with the greatest income disparity between the top 20 per cent and the bottom 20 per cent fare significantly less well according to a wide range of well-being indicators: such as mental health and drug use, obesity, teenage births, violence, incarceration rates, social mobility and reported levels of trust in the integrity of other people. Japan and the Scandinavian countries come out best; the US, Singapore and Portugal worst – a provocative triad. The authors make a point of stressing that no one story-line can explain the variation in top–bottom polarization, including what would seem the most likely explanation *prima facie*: public expenditure on social welfare as a percentage of Gross Domestic Product, on which Japan (for instance) ranks near the bottom. 'How a society becomes more equal', they claim, 'is less important than whether or not it actually does so' (Wilkinson and Pickett 2010:177).

At many points the data and inferences can be questioned; but *The Spirit Level*'s big claim seems persuasive, including the sub-claim of the 'Equality and Sustainability' chapter: that greater inequality increases 'pressure to consume' (ibid.:208) and the percentage of unrecycled waste. If so, then some of bio-regionalism's precepts would seem to make for better outcomes at a pan-national level too. If Wilkinson and Pickett are right, equality of condition correlates with social cohesion, a broad-based sense of socio-environmental accountability and interdependence, personal moderation and inclination to environmental thrift.

But to what extent dare we expect large-scale behavioural shifts of such kind on a national scale, let alone international? Here ethical and political will lag far behind the resources of ethical and aesthetic imagination.

To be sure, even in the US, where economic inequalities between top and bottom are now the most extreme in the entire rich world next to Singapore, there is a long and strong history of egalitarianism despite the more libertarian understanding that now prevails of our Declaration of Independence's pro-clamation of 'life, liberty, and the pursuit of happiness' as fundamental human rights. So, for example, the state of New Hampshire, whose automobile license plate bears the motto 'Live Free or Die', also ranks according to Wilkinson and Pickett as one of three or four among the 50 states with the smallest gap between the top and bottom 20 per cent. Jefferson's agrarian vision of a nation of moderately prosperous small farmers; Alexis de Tocqueville's observation of neighbourly cooperation on the frontier in *Democracy in America*; our national poet Walt Whitman curbing the potential self-aggrandizement of his poetic persona by insisting 'By God! I will accept nothing which all cannot have their counterpart of on the same terms' (2002:46); the Homestead Act of 1862 that made available generous-sized equal parcels of the vast public lands in the mid-continent and west for would-be settlers – these are a few notable expressions of the same kind.

In US literary history, the most striking embodiment of this cast of thinking is Edward Bellamy's late-nineteenth-century utopian novel *Looking Backward: 2000–1887* (2007), an international best-seller among whose distinctions was to become the first work of American literature translated into Chinese. Bellamy wrote it in the midst of a techno-economic boom the likes of which the world had never seen, which transformed the US into the world's leading industrial as well as agricultural powerhouse by 1900 – a transformation surpassed in scale and rapidity only by contemporary China. The telephone, the elevator, the electric light had all been invented the decade before. But no less was this a time of social upheaval, of stark economic polarization and intensified class conflict: rampant capitalism versus insurgent labour. *Looking Backward*'s vision of a future America transformed into an egalitarian utopia after somehow getting past this crisis reads like a preparatory script for *The Spirit Level*, except for its explicitly socialist solution, whereas Wilkinson and Pickett studiously refrain from favouring any specific type of regime.

In Bellamy's imagined year 2000, education is universal; everyone works, both women and men, though only for a stipulated number of years and never to excess; and every job is equally honoured, with a system of proportional remuneration that minimizes extremes at both ends, that scrupulously matches talent to role, that calibrates supply to demand. Money has been replaced by a system of annually renewed individual credit cards that expire at death. An ethic of enoughness prevails because ostentation is scorned, efficiency is optimized and the system guarantees more or less the same sustenance for all. What's enabled all this is the displacement of the ideology of possessive individualism by one of interdependent egalitarian cooperation that sets supreme value on minimizing the gap between haves and have-nots. Of course the great mystery is how so amazing a transformation could have happened. Nearly to the same extent as *The Spirit Level*, *Looking Backward* emphasizes the 'is' rather than the 'how', except for a few hasty generalizations about worsening capital-labour antagonism becoming so dreadful as to produce a massive ethical paradigm shift leading in turn to peaceable, consensual evolution of this radically different social order.

Ironically, the early twenty-first century US has seen almost the opposite outcome from the New Jerusalem of *Looking Backward*, so far at least: a new Gilded Age with a 'growing inequality crisis' (Noah 2012) redressed only in part by 2013 tax law changes, with the top tier benefitting disproportionately during the past several decades from lower rates of taxation than during the mid-twentieth century, financial deregulation and economic globalization.[10] This repolarization of privileged versus disprivileged mirrors the gap between the global North and global South at the planetary level. That in turn has generated or reinforced polarized conceptions (or assumptions) about what counts as requisite human needs. The relatively well-off form exaggerated images of their material needs even as the world's disprivileged risk being denied what in former times would have been considered universal sustenance entitlements, as with the trend towards commodification of water resources such that more poor, place-based people are going thirsty or malnourished.

All that helps explain why the most dynamic push today in environment-and-literature studies, my own disciplinary home base, is so-called environmental justice ecocriticism, which has been steadily broadening out from its original focus on 'environmental racism' in North America and is on the way to achieve its full potential by going transnational and cross-pollinating with postcolonial studies.[11] Something like a new contemporary canon of transnational environmental justice (EJ) literature has come into view, including such works as Michiko Ishimure's *Paradise in the Sea of Sorrow* (1969), Linda Hogan's *Solar Storms* (1995), Helen María Viramontes' *Under the Feet of Jesus* (1995), Sandra Steingraeber's *Living Downstream* (1997), Zakes Mda's *The Heart of Redness* (2003), Rong Jiang (Lü Jiamin)'s *Wolf Totem* (2004), Amitav Ghosh's *The Hungry Tide* (2004), Alexis Wright's *Carpentaria* (2006) and Indra Sinha's *Animal's People* (2007). At the risk of oversimplifying so diverse a group of works, one can nonetheless usefully see them all as more or less sharing the following emphases. First, they testify to the sharply unequal distribution of environmental benefits and risks across different population groups. Second, they are witness to land degradation and/or the imperilment of nonhuman species and/or habitat loss by dominant national and transnational regimes, both political and economic. Third, and as a consequence, they dramatize the dire long-run consequences of bad ecological stewardship, potentially resulting in the 'revenge of Gaia' as James Lovelock (2006) calls it: whether it be the desertification of inner Mongolia owing to destruction of the traditional grasslands herding economy (*Wolf Totem*), devastation of First Peoples' lands in northern Canada by timber and hydropower interests (*Solar Storms*), or the devastation of the ecosystem and ecosystem-dependent people of the Delta region of the Bay of Bengal by forms of encroachment that disregard local knowledge (*Hungry Tide*).

To some extent, EJ literature is open to the same charge of provincialism to which, as we've seen, bioregionalism is vulnerable. Marxist geographer David Harvey's assessment of the characteristic limitation of EJ agendas broadly applies to both forms of counter-hegemonic of insurgency:

> as a movement embedded in multiple "militant particularisms," it has [yet] to find a way to cross that problematic divide between action that is deeply embedded in *place*, in local experience, power conditions and social relations to a much more general movement
>
> (1996:399)

that would 'transform the processes that gave rise to the problem in the first place' (ibid.:401). Harvey might plausibly contend that Viramontes' scenario of an extended family of Hispanic agricultural workers condemned to suffer horribly without prospect of relief is nothing more than a mirror image of the apocalyptic denouement of *Carpentaria*, in which Will Phantom and his band of aboriginal guerillas (aided by a monster typhoon) succeed in destroying a northern

Australian mining enterprise and its enclave of racist white settlers. For the emphases of both novels is on misery from or recourse against predatory master-class-dominated capitalist institutions operating at this or that ethno-regional level rather than on dismantling the underlying systemic inequities that produced the pathologies of ethnic and economic stratification to begin with.

Likewise, in *Heart of Redness* the plot turns on disputes within a poor South African coastal community, aggravated by ancient tribal feuds, over whether to recoup itself by accepting transformation into an ecotouristical playground. Although the novel deploys satire with considerable success to keep sentimental melodrama at arm's length, the community's eventual decision to opt instead to develop itself as an enterprise zone based on uniquely local crafts and materials amounts to a somewhat wishful romanticization of local empowerment defying vested interests. By contrast, *Wolf Totem* – which focuses on the losing battle of isolated bands of inner Mongolian herders to maintain their traditional way of life as the grasslands becomes appropriated for central government-sponsored agro-expansion certain to ruin the land – delivers a more pointed indictment of the folly of ecologically insouciant top-down Maoist social engineering – but, again, without envisaging any alternative path except for the one that's clearly no longer possible, of leaving the grasslands intact.

But just how culpable are such limitations, really? Can works of environmental imagination, whether of literature or of any other expressive genre, be fairly judged by the standard of whether they do or do not spell out a coherent, articulated conception of an alternative socio-economic order to the bad *status quo* they critique? Surely diagnostic prescriptivism of this kind is more the province of social theory than of the thought experiments of the creative arts.[12] That is not to say that the expressive arts are any less important forms of social intervention, only to point towards the distinctive kinds of contribution they stand to make to that end. In particular: affect, which is potentially one of literature's strongest suits, is as ecocritic Heather Houser declares, 'central to whether action flourishes or withers' (2014: 18). The very recalcitrance of global problems of the first magnitude to clear-cut programmatic solutions arguably makes it all the more so. As Houser elaborates: 'affect is pivotal to the complexity of emergent concerns about climate change, species extinction, pervasive toxicity, population growth, capitalist expansion, and technoscientific innovation' (ibid.:8) – the whole menu of today's preeminent environmental(ist) challenges.

For our purposes, what more specifically is most worthy and notable above all about EJ literature's cultural work is its prevailing aesthetic of frustrated vexation dramatized by scenarios that probe the confusions, impediments and complexities that stand in the way of fulfilment of Eckersley's key prerequisite for an ecologically responsive democratic order worthy of the name: that 'the demos' must be re-understood

> as the affected community or [transnational] community at risk, tied together
> not by common passports, nationality, blood line, ethnicity, or religion but

by the potential to be harmed by the particular proposal, and not necessarily all in the same way or to the same degree.

(2004:113)

This the narratives just named all do by conjuring up images of ecologically endangered little people the world has overlooked, seen through the eyes of more cosmopolitan observers (narrators or other proxy characters) who find themselves involved, identifying with and experiencing and indeed suffering from their pain. As with bioregionalism at its most expansive, all these texts concentrate in the first instance on dramatizing local conditions in remote districts scantly understood if ever noticed at all by their cosmopolitan, metro-centric target audiences; but they do so in such a way as also to dramatize their enmeshment within larger ecological, economic and ethno-racial forces that are ultimately planetary in scope.

In its prioritization of *human* communities at risk, EJ imagination predictably distributes its attention and its sympathies somewhat asymmetrically between human and the nonhuman. The underlying ideology of EJ literature is not 'deep ecology' as Næss generally defined it: i.e. the conviction 'that all living creatures have their own intrinsic value . . . irrespective of the use they might have for mankind' (Næss and Haukeland 2002: 6). Only intermittently and secondarily is the thrust of the aforementioned narratives biocentric. Ecosystemic degradation is seen as subsidiary to human immiseration. The sense of the humanitarian emergency predominates. But they also lean somewhat in that other direction by dramatizing the plight of 'ecosystem people', as Indian environmental historians Mahdav Gadgil and Ramachandra Guha call them. In the process, they thereby define the human being itself as effectively 'transcorporeal' (1995:4), as inseparable from the material environment that humans inhabit and must navigate.[13] Human flourishing is tied inextricably to ecosystemic health, or degradation. The implication is always that social and environmental inequalities are inextricably conjoined.

Altogether, then, the literature – perhaps one should rather say 'literatures' – of EJ showcase the cultural work that aesthetic texts can perform at a time of ecological crises of planetary scale. They give visibility and voice to overlooked communities of risk, including at least implicitly if not explicitly the other-than-human: to the endangered plants or mammals that might nonetheless be keystone species for whole ecosystems, aboriginal pocket cultures, slum dwellers in the megacities of the global South and in marginalized communities within the rich world that (as Wendell Berry has often pointed out) might just as well be the Third World. Such interventions obviously are not the only path to awakening public conscience. But neither can one set an outer limit to the catalytic power of aesthetic affect to effect changes in the actual world.

Concluding thoughts

The recognition that a 'good life' worthy of the name requires redirecting the behaviour and lifestyle of twenty-first century humans towards a more environmentally sustainable and socio-economically equitable path is almost certainly shared by a large number, and very likely a majority, of affluent persons today worldwide, especially in the world's more economically developed countries. But to act nontrivially upon that recognition is quite another matter. As this chapter has suggested, action at the individual level is a far simpler, more straightforward matter than action at a collective level, especially in proportion to the size, heterogeneity and jurisdictional complexity of the level of the collective in question. At this point in history, the prospect of an increasing cadre of practitioners of VS at whatever degrees of rigour seems far more feasible than the prospect of a whole nation, much less an international body, committing itself anytime soon to a goal of environmental sustainability worthy of the name. And even the former prospect – the prospect of anything more than scattered cases of individuals or families following the Beavans or the Kingsolvers wholeheartedly – is by no means assured.

That infinitely distressing gap between what educated, affluent humans 'know' to be right and the lamentably inadequate measures so far taken to act upon that recognition is precisely the space in which the work of environmental aesthetics and the critiques of environmental humanists stand to make their distinctive contribution, however. To them falls the responsibility of serving as consciences and guardians of environmental sustainability – as envisioners and articulators of a good life worthy of the name – at this time in history when the ideology of scientific research (for legitimate reasons of its own) remains guardedly neutral, technology a two-edged sword, economic globalism addicted to growth as the crucial measure of health, and political processes and institutions gridlocked, the parties mutually at odds and the politicians (however decent in their private lives) forever susceptible to manipulation by interest groups. For in the arts and the humanities, although by no means always recognized by others or even by the practitioners themselves, lie the best hope for fathoming, articulating, dramatizing the qualitative factors that shape human motivations: affects, dreams, attitudes, values, convictions.

What result can be expected from those interventions? Will the environmental arts and humanities go down in history as nothing more than Cassandras to whom the denizens of the Anthropocene chose not to listen? Maybe so. But far better to make the attempt than to succumb to indifference or despair.

Notes

1   Some portions of the first part of this chapter were previously published in Lawrence Buell, 'Does Thoreau Have a Future?' *Ecologies of Human Flourishing*, eds Donald K. Swearer and Susan Lloyd McGarry (Cambridge MA: Center for The Study of World Religions, Harvard Divinity School, 2011). I am grateful to the CSWR and to the President and Fellows of Harvard College for permission to reprint.

2 'Ecological footprint' denotes to the relation between biocapacity and actual expenditure of natural capital or resources on human production and absorption of waste. A 'light' ecological footprint means that the latter is little if any greater than the former.

3 For the world's largest economy, a pithy summation of the latter is Timothy Noah, *The Great Divergence* (New York: Bloomsbury, 2012).

4 For a more positive interpretation of consumption as a pathway toward ecological responsibility, see Kate Soper's chapter 'Towards a sustainable flourishing: democracy, hedonism and the politics of prosperity' on alternative hedonism later in this volume.

5 Even Layard's many critics do not seem to dispute the finding that for the wealthiest incremental gains in income mean smaller incremental gains in happiness than is the case for those lower down the economic ladder.

6 For further reflections on this subject, see Bengt Brülde's chapter 'Well-being and environmental responsibility' later in this volume, which after citing the Beavan family case pertinently observes, 'even if it were possible for *each* to adopt a sustainable lifestyle without loss of any well-being, it might not be possible for *all* (or *sufficiently many*) to do this'.

7 For definitions, see Lawrence Buell, *The Future of Environmental Criticism* (Oxford: Blackwell, 2005), 135; Michael Vincent McGinnis (ed.) *Bioregionalism* (London: Routledge, 1999), especially the editorial introduction; Robert L. Thayer, Jr., *LifePlace* (Berkeley, CA: University of California Press, 2003); Mike Carr, *Bioregionalism and Civil Society* (Vancouver: University of British Columbia Press, 2004), 70–100; and Tom Lynch, Cheryll Glotfelty and Karla Armbruster (ed.) *The Bioregional Imagination* (Athens, GA: University of Georgia Press, 2012).

8 Note Berry's obvious reliance on etymology here: 'economy' as secular discipline derived from the concept of 'divine economy'.

9 For a very thoughtful account of 'ecological modernization' as a more sceptically pragmatic semi-synonym for 'sustainable development' that acknowledges without conceding the possibility of 'development' trumping 'sustainability', see Maarten A. Hajer (1995) *The Politics of Environmental Discourse*. Oxford: Clarendon Press.

10 Quotation from the book's subtitle. The main title, as Noah explains, is a phrase coined by Nobel laureate in economics, Paul Krugman. More recent studies question such aspects of this book's argument such as its contention that upward mobility for Americans has significantly diminished in recent years, but without questioning Noah's assertions of widening inequality between the economic top and bottom and the US's strikingly low rate of upward mobility compared to that of other developed economies, not to mention the myth of the US as a land of opportunity. See for example, Raj Chetty, Nathaniel Hendren, Patrick Kline, Emmanuel Saez and Nicholas Turner, 'Is the United States Still a Land of Opportunity? Recent Trends in Intergenerational Mobility', *NBER Working Paper 19844* (January 2014).

11 'Environmental injustice' can be briefly defined as inequitable distribution of environmental benefits and hazards across population groups, with special concern for the plight of poor and/or ethno-racial minority groups. As a social movement, it has been striking for the leadership of groups represented marginally if at all in previous waves of environmental activism: the disprivileged, ethno-racial minorities and women. For the initially North American-centric phrase of ecocriticism, see Joni Adamson, Mei Mei Evans and Rachel Stein (eds) *The Environmental Justice Reader* (Tucson, AZ: University of Arizona Press, 2002). An influential analysis of the worldwide scope of environmental justice (EJ) social activism is Joan Martínez-Alier, *The Environmentalism of the Poor* (Cheltenham, UK: Elgar, 2002). The most influential example to date of the cross-pollination of EJ ecocriticism and postcolonial studies is Rob Nixon, *Slow Violence and the Environmentalism of the Poor* (Cambridge, MA: Harvard University Press, 2011). For summary reflections on the 'worlding' of EJ

ecocriticism, see Lawerence Buell, 'Ecocriticism: Some Emerging Trends', *Qui Parle*, 19 (Spring/Summer 2011): 97–101.

12 For more on this point, see Lawrence Buell, 'Literature as Environmental(ist) Thought Experiment', in Donald K. Swearer *Ecology and the Environment: Perspectives from the Humanities* (Cambridge, MA: Center for the Study of World Religions, 2009), 21–36.

13 For the theory of transcorporeal being, see Stacy Alaimo, *Bodily Natures* (Bloomington, IN: Indiana University Press, 2010), 2–3, 113–114.

Bibliography

Adamson, J., Evans M. M. and Stein, R. (eds) (2002) *The Environmental Justice Reader*. Tucson, AZ: University of Arizona Press.

Alaimo, S. (2010) *Bodily Natures: Science, Environment, and the Material Self*. Bloomington, IN: Indiana University Press.

Aristotle (1962) *Nichomachean Ethics*. Trans. Martin Ostwald. Indianapolis, IN: Bobbs-Merrill.

Beavan, C. (2009) *No Impact Man: The Adventures of a Guilty Liberal Who Attempts to Save the Planet and the Discoveries He Makes about Himself and Our Way of Life in the Process*. New York: Farrar, Straus.

Beavan, C. (n.d.) http://noimpactman.typepad.com (accessed 29 January 2014).

Bellamy, E. (2007) *Looking Backward: 2000–1887*. Beamont, M. (ed.). Oxford, NY: Oxford University Press.

Berry, W. (1972) *A Continuous Harmony: Essays Cultural and Agricultural*. San Diego, CA: Harcourt.

Berry, W. (1977) *The Unsettling of America: Culture & Agriculture*. San Francisco, CA: Sierra Club.

Berry, W. (1987) *Home Economics*. San Francisco, CA: North Point.

Biswas-Diener, R. M. (2008) 'Material Wealth and Subjective Well-Being' in Eid, M. and Larsen, R. J. (eds) *The Science of Subjective Well-Being*. New York: Guilford, 307–322.

Buell, L. (2005) *The Future of Environmental Criticism*. Oxford: Blackwell.

Buell, L. (2009) 'Literature as Environmental(ist) Thought Experiment' in Swearer, D. (ed.) *Ecology and the Environment: Perspectives from the Humanities*. Cambridge, MA: Center for the Study of World Religions, 21–36.

Buell, L. (2011) 'Ecocriticism: Some Emerging Trends' in *Qui Parle*, 19 (Spring/Summer), pp. 97–101.

Callenbach, E. (1975) *Ecotopia: The Notebooks and Reports of William Weston*. Berkeley, CA: Banyan Tree Books.

Carr, M. (2004) *Bioregionalism and Civil Society: Democratic Challenges to Corporate Globalism*. Vancouver: University of British Columbia Press.

Chetty, R., Hendren, N., Kline, P., Saez, E. and Turner, N. (2014) 'Is the United States Still a Land of Opportunity? Recent Trends in Intergenerational Mobility' in *National Bureau of Economic Research Working Paper 19844* (January). www.nber.org/papers/w19844 (accessed 29 January 2014).

Child, L. M. (1835) *The American Frugal Housewife*. Boston, MA: Carter, Hendee.

Cohen, L. (2003) *A Consumer's Republic: The Politics of Mass Consumption in Postwar America*. New York: Knopf.

Eckersley, R. (2004) *The Green State: Rethinking Democracy and Sovereignty*. Cambridge, MA: MIT Press.

Epictetus. (1944) *Discourses and Enchiridion*. Trans. Higginson, T. W. New York: Walter J. Black.

Emerson, E. W. (ed.) (1903–4) *Complete Works of Ralph Waldo Emerson: Lectures and Biographical Sketches*. Boston, MA: Houghton.

Evanoff, R. (2011) *Bioregionalism and Global Ethics: A Transactional Approach to Achieving Ecological Sustainability, Social Justice, and Human Well-Being*. New York: Routledge.

Gadgil, M. and Guha, R. (1995) *Ecology and Equity: The Use and Abuse of Nature in Contemporary India*. London: Routledge.

Ghosh, A. (2004) *The Hungry Tide*. London: HarperCollins.

Gray, C. (1995) 'The World Equity Budget or Living on about $142 per Month' in Anderson, D. (ed.) *Downwardly Mobile for Conscience's Sake: Ten Autobiographical Sketches*. Eugene, OR: Vesta, 97–124.

Gregg, R. B. (1936) *The Value of Voluntary Simplicity*. Wallingford, PA: Pendle Hill.

Hajer, M. A. (1995) *The Politics of Environmental Discourse: Ecological Modernization and the Policy Process*. Oxford: Clarendon Press.

Harvey, D. (1996) *Justice, Nature & the Geography of Difference*. Malden, MA: Blackwell.

Heise, U. (2008) *Sense of Place and Sense of Planet: The Environmental Imagination of the Global*. New York: Oxford University Press.

Hogan, L. (1995) *Solar Storms: A Novel*. New York: Scribner.

Houser, H. (2014) *Ecosickness in Contemporary U.S. Fiction: Environment and Affect*. New York: Columbia University Press.

Ishimure, M. (2003) *Paradise in the Sea of Sorrow: Our Minimata Disease*. Trans. Livia Monnet. Ann Arbor, MI: University of Michigan Press.

Jiang, R. (Lü Jiamin). (2004) *Wolf Totem*. Trans. Harold Goldblatt. New York: Penguin.

Kingsolver, B. (2007) *Animal, Vegetable, Miracle: A Year of Food Life*, with Hopp, S. L. and Kingsolver, C. New York: HarperCollins.

Land Institute (n.d.). http://landinstitute.org (accessed 29 January 2014).

Layard, R. (2005) *Happiness: Lessons from a New Science*. New York: Penguin.

Lovelock, J. (2006) *The Revenge of Gaia: Earth's Climate in Crisis and the Fate of Humanity*. New York: Basic.

Lynch, T., Glotfelty, C. and Armbruster, K. (eds) (2012) *The Bioregional Imagination: Literature, Ecology, and Place*. Athens, GA: University of Georgia Press.

McGinnis, M. V. (ed.) (1999) *Bioregionalism*. London: Routledge.

Martínez-Alier, J. (2002) *The Environmentalism of the Poor: A Study of Ecological Conflicts and Valuation*. Cheltenham, UK: Elgar.

Mda, Z. (2003) *The Heart of Redness*. London: Picador.

Næss, A. (2008) *The Ecology of Wisdom: Writings by Arne Næss*. Drengson, A. and Devall, B. (eds) Berkeley, CA: Counterpoint.

Næss, A, with Haukeland, P. I. (2002) *Life's Philosophy: Reason and Feeling in a Deeper World*. Trans. Ronald Huntford. Athens, GA: University of Georgia Press.

Neilan, T. (2010) *Millionaire Is Giving Away His Entire Fortune*. (14 February 2010). www.aolnews.com (accessed 29 January 2014).

Nixon, R. (2011) *Slow Violence and the Environmentalism of the Poor*. Cambridge, MA: Harvard University Press.

Noah, T. (2012) *The Great Divergence: America's Growing Inequality Crisis and What We Can Do about It*. New York: Bloomsbury.

Schumacher, E. F. (1973) *Small is Beautiful: A Study of Economics as if People Mattered*. London: Blond and Briggs.

Serres, M. (1995) *The Natural Contract*. Trans. MacArthur, E. and Paulson W. Ann Arbor, MI: University of Michigan Press.

Shi, D. E. (1985) *The Simple Life: Plain Living and High Thinking in American Culture*. New York: Oxford University Press.

Sidalsky, R. and Sidalsky, E. (2012) *How Much Is Enough? Money and the Good Life*. New York: Other Press.

Singer, P. (2002) *One World: The Ethics of Globalization*. New Haven: Yale University Press.

Sinha, I. (2007) *Animal's People*. New York: Simon & Schuster.

Steingraeber, S. (1997) *Living Downstream: An Ecologist Looks at Gender and the Environment*. Reading, MA: Addison-Wesley.

Thayer, R. L., Jr. (2003) *LifePlace: Bioregional Thought and Practice*. Berkeley, CA: University of California Press.

Thoreau, H. D. (1971[1854]) *Walden; or, Life in the Woods*. Lyndon Shanley, J. (ed.) Princeton, NJ: Princeton University Press.

UNEP (United Nations Environment Program). *Global Environment Outlook-1: Chapter 2: Regional Perspectives*. www.unep.org/geo/geo1/ch/ch2_12.htm (accessed 29 January 2014).

Viramontes, H. M. (1995) *Under the Feet of Jesus*. New York: Dutton.

Whitman, W. (2002) *Leaves of Grass and Other Writings*. Moon, M. (ed.). New York: Norton.

Wilkinson, R. and Pickett, K. (2010) *The Sprit Level: Why Greater Equality Makes Societies Stronger*. New York: Bloomsbury Press.

Wright, A. (2006) *Carpentaria: A Novel*. Sydney: Giramondo.

Wuthnow, R. (1996) *Poor Richard's Principle: Recovering the American Dream Through the Moral Dimension of Work, Business, and Money*. Princeton, NJ: Princeton University Press.

**The essayistic spirit
of *Utopia***

Thorunn Gullaksen Endreson

What a book can do

How to be Idle. This is the title of Tom Hodgkinson's[1] 2004 book on the benefits
of a slower and more contemplative life. In an essayistic manner, Hodgkinson
muses on such idle pleasures as "Sleeping In", "The Ramble", "On Fishing", and
"The Art of Conversation", to mention some of the chapters of the book. Reading
How to be Idle for the first time in 2004, I was writing a master's thesis in literature
on Virginia Woolf as an essayist in a predominantly male tradition. Paying
perhaps more attention to form than content, Hodgkinson's book served as a
contemporary example of the English essay – he even borrowed the title of
Virginia Woolf's essay "On Being Ill" for one of the chapters – and it was highly
amusing. Never did it occur to me that his thoughts on an idle lifestyle were
something to consider seriously, and I viewed the book more as (idle) entertainment than as severe civilization critique; I certainly did not consider Hodgkinson
as another Rousseau. For Tom Hodgkinson in 2004 his reactions on the work and
consume culture was mainly motivated by self-interest and quest for the good life:
'The purpose of this book is both to celebrate laziness and to attack the work
culture of the western world, which has enslaved, demoralized and depressed so
many of us' (Hodgkinson 2004:Preface), exposing a hedonistic and individualistic
perspective. Sustainability or environmental responsibility is not on the agenda
here.

Eight years later I picked up the book again. Today *How to be Idle* appears in a
different light, as a cultural critique, and as a (positive) vision of a new way of
thinking about life and what life has to offer, thought-provoking and relevant as
awareness regarding the perils of our work and consumer society slowly starts to
seep in. Being an idler is one way of combining a good life with environmental
responsibility. By sleeping in, rambling around, improving our mind, and taking
long leisurely lunches, we could both enjoy ourselves more and lead more
sustainable lives, reducing the number of working hours and having less money to
spend. The philosopher Kate Soper, who has written extensively on consumer
culture[2], refers to Hodgkinson's book as one among several more "serious" works,
in order to illustrate that 'the affluent lifestyle is generating its own specific form
of disaffection, either because of its negative by-products or because it stands in

the way of other enjoyments' (Soper 2008:571). For an increasing amount of people, consumerism is tainted by the pollution and stress it causes, by the congestion, the bad health effects and loss of community and personal forms of contact. Certainly, the good life pursued by the idler, as described in Hodgkinson's book, can be both a good life and a more sustainable lifestyle. And this is exactly the point of Kate Soper's concept of "alternative hedonism". I will get back to this concept later.

What is the point of revealing my personal reading experience in this context? To begin with, this anecdote shows that a book's impact relies on your personal situation, your mindset, as well as the state of the world and on cultural, political, and economic factors. As Kenneth Roemer points out, '[t]exts invite the creation of meaning, and readers give meaning to the texts. Before, during, and after the reading experience, this process of meaning creation is constrained, guided, and encouraged by powerful cultural, historical, and personal situations and forces' (Roemer 2003:4). These forces are diverse, spanning from broad categories such as gender roles, historical circumstances, and world views to more narrow categories as, for example, conventions of reading and individual psychologies. When any of these factors change, readers might give different meaning to a text. Hodgkinson's book appeared as a different book during a time span of only eight years as both historical and personal circumstances changed. My research interests have taken a turn and the state of the world has changed, along with our mindset: we are becoming increasingly more aware of the urgency of the environmental crisis, and climate change has become a major policy issue. Science and technology alone are not sufficient to save the world; cultural and literary studies are equally important to induce awareness and change our values and perceptions in a more environmental friendly direction, a point Lawrence Buell makes in *The Future of Environmental Criticism* (2005). The question is: What kind of books might turn into transformative reading experiences in a time of environmental crisis?

Books can certainly make a difference. Rachel Carson's *Silent Spring* (2000) is one potent example of a book as an agent of change. Carson (1907–1964) was a biologist, specializing in marine zoology, and also an acclaimed writer of non-fiction, for example the best-selling *The Sea Around Us* (1951)[3], and articles on natural history in reputable periodicals such as *The Atlantic Monthly* and the *New Yorker*. A version of *Silent Spring* first appeared as a series of articles in the *New Yorker*, later as a book. In *Silent Spring* Carson shows the hazards of poisonous pesticidal chemicals, comparing them to the threat of radioactive fallout from atomic bomb testing, and towards the end of the book she suggests some biological alternatives to the chemical control of insects. In 1962, *Silent Spring* led to widespread public debate on the abuse of pesticides and the effect on both humans and the environment. Her single voice of warning spread through media, created debate, controversy and even condemnation. The chemical industry tried to ban the book. With *Silent Spring*, Carson created public awareness of the environment as well as changes in government policy. It is generally agreed that Carson's book is the founding text of modern environmentalism, and it is also widely appreciated that Carson's reliance on literary qualities, most obvious in the introductory poetic parable, is an important reason for the book's success (see for example Gartner 2000). Carson's apocalyptic vision made a severe impact on the world. We do not know, however, if this would have been the case in our society today. A number of dystopian visions of future doom have manifested themselves the last couple of decades, in literature, both fiction and non-fiction, and in film, such as Al Gore's documentary film *An Inconvenient Truth* (2006). A couple of years earlier the fictional film *The Day After Tomorrow* (2004) was released, and the film was widely believed to have severe impact on people's perception of climate change. Surprisingly, surveys conducted on the film audience show that 'any increase in concern about climate change induced by the film appeared short lived, with most viewers treating the film purely as entertainment' (Hulme 2009:213)[4]. Cormac McCarthy's novel *The Road* (2006) is another forceful example of the dystopian genre. The novel is a portrait of a father and his son, walking through a burned out landscape in an imagined apocalyptic future. They have to fight for food and for their life, being constantly alert and afraid. Love and care for each other are the only things that sustain them in a world totally destructed. *The Road* was proclaimed by the environment activist, writer, and *Guardian* columnist George Monbiot to be the most important environmental novel ever. It will change how we view the world, was his prediction. The narrative was even more hyped as the novel was made into a film. Half a decade later environmental action is still not sufficient.

The mobilizing effect of dystopian narratives seems to be small, or only short-term. There are a number of possible explanations. First, some of these narratives are told in ways that reduce a serious message to entertainment, such as the reactions on the film *The Day After Tomorrow* indicate. We watch or read, experience *catharsis*, and then we go home and do nothing about it. Another explanation might be that we have too much information to make sense of it. As the media environment has expanded we are drowning in information, and 'the attention needed to make sense of the information has become our scarce resource', as Richard Lanham writes in the *The Economics of Attention* (2006:xi). Information is not in limited supply in our "information economy", but we have a limited amount of attention: 'Attention is the commodity in short supply' (ibid.). Human attention is the scarce commodity in an information economy; it does not grow with the increase of information. Shorter attention span due to a completely changed media environment could be one likely reason why a 2012 equivalent to *Silent Spring* would not be mobilizing in the same way. And climate change is but one of several pressing problems demanding attention and action; it does not exist in isolation, as Susanne C. Moser (2007) points out.

A third possible reason could be that we are in a state of climate change denial. Could our ignorance of dystopian vision's environmental messages be seen as a form of denial? In her book *Living in Denial* (2011), the sociologist Karen Marie Norgaard has conducted research on the public's lack of response to environmental problems. In her study of a small Norwegian community, she asks why awareness did not translate into social action (Norgaard 2011:xvii). Norgaard attributes public apathy towards significant environmental issues such as global warming to the phenomenon of socially organized denial; disturbing information is actively muted and disconnected from both political and private life. Only by mechanisms of repression are we able to go on living our daily lives in spite of serious threats to the environment. In her study of the Norwegian community, she found that global warming was not a common topic of either political or private conversation, despite wide knowledge and concern regarding climate change. Similarly, in the US, especially since the extensive viewing of Al Gore's *An Inconvenient Truth* as well as the events of Hurricane Katrina, there is widespread knowledge and concern regarding climate change, but still too little action, she claims. Norgaard's conclusions are in line with both philosopher and psychotherapist Shierry Weber Nicholsen's and sociologist Stanley Cohen's views on apathy, as 'a way of adapting, of defending oneself in a situation that is utterly overwhelming and where there is no end in sight' (Nicholsen 2002:147). Inaction does not necessarily mean indifference and lack of concern: 'Passivity and silence may *look* the same as obliviousness, apathy and indifference, but may not be the same at all. We can feel and care intensely, yet remain silent' (Cohen 2001:9).

Even if we do not know for sure the effect of fictional dystopian visions, there are several studies exploring the effect of "dystopian" climate change communication. Initiated by Carson's *Silent Spring*, '[e]nvironmental discourses have long been clothed in the language of Apocalypse' (Hulme 2009:345). Mike Hulme, in his book *Why We Disagree About Climate Change*, delivers some relevant insights. The book was actually written as a response to the pejorative discourse on climate change: 'I feel uncomfortable that climate change is widely reported through the languages of catastrophe and imminent peril, as "the greatest problem facing humanity", which seeks to trump all others' (ibid.:xxxiii). He questions what the myth of Apocalypse does to us:

> It undoubtedly lends a sense of danger, fear and urgency to discourses around climate change captured in such claims such as we only have ten years "to reduce emissions" or to "save the climate". Yet the counterintuitive outcome of such language is that it frequently leads to disempowerment, apathy and scepticism among its audience.
>
> (ibid:347–348)

Promoting fear is often both ineffective and counterproductive as a tool to change behaviour. As Susanne Moser points out, fear appeals can usually not 'generate a sustained and constructive engagement with climate change' (Moser 2007:70). And she continues: 'Empirical studies show, for example, that fear may change attitudes and verbal expressions of concern but not necessarily increase active engagement or behaviour change' (ibid.). It seems, then, that not only does the problem of climate change in itself induce apathy and denial, but the communication of climate change in dystopian visions and language amplifies the effect.

It makes sense to conclude that dystopian apocalyptic visions do not seem to work as mobilizing narratives. Fictional narratives of apocalypse are both entertaining and promote fear. Doomsday visions are certainly disturbing information. The ecocritic Greg Garrard suggests that we need more positive visions in order to act: 'Only if we imagine that the planet *has* a future, after all, are we likely to take responsibility for it' (Garrard 2012:116). His comment is in line with Susanne Moser's conclusion: 'it will be critical to engage people in envisioning a future worth fighting for' (Moser 2007:75). Is it time to reconsider utopian visions? And, in line with the example of my own reading experience of *How to be Idle*: Could it be that readers in a time of environmental crisis are more receptive to the "message" of utopias? Could this time of environmental crisis be the time when the utopian novel experiences a renaissance? Utopian narratives might prove to speak more compellingly and persuasively than narratives of future gloom.

Utopian narratives may, under the right historic, cultural, and personal conditions, turn out to be transforming reading experiences. Let me illustrate with an historical example. Edward Bellamy published the utopian novel *Looking Backward* in 1887. The book was immensely popular and influential. Of American nineteenth-century fiction, only *Uncle Tom's Cabin* and (possibly) *Ben Hur* sold more than *Looking Backward* (Roemer 2003:9). The novel is framed by a preface dated 26 December 2000, and written by the "author", a fictional historian in a Boston college. He tells us that the author 'has sought to alleviate the instructive quality of the book by casting it in the form of a romantic narrative' (Preface). The "author" then steps aside and leaves Mr Julian West, the narrator of the novel, to speak for himself. He tells us his story after he wakes up in Dr Leete's house in the year 2000, apparently having slept since 1887. He is given information about the organization of the society by the doctor, and the narrative is sweetened by the love story between Julian and Dr Leete's daughter. The conversation between Dr Leete and Julian reveals the new society as well as the contrasts between the old and the new. In the last chapter of the novel Julian wakes up, this time in his old room in the capitalist society of 1887. He realizes what had happened to him:

> All about the twentieth century had been a dream. I had but dreamed of that enlightened and care-free race of men and their ingeniously simple institutions, of the glorious new Boston with its domes and pinnacles, its gardens and fountains, and its universal reign of comfort.
>
> (Bellamy 2011:123)

However, he wakes up yet again, this time back in Dr Leete's house and it turns out that it was the return to the nineteenth century that was the dream. As Darko Suvin points out, Bellamy's novel was innovative in the utopian tradition in terms of the development of the hero: 'The construction of the social system for the reader is also the reconstruction of the hero', answering Shakespeare's challenge 'that changing the world entails changing the "nature" of men' (Suvin 1979:174). Julian West changes from a quite self-centred and wealthy man to a person that supports a 'centralized, socialized, egalitarian economy and a concept of self that merges the individual and society' (Roemer 2003:10).

Presenting an economic blueprint, an improved utopian society, through a romantic narrative turned out to be a success, not only in terms of sales. The novel had a mobilizing impact as well. Kenneth Roemer investigates why and how American readers transformed 'a book by a relatively unknown author into an agent of national and even international change' (ibid.:xii). The financial panic of 1873, the depression 20 years later, political corruption, unequal distribution of wealth leading to strikes, and labour disturbances are some of the historical conditions that contributed to making the readers ready for a brave new world; they sought answers and new political solutions. The historical circumstances played an important role in making the reading of Bellamy's utopian novel a transformative reading experience. As Roemer and Phaelzer found, utopian literature articulated anxieties about the historical conditions and at the same time gave answers and solutions. Textual invitations inherent in the novel answered a strongly felt belief or value of the reader. To put Umberto Eco's concept of the model reader into play, we might say that the model reader turned out to match the (real) historical reader (Eco 1984). In 1935 the philosopher John Dewey, Edward Weeks (editor of *The AtlanticMonthly*[5]), and the historian Charles Beard claimed that since the publication in 1885, 'only Marx's *Das Kapital* had done more to shape the thought and action of the world' (Roemer 2003:10). It inspired reform movements worldwide. Numerous politicians during the twentieth century – socialist, Progressive, and New Deal – referred to Bellamy's *Looking Backward* as influential. *Looking Backward* is both entertaining and didactic, like most literary utopias. Today, however, Bellamy's novel is not widely read, maybe not surprising as it was received as a response to the specific historical conditions of the late nineteenth century. With the portrayed society's reliance on abundant consumption it is certainly not a suitable candidate for a mobilizing narrative for environmental responsibility.

Ecotopias and the concept of alternative hedonism

In *The End of Over-consumption* (2003), Marius de Geus distinguishes between two different types of utopias: "ecological utopias" or "utopias of sufficiency" versus "technological utopias" or "utopias of abundance"; in other words, ecotopias versus technotopias. The first group includes Thomas More's *Utopia* (1516), Thoreau's *Walden* (1854) and William Morris' *News from Nowhere* (1891), to mention a few. The second group encompasses such work as Francis Bacon's *New Atlantis* (2008) and Edward Bellamy's *Looking Backward* (1887).

> The basic difference between these utopias lies in the notion of whether an ideal society should enjoy material abundance and luxury or be based on satisfaction and sufficiency. [. . .] The utopian ecological thinkers show themselves as opponents of abundant production and consumption. They emphasize that a perfect situation is not compatible with excess: abundance does not make people happy. [. . .] This approach consistently emphasizes the

advantages of a simpler life, and insists that humans should treat and use the natural surroundings with care.

(de Geus 2003:84–85)

To emphasize 'the advantages of a simpler life' echoes Soper's concept of "alternative hedonism". Alternative hedonism is the pursuit and enjoyment of pleasures with less emphasis on consumption, such as walking or biking instead of driving a car; shorter working hours and more time to enjoy life; not having to drive to the gym to exercise indoors on a bike or treadmill; having time to take a walk in the woods or gardening and getting the added bonus of fresh air and a healthy body. Growing your own vegetables does not only give the pleasures of fresh air and closeness to nature, but enhances health and enables you to eat and prepare slow food instead of fast food. '[A]lternative hedonism is premised on the idea that even if consumerism were indefinitely sustainable it would not enhance human happiness and well-being' (Soper 2009:3). As Soper argues, alternative hedonism emphasizes 'the pleasures of escaping the consumerist lifestyle', but at the same time 'chimes with those calling for a redefinition of prosperity' (Soper 2009:5). It also provides a theoretical framework to understand the increase in movements such as the Voluntary Simplicity movement in the US, embracing a lifestyle that is 'outwardly simple, inwardly rich', (a slogan the philosopher Arne Naess gave a new impetus and a thorough interpretation, often quoted as 'simple in means, rich in ends'). Replacing consumption as the main source of well-being, the philosophy of alterative hedonism makes it possible to pursue the good life and at the same time act environmentally responsibly.

Thomas More's[6] *Utopia* (1516) is 'regarded as a foundation stone of the utopian ecological way of thinking' (de Geus 2003:84). As an ecotopia *par excellence*, *Utopia* is worth considering as a mobilizing narrative for sustainability. My own provisional understanding of More's *Utopia* relies on the conformity of More's good place or no-place with Kate Soper's ideas of alternative hedonism. More portrays a universe displaying shorter working hours, emphasis on the beauty of nature and gardens and the pleasures of gardening, disregard for consumption, no stress, and ample opportunity for learning and self-development. Could Thomas More's *Utopia* function as an inspiration for action, a transformative reading experience? Can a sixteenth-century utopian narrative appeal to the (post)modern reader?

Utopias as boundary works

As Peter Ruppert (1986) points out, fictional utopian narratives are generally seen as poor literary works, lacking in psychological complexity, drama, and humour. However, utopian fictional narratives can usually not be seen as "pure" works. Robert Elliott calls fictional utopias a 'bastard form' (Elliott 1970:10), Gary Saul Morson, in *Boundaries of Genre* (1981), identifies literary utopias as "boundary works", they are heterogeneous works, combining fiction and non-fiction. These boundary or threshold texts might cast the reader into a kind of 'hermeneutic perplexity', to use Morson's (1981:93) wording. Contrary to his argumentation, I will argue that this hermeneutic perplexity might prove productive. The reader is thus given an important role; 'utopias are able to generate some complexity and ambiguity in the act of reading – they become multifaceted texts whose significance depends in part on how we read them' (Ruppert 1986:34). The difficulty of genre, the ambiguity and complexity of the text, and the role of the reader ties utopian narratives to another "unclean" genre: the essay. Claire de Obaldia coins the essay as "literature *in potentia*", building on Alastair Fowler's concept (de Obaldia 2002:5). The genre is ambiguous, open, and indeterminate; a hybrid. The essay is in a borderline position between knowledge and art; it is neither purely literary, nor purely scientific or philosophical, but something in between, oscillating between the two positions. There is something of an essayistic spirit in utopian narratives such as Thomas More's *Utopia*, as I will elaborate on later. An appealing aspect of the concept "boundary work" is 'that it seems to rescue literary utopias from their one-dimensional status as either reductive arguments for socialism or escapist fantasies' (Ruppert 1986:42–43). Thomas More's *Utopia* has been called both.

Even if there are several examples of earlier utopian narratives – such as Plato's *Republic*, Pliny's *Natural History*, and Lucian's satirical *True History* (2012) – Thomas More is the inventor of the term "utopia", playing on the two Greek words *outopia* – "not-place" – and *eutopia* – "good place". Later utopian visions are often placed in the future, as for example William Morris' *News from Nowhere* (1890) and Edward Bellamy's *Looking Backward* (1887). Thomas More situated his "good place" on an island, a tradition of the early utopia. Another early utopian ingredient, found in both Pliny and Lucian, is the fantastic traveller's tale. More followed his predecessors, but his good place, and especially the discussions framing the fantastic traveller's tale, is quite realistic, relying on real names and situations. To increase the sense of the real, More enclosed the Utopian alphabet and some Utopian poetry; "Lines on the Island of Utopia by the Poet Laureate, Mr. Windbag Nonsenso's Sister's Son":

> NOPLACIA was once my name,/ That is, a place where no one goes./ Plato's Republic now I claim/ To match, or beat at its own game;/ For that was just a myth in prose,/ But what he wrote of, I became,/ Of men, wealth, laws a solid frame,/ A place where every wise man goes; / GOPLACIA IS NOW MY NAME.

> (More 2003:5)

This particular translation[7] has replaced the original Greek names. The original pun is on *Outopia* and *Eutopia*. By the explicit mentioning of Plato's *Republic*[8], More displays his place in a tradition of utopian thinkers; Plato represents both his ideal and his competition as he imitates and improves, as in the old literary concept of *imitatio*. Plato is mentioned and referred to frequently, especially by Raphael, who promotes Plato's views on communal ownership (More 2003:42). In "Gilles's Letter to Busleiden", another of More's multiple framing devices, Peter

Gilles introduces the island Utopia 'like Plato's *Republic*, only better – especially as it's described by such a talented author' (ibid.:11). The reader should be in no doubt as to the superiority of More's *Utopia* to Plato and his *Republic*.

Thomas More's *Utopia* can be described as a combination of a philosophical discussion and an imaginative narrative, certainly a boundary work. On the title page of the first edition in 1516 it was announced as 'a really splendid little book, as entertaining as it is instructive', so like Lucian's *True History*, 'not merely to be witty and entertaining, but also to say something interesting' (Turner 2003:xi). The structure of the book was probably inspired by the dialogues in Lucian's *Satirical Sketches*; More was a big fan and translator of Lucian (Turner 2003). *Utopia* consists of two books. In Book One we are given an insight into More's contemporary English society, focusing on the problems of poverty, the injustices of the penalty system, and inequality. This complex introduction is given the form of a conversation between Peter Gilles, secretary of the city of Antwerp (who really existed and was a good friend of the author), Thomas More "himself", who is also the first-person narrator, and a fictional Portuguese seaman named Raphael Hythlodaeus. By being placed in a setting of Americo Vespucci's historical travels, Raphael is given a hint of the real as well. In Book Two, the problems presented in Book One are (supposedly) solved. We are served a fantastic traveller's tale describing an imaginary place: an island society called Utopia. In effect, the remedy of an unhealthy society is presented in the form of an ideal utopian island society. He effectively contrasts the "bad" place of England against the "good" place of Utopia. The traveller is the same Raphael we met in Book One. He is not only a seaman and a traveller, but also, perhaps not surprisingly, a student of philosophy. Raphael stayed on the island for more than five years: 'I lived there for more than five years, you know, and the only reason why I ever left was that I wanted to tell people about the New World – [. . .] you'd never seen a country so well organized' (More 2003:46).

The character More does not visit the island himself, he merely experiences Utopia through Raphael's narrative. More is thus both a first-person narrator and a narratee, he listens and he is a conversation partner. Raphael is both a visitor and guide, and in Book Two he is a narrator as well. In Turner's translation, Raphael Hythlodaeus is suitably called Raphael Nonsenso; Hythlodaeus means "dispenser of nonsense". Obviously, More had a passion for jokes, but the names are not only meant to be funny. They remind the reader of the imaginary quality of the narrative, and enable More to pass severe critique without the risk of ending up in the Tower. The subversive quality of the discourse is disguised by playing the role of the fool. And, Raphael is the only character in the book which passes serious critique, the persona More is more careful, remaining (throughout the book) a sceptic towards Raphael's "revolutionary" ideas and subversive thinking. In effect then, the author More has constructed a form both entertaining and instructive, as promised in the first edition's title page, but also safe; a 'sanctuary of ambiguity constructed by its form', as Turner phrases it (Turner 2003:xiv).

An ecotopia to wish for?

What kind of ecotopia is Raphael's island? Let us visit this imaginary society and see for ourselves. If we look for sustainable visions for a good life, Utopia seems at first to comply. In contrast to our growth economy, the inhabitants of Utopia work only six hours a day[9]: 'In Utopia they have a six-hour working day – three hours in the morning, then lunch – then a two hour break – then three more hours in the afternoon, followed by supper' (More 2003:56). The organization of the working day and the short working hours has several positive side effects. The shorter working hours gives ample free time to expand the mind: 'Most people spend these free periods on further education' (ibid.:56). Cultivation of the mind is regarded as 'the secret of a happy life' (ibid.:59) in Utopia. And, as everybody is working less, there is no unemployment. Production and consumption of clothing is kept at a minimum; this is no work-and-spend economy where consumers find themselves trapped in an escalation of desire, or in Colin Campbell's words, a 'cycle of desire-acquisition-use-disillusionment-renewed desire' (Campbell 2005:90):

> So whereas in other countries you won't find anyone satisfied with less than five or six suits and as many silk shirts, while dressy types want over ten of each, your Utopian is content with a single piece of clothing every two years.
> (More 2003:59)

Utopian austerity is effectively contrasted with the vanity and greed of inhabitants of "real" countries. The frivolous pleasure of dressing up is not valued in Utopia. Certainly this pattern of consumption is sustainable and likely to be embraced by green radicals. Most people, however, would not appreciate the lack of beauty and glamour in wearing only a cloak, always in the same 'natural color of wool' (ibid.:59), thrown over loose-fitting leather overalls, valued for their durability and practicality. Beauty in nature and gardens, however, is highly valued. The visitor is especially impressed with the gardens of Utopia, in which pleasure is combined with profit. This aspect of the island community fits perfectly well with the philosophy of alternative hedonism:

> They're extremely fond of these gardens, in which they grow fruit, including grapes, as well as grass and flowers. They keep them in wonderful condition – in fact, I've never seen anything to beat them for beauty or fertility. [. . .] Certainly it would be hard to find any feature of the town more calculated to give pleasure and profit to the community.
> (ibid.:53)

The nature of human happiness in Utopia is discussed at length by Raphael. 'Here they seem rather too much inclined to take a hedonistic view, for according to them human happiness consists largely or wholly in pleasure' (ibid.:71). However, as it turns out, the concept of hedonism in Utopia is rather long term. Utopians are expected to forego a range of earthly pleasures in return for 'an eternity of perfect joy' (ibid.:73).

Like Plato's imaginary *Republic*, More's *Utopia* is based on communal ownership instead of private property. 'I don't see how you can ever get any real justice or prosperity, so long as there's private property, and everything is judged in terms of money' (ibid.:44), argues Raphael in Book One, and in Utopia '[e]veryone gets a fair share, so there are never any poor men or beggars. Nobody owns anything, but everyone is rich' (ibid.:110). Considering its historical setting, the equality of the inhabitants is one of the most radical features of More's imaginary island. However, if we study Utopia more thoroughly, we discover that some are more equal than others. The elders enjoy an elevated position in the society, they have political power: 'Each town sends three of its older and more experienced citizens to an annual meeting at Aircastle, to discuss the general affairs of the island' (ibid.:50). The elders also rule the household: 'Each household [. . .] comes under the authority of the oldest male' (ibid.:60). Even an innocent activity like meandering in the countryside in the outskirts of the towns needs to be cleared with the head of the family. The patriarchal character of the society is illustrated further by the superior position of men over women. The ideal of equality does not apply to them. Wives have to wait on their husbands, and once a month, 'wives kneel down at home before their husbands [. . .] to confess all their sins of omission and commission, and ask to be forgiven' (ibid.:107). The law system further illustrates the patriarchal nature of the island, as 'husbands are responsible for punishing their wives' (ibid.:85). The least equal of all inhabitants are the slaves, consisting of utopian convicts and acquired (!) criminals from other countries. 'Both types of slaves are kept hard at work in chaingangs' (ibid.:82). There is even a third type of slave: 'the working-class foreigner who, rather than live in wretched poverty at home, volunteers for slavery in Utopia' (ibid.). These slaves have to work harder than "ordinary" people, because, as Raphael informs us, 'they're used to it' (ibid.). The slaves are treated more like beasts than humans, set to perform tasks unworthy of the other inhabitants: 'The slaughtering of livestock and cleaning of the carcasses are done by slaves. They don't let ordinary people get used to cutting up animals, because it tends to destroy one's natural feeling of humanity' (ibid.:61). And even worse, if convicts do not respond to any sort of prison discipline 'they are just slaughtered like wild beasts' (ibid.:85). Slaves are clearly not considered humans. The seemingly classless society based on equality turns out to be hierarchical, patriarchal, and inhuman. The Utopians think of themselves as free men, however, '[e]veryone has his eye on you, so you're practically forced to get on with your job, and make some proper use of your spare time' (ibid.:65), connoting the omnipresent "Big Brother" of George Orwell's dystopian *1984*. The examples unveiled here are just some of the many contradictions and paradoxes within the text, in line with the oxymoronic title of More's work; a place that is no place.

Even if certain aspects of Utopian life correspond to the concept of alternative hedonism, Utopia is hardly an ideal society or even a good place. It becomes increasingly difficult to fathom why Thomas More's *Utopia* (1516) is 'regarded as a foundation stone of the utopian ecological way of thinking' (de Geus 2003:84), and even de Geus himself 'would not be very anxious to move there' (de Geus 1999:67). He argues, nonetheless, that the ecological dimensions of the utopian society cannot be overlooked. As I have already pointed out, Utopia certainly has ecological dimensions. However, the value of More's Utopia lies, I will argue, not as a model of green living, but in its ability to bring the reader into play.

Essaying a society

More's book is trying out or essaying a society through constant dialogue, both within the text and between the fictional personas in the text, and consequently, as in the essay, with the reader. The reader is brought into play by negotiating both the paradoxes in the text, and the incongruous views presented by the characters in the book. Through the reader, More's island becomes a society *in potentia*, to borrow Claire de Obaldia's expression about the essay. Ruppert (1986) argues that Utopia is a static place. However, the permeability of its boundaries is symbolized by the interplay between the text and its paratexts, or to be more precise, peritexts. These are texts within the book that mediate the book to the reader, such as forewords, dedications, notes, epilogues, etc. Genette (1997) distinguishes between peritexts, within the book, and epitexts, outside the book. These framing elements of the text, these 'thresholds of interpretation', in Genette's terms, cannot be isolated, but may be seen as an integral part of More's work. The utopian island presented in Book Two is not an isolated and static island; its borders are permeated by its frames, and by the reader's constant negotiation between the different levels. This is the transformative reading experience. The discrepancies, paradoxes, and contradictions within the text bring the reader into play. The text enters into an imaginary dialogue with the reader, keeping the reader alert, in the spirit of the dialogism of Plato and the essays of Montaigne.

This open-endedness, which enables a dialogue with the reader, is not a distinct feature of More's work, but characterizes some important utopian fictional narratives. According to Darko Suvin: 'significant utopian writings are in permanent dialogue with the readers, they are open-ended – as in More' (Suvin 1979:96). The many conflicting interpretations and controversies that More's book has generated over the years is indeed a sign of its open-endedness, as Ruppert (1986) points out. The conversation between the persona, More, and the traveller and student of philosophy, Raphael, represents one important aspect of the open-endedness of More's narrative. The views of the two characters are in constant negotiation, offering the reader no reconciliation, even at the end of the book, keeping her alert and in dialogue. In spite of Raphael's enthusiasm about the Utopian society, and More's willingness to listen and discuss, More remains sceptical throughout the book: 'while Raphael was telling us all this, I kept thinking of various objections. The laws and customs of that country seemed to me in many cases perfectly ridiculous' (More 2003:113). However, after thanking Raphael for his interesting talk, More replies: 'Well, I must think it over. Then perhaps we can meet again and discuss at greater length' (ibid.:113). He is sceptical and open, he admits there are many good features of Utopia, although he hardly expects to see these features adopted in Europe. These conflicting arguments, radical change against careful consideration, scepticism, prolonged discussion, and, maybe, gradual reform are presented to the reader, forcing her to be alert, critical, and, hopefully, imaginative.

Even if Raphael's forceful argumentation appears persuasive it is useful to be reminded of the meaning of Raphael Hytlodaeus' name. Hythlodaeus means "dispenser of nonsense", and he is just a *student* of philosophy. Turner, in his introduction to More's *Utopia*, gives an interesting interpretation of the traveller's first name.

> [I]n the Apocryphal *Book of Tobit* the Archangel Raphael guides Tobit's son Tobias on a journey, which ends with the curing of Tobit's blindness, and the recovery of his property. So the name is quite appropriate for a character who tries to open up people's eyes to the causes of social evils, and the sources of prosperity.
>
> (Turner 2003:xii)

His name, then, as it turns out, is an oxymoron, a compressed paradox. He is both a seer and a dispenser of nonsense, and this compressed paradox serves as a foreshadowing, or symbol, of the nature of the discourse in the book, a reminder to the reader to remain alert and sceptical, to expect paradoxes and discrepancies. And, as mentioned earlier, even the title of More's work is a paradox, a good place that is no place.

Michel de Montaigne, the father of the essay[10], used his experiences as the basis for asking himself questions, and the overall question that he posed was "How to live". But he was always ready to admit: "What do I know?". These words – in the French original *"Que scay-je?"* – was indeed his motto, 'inscribed over a pair of scales' (de Montaigne 2003:477). A sceptical approach is underlying his essays, there is not one true answer, or there is no answer at all. And as I have argued, this questioning, this underlying scepticism, is a significant part of Thomas More's *Utopia*. The conversation with the reader inherent in Montaigne's essays is not so much a direct conversation as an effort to keep the reader alert by a similar exercise as More does in *Utopia*; Montaigne's essays are full of paradoxes and contradictions. This willingness to question, to play, and to argue is a common feature in Montaigne and More; More in the early sixteenth century (1516) and Montaigne in the late sixteenth century (1580). Both are ambiguous "boundary works", both are able to influence the act of reading, to force the reader to remain both sceptical and imaginative.

Marius de Geus, in his *Ecological Utopias: Envisioning the Sustainable Society* (1999), argues that ecological utopias could function as a compass to steer by. I do not find the compass metaphor useful to think with. In line with my argumentation, I propose that we should take an essayistic approach, read utopian narratives as a dialogue, to remain sceptical and open-minded. In French, *essayer* literally means to try. *Essai* is derived from Latin *exagium*; "the controlling of weight". *Exagito* means to set in motion or to unrest or agitate. This would be just what we need in a time where the prevailing attitude is lack of response, denial, and apathy. Reading More's *Utopia* is an experience, a stimulation of our thoughts, a test case, but not a final answer or a blueprint for a sustainable society. Only by being challenged, by considering visions for sustainability, by envisioning that we have a future, can we start to mobilize towards a sustainable future. It is precisely the contradictory and paradoxical features of the book that is its force. Let us embrace the utopian visions in an essayistic spirit.

Roemer defines a utopia as a description of an imaginary culture:

> · a fiction that invites readers to experience vicariously an alternative reality that critique theirs by opening cognitive and affective spaces that encourage readers to perceive the realities and potentialities of their culture in new ways. If the author or reader perceive the alternative imaginary culture as being significantly better than the "present", then the work is a [. . .] utopia; if significantly worse, it is a dystopia.

(Roemer 2003:20)

His definition accentuates the role of the reader, by emphasizing "imagination" and "opening cognitive spaces". Can we be sure that readers respond to the challenge in the "right" green, sustainable way? Reading in an essayistic spirit might lead the reader into the "wrong" conclusions, opting for an unsustainable society. This is a risk we have to take. As Roemer points out:

> [No] writer can satisfy the readers' desire for all the details they need to construct convincing images of entire alternative cultures. There are always enormous indeterminacies or gaps, to use Iser's terms, that leave ample room for the readers' affirmative and/or critical projections and for multiple questions.

(ibid.:28)

We cannot afford to lose 'the inspiration and innovative power of the utopian ecological imagination' (de Geus 1999:260). According to Tzvetan Todorov, literature's most important task is to uncover and clarify (new) aspects of reality, to construct models of experience. The fiction of Thomas More's *Utopia* may or may not contribute to environmental change, but it might wake up the reader. And, as Mike Hulme observes, climate change does not lend itself to a grand and easy solution. He presents climate change as an imaginative resource, 'which can be made to do work for us' (Hulme 2009:359). We, the readers, can treat Thomas More's *Utopia* as an imaginative resource, but in the essayistic spirit we need to do some of the work ourselves.

Notes

1 Tom Hodgkinson is the founder of the periodical the *Idler*, and he is also known from the lifestyle magazine *Country Living* as a columnist, writing on how to grow your own vegetables and enjoy nature's various pleasures.
2 See Soper's chapter in this collection.
3 *Under the Sea Wind* (1941), *The Sea Around Us* (1951), and *The Edge of the Sea* (1955) comprised her biography of the sea. The two last books were best-sellers.
4 For a summary of the research conducted on the film, see Hulme (2009:211–214).
5 Established in 1857 in Boston as a literary and cultural magazine; now called *The Atlantic Monthly*.
6 Thomas More (1478–1535) was an English philosopher and statesman.
7 Translation Paul Turner (2003).
8 Plato: 'What is the best form of organization for a community and how can a person best arrange his life' (Laws 3, 702b, quoted from Suvin 1979:37).
9 The eight-hour working day was established with Henry Ford and Ford Motor Company in 1914. Before that, from the early days of the industrial revolution, 10–16 hours was considered normal. John Maynard Keynes was an early promoter of a six-hour working day, and in recent years both individuals, such as Tom Hodgkinson, and political parties have suggested a six-hour working day. More free time, less unemployment and reduced consumption are some of the benefits from reducing the number of hours. A decrease in growth is good from an environmental perspective, but most politicians are in favour of a steady increase in growth.
10 Michel de Montaigne (1533–1592) is considered the founder of the essay, but there are several antecedents or kindred forms, such as in Plato, Cicero, Seneca, and Horace. All of them have contributed to the spirit and the form of the essay, as de Obaldia (2002) remarks. Montaigne was the first to use the term "essay".

Bibliography

Bacon, F. (2008) *New Atlantis*. In *Three Modern Utopias*. Susan Bruce (ed.). New York: Oxford University Press: 149–186.

Bellamy, E. (2011) *Looking Backward: 2000–1887*. Seattle, WA: Pacific Publishing Studio.

Buell, L. (2005) *The Future of Environmental Criticism*. Malden, MA; Oxford; Carlton, Victoria: Blackwell Publishing.

Campbell, C. (2005) *The Romantic Ethic and the Spirit of Modern Consumption*. Great Britain: Alcuin Academics.

Carson, R. (2000) *Silent Spring*. London: Penguin Books.

Cohen, S. (2001) *States of Denial: Knowing About Atrocities and Suffering*. Cambridge, MA: Polity Press.

Eco, U. (1984) *The Role of the Reader: Explorations in the Semiotics of Texts*. Bloomington, IN: Indiana University Press.

Elliott, R. C. (1970) *The Shape of Utopia: Studies of a Literary Genre*. Chicago, IL: University of Chicago Press.

Garrard, G. (2012) *Ecocriticism*. London: Routledge.

Gartner, C. B. (2000) 'When Science Writing Becomes Literary Art: The Success of *Silent Spring*' in Waddell, C. (ed.) *And No Birds Sing: Rhetorical Analyses of Rachel Carson's Silent Spring*. Carbondale and Edwardsville, IL: Southern Illinois University Press: pp. 103–125.

Genette, G. (1997) *Paratexts: Thresholds of Interpretation*. Cambridge; New York; Melbourne: Cambridge University Press.

Geus, M. de. (1999) *Ecological Utopias: Envisioning the Sustainable Society*. Utrecht: International Books.

Geus, M. de. (2003) *The End of Over-consumption: Towards a Lifestyle of Moderation and Self-restraint*. Utrecht: International Books.

Hodgkinson, T. (2004) *How to be Idle*. London: Hamish Hamilton, Penguin Books.

Hulme, M. (2009) *Why We Disagree About Climate Change: Understanding Controversy, Inaction and Opportunity*. Cambridge: Cambridge University Press.

Lanham, R. (2006) *The Economics of Attention: Style and Substance in the Age of Information*. Chicago, IL; London: University of Chicago Press.

Lucian of Samosata. (2012) *Lucian's True History*. U.K.: Lightning Source.

McCarthy, C. (2006) *The Road*. London; Basingstoke; Oxford: Picador.

Montaigne, M. de. (2003) *The Complete Works: Essays, Travel Journal, Letters*. Trans. D. M. Frame, New York; London; Toronto: Alfred A. Knopf.

More, T. (2003) *Utopia*. Trans. P. Turner, London: Penguin Books.

Morris, W. (2004) *News from Nowhere and Other Writings*. Wilmer, C. (ed.) London: Penguin Books.

Morson, G. S. (1981) *The Boundaries of Genre: Dostoevsky's Diary of a Writer and the Traditions of Literary Utopia*. Evanston, IL: Northwestern University Press.

Moser, S. C. (2007) 'More Bad News: The Risk of Neglecting Emotional Responses to Climate Change Information' in Moser, S. and Dilling, L. (eds) *Creating a Climate for Change: Communicating Climate Change and Facilitating Social Change*. New York: Cambridge University Press: pp. 64–80.

Nicholsen, S. W. (2002) *The Love of Nature and the End of the World: The Unspoken Dimensions of Environmental Concern*. Cambridge, MA: MIT Press.

Norgaard, K. M. (2011) *Living in Denial: Climate Change, Emotions, and Everyday Life*. Cambridge, MA; London: MIT Press.

Obaldia, C. de. (2002) *The Essayistic Spirit. Literature, Modern Criticism, and the Essay*. Oxford: Clarendon Press.

Plato. (2012) *Republic*. Trans. C. Rowe, London: Penguin Books.

Pliny The Elder. (1991) *Natural History*. Trans. J. Healey, London: Penguin Books.

Roemer, K. M. (2003) *Utopian Audiences: How Readers Locate Nowhere*. Amherst and Boston: University of Massachusetts Press.

Ruppert, P. (1986) *Reader in a Strange Land: The Activity of Reading Literary Utopias*. Athens and London: The University of Georgia Press.

Soper, K. (2008) 'Alternative Hedonism, Cultural Theory and the Role of Aesthetic Revisioning' in *Cultural Studies*, 22:5, pp. 567–587.

Soper, K. (2009) 'Introduction: The Mainstreaming of Counter-Consumerist Concern' in Soper, K., Ryle, M. and Thomas, L. (eds) *The Politics and Pleasures of Consuming Differently*. Basingstoke: Palgrave Macmillan: pp. 1–21.

Suvin, D. (1979) *Metamorphoses of Science Fiction: On the Poetics and History of a Literary Genre*. New Haven and London: Yale University Press.

Thoreau, H. D. (2008) *Walden*. Oxford: Oxford University Press.

Turner, P. (2003) 'Introduction' in More, T. *Utopia*. London: Penguin Books: xi–xxiv.

3 Towards a sustainable flourishing

Democracy, hedonism and the politics of prosperity

Kate Soper

Human needs, global distribution and sustainable consumption

Until recently, few have questioned the concept of prosperity associated with the market-driven 'consumerist' way of living. Many indeed continue to view it as both the sole means to a 'high' standard of living, and the only reliable vehicle of 'freedom and democracy'. Government and corporate elites believe – or hope – that eco-modernising technologies will allow it indefinitely to continue and that we can have unending economic expansion with little alteration in lifestyle. The common presumption is that the consumerist model of the 'good life' is the one we want to hold on to as far as we can, and that any curb on that will necessarily prove unwelcome.

Yet this sanguine outlook is now increasingly vulnerable to the contradictions between economic and ecological imperatives. It is also failing to address the anger – and anxiety – many now feel about living in a world that has so plainly favoured the greed and ever more conspicuous, and environmentally vandalising, consumption of the already very wealthy, and allowed the gap between richer and poorer to grow to inflammatory proportions both within the nation state and globally. Indeed there is now a growing fear of the potentially explosive consequences of a system that is so deeply troubled, both socially and environmentally. To this we may add the evidence – to which I shall return shortly – of a certain disenchantment with 'consumer culture' even within the more affluent nations; of a growing disquiet over the negative legacy of the consumerist lifestyle itself.

I shall begin, however, with some – necessarily very bald – reflections on what is probably the most intractable conceptual issue that arises in this general area: that of the criteria and norms of a so-called 'sustainable' consumption.

And here my first point is that the longer we continue with the growth economy and the conception of the 'good life' it supports (and depends upon), the more intense the competition for dwindling resources will become, and the more uncivil the methods to which richer societies are likely to have recourse in defending their advantage. These could include measures that most of us would currently regard as deeply repugnant, indeed they could spell an end to rights-based humanitarian morality as we know it – the manipulation of poverty, disease and famine to control global population; the coercion of the poorest economies into servicing of First World needs for bio-fuels and other energy substitutes; ever more restrictive policies on immigration in privileged regions such as the EU to check the flow of eco-refugees from the more devastated areas of the globe. Such measures are likely to encourage ever more desperate forms of terrorist activity and could well end in genocidal and even terminal forms of global warfare.

Now since no global economic order can be said to be sustainable unless it can avoid those kinds of outcome, what is more truly sustainable will necessarily involve a more co-operative, less competitive global order, and a significant re-distribution of wealth and access to resources.

Yet even if we accept that greater equality is essential to enduring global peace and security, and hence sustainability, we still have to confront the question about what this sustainable – because enduring and universalisable – level of consumption might consist in. What kind of norm of human gratification are we aspiring to? What standard of living might be indefinitely viable – in the sense that it could be enjoyed by everyone here and now and by all future generations? Given the global diversity of cultures and conceptions of the 'good life' and the number of over-determining variables of which any projected assessment would need to take account, the question becomes well-nigh imponderable. Hence the understandable inclination to shift the discussion onto human needs – to think instead in terms of some level of basic needs provision that can serve as the enabling condition of differential forms of flourishing in diverse social settings.[1]

However, observant as this type of approach is of cultural difference, the resistance to specifying anything 'thicker' than *in perpetuo* basic need provision for all is actually in many ways an evasion of the key issues we need to address in thinking about sustainable consumption.[2] For it is clear that 'basic' needs for food, shelter and the like can be provided in variously ascetic or luxurious ways; and many of those more luxurious ways – those associated, for example, with Western consumerist forms of affluence – are clearly not sustainable. The emphasis on providing for abstract basic or common needs (for food, shelter, etc.), while important, does not, in other words, engage with the highly charged discriminations which are also needed in respect of the specific 'satisfiers' (the *forms* of provision for food, housing or clothing, etc.) of basic needs that might qualify as sustainable. And if we focus too exclusively on provision for common and basic human needs, we risk overlooking the critical role of the form taken by the specific satisfiers of those common needs in the affluent and 'best performing' nations in creating deprivation elsewhere. What therefore has to be targeted by a global politics of need is not only what we share in the way of basic needs but the causal relationship between the highly elaborated and luxurious forms in which the more globally privileged are meeting their 'developed' needs and securing the protection of their affluent lifestyles, and the forms in which other communities are being deprived of even the more reduced forms of satisfaction of 'basic' needs, let alone provided with the wherewithal to conserve for the future (Martinez-Alier, 1995; Redclift, 1996; 2005; Dobson, 1998; Dobson, 1999; Miller, 1995; Goodland and Daly, 1992).

What adds to the problem here is that 'development' has been so closely associated with the promotion of consumerist standards of living. Those seeking to extend commercial access in the provision of 'basic' utilities in 'developing' countries are usually not interested in re-thinking the 'good life' along less acquisitive and ecologically rapacious lines, but rather in fostering new potential markets for the goods associated with the consumer culture of the 'developed' world. For importantly included among the market 'freedoms' is the license for producers to pursue profit, develop new wants and thus expand consumption wherever that proves possible. But this is a dynamic that thrives best on the expansion of the market for consumer goods in the already relatively affluent nations, and is thus at odds with the redistribution of wealth and resources that is essential to meeting basic needs in the poorest nations.

'Development', as currently construed, is thus a key factor in the creation of underdevelopment and the ecological and social exploitations associated with it. Charities and human rights activists concerned with these exploitations might do better, therefore, to link their demands for the universal satisfaction of basic human needs to a critique of the conception of human flourishing that has been promoted through the neo-liberal market, and that needs now itself to be re-thought in the light of its deleterious consequences. To be genuinely interested in the promotion of basic needs satisfaction on a global scale is also to be interested in promoting an alternative 'political imaginary' in respect of human pleasure and fulfilment – especially if the interest in meeting needs extends into the indefinite future and includes a concern with the welfare of future generations.

When considered in this light, we might also take note of a fundamental ambivalence in the very concept of 'basic' needs, given that it seems to point only to the essentials of survival and minimal well-being, while implying that a distinctively human *flourishing* would require something altogether more evolved and elaborate in the way of material provisioning. After all, given current rates of population growth it might seem overly optimistic to expect the universal gratification *in perpetuo* of even this minimum. (As Adorno (1974:16) suggested some while ago, it seems utopian enough simply to hope that no one will go hungry any more.) But if some reasonable provision for basic needs is the best we can hope to realise globally over time, then what should we make of the idea of these needs being designated as 'basic'? Does this not expose a partial – Western and ethnocentric – perception of human potentialities of a kind to give us pause for thought? If an indefinitely sustainable consumption for all can only be had at the cost of reneging on 'wants' (or even on that other class of 'non-basic' needs which the concept of 'basic' needs implies), should we not seek to discourage the prospect of any further flourishing as unrealistic? Relatedly, should we not submit ourselves to the somewhat sobering thought that it is an awareness, however subliminal, that a more egalitarian global order will cut off the prospects of any further human 'flourishing' beyond that provided through universal 'basic' need satisfaction, that underlies the nonchalance of affluent governments and many of their citizens, in regard to matters of global justice, especially in relation to ecological sustainability? There is an unspoken sense here, one feels, that it is better that some should flourish, even at the cost of the survival of others, than that all should manage little more than to live 'by bread alone'.

But the appropriate response to such speculations is that they are based on an overly conservative conception of what constitutes a distinctively human flourishing. That they have force only if we assume that not 'living by bread alone' always means, shall we say, 'eating cake' – that is to say, it would always involve a more refined and luxurious level of *material* satisfaction. It is only if we adopt a 'materialist-consumerist' conception of what it means to flourish or expand on 'basic' need provision that we shall share rather than challenge the standard liberal-economic anxieties about the 'stagnating' effects of an essentially stable and reproductive provision of basic material needs for all. If we break with the idea of an 'improved living standard' engendered by consumer culture, then we need no longer think of 'wants' or 'non-basic' needs always as extensions of, or ever more baroque and resource-hungry constructions upon, primary physical needs but as an altogether less materially encumbered and encumbering source of fulfilment.

In other words, a 'decent and humane' standard of living for all is in principle compatible with the furthering of human flourishing conceived as the gratification of desires (or less basic needs), provided these latter cease to be so fixated on tangible goods, and more directed to so-called 'spiritual' dimensions of satisfaction. Moreover (and I'll return to this shortly) by restraining our more 'consumerist' forms of consumption we could enhance even our more directly sensory pleasures through the enjoyment of better health, more free time and a slower pace of living. In this sense the call for sustainable consumption is also a call for a different vision of human prosperity. If the more affluent peoples of the world need to restrain their material desires in order to secure a socially just and sustainable global order, then it is surely also true that a condition of the emergence of a will to sobriety in material consumption will be the fostering of an altered conception of pleasure and enjoyment. In this sense, being practical about human needs and natural limits may require us to be highly imaginative about wants, and the realism of any theory of sustainable development may prove dependent on our capacities for utopian projection at the level of desire (cf. Soper 1993:127–128).

Rethinking 'prosperity': the 'alternative hedonist' approach

My argument around the concept of 'alternative hedonism' is designed to highlight the need for such utopian projection while at the same time indicating the likely influences upon its formation, and the possible agents of its promotion. It responds to the current situation not only as a crisis, and by no means only as presaging future gloom and doom, but as offering an opportunity to advance beyond a mode of life that is not only environmentally doomed but also in many respects unpleasurable and self-denying.

There are two main claims to the 'alternative hedonist' argument.[3] The first is that the affluent, 'consumerist', Euro-American mode of consumption that has become the model of the 'good life' for so many other societies today is unlikely to be checked in the absence of a seductive alternative – an altered conception of what it is to flourish and to enjoy a 'high' standard of living.[4] In this sense, the chances of developing or reverting to a more ecologically sustainable use of resources, and hence of removing some of the key sources of social and environmental exploitation, are dependent on the emergence and embrace of new modes of thinking about human pleasure and self-realisation, especially, in the first instance, within the relatively affluent global societies. This is not to suppose that any ambivalence towards consumer culture will be experienced only by those who already have access to it. Nor is it to assume that less affluent societies will necessarily be influenced by any 'alternative hedonist' revision of thinking that might emerge over time within the more affluent. The claim is only that an important stimulus of any change of direction, if there is to be one, will be the compulsion exercised by an alternative vision of the 'good life'. An anti-consumerist ethic and politics should therefore appeal not only to altruistic compassion and environmental concern but also to the more self-regarding gratifications of consuming differently: to more personally rewarding ways of consuming.

The more substantive claim is that we are indeed seeing the beginnings of this particular counter-consumerist trend, both in the sense that other conceptions of the 'good life' appear to be gaining more of a hold among some affluent consumers, and in the sense that there is a more pervasive disenchantment with the supposed blessings of consumerism. Shopping may still be a very favoured way of spending time, and there has been precious little reform in the use of the car and air flight, yet there are also some signs now that the affluent lifestyle is generating its own specific forms of disaffection, either because of the pollution, congestion, ill health, loss of community and personal forms of contact it entails or because it stands in the way of other enjoyments (Schor, 2004; Levett, 2003; Bunting, 2004; Honore, 2005; Shah, 2005; Thomas, 2008; 2009).

There is, for example, general agreement today that the 'consumerist' lifestyle is a major cause of stress and obesity. It subjects us to high levels of noise and stench, and generates vast amounts of junk. Its work routines and modes of commerce mean that many people for most of their lives begin their days in traffic jams or overcrowded trains and buses, and then spend much of the rest of them glued to the computer screen, often engaged in mind-numbing tasks. A good part of its productive activity locks time into the creation of a material culture of ever faster production turnovers and built-in obsolescence, which pre-empts more worthy, enduring or entrancing forms of human fulfilment. Instead of enhanced productive efficiency being used to shorten the working-week so as we could enjoy growing and preparing more food for ourselves, companies profit from selling us back 'fast food' and ready-cooked meals; instead of giving us the leisure and facilities to walk or go by bike, we are co-opted into buying short-sharp exercise sessions in the gym; instead of longer holidays in which we could travel more slowly and experience more genuine relaxation, the tourist and therapy industries profit hugely from their provision for mini-breaks and stress-relieving services.

Now more than ever, in fact, the consumer society is dependent on a collective preparedness to spend the money we earn by working too hard and too long on provision to compensate for the more diverse, enriching and lasting satisfactions we have sacrificed through over-work and over-production. Yet it is far from clear that this reflects some innate desire of people constantly to work and consume more. If it did, the billions spent on advertising, and especially now on grooming children for a life of consumption, would hardly be necessary (Schor, 2004; Williams, 2008); and nor would the government pressure people to keep spending (the injunctions to 'patriotic shopping' in the aftermath of 9/11 as a means of defending the 'Western way of life'; or the car scrappage schemes to keep the motor industry on track; or the anxieties in the UK lest increased VAT reduces sales in the malls). Nor would politicians keep warning us of the terrible regression in any departure from the consumerist lifestyle. Alternative hedonism challenges that notion of regression. It is premised on the idea that even if the consumerist lifestyle were indefinitely sustainable it would not enhance human happiness and well-being (or not beyond a certain point that has already passed). And it claims that it is emergent forms of desire rather than fears of ecological disaster that are likely to have most impact in any move towards more sustainable modes of consuming. Such desires, for example, are already implicit in the common laments over lost spaces and communities, the commercial battening on children, the vocational dumbing-down of education, the ravages of 'development', the 'cloning' of our cities, and so forth; and they indicate an interest in a society no longer subordinate to the imperatives of growth and consumerist expansion. Diffuse and politically unfocussed though they may be, they speak to a widely felt sense of the opportunities squandered in recent decades for creating a fairer, less harassed, less environmentally destructive and more enjoyable way of life. To defend the progressive dimension of this kind of yearning (one might term it 'avant-garde nostalgia') against the exigencies of 'progress' is not to recommend a more ascetic existence. On the contrary, it is to highlight the puritanical, disquieting and irrational aspects of contemporary consumer culture. It is to speak for the forms of pleasure and happiness that people might be able to enjoy were they to opt for an alternative economic order. It is to open up a new 'political imaginary': a seductive vision of alternatives to resource-intensive consumption, centred on a reduction of the working-week and a slower pace of living. By working and producing less we could improve health and well-being, and provide for forms of conviviality which our harried and insulated travel and work routines make impossible. A cultural revolution along these lines would challenge the advertisers' monopoly on the depiction of prosperity and the 'good life'. It would make the stuff that is now seriously messing up the planet – more cars, more planes, more roads, more throwaway commodities – look ugly because of the energy it squanders and the environmental damage it causes.

By focussing on these new developments and shifts of feeling in constituting an immanent critique of consumer culture, the 'alternative hedonist' perspective aims to avoid the moralising about 'real' needs that has often characterised earlier critiques of consumer culture (Miller, 2001). It engages with ambivalence or disaffection towards consumerism as this comes to the surface and finds expression in the sensibility or behaviour of consumers themselves. The concern is not to prove that people 'really' need something quite other than what they profess to need (or want) – a procedure which is paternalistic and undemocratic – but to reflect on the hedonist aspirations prompting changes in experienced or imagined need, and their implications for the development of a new electoral mandate for the forms of self-policing essential to sustainable living. Those espousing the ecological cause are in general pretty good at diagnosing what has gone wrong and informing us of what is needed in order to put it right. In the *Limits to Growth* (Meadows et al., 1972:216) we are told, for example, that:

> People don't need enormous cars; they need respect. They don't need closetfuls of clothes; they need to feel attractive and they need excitement and variety and beauty. People don't need electronic entertainment; they need something worthwhile to do with their lives. And so forth.

But it is one thing to claim knowledge of what is 'really' needed. It is quite another thing to reveal in what sense, if any, these are indeed the 'needs' of consumers; and another again to show by what agencies and transitional means they might be more universally acknowledged and acted upon. An anti-consumerist argument, in short, cannot be effective or democratically sensitive if it disregards the expressed feelings of consumers or treats them as unthinking 'dupes' of consumer culture. In contrast to this emphasis on people's 'real', but unacknowledged, needs, the alternative hedonist seeks both to respect what people themselves say about their needs, and to credit them with a degree of autonomy and self-knowledge. Its main interest is thus in the hedonic aspirations prompting changes at the level of actual experience – or, to invoke Raymond Williams's concept – in an emerging 'structure of feeling' that is both troubled by what was previously taken much more for granted, and aware, if only dimly, of former pleasures that are going missing, or other possible gratifications that are unlikely now to become available (Williams, 1977:132; cf. 128–136).

In pointing to an emergent form of resistance to consumer culture, the alternative hedonist position differs substantially from earlier leftwing – Marxist and Critical Theory – critiques of commodification whose emphasis has been on the construction or manipulation of consumer 'needs' and wants rather than on the critical reflexivity of consumers themselves (Adorno, 1974; 1991; Marcuse, 1964; 1955/1972; Leiss, 1978; Haug, 1986; 2006; Lodziak, 1995; Gorz, 1989; Bauman, 1988; 1991; 1998). It followed from these critiques that production alone was viewed as the site of potential mobilisation against the capitalist order through the agency of worker militancy. Political efforts had therefore to be directed to transforming the relationships of ownership and control over industrial production rather than at the quality and methods of production as such. The objective was to equalise access to consumption, rather than to revolutionise its culture. And today, labour militancy and trade union activity have largely become confined to protection of income and employees' rights within the existing structures of globalised capital, and have not sought to challenge, let alone transform, the 'work and spend' dynamic of affluent cultures.

Even when the left has in the past addressed issues of need and consumption more directly, it has veered towards asceticism and paternalism (suggesting baldly that people are misled into thinking they need more than they really do), or proved divided and confused on issues of consumer autonomy and accountability (both endorsing popular choice and exposing its false forms of construction by the market). This is because it has been anxious to claim both that its critique of the 'falsity' of consumerism (together with its implied knowledge of what people 'really' need) is democratically representative, *and* to explain the mismatch at any point in time between what consumers *actually* demand and what it is claimed they *really* want, by reference to their unfreedom, in other words, their ideological manipulation. But it seems no more convincing to view shopping enthusiasts as merely the unfortunate and unaccountable dupes of the consumer society, than to view them as fully autonomous and self-knowing beneficiaries of it. There is, in short, a tension around the issue of consumer needs and desires that it would be more honest to admit and openly discuss, rather than seek to suppress.

As it is, Marxist critics of consumer culture have tended to offer reductive 'simple life' versions of human need and fulfilment rather than provide more complex imaginative reflection on the potentialities of human pleasure, and the rich and subtle forms of their possible realisation in a post-capitalist society.

To avoid misunderstanding, I would emphasise the role in this form of 'utopian projection' of conceptual reconstruction, and the break with earlier notions of both 'spirituality' and of 'material' well-being that would necessarily be involved. In my opinion not least of the difficulties in conceptualising these shifts is the lack of a vocabulary of the 'spirit' that does not come loaded with either religious, or mystical or ascetic connotations. But conversely, it is almost impossible today to engage in critique of an overly 'materialist' consumption without it being assumed that one is advocating some less complex and sensually enriching mode of existence. Let me make clear, too, that counter to some anti-consumerist critiques, I do not presume that the 'excesses' of modern consumption can be corrected through a return to a simpler, objectively knowable, and supposedly more 'natural' *modus vivendi*. The critique associated with 'alternative hedonism' does not deny the complexity of human desires, nor the need to accommodate the distinctively human quests for novelty, excitement, distraction, self-expression and the gratifications of *amour propre*. It can even allow that the gratification of what Rousseau termed the '*fureur de se distinguer*' – the zeal for self-distinction which he associated with *amour propre* – is most easily supplied through material acquisition (at least if you have the money for it). But what comes easiest, of course, is not necessarily the most rewarding or fulfilling, and in deflecting complex needs and demands onto commodified sources of satisfaction, consumer culture is hedonistically more restrictive than permissive.

Today, I would argue, we need to overcome the reluctance to address the 'politics of pleasure', and to associate it with the promotion of a steady state economy and 'alternative hedonist' political imaginary (cf. Jackson, 2004; 2009;

Victor, 2008). This would be consistent with the critique of consumer culture that is implicit in much discourse on sustainable consumption, and allow it to connect with and give voice to the political desires suggested by the forms of disaffection with consumerism outlined above. It would also be consistent with the recent empirical research that has undermined the presumption that increased wealth leads to increased happiness and indicated that there is something inherently self-defeating in the pursuit of ever more consumption (Brown and Kasser, 2005; Kasser, 2002; 2007).

It is true that the simple lack of a correlation between higher income and increased reported life satisfaction does not in itself entail that more consumption has not improved well-being. The standards used by people in assessing their level of satisfaction may themselves become more stringent as their life experience changes with increased income. Nor are feelings of satisfaction always the best guide to how well people may be faring. Education has often exposed alienation and served the cause of personal emancipation precisely by generating discontent. The learning of skills may lead to increased dissatisfaction and demands on the self as one makes progress in their acquisition.

All this indicates that happiness is an elusive concept, and it is difficult to pronounce on its quality or the extent to which it (and its associated states of pleasure, well-being or satisfaction) has been achieved. What should count in the estimation of the 'good life': the intensity of its isolated moments of pleasure, or its overall level of contentment? Should it be the avoidance of pain and difficulty or their successful overcoming? And who, finally, is best placed to decide on whether personal well-being has increased: is this entirely a matter of subjective report, or is it open to objective appraisal?

Such issues have long been at the centre of debates between Utilitarianism and Aristotelianism. Where the former has looked to a 'hedonic calculus' of subjectively experienced pleasure or avoidance of pain in assessing life satisfaction, the more objectively oriented Aristotelian focus has been on capacities, functions and achievements (with what one has been enabled to do with one's life) rather than with its more immediate feelings of gratification. Hence its attention to the overall fulfilment and happiness (eudaimonia) of a life taken as a whole. In defence of this stance, Aristotelians will argue that if we disallow any objective knowledge of another person's well-being or of what makes for a life well spent, we shall also be deprived of grounds to criticise personally self-destructive or selfish and environmentally vandalising forms of pleasure seeking. It has also been claimed, relatedly, that a 'happiness' conceived or measured in terms of subjective feeling discourages the development of the republican sentiment and inter-generational solidarity essential to social and environmental well-being (O'Neill, 2006; 2008).

On the other hand, the 'hedonic calculus' for its part need not rule out the more civically oriented forms of felt pleasure, or the subjective gratifications of consuming in socially and environmentally responsible ways. The pleasure of many activities, after all, riding a bike, for example, include both immediately personal sensual enjoyments and those which come from not contributing to social harms – in this case, the danger and damage of car driving. Moreover, it is difficult in the last analysis to legitimate claims about well-being without some element of subjective endorsement on the part of those about whom they are being made.

There is, then, a tension in discussions of hedonism and the good life between the Utilitarian privileging of experienced pleasure and the objective bias of the eudaimonic tradition. The focus on the having of good feelings risks overlooking the more objective constituents of the 'good life' and the 'good society'; the Aristotelian emphasis does justice to those constituents but runs the risk of patronage and condoning the superior knowingness of experts over individuals themselves.

But to accept the complexity of gauging claims about the quality of life and personal satisfaction is one thing. To deny that today there is any evidence of the self-defeating nature of ever expanding consumption would be quite another, and both sides to the hedonist debate are, in fact, in general agreement that happiness does not lie in the endless accumulation of more stuff. And, as indicated earlier, although it does not – and cannot – aspire finally to resolve the philosophical issues in this area, the alternative hedonist perspective, by highlighting the narratives about pleasure and well-being that are implicit in the emerging forms of disaffection with affluent culture, seeks to open up a post-consumerist optic on the 'good life' while still respecting felt experience.

Notes

1   This has been the general approach adopted, for example, by Doyal and Gough, 1991; cf. Sen, 1984; 1985; 1992; Nussbaum, 1992; Soper, 2007a. It is represented in this volume by Hellevik as well as by Rauschmayer and Omann.
2   So-called 'thin' theories of need are universalist, specifying needs held in common by all humans (for basic nutrition, shelter and the like). 'Thin' theorists tend to emphasise the objectively knowable status of needs. 'Thicker' theories emphasise, by contrast, the subjectively acknowledged and culturally relative nature of needs, and are sceptical about allowing 'experts' to know better than people themselves about their needs.
3   For further discussion, see Soper 2007a; 2007b; 2008a; 2008b; 2009.
4   The concept of 'affluence' and of the 'affluent consumer' is here used rather generally to refer to the Western standard of living and those who participate in it. It refers, that is, to a lifestyle that in material terms is very prosperous relative to that of the majority of the world's population. This is not to deny, however, the economic divisions within 'affluent' societies themselves and the very differing levels of access to affluence within them.

Bibliography

Adorno, T. (1974 [German 1951]) *Minima Moralia*. London: NLB.
Adorno, T. (1991 [German 1947]) *The Culture Industry: Selected Essays on Mass Culture*. Bernstein, J.M. (ed.) London: Routledge.
Bauman, Z. (1988) *Freedom*. Milton Keynes: Open University Press.
Bauman, Z. (1991) *Modernity and Ambivalence*. Cambridge: Polity.
Bauman, Z. (1998) *Work, Consumerism and the New Poor*. Milton Keynes: Open University Press.

Brown, K.W. and Kasser, T. (2005) 'Are psychological and ecological well-being compatible? The role of values, mindfulness, and lifestyle' in *Social Indicators Research*, 74, pp. 349–368.

Bunting, M. (2004) *Willing Slaves: How the Overwork Culture is Ruling Our Live*. London: Harper Collins.

Dobson, A. (1998) *Justice and the Environment*. Oxford: Oxford University Press.

Dobson, A. (ed.) (1999) *Fairness and Futurity: Essays on Sustainability and Justice*. Oxford: Oxford University Press.

Doyal, L. and Gough, I. (1991) *A Theory of Human Need*. London: Macmillan.

Goodland, R. and Daly, H. (1992) *Ten Reasons Why Northern Income is not the Solution to Southern Poverty*. Washington D.C.: Environment Department, World Bank.

Gorz, A. (1989) *Critique of Economic Reason*. London: Verso.

Haug, W.F. (1986) *Critique of Commodity Aesthetics*. Cambridge: Polity.

Haug, W.F. (2006) 'Commodity aesthetics revisited' in *Radical Philosophy*, 135.

Honore, C. (2005) *In Praise of Slowness: Challenging the Cult of Speed*. New York: Harper One.

Jackson, T. (2004) *Chasing Progress: Beyond Measuring Economic Growth*. London: New Economics Foundation.

Jackson, T. (2009) *Prosperity without Growth*. Sustainable Development Commission.

Kasser, T. (2002) *The High Price of Materialism*. Cambridge MA: MIT Press.

Kasser, T. (2007) 'Values and Prosperity' paper to the SDC seminar on 'Visions of Prosperity', 26 November 2008.

Leiss, W. (1978) *The Limits to Satisfaction: On Needs and Commodities*. London: Marion Boyars.

Levett, R. (2003) *A Better Choice of Choice: Quality of Life, Consumption and Economic Growth*. London: Fabian Society.

Lodziak, C. (1995) *Manipulating Needs, Capitalism and Culture*. London: Pluto.

Marcuse, H. (1955/1972) *Eros and Civilisation*. London: Abacus.

Marcuse, H. (1964) *One-Dimensional Man*. London: Beacon Press.

Martinez-Alier, J. (1995) 'Political ecology, distributional conflicts and economic incommensurability' in *New Left Review*, 9 (3), pp. 295–323.

Meadows, D. et al. (1972) *Limits to Growth*. New York: Universe Books, Transaction Publishing.

Miller, D. (1995) 'Consumption as the vanguard of history' in Miller, D. (ed.) *Acknowledging Consumption*. London & New York: Routledge, pp. 1–57.

Miller, D. (2001) 'The poverty of morality' in *Journal of Consumer Culture*, 1 (2), pp. 225–243.

Nussbaum, M. (1992) 'Human functioning and social justice: in defence of Aristotelian essentialism' in *Political Theory*, 20 (2), pp. 202–246.

O'Neill, J. (2006) 'Citizenship, well-being as sustainability: Epicurus or Aristotle?' in *Analyse & Kritik*, 28 (2), pp. 158–172.

O'Neill, J. (2008) 'Sustainability, well-being and consumption: the limits of hedonic approaches', in Soper K. and Trentmann F. (eds) *Citizenship and Consumption*. London: Palgrave, pp. 172–190.

Redclift, M. (1996) *Wasted: Counting the Costs of Global Consumption*. London: Earthscan.

Redclift, M. (2005) 'Sustainable development (1987–2005). An oxymoron comes of age' in *Sustainable Development*, 13, pp. 212–227.

Schor, J. (2004) *Born to Buy*. New York: Schribner.

Sen, A. (1984) *Resources, Values and Development*. Oxford: Oxford University Press.

Sen, A. (1985) *Commodities and Capabilities*. Amsterdam: Elsevier.

Sen, A. (1992) *Inequality Reexamined*. Cambridge MA: Harvard University Press.

Shah, H. (2005) 'The politics of well-being' in *Soundings*, 30, pp. 33–44.

Soper, K. (1993) 'To each according to their need ?' in *New Left Review*, 197, pp. 113–128.

Soper, K. (2007a) 'Conceptualising needs in the context of consumer politics' in *Journal of Consumer Policy*, 29, pp. 355–372.

Soper, K. (2007b) 'Re-thinking the "good life": the citizenship dimension of consumer disaffection with consumerism' in *Journal of Consumer Culture*, 7 (2), pp. 205–230.

Soper, K. (2008a) 'Alternative hedonism, cultural theory and the role of aesthetic revisioning' in *Cultural Studies*, 22 (5), pp. 567–587.

Soper, K. (2008b) 'Alternative hedonism and the citizen consumer' in Soper, K. and Trentmann, F. (eds) *Citizenship and Consumption*. New York and Basingstoke: Palgrave Macmillan, pp.191–205.

Soper, K. (2009) 'Introduction' in Soper, K., Ryle, M. and Thomas. L. (eds) *The Politics and Pleasures of Consuming Differently*. London: Palgrave, pp.1–21.

Thomas, L. (2008) 'Alternative realities: downshifting narratives in contemporary lifestyle television' in *Cultural Studies*, 22 (5), pp. 680–699.

Thomas, L. (2009) 'Ecochic: green echoes and rural retreats in contemporary lifestyle magazines' in Soper, K., Ryle, M. and Thomas, L. (eds) *The Politics and Pleasures of Consuming Differently*. London: Palgrave, pp. 59–73.

Victor, P. (2008) *Managing without Growth, Slower by Design, Not Disaster*. London: Edward Elgar.

Williams, R. (1977) *Marxism and Literature*. Oxford: Oxford University Press.

Williams, Z. (2008) 'The commercialisation of childhood', *Compass UK report*, February. www.compassonline.org/publications (accessed 21 July 2014).

4 Is the good life sustainable?

A three-decade study of values, happiness and sustainability in Norway

Ottar Hellevik

Introduction

The key concepts in this chapter are values, subjective well-being and sustainability. *Values* refer to our ideas of how we want to live our lives, our conceptions of basic goals and means to attain them. Values may thus be said to constitute an individual's own recipe for a good life. Whether that recipe actually works, in the sense of increasing his or her *subjective well-being* (happiness and satisfaction with life), turns out to depend on which values are pursued. Finally *sustainability* concerns the question of how our way of life affects the chances for solving basic problems facing mankind today. Not surprisingly value preferences strongly influence attitudes towards protecting the environment and improving the situation for the underprivileged. They are also relevant for the discussion of the sustainability of the welfare state, fuelled by the current economic crisis in Europe.

The question – is the good life sustainable? – is thus a question of how the choices we make based on our values affect our chances of becoming happy and satisfied with our lives, as well as the sustainability of this way of life. This chapter attempts to answer these questions through analyses of survey data from Norway for the period 1985–2011.

It starts out by describing contrasting conceptions of the good life in the Norwegian population by means of a dimensional analysis of 25 value measures. The results show the opposition between modern and traditional values to be the most differentiating one, followed by materialistic versus idealistic values. The latter dimension turns out to be especially important in relation to both subjective well-being and sustainability, as it is strongly correlated with happiness and satisfaction as well as with attitudes towards environmental protection, redistribution of wealth and support for the welfare state.

The answer to the question "is the good life sustainable?" thus turns out to depend on what *kind* of "good life" is preferred, whether idealistic or materialistic values are pursued. The main conclusion of the chapter is that an idealistic idea of the good life is superior, both with regard to feelings of happiness and satisfaction and with regard to support for sustainable policies and practices.

An important question is how rising income and material standard of living affect the value formation in a population. In this regard Norway is a case of special interest, since here the trend of rising prosperity has continued over decennia without the major setbacks that many other countries have suffered in recent years. We will look at how value preferences, subjective well-being and sustainability-relevant attitudes and behaviour have developed since 1985. Is the tendency that increasing wealth has lead to rising material desires and expectations, or do we see a growing feeling that enough is enough and that other aspects of life are more important?

The Norwegian Monitor study

The data analysed is from the Norwegian Monitor study (NM). This is a series of large surveys, both in terms of sample size and number of questions asked, carried out by the market research institute Ipsos MMI every second year since 1985.[1] The introductory questions are asked by an interviewer, from 1997 over the phone, earlier in the home of the respondent, while the major part is included in a self-completion questionnaire. The samples are representative for the Norwegian population aged 15 and above (from 1997 simple random sampling from telephone directories has been used, earlier two-stage cluster sampling). The problem of non-response has increased over the years, but comparisons of sample results with known population statistics so far indicate a random rather than systematic pattern of refusals.[2] A substantial part of the survey is devoted to describing the value preferences of the Norwegian population.

Values and value dimensions of the Norwegian Monitor

To measure value preferences, 62 questions – mostly propositions with agree/disagree responses – are used to construct 25 additive value indexes, with two or more items each, as shown in the appendix (Hellevik 1996). The propositions are worded in opposite directions, to control for "yes-saying" tendencies, which for some questions are quite strong (Hellevik 1995). The index positions the respondents on a scale between opposite value poles, e.g. protection of the environment versus economic growth, with scores ranging from 0–8 or more. A factor analysis of the index scores yields value dimensions with a clear substantive interpretation.[3]

The dimension which best captures differences in value preferences in the Norwegian population, contrasts those who are positive to technological innovations, risk taking, spontaneity, urban life, new social mores such as gender equality, to those who believe in established traditions, religion, authority, conformity, frugality, respect for law and order. The terms *modern* versus *traditional* value orientation or change oriented versus stability oriented have been used to characterize the first value dimension (Hellevik 1993). Not surprisingly, it is clearly correlated with age. Cohort analyses indicate that the age pattern is a result of generational differences as well as life cycle processes (Hellevik 2002).

The second dimension has been called *materialistic* versus *idealistic* value orientation, or outer versus inner directed. On one side we find people who value economic growth, material possessions and consumption, immediate and conspicuous, and who put their own needs above concern for others. On the other side we find people valuing self-realization, close interpersonal relations, religion, good health and concern for the environment. Women and those with a higher education tend to be more idealistic in their value orientation than men and those with less education (Hellevik 2002).

The two value dimensions are independent (orthogonal). They define a two-dimensional cultural space as shown in Figure 4.1, where persons with a modern value orientation are located at the top and traditionalists at the bottom of the vertical axis, and materialists to the left and idealists to the right on the horizontal axis.

The position of a value in the map represents the average score on the two dimensions for those members of the sample who hold this value, in the sense that they belong to the quarter of the sample located at one extreme of the value index.[4] An appendix lists the values and the questions used as indicators for the 25 indexes.

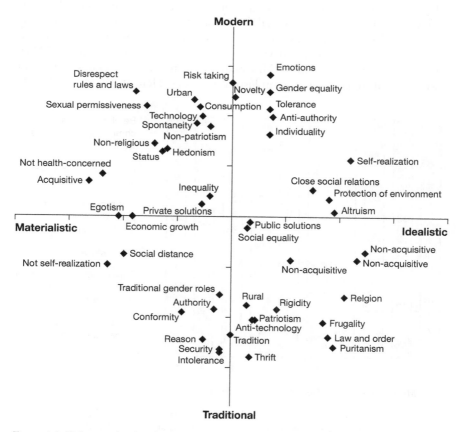

Figure 4.1 Values and value dimensions of the Norwegian Monitor

We may further illustrate the content of the materialism–idealism value dimension by showing the responses to a question asking which of five alternative wishes one would most want to have fulfilled. The value dimension is divided into ten categories with an equal number of respondents in each (Figure 4.2). The alternative choices serve as indicators for five different value indexes (as shown in the appendix). By combining the last five waves of the survey, we get solid bases for the percentages, with approximately 2,000 respondents within each of the deciles.

The wishes of materialists and idealists are clearly contrasting. Being able to afford something one has always wanted and feeling safe and fearless for the future dominate at the materialistic end, while leading a life with opportunity to develop as a person and experiencing more warmth and friendship are preferred at the idealistic end.

Other descriptions of basic value dimensions

The NM is one of several efforts to describe the value preferences of individuals empirically. In contrast to social background variables, where a relatively standardized set of measures are included in most opinion surveys, a similar consensus has yet to be reached with regard to values (Hitlin and Piliavin 2004). But the value dimensions in the NM study clearly resemble other descriptions of basic cultural divisions in post-industrial societies. Here the works of Ronald

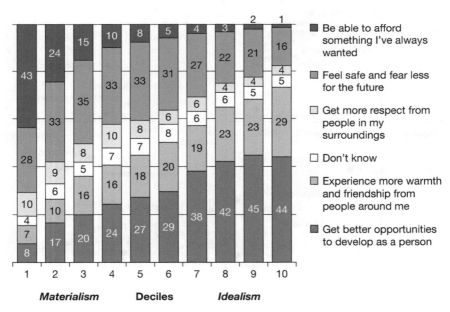

Figure 4.2 Position on the materialism–idealism dimension and choice between five wishes one would most like to have fulfilled (per cent; NM 2003–2011 combined)

Inglehart (1977, 1990, 1997, Inglehart and Baker 2000) are central. His index of materialism–postmaterialism has been included in numerous surveys in several countries. A materialist value orientation emphasizes economic and physical security, while a postmaterialist gives higher priority to nonmaterial needs, such as a sense of community and quality of life. His original measure is a ranking of four alternatives regarding what should be the goals of the country for the next ten years. A respondent ranking "Maintain order in the nation" and "Fight rising prices" as the top two is classified as a materialist, while ranking "Protect freedom of speech" and "Give people more say in the decisions of the government" on top makes you a postmaterialist. When this empirical measure is entered into the two-dimensional space of the NM, the average for postmaterialists falls in the upper right quadrant of modern idealists, while his materialists are located in the lower left quadrant of traditional materialists (Hellevik 1993).[5] Inglehart's materialist–postmaterialist dimension seems to correspond to the main diagonal of the NM axes (Figure 4.3).

Scott Flanagan (1982a, 1982b) discusses two orthogonal value dimensions, called authoritarian–libertarian and materialism–nonmaterialism. The indicators used by Flanagan vary between the surveys, and has not been included in the NM. Their content suggests that his dimensions closely resemble the two NM axes. This is striking when one considers what Flanagan calls two sub-dimensions of the authoritarian–libertarian dimension: strong versus weak social and moral constraints on the self-actualization of members of a society (1982a). The first – degree of social constraints, opposing authority and conformity to autonomy and independence – clearly corresponds to the main diagonal of the NM axes and Inglehart's materialism–postmaterialism dimension. The second corresponds to the NM bi-diagonal with, in Flanagan's terms, piety and self-discipline in the lower right corner and self-indulgence, secularism and permissiveness in the upper left.

Shalom Schwartz (1992, 1994) has proposed a comprehensive instrument for measuring values. His main dimensions are openness to change versus conservation, and self-enhancement versus self-transcendence. Within the space defined by these two orthogonal dimensions, ten motivational types of values are located: stimulation and self-direction at the openness to change pole; universalism and benevolence at the self-transcendence pole; conformity, tradition and security at the conservation pole; and finally power, achievement and hedonism near the self-enhancement pole. The dimensions and values discussed by Schwartz also clearly resemble the NM axes. This was evident when his empirical measure was included in the Monitor survey.

These results suggest that there is a convergence in the findings of value research in post-industrial societies (Hellevik 2008a, 2008b). Allowing for variations in precisely which values are included, how they are measured and how the data are analysed, the resulting value dimensions seem to constitute axes and diagonals within the same basic cultural space. This convergence makes it all the more interesting to study the relationship between the Monitor materialism–idealism dimension on the one hand, and subjective well-being and sustainability on the other.

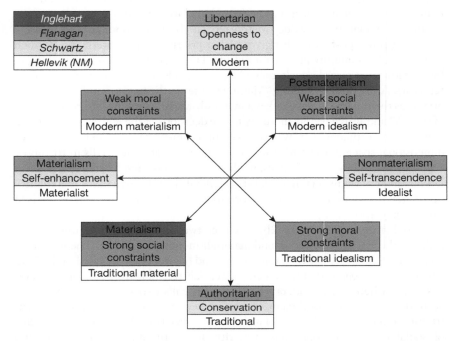

Figure 4.3 Dimensions of value preferences as discussed by Inglehart, Flanagan, Schwartz and Hellevik

Values as causes of subjective well-being

Within the field of happiness research the importance of such a value dimension has been focused. The distinction between extrinsic and intrinsic goals (Kasser and Ryan 1993, 1996) clearly resembles the materialism–idealism dimension. Richins and Dawson (1992:308) consider materialism as 'a set of centrally held beliefs about the importance of possessions in one's life'. They have developed measures of 'acquisition centrality, the role of acquisition in happiness, and the role of possessions in defining success', using indicators which in many cases resemble questions central in defining the NM materialism–idealism dimension.

Since the start of the NM project in 1985, a standard question on subjective well-being has been asked: "Would you on the whole describe yourself as very happy, quite happy, not particularly happy or not at all happy?" From 1999 another often used question was included: "How satisfied are you with the life you live: very satisfied, quite satisfied, neither satisfied nor dissatisfied, a little dissatisfied or very dissatisfied?" The first concerns the emotional aspect of subjective well-being, the other the cognitive-evaluative aspect. The former may be expected to depend on the latter; the feeling of happiness reflects whether one sees life as fulfilling ones hopes and expectations.

To compare groups, the balance of positive over negative answers is calculated for the two well-being questions. The *level of happiness* is defined as (% very happy) – (% not particularly or not at all happy) – and the *level of satisfaction* as (% very satisfied) – (% very or somewhat dissatisfied or neither satisfied nor dissatisfied). We then may compare the level of subjective well-being within the deciles on the materialism–idealism dimension (Figure 4.4).[6]

There is a clear, nearly linear relation between the position on the value dimension and subjective well-being. For the level of happiness the distance between the extreme groups of materialists and idealists is 27 points, and for the level of satisfaction with life nearly twice as much, 52 points. A similar relationship between a materialistic or extrinsic value orientation and reduced happiness has been documented with American data.[7] What may be the reason for such a tendency?

The reason for lower subjective well-being among materialists does not seem to lie in inferior objective circumstances. NM data show materialists and idealists to be fairly equally situated with regard to income, with idealists only slightly better off (Figure 4.5). Comparing the two extreme groups, the actual income of idealists is 7 per cent above that of materialists. With regard to material possessions, there is no difference (Hellevik 2003). Their felt economic needs differ more, however. The amount of income perceived necessary to live a satisfactory life is on average 35 per cent higher among the extreme materialists than among their idealist counterparts. The gap between actual and perceived necessary income goes from negative at the materialist end of the dimension to positive on the other. Among the extreme idealists the "surplus" equals one quarter of the actual income.

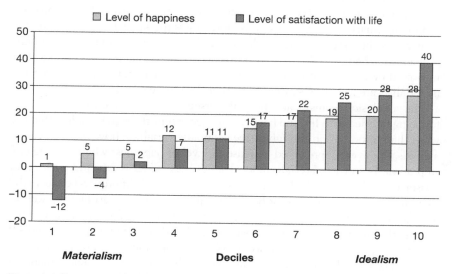

Figure 4.4 Position on the materialism–idealism value dimension and subjective well-being (per cent; NM 2003–2011)

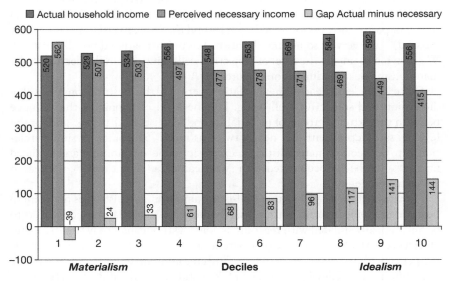

Figure 4.5 Position on the materialism–idealism dimension and actual versus perceived necessary income (in NKr 1,000; NM 2003–2011)

A similar difference in how one's economic situation is experienced is evident also when we look at other subjective economic indicators (Table 4.1). Satisfaction with income, possessions and the personal economy in general varies strongly along the materialism–idealism dimension, even though the objective economic situation as we have seen is more or less the same. How one's situation relative to others is evaluated also differs. And so does the fear of facing economic problems in the future. With such differences between materialists and idealists in how they experience their economic situation, it is not surprising that the materialists are less often satisfied with their lives or feeling happy.

The conclusion seems clear. The goals pursued by idealists increase the chances for being satisfied with life and happy, to a large extent through the effect that the value dimension has on the subjective economic variables. If we do a regression analysis, the average predicted increase in level of happiness when moving one step upwards on the materialism–idealism deciles ladder is 2.6, and for level of satisfaction 5.1. Multiplied by 10 we get an expected difference between the extreme deciles of 26 points for happiness and 51 points for satisfaction, well in accordance with the actual figures of 27 and 52. Controlling for household income reduces the effect of the value dimension only slightly to 2.5 for happiness and 4.9 for satisfaction. A control for the five subjective economic variables dichotomized as in Table 4.1 indicates that the main part of the effect of the value dimension on happiness and satisfaction is indirect via these variables, leaving a direct effect of 0.9 and 2.1, respectively.

Table 4.1 Position on the materialism–idealism dimension and subjective economic situation (per cent; NM 2003–2011); satisfied with own economic situation: 2005–2011

Value orientation:	Materialistic								Idealistic	
Deciles:	1	2	3	4	5	6	7	8	9	10
Income sufficient/more than sufficient	50	63	69	76	77	84	83	88	91	95
Do not lack material possessions	16	32	39	50	56	65	70	79	84	93
Satisfied with own economic situation	44	50	54	63	65	71	71	77	78	86
Compared to others: as well or better off	64	68	71	74	72	79	78	80	82	83
Little or no fear of not coping financially	28	35	42	47	50	55	55	63	66	75

We now turn the attention to the relationship between value preferences and sustainability, by looking at variations in attitudes towards issues of environmental protection, redistribution of wealth and support for the welfare state.

Values and sustainability

While a majority of the extreme idealists considers the environmental situation to be grave and requiring immediate action, the same applies to little more than one-fifth of the extreme materialists. In line with such a difference in outlook, the willingness to do a personal effort or accept anti-pollution taxes or higher energy prices vary greatly along the value dimension, with percentage differences of more than 40 points between the extreme deciles (Table 4.2). Environmentally friendly

Table 4.2 Position on the materialism-idealism dimension and environmental attitudes and behaviour (per cent; NM 2003–2011)

Value orientation:	Materialistic								Idealistic	
Deciles:	1	2	3	4	5	6	7	8	9	10
Positive to anti-pollution taxes and fees	37	45	52	56	62	67	70	77	79	81
Wants to make a personal effort to protect the environment	28	39	42	51	54	61	63	65	73	75
Often/sometimes uses public transportation to protect the environment	34	39	43	47	50	56	55	60	63	62
Agree: make energy more expensive to reduce consumption	13	19	22	29	30	35	41	45	53	55
The grave situation of the environment requires immediate and drastic action	22	26	29	34	36	38	39	43	47	51

64   Ottar Hellevik

behaviour, as measured by the propensity to use public transportation instead of driving a car, is also more common among idealists, even if the difference is somewhat smaller (28 points).

These results are not surprising, since the value index for environmental concern versus economic growth is a main contributor to (highly correlated with) the materialism–idealism dimension. They indicate that popular support for environmentally responsible policies will fluctuate with trends in value preferences. The same holds for attitudes towards policies aiming at reducing global inequalities in wealth and living conditions.

Norway has reached the goal of giving 1 per cent of its GNP in aid to poorer nations. Such a policy has been supported by nearly all political parties, and had broad support in the population. In 2011 a majority of 64 per cent wanted to keep foreign aid at its present level (47 per cent) or increase it (17 per cent), while 27 per cent wished to reduce it. Popular support varies strongly along the materialism–idealism dimension, with 59 per cent preferring reduced and only 5 per cent increased aid at the extreme materialist end, compared to 7 per cent reduced and 48 per cent increased at the idealist end of the dimension (Figure 4.6).

Similar patterns are found also for other indicators of willingness to give priority to the needs of others over one's own desires. The value index egotism versus altruism is strongly correlated with the materialism–idealism dimension. Also for sustainability as regards redistribution of wealth between nations to improve conditions for those living below minimum standards, we may conclude that popular support will depend on changes in the value climate.

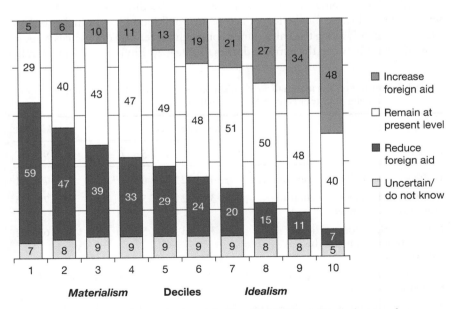

Figure 4.6 Position on the materialism–idealism dimension and attitude towards Norwegian aid to developing countries (per cent; NM 2003–2011)

Is the extensive welfare state as exemplified by the Scandinavian countries sustainable? The current economic crisis in Europe, as well as the aging of European populations, has raised doubts about whether it will be possible to keep up the level of public services and redistribution of wealth in the future. An important factor will be the support for the welfare state in the population, which will determine the willingness among voters to pay the taxes necessary to keep the system running. As shown in Table 4.3, such a support is highly dependent on the value orientation of the voters. The pattern for civic attitudes is similar, with motivation to engage actively in social affairs increasing from 29 per cent at the materialistic end of the value dimension to 78 per cent at the idealistic end.

We have found that values are important for subjective well-being as well as for attitudes that affect sustainability. An idealistic value orientation increases the chances for being satisfied with one's life and happy. The "good life", as defined by idealist values, is good in the sense of actually promoting subjective well-being, compared to the effect of a materialistic value orientation. It is sustainable in the sense that it increases support for policies to protect the environment and improve living conditions globally. It also affects the support for an extensive welfare state like the Norwegian. The future development for subjective well-being as well as all three kinds of sustainability accordingly will be influenced by changes in the value preferences of the population.

Such changes in value orientation may be brought about by changes in living conditions. The long-term trend in affluent nations has been one of steadily rising income and material standard of living. The question is how increasing wealth in a nation will affect the value preferences in its population. Two theories have been put forward that give an answer to this question.

Prosperity and value change: two theories

What long-term trends of value change can be expected in modern affluent societies such as the Norwegian? According to Inglehart's so-called postmaterialism theory, the values of individuals reflect the conditions that prevailed during their

Table 4.3 Position on the materialism–idealism dimension and support for the welfare state (per cent; NM 2003–2011)

Value orientation:	Materialistic									Idealistic
Deciles:	1	2	3	4	5	6	7	8	9	10
Tax evasion unacceptable	54	62	65	67	70	75	76	77	82	89
Reducing public expences not a political priority	60	70	73	76	81	82	85	87	91	95
Agree: high taxes necessary to keep up important public services	43	49	52	53	56	58	61	66	68	68
Want to participate actively and contribute to society	29	37	39	44	47	51	56	60	66	78

adolescence, whether these values satisfied basic needs for physical and economic security or not (Inglehart 1977, 1990, 1997). When these needs are not met, the individual will be preoccupied with such concerns for the rest of his or her life. Increasing prosperity, giving the new generations a feeling of economic security during their formative years, should produce a shift for the population as a whole along the main diagonal in Figure 4.3, with a growing number of postmaterialists and a declining number of materialists as a result of the ongoing process of generational replacement.

Flanagan has launched an alternative theory for the direction of value change (Flanagan 1982a, 1982b). Instead of fulfilment of individual needs for security, his point of departure is the functional requirements of a society. When resources are scarce, survival demands that society must restrict the activities of its members in order to economize with scarce resources. This is done through strong moral and/or social restrictions on their behaviour. As a society grows more affluent, the moral and social restrictions will become weaker, leaving individuals free to pursue their personal interests and desires. This results in a movement over time, along the vertical axis of Figure 4.3, from traditional to modern values, or, to use Flanagan's own terms, from authoritarian to libertarian values.

If increasing income and standards of living stimulated materialist desires and cravings, the prospects for subjective well-being and a sustainable development would seem bleak in affluent societies. Here the theory of Inglehart strikes an optimistic cord, predicting an opposite trend in the direction of idealism. Flanagan does not envisage changes in either direction with regard to the materialism–idealism dimension, but a movement towards libertarian/modern values along the first dimension of the NM. This means that neither Inglehart nor Flanagan expects economic growth to stimulate materialism.

Value change in Norway

What is the actual trend for value development in Norway? This is traced by positioning each wave of the NM on the value dimensions of the first wave in 1985.[8] Inglehart (1990) has presented ample empirical evidence in support of his theory from analyses of longitudinal data for several countries in the 1970s and 1980s. Also the NM results from 1985 to 1989 show a trend in an idealistic direction (Figure 4.7). But during the 1990s the trend changed direction towards materialism. Combined with a trend towards modern values, the movement of the Norwegian population followed the bi- rather than the main diagonal in Figure 4.1, towards a new kind of pleasure-seeking materialism (Hellevik 2002). An improving economy has meant moving from a state of material security during adolescence to one of affluence and immediate gratification of desires for many Norwegian families. This may have led to more, rather than less, interest in and dependence on possessions and consumption among the young, contrary to what Inglehart's theory predicts.

The trend towards materialistic values continued until 2003. From 2003 to 2007 there was a marked movement towards a more idealist position, where the

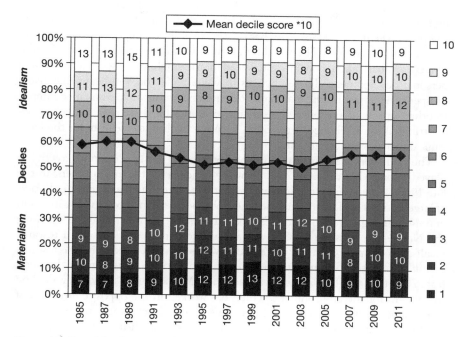

Figure 4.7 Trend for the materialism–idealism dimension (per cent deciles distribution and average deciles score times 10; NM 1985–2011)

population average has remained in 2009–2011. This idealist trend is in line with Inglehart's postmaterialism theory, but closer scrutiny reveals that it is *not* a result of idealist younger cohorts replacing materialist older ones, as the theory assumes. On the contrary, a cohort analysis shows that the generational replacement effect works in the direction of materialism (Hellevik 2008b:231–235). The young are more, not less, in favour of materialist values than older generations. A reason for this seems to be uncertainty of how they will get by financially and fear of not doing as well as their parents.

The trend towards idealism since 2003 is thus the result of a period effect strong enough to more than offset the effect in the opposite direction of generational replacement. We shall now look at possible causes for such a period effect, and its consequences for subjective well-being and the various kinds of sustainability.

Possible causes of the changes in basic value preferences

The direction of the movement of the Norwegian population along the materialism–idealism dimension is produced by changes in the support for particular values. Figure 4.8 shows the trends for important contributors, with the value indexes transformed so as to vary between 0 and 100. While the preoccupation with acquiring material goods was on the rise until the mid-1990s – a paradoxical trend considering the dramatic improvements in the material standard of living for Norwegians during this period (Hellevik 2008b) – this has become steadily less important as a goal after the turn of the century. The trend for altruism is of the same kind, and a similar tendency, albeit much more modest, is seen for the emphasis on self-realization and personal development. These changes in value preferences indicate that rising prosperity no longer inspire materialistic desires, but rather have stimulated interest in other aspects of existence. The change of trends for these separate values has contributed to the change of direction from materialism to idealism for the basic value dimension in recent years.

The value opposition of environmental protection versus economic growth has played a somewhat different role. Growing concern for the environment in the late 1980s – caused by fear following dramatic incidents such as nuclear pollution of large districts of Norway after the Chernobyl accident in 1986, and the invasion of poisonous algae from polluted European rivers threatening life in the sea along the Norwegian coast in 1988 – was a main contributor to the trend towards idealism in this period. In the 1990s and onwards until 2003 the trend was towards giving higher priority to growth, but the focus on climate change turned the trend from 2003 to 2007. The last two waves of the NM once again show a new decline in concern for the environment, which has worked in the opposite direction of the changes for the other values in Figure 4.8. These opposing tendencies have resulted in stability for position on the materialism–idealism dimension for the Norwegian population.

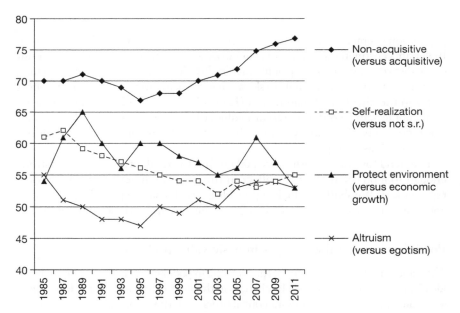

Figure 4.8 Trends for selected value indexes (transformed to vary 0–100; NM 1985–2011)

Consequences for subjective well-being of the value changes

The level of happiness in Norway remained stable in the period 1985–2001, with on average a positive balance of 10 percentage points of people declaring themselves to be "very happy" as compared to "not particularly happy" or "not at all happy". Then a shift occurred, raising the average level of happiness to 13 percentage points for the period 2003–2011. The change in value orientation seems to have been a main contributor to this modest rise in the happiness level in Norway (Hellevik 2008b). The level of satisfaction shows an increasing trend since it was first measured in 1999.

We have earlier discussed the importance of how one's economic situation is perceived for happiness and satisfaction as a major explanation for the correlation between values and well-being. In accordance with this we find that the recent change in value preferences is accompanied by a change in what income is deemed necessary. Actual household income has increased more in the period 2003–2011 than the income perceived necessary to lead a satisfactory life (Figure 4.10). This means that the surplus gap in income has been increasing.

The different subjective indicators of how one's economic situation is experienced also exhibit a change to the better after the turn of the century (Figure 4.11). For satisfaction with material possessions this happened after a decline in the first half of the 1990s, at the same time as the actual number of possessions increased substantially (Hellevik 2003, 2008b). The other indicators show more modest improvements in recent years.

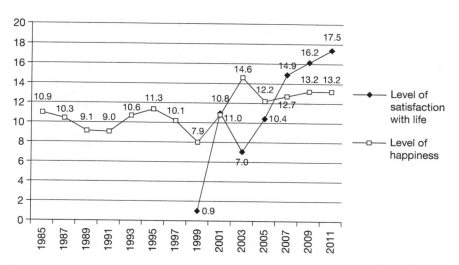

Figure 4.9 Trends in subjective well-being (level of happiness and level of satisfaction; NM 1985–2011)

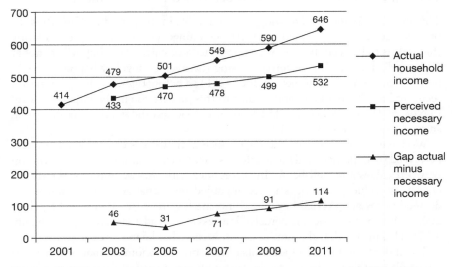

Figure 4.10 Trends in average actual and perceived necessary income (in NKr 1,000; NM 2001–2011)

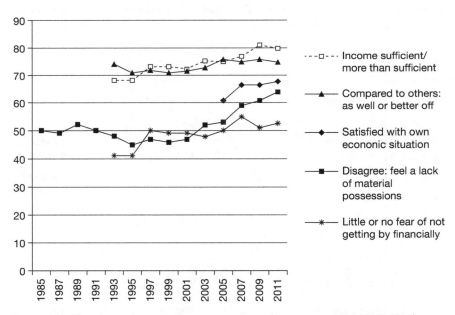

Figure 4.11 Trends in subjective economic situation (percentages; NM 1985–2011)

Consequences of the value changes for sustainability

Since an idealistic value orientation goes together with attitudes and behaviours that are favourable for the three aspects of sustainability considered here, a positive trend for sustainability is to be expected after the turn of the century. Since the actual development will be influenced by a number of other factors, however, this cannot be taken for granted. The Monitor data make it possible to investigate empirically what has actually happened.

All indicators of environmentally friendly attitudes and behaviours are at a higher level in 2011 than they were in 2001 (Figure 4.12). Some of them have declined somewhat in recent years, however. This a sign of the importance of media-focused events influencing how people experience the environmental situation, creating what is known as period effects.

The trend for willingness to share Norway's wealth with less fortunate nations follows the pattern for the trend in the materialism-idealism value dimension, decreasing until the mid-1990s and then increasing again (Figure 4.13).

Also attitudes relevant for the sustainability of the Norwegian welfare state show a tendency towards increasing levels of support in recent years (Figure 4.14). In particular the willingness to pay taxes and the acceptance of high public expenditure has risen.

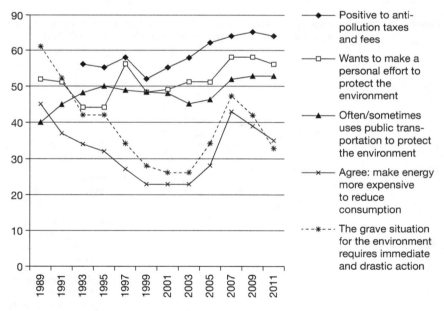

Figure 4.12 Trends in environmental attitudes and behaviour (percentages; NM 1989–2011)

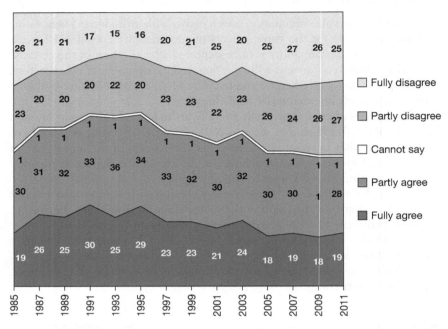

Figure 4.13 Percentage agreeing to the statement: "We should solve the problems in our own country before spending money on helping other countries" (NM 1985–2011)

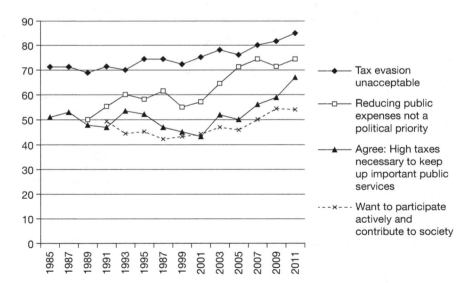

Figure 4.14 Trends in civic attitudes (percentages; NM 1985–2011)

Conclusion

'Happiness and ecological well-being are often portrayed as conflictual pursuits, but they may actually be complementary' (Brown and Kasser 2005:349). This is fitting as a conclusion to be drawn from the findings presented here. Individuals with attitudes and behaviour conducive to a sustainable lifestyle also have the highest levels of subjective well-being. They more often feel happy and satisfied with their life than people with a less sustainable way of life.

The explanation for this complementarity lies in the values people pursue, or in other words, what they see as the good life. We have described an opposition in value orientation between what may be called *idealism* and *materialism*. The former have goals that put less strain on the environment and leave room for considering the well-being of others. For idealists, income and possessions are means, in contrast to materialists, who see consumption and acquisition as central goals in life. For them the conflict between well-being and sustainability is experienced as a real one. Demands to abstain from materialist desires will be seen as a negative and unwanted interference in their pursuit of happiness. They are unaware that such a pursuit may have a negative effect on their subjective well-being. The goals of materialists are harder or even impossible to reach – not everyone can be the proud owner of the most expensive car in the neighbourhood – and may be less fulfilling if they are reached than the goals of idealists.

Improving the subjective quality of our lives as well as the sustainability of this way of life may thus be seen as a question of value formation, how to influence it in the direction of idealism and away from materialism. How can this be done? Inglehart's optimistic idea – that increased prosperity would create economically secure adolescents with a postmaterialist value orientation – does not seem to be correct. Young people in Norway today are more preoccupied with consumption and acquisition than older generations. There are many possible reasons for this. Advertising directly aimed at children, parents using their increasing affluence to indulge themselves and spoil their children, media glorifying the lifestyle of the super-rich, to mention a few.

What is less obvious is what has caused the recent change towards idealism in Norway. What are the events that have led some people to change their value preferences resulting in such a period effect? Fear of climate change and environmental degradation may play a role, but the indications here are contradictory. Perhaps exposure through the media to the sufferings of people in other parts of the world is eventually having an effect, making it difficult to go on indulging oneself. Maybe more people have experienced for themselves what the results of the surveys presented here show, that consumption and material goods are not the recipe for satisfaction and happiness they once thought. What is certain is that a better understanding of the basis for the idealism trend will be important for the success of efforts to strengthen such a change in value preferences.

An idealistic conception of the good life creates the fortunate situation that our pursuit of the good life does not have to be at the expense of others. We do not have to choose between our own happiness and that of coming generations, who will suffer if we do not live environmentally responsibly, or that of the under-privileged in the world today, who will go on suffering if we are not willing to share our wealth in order to improve their situation.

Appendix

Value measures in the Norwegian Monitor (questions abbreviated)

Altruism – egotism

- The needs of others should be put before own desires.
- The problems in own country should be solved before spending money on helping other countries.

Authority – anti-authority

- Children must be taught obedience and respect.
- One should find other ways of influencing people than commanding or ordering them about.

Health concerned – not health concerned

- How food tastes is more important than how healthy it is.
- Focus on a healthy way of living and on staying in good physical shape.

Acquisitive – non-acquisitive

- Feel a lack of material goods needed to live a satisfactory life.
- One wish fulfilled: be able to buy something one has always wanted.
- Spend unexpected day off: go shopping.

Status – anti-status

- Want to get hold of things that will impress others.
- Think that people are impressed by a grand house, an expensive car, etc.
- One wish fulfilled: be more respected by other people.

Technology – anti-technology

- Positive to new technology.
- Are frightened by computers and other forms of modern technology.

Social distance – close social relations

- Prefers to keep a certain distance to other people.
- One wish fulfilled: experience more warmth and friendship from other people.
- Spend unexpected day off: with friends or family.

Consumption – thrift

- Spend money on things that last rather than pleasures of the moment, e.g. restaurants, holidays.
- Like to buy things using part-payment.

Reason – emotions

- Important not to let oneself be carried away by feelings.
- On the outlook for new emotional experiences.

Sexual permissiveness – puritanism

- Sees sexual experiences before marriage as positive.
- Pornography should be prohibited.

Hedonism – frugality

- Wants to follow own desires and enjoy the pleasures of life in the future.
- It is not good for an individual to have all its wishes fulfilled.

Patriotism – non-patriotism

- Prefers to buy Norwegian products even if they are more expensive.
- Proud to be a Norwegian.
- Sees it as a negative development that special national characteristics are disappearing.

Religion – non-religious

- Regards oneself as a religious person.
- Frequency of participation in church services and other religious meetings.

Self-realization – not self-realization

- Attempts to obtain a richer inner life.
- A dull job is OK as long as it is well paid.
- One wish fulfilled: be able to live so as to develop as a person.
- Choice between opportunity to be more creative or to have more economic security.

Individuality – conformity

- Importance of following rules of good behaviour.
- Important to be just like other people.

Economic growth – environmental protection

- Economic growth should be given priority over protecting the environment.
- Willing to cut down on own consumption in order to save natural resources.

Tolerance – intolerance

- Some opinions should be censored from the media.
- People should be allowed to live as they wish to, no matter what other people think.
- One may demand that foreigners who come to live in Norway adapt to Norwegian ways of life.

Gender equality – traditional gender roles

- Partners should share responsibility for housework and children equally.
- Choice between three types of families: equal roles at home and at work, some differentiation with the man as main provider, completely different roles with the woman staying at home.

Social equality – social inequality

- Distribute wealth more evenly versus increase wealth of country.
- Positive that those who want to may buy better health and educational services.

Law and order – disrespect laws and rules

- Is it acceptable or not to drive above the speed limit or under the influence of alcohol, smoke pot, keep money one finds, not pay on public transportation, cheat on the taxes, produce illegal liquor.

Novelty – tradition

- Wishes to be among the first to make use of new products and services.
- Prefer the old and well-tested ways of doing things.

Public solutions – private solutions

- More public services should be privatized.
- A high level of taxation is necessary to finance important public activities.
- Government must control private enterprises to ensure quality of products and services.
- There is too much government interference and regulations.

Rigidity – spontaneity

- Prefer detailed planning of everyday life.
- One should follow ones inclinations and not be restricted by rules and routines.

Notes

1 The sample size has increased from 2,200 in the first wave, to around 3,000 from 1987 to 1995, and around 4,000 in later waves. The number of questions is close to 3,000 and many have been part of the interview for the entire period.

2 The most recent figures show that approximately one in four of those contacted by telephone agree to be interviewed. Two-thirds of those interviewed say yes to receiving the self-completion questionnaire in the mail, and of them again two-thirds answer the questions and return it. This means that the final sample only includes around one-tenth of those originally contacted. Election results, population statistics and other forms of control of the sample quality indicate that it does not deviate form the population in a systematic way (Hellevik 2008b:132–136).

3 The method is principal component analysis with orthogonal varimax rotation. Earlier multiple correspondence analysis of dichotomized indexes was used. The resulting dimensions are highly similar for the two techniques.

4 Exactly 25 per cent are defined as holders of a value, which means that one-quarter of the sample are located at each extreme of the index as holders of the opposite values (e.g. altruism versus egotism), while half of the sample is located in the middle. To obtain this when the distribution on a value index does not give such a split, which is almost always the case, those with the index score where the split falls are ranked according to how they score on other value indexes correlated with the one in question. There are minor variations between waves in the exact location of the values in the map. The map shown is from the 2005 wave (Hellevik 2008b:179).

5 Inglehart's original four-item index has been included in the NM survey, and the average position of his materialists and postmaterialists on the two Monitor dimensions calculated (Hellevik 1993).

6 The deciles are calculated for all years combined, meaning that the total distribution for the data is one-tenth in each decile. Scored 1–10 the average decile score is 5.5.

7 Richins and Dawson 1992 and Diener and Biswas-Diener 2002 (materialistic); Ryan et al. 1996 and Kasser 2000 (extrinsic value orientation).

8 Regression analyses with the 25 value indexes as independent and the value dimensions from the factor analysis in 1985 as dependent variables are carried out. The coefficients from these regression equations are then used to position respondents from the other waves on the 1985 dimensions. The average position for each wave then shows the trend for the population. The results have been transposed so as to place the last wave of 2011 in origo.

Bibliography

Brown, K. W. and Kasser, T. (2005) 'Are psychological and ecological well-being compatible? The role of values, mindfulness, and lifestyle' in *Social Indicators Research* 74. pp. 349–368.

Diener, E. and Biswas-Diener, R. (2002) 'Will money increase subjective well-being? A literature review and guide to needed research' in *Social Indicators Research* 57. pp. 119–169.

Flanagan, S. C. (1982a) 'Changing values in advanced industrial society' in *Comparative Political Studies* 14. pp. 403–444.

Flanagan, S. C. (1982b) 'Measuring value change in advanced industrial society: A rejoinder to Inglehart' in *Comparative Political Studies* 15. pp. 99–128.

Hellevik, O. (1993) 'Postmaterialism as a dimension of cultural change' in *International Journal of Public Opinion Research* 5 (3). pp. 211–233.

Hellevik, O. (1995) '"Fra tilskuere til deltagere"'. Utdrag av opposisjonen ved Lise Togebys doktordisputas' in *Politica* 27(2). pp. 213–222.

Hellevik, O. (1996) *Nordmenn og det gode liv. Norsk Monitor 1985–1995* (Norwegians and the good life. The Norwegian Monitor 1985–1995). Oslo: Universitetsforlaget.

Hellevik, O. (2002) 'Age differences in value orientation – life cycle or cohort effect?' in *International Journal of Public Opinion Research* 14(3). pp. 286–302.

Hellevik, O. (2003) 'Economy, values and happiness in Norway' in *Journal of Happiness Studies* 4(3). pp. 243–283.

Hellevik, O. (2008a) 'Assessing long-term value changes in societies' in Donsbach, W. and Traugot, W. (eds) *Handbook of Public Opinion Research*. London: Sage. pp. 556–569.

Hellevik, O. (2008b) *Jakten på den norske lykken* (The pursuit of happiness in Norway). Oslo: Universitetsforlaget.

Hitlin, S. and Piliavin, J. A. (2004) 'Values: Reviving a dormant concept' in *Annual Review of Sociology* 30. pp. 359–393.

Inglehart, R. (1977) *The Silent Revolution – Changing Values and Political Styles Among Western Publics*. Princeton: Princeton University Press.

Inglehart, R. (1990) *Culture Shift in Advanced Industrial Society*. Princeton: Princeton University Press.

Inglehart, R. (1997) *Modernization and Postmodernization. Cultural, Economic and Political Change in 43 Societies*. Princeton: Princeton University Press.

Inglehart, R. and Baker, W. E. (2000) 'Modernization, cultural change, and the persistence of traditional values' in *American Sociological Review* 65. pp. 19–51.

Kasser, T. (2000) 'Two versions of the American dream: Which values and goals make for a high quality of life', in Diener, E. and Rahtz, D. R. (eds) *Advances in Quality of Life Theory and Research*. Dordrecht: Klüwer Academic. pp. 3–12.

Kasser, T. and Ryan, R. M. (1993) 'A dark side of the American dream: Correlates of financial success as a central life aspiration' in *Journal of Personality and Social Psychology* 65. pp. 410–422.

Kasser, T. and Ryan, R. M. (1996) 'Further examining the American dream: Differential correlates of intrinsic and extrinsic goals' in *Personality and Social Psychology Bulletin* 22. pp. 280–287.

Richins, M. L. and Dawson, S. (1992) 'A consumer values orientation for materialism and its measurement: Scale development and validation' in *Journal of Consumer Research* 19(3). pp. 303–316.

Ryan, R. M., Kennin M. S., Kasser, T. and Deci, E. L. (1996) 'All goods are not created equal. An organismic perspective on the nature of goals and their regulation' in

Gollwitzer, P. M. and Bargh, J. A. (eds) *The Psychology of Action: Linking Cognition and Motivation to Behaviour.* New York: Guilford Press. pp. 7–26.

Schwartz, S. H. (1992) 'Universals in the content and structure of values: Theoretical advances and empirical tests in 20 countries' in Zanna, M. P. (ed.) *Advances in Experimental Social Psychology.* San Diego: Academic. pp. 1–65.

Schwartz, S. H. (1994) 'Are there universal aspects in the structure and content of human values?' in *Journal of Social Issues* 50. pp. 19–45.

Schwartz, S. H., Melech, G., Lehmann, A., Burgess, S., Harris, M. and Owens, V. (2001) 'Extending the cross-cultural validity of the theory of basic human values with a different method of measurement' in *Journal of Cross-Cultural Psychology* 32(5). pp. 519–542.

5 Well-being and environmental responsibility

Bengt Brülde

Introduction

The average level of well-being is pretty high in wealthy countries, and it has been increasing in many parts of the global South. However, there are several developments that might have a negative effect on many people's well-being (that might make their lives worse),[1] one of which is global warming, and the changes in climate to which it will give rise.

In a 2012 report from the World Bank, the authors argue that:

> [w]ithout further commitments and action to reduce greenhouse gas emissions, the world is likely to warm by more than 3°C above the preindustrial climate. Even with the current mitigation commitments and pledges fully implemented, there is roughly a 20 percent likelihood of exceeding 4°C by 2100. If they are not met, a warming of 4°C could occur as early as the 2060s.
>
> (World Bank, 2012, p. xiii)

A 4°C world would have dramatic effects on people's well-being, especially in many of the world's poorest regions, e.g. it would be a world of 'unprecedented heat waves, severe drought, and major floods in many regions, with serious impacts on human systems, ecosystems, and associated services' (ibid., pp. xiii–xiv). The question of how the well-being of future generations might be affected in different scenarios is of course very important, and so is the question of how future societies might best adapt to global warming. However, this chapter will focus on how the well-being of *present* people might be affected *if* we decide to lead our lives in a more environmentally responsible way and reduce our greenhouse gas (GHG) emissions to a more sustainable level.[2]

The necessary reduction and its achievement

According to experts in emission pathways, the 2°C goal can only be reached if our total GHG emissions are reduced from the present 48 gigatonnes (Gt) of CO_2 equivalent to 20 Gt by 2050 (Rogelj et al., 2011). If we assume that the world population will increase to around 9 billion by 2050, this means that we need to reduce emissions from 6–7 tonnes to 2 tonnes per person a year by 2050. It is worth noting that 6–7 tonnes is the global average, and that emissions are very unequally distributed between nations, e.g. the annual per capita emissions of the US was 18 tonnes in 2010, while India emitted 1.7 tonnes and Bangladesh only 0.34 tonnes per person a year.

At present, the necessary decrease in GHG emissions cannot be achieved by technological change alone: a more sustainable lifestyle is also needed. This assumption is well corroborated by the findings of the 'One tonne life' project that was conducted in Sweden a few years ago (Hedenus & Björck, 2011). The purpose of this project was to help a test family reduce their private emissions from 7 tonnes per person to 1 tonne. To achieve this goal, they were assisted by companies and experts. It was relatively easy for them to reduce emissions to 2.8 tonnes, since this reduction was mainly due to technological changes. Their petrol-powered cars were replaced by an electric car, and they got an exceptionally energy-effective house and energy-effective household appliances. But some changes in lifestyle were also necessary, e.g. vacations by airplane were replaced by vacations by train, and their meat consumption was reduced. These changes were not perceived as sacrifices, but major sacrifices were required to reduce emissions from 2.8 to 1.5 tonnes (this is how far they got). To get this far, the family had to adopt a fully vegan diet, and bring their own food to work. They also had to reduce their living space, use very little water, stop travelling, and reduce their shopping radically. The energy system of the future might be much better than today's system, however, and Hedenus and Björck speculate that it might be possible to reach a 'comfort level' at less than 2 tonnes by 2050, at least in countries with rich access to hydropower (like Sweden).

This project strongly suggests that major behavioural changes are necessary to reduce per capita emissions to 2 tonnes by 2050, especially with regard to diet and transportation. If we assume that emissions should be distributed equally between nations, this means that the average American needs to reduce their emissions by 16 tonnes per year, whereas the average Indian is allowed to increase their emissions somewhat.

The questions of this chapter

Different strategies can be used to get people to behave in a more environmentally responsible way, e.g. to fly less or consume less red meat. Some strategies are political, like taxation of unsustainable consumption. In these cases, people are given incentives to behave differently through changes in their external situation. Other strategies are 'psychological'. In this case, attempts are made to change people's behaviour by changing their beliefs or attitudes. As far as attitudinal change is concerned, we can distinguish between moral and non-moral change. In the moral case, I get to believe that it is morally right, e.g. to stop flying, even if this does not benefit me. In the non-moral case, we get to believe that it is in our own interest to adopt a more sustainable lifestyle.

To try to change people's behaviour by influencing their non-moral values is not very common in this context, but the belief that a sustainable lifestyle would constitute a big sacrifice may well constitute a major obstacle to behavioural change (Holmberg et al., 2011). For this reason, it is worth investigating what role considerations of well-being might have in a sustainability context. It is not just that people's willingness to adopt a more sustainable lifestyle depends on how this would (in their own view) affect their own well-being. These beliefs also affect how willing we are to endorse climate-friendly political interventions. In my view, this is the most important pragmatic reason why we need to find out how a more environmentally responsible lifestyle (and a more sustainable society) would actually affect our well-being.

If the question is formulated like this (in terms of 'would'), it is about what effects certain morally desirable changes or policies are *likely* to have on our well-being. For example, how would our well-being be affected if we (people living in wealthy countries) make the behavioural changes that are necessary to keep the increase in global warming below 2°C, or if we (at least) make changes *in this direction*? Are those lifestyle changes that are beneficial from a climate perspective – like less air travel and meat consumption – also conducive to well-being, or would they rather make us worse off?

We might also ask ourselves what is *possible* (rather than probable), however, e.g. whether it is *possible* for us to live lives that are both good and sustainable. One question is whether it is possible for us *as individuals* to maintain (or increase) our present level of well-being if we would lead more sustainable lives. Is it possible to live a sustainable and good life in wealthy countries, e.g. if we set the limit at 2 tonnes per person a year? That it is possible *for some of us* has already been shown in connection with the 'One tonne life' project,[3] but there are other successful examples of voluntary simplicity as well, e.g. as in the case of the Manhattan-based Beavan family (Beavan, 2009). These examples might be inspiring to some, but they do not show that it is possible for *each of us* to live a sustainable good life. Given our present needs and desires, it might simply be too hard for most of us, even if we disregard how expensive the new sustainable technology is.

On the collective level, the question is whether it is possible to create a society where all (or sufficiently many) citizens have lives that are both good and sustainable. It is worth noting that even if it were possible for *each* to adopt a sustainable lifestyle without any loss of well-being, it might not be possible for *all* (or *sufficiently many*) to do this. Perhaps I can only lead a simple life if the economy works, which presupposes that sufficiently many others maintain their present levels of consumption?

The global nature of the problem suggests that the question of what is possible for *all* (or sufficiently many) is more important than what is possible for *each*, which is (in turn) more important than what is possible for *some*. It also suggests that 'the question of probability' (how a sustainable lifestyle is likely to affect well-being) is more important than the question of what is possible for individuals. But regardless of which question we consider more important, we need (as a matter of 'method') to be realistic. We need to start from the present situation – i.e. look at how we actually live our lives, and take the economic and political realities into account – and then ask ourselves what changes are feasible. Above all, we must acknowledge that people's values might be difficult to change. Discussions of what is possible for individuals are often based on unrealistic assumptions, however, e.g. that if sustainable lives can be good in some cases, they can also be good in most cases. It is also highly unrealistic to assume that we can shape our lives 'from scratch'. It is tempting to believe that once we have knowledge about the determinants of happiness, we simply need to investigate whether these determinants can be realized in a sustainable way. However, this approach is only relevant if it is falsely assumed that we are malleable like infants, or if we take a really long view and ask what is possible for individuals in the next generation. But if we have existing adults in mind, the question is not what could be achieved if we started afresh, but what is feasible given what we are.

A third and related question is whether considerations of well-being can influence us in a more climate-friendly direction, both with regard to our willingness to change our own behaviour, regardless of what others do, and with regard to our willingness to support policies that give everyone, including ourselves, strong incentives to change our behaviour. This is practically important, just as we need to find out what moral reasons can increase people's acceptance of radical policies.

Now, to be able to answer the first two questions, we need to know what a person's well-being consists in. To answer the third question, we rather have to know what people *believe* makes their lives good: to know what actually makes a life good can only help us influence people's behaviour if they already endorse some plausible conception of well-being (like the happiness theory), or if they can be influenced in this direction.

The nature of well-being

The question of well-being (the good life, or quality of life) is a classical philosophical question. This question has been formulated in somewhat different ways, e.g. 'What makes a life good for the person who lives it?', or 'What does ultimately make a life worth living?'. To make the question more precise, philosophers have formally defined 'well-being' in terms of what has *final value for a person* (Brülde, 2007a). On this view, a person's well-being is constituted by those conditions which are desirable for her *as ends* rather than as means, and the question of well-being is really a question of what is good for us *as ends*, i.e. what has *final value* for us. To be on a high level of well-being (to have a good life) is simply to have a lot of positive final value (and little or no negative final value) in one's life.

Over the years, philosophers have defended a number of *theories of well-being*, i.e. substantive general claims about what has final value for us, and why. These theories can be classified in different ways, but most of the modern discussion is based on Parfit's (1984) distinction between three kinds of conceptions of the good life, namely Hedonistic Theories, Desire-Fulfilment Theories, and Objective List Theories. These general theories should be carefully distinguished from specific 'visions' of well-being, such as 'the simple life'. No such vision is sufficiently flexible to be universally valid. As Sumner puts it, no adequate theory of well-being can simply 'favour complexity over simplicity, [. . .] excitement over tranquillity, [. . .] perpetual striving over contentment, [. . .] companionship over solitude, [. . .] religious conviction over atheism, [. . .] the intellectual life over the physical, or whatever' (1996:18).

This suggests that the different theories of well-being also need to be distinguished from the folk conceptions of well-being that are endorsed in different cultures, e.g. well-being as a high standard of living or as a healthy life. Although these conceptions might have some relevance in relation to our third question, they are too specific, and most probably never take the distinction between final and instrumental value into account.

The three theories identified by Parfit can be characterized as follows (cf. Brülde, 2007a): On the *hedonistic theory*, the good life is identical with the pleasant life. The only thing that has positive final value for a person is feeling good, and the only thing that is 'bad as an end' is feeling bad. This theory can be regarded as a *happiness theory* of well-being. According to the pure happiness theory, a person's well-being depends on one thing only, namely how happy she is. Nothing but happiness has final value for a person. But the happiness theory of well-being is only identical with hedonism if a hedonistic conception of happiness is incorporated, i.e. if happiness is conceived of as feeling good on the whole, as a kind of affective state (ibid.).

There are other conceptions of happiness, however, e.g. the *life satisfaction view*. On this view, happiness is regarded as a positive attitude (in the philosophical sense) towards one's life as a whole, and this attitude (or cognitive state) need not (at least not by definition) be accompanied by any pleasant feeling whatsoever. To be happy is simply to evaluate one's own life in a positive manner, to approve of it, or to regard it favourably (Brülde, 2007a).[4]

In my own view, happiness is best conceived of as a complex mental state consisting both of an affective and a cognitive component. To be happy is a matter of cognitively evaluating one's life as a whole in a positive manner, *and* to feel good on the whole. If we incorporate this *hybrid view* of happiness into the happiness theory, we get a theory that is in part hedonistic, but that also makes a person's level of well-being depend directly (and not just causally) on how satisfied she is with her life as a whole.

According to the *desire-fulfilment theory* (desire theory, or preferentialism), a person has (roughly) a good life if she has the kind of life that she herself wants to have. The only thing that has positive final value for a person is that her (intrinsic) desires are fulfilled, and the only thing that has negative final value for a person is that she gets what she does not want. This is not a mental state theory, since whether a desire is actually satisfied depends in part on the state of the world. It is worth noting that most desire theorists endorse some kind of *modified* version of the theory, e.g. the view that it is only good for us to have our desires satisfied if these desires are rational or informed. (See Brülde, 1998, for a number of possible modifications.)

Finally, according to *objectivist pluralism* (the objective list theory), there are several objective values (besides happiness or enjoyment) that make a life good for a person, independently of what she herself thinks of the matter, and to have a good life is to have these values present to a high degree. Classical examples of such alleged objective values are knowledge, contact with reality, friendship, love, freedom, to function well (e.g. virtuously), personal development, meaningful work, and rational activity.[5]

In my own view, well-being consists in *authentic happiness*. On this modified happiness theory of well-being, it is necessary but not sufficient for maximal well-being that the person evaluates her life as a whole in a positive manner and feels good on the whole. The happy state must also be *authentic*, which roughly means that (a) the person's positive evaluation of her own life is based on a correct perception of this life, and (b) that the evaluative standard on which her evaluation is based is reasonable (Brülde, 2007b; Brülde, 2009).[6] It should be noted that fully inauthentic happiness is probably quite rare. It is also worth noting that environmental awareness or environmental concern cannot be included in 'authenticity'. In this context, full authenticity only presupposes full information about one's own life, not about the world.

In the following, I will not assume that (authentic) happiness is the only final value, but only that it is a central prudential value. After all, every reasonable theory of well-being seems to regard happiness as desirable as an end. For example, happiness is something that most of us desire intrinsically, and most pluralists tend to regard happiness as one of the relevant objective values.

The three questions revisited

This suggests that our first two questions can to a large extent be specified in terms of happiness. If we do this, we get: (1) If we decided to live in a more environmentally responsible way, e.g. adopt a 'two tonnes lifestyle', how would this (likely) affect our happiness? (2) Is it possible for us to maintain (or improve) our present level of happiness if we make these changes? Is it possible for some, for many, and for each? And is it possible for all or for sufficiently many?

There might be other prudential values besides happiness, however, and it is also worth investigating how a more environmentally responsible lifestyle would affect these values. Examples of such values are intimate relationships, freedom, personal development, and meaningful work.

Our third question is whether there is any reason to believe that considerations of well-being can make us more willing to live in a more environmentally responsible way, or to accept more radical environmental policies. This question can most probably *not* be specified in terms of happiness, however, for the simple reason that most people do not seem to endorse the happiness theory of well-being. First, it is far from certain that most people have determinate conceptions of well-being at all, e.g. because they are not familiar with the distinction between final and instrumental values. Second, many people might care more, e.g. for their material welfare than their happiness (as far as their self-interest is concerned), and it might thus be more effective to appeal to a broader conception of 'welfare', that also includes e.g. health and intimate relationships. In short, it might be better to appeal to some folk's conception of well-being in this context. But to the extent that people care about their own happiness, it is of course worth asking whether there is any reason to believe that considerations of happiness can make people think and act in a more environmentally responsible way. Moreover, people's conceptions of well-being are not written in stone, and it may well be possible to convince people that health or a high living standard is only valuable to the extent that it makes us happier.

The fact that happiness is perceived as a central value is not the only advantage of specifying the first two questions in terms of happiness. This move also makes it possible to use the empirical findings from happiness studies to answer these questions, especially question (1).

When asking how a more sustainable lifestyle would affect happiness, it is important to distinguish between individual lifestyle changes and politically induced changes. In the first case, the question is how the happiness of the individual would be affected if she e.g. stopped eating meat, *regardless of what others do*. In the political case, the question is rather what effects certain policies would have on society at large, e.g. how people's happiness would be affected if a high meat tax was introduced. It is worth noting that many might be willing to change their lifestyle if others do the same (given that the distribution of burdens is reasonably fair), but not unilaterally. This is one reason why political solutions are attractive. Another reason is that the relevant 'sacrifices' would probably be perceived as smaller if shared by others.

We also need to distinguish between different temporal perspectives, both within particular lives and between generations. If we adopt a more sustainable lifestyle, this may well make us less happy for a few years, but we might then adapt to the new situation and return to our previous happiness level (see below). It is also likely that the next generation will be better equipped than the present generation to live a life that is both happy and sustainable. In short, it is important to distinguish between short-term effects and different kinds of long-term effects, even with regard to the third question, since at least some people might be more willing to make sacrifices if they believe that they are limited in time.

It should be noted that the available empirical data are mostly cross-sectional, and that they can only tell us how people live and feel under the present circumstances. These data might *at best* tell us how individual (voluntary) changes in behaviour might affect happiness, mainly in the short run. The effects of politically induced lifestyle changes cannot be studied empirically before they have been introduced, especially not the long-term effects, and if the available findings allow us to speculate about policy outcomes at all, it is mainly about the possible *direct* effects of different policies.[7]

It is also worth noting that the existing knowledge of the determinants of happiness (and their relative weight) has been generated by investigating how different factors are related to happiness in people's actual lives, mainly in wealthy countries. For this reason, we cannot assume that all determinants have the same weight in a sustainable context as in a non-sustainable context, and it might be of limited value to ignore the context of the findings and simply investigate whether the different determinants can be realized in a sustainable way.

In search of answers: seven potentially relevant considerations from the happiness research

So, are there any empirically based considerations that suggest that we would be happier if we lived more sustainable lives, or that we (at least) would not feel significantly worse? It is of practical interest to find factors that are both beneficial from a climate perspective and conducive to happiness, but it is also important to gain knowledge about what determinants of happiness are neutral or harmful from a climate perspective (Holmberg et al., 2011).

The considerations have been generated as follows: It is well known what factors give rise to high GHG emissions, and we also know what factors are harmless from a climate perspective. Once these factors are identified, we can investigate what (if anything) happiness studies have to say about the relation between these different factors and happiness. (For an overview of the field, see e.g. Argyle, 2001; Brülde 2009; Frey, 2008; Layard, 2005.) However, considerations can also be generated by reflecting on proposed policies, e.g. the idea that we can reduce emissions by shortening working hours. We can then ask if there are any relevant studies that can help us determine what direct effects these suggested policies would have on happiness or other values, e.g. whether employees would be happier or have better intimate relationships if they worked less. Let us now take a closer look at the seven considerations.

1. The connection between wealth and happiness on the national level

We know that GHG emissions are considerably higher in wealthy industrialized nations than in low- and middle-income countries. (The differences within each group are considerable, however.) Average happiness levels are also significantly higher in rich countries than in lower-income countries (even though there are exceptions), and this is to a large extent due to a higher level of consumption (but not just private consumption).[8] However, the dramatic increase in material welfare in the richest countries during the last 50 years has not resulted in any significant increases in happiness (Easterlin, 1974; Hellevik, 2003; Layard, 2005). This is sometimes taken to suggest that reduced economic growth (or even 'degrowth') would not jeopardize our happiness, but this inference may well be invalid. First, it has been argued that economic growth is conducive to happiness even in affluent countries (Stevenson & Wolfers, 2008). And second, even if economic growth does not have positive effects on happiness in wealthy countries, it might be necessary to maintain present happiness levels, e.g. because it promotes employment and helps finance important welfare services.

So, can the relevant findings on wealth, happiness, and ecological footprint tell us whether it is *possible* to create a society that is both reasonably happy and sustainable? Well, it is easy to find examples of relatively poor low emission countries (e.g. in Latin America) that are just as happy as wealthy high emission countries in the global North (like the US or Japan), but this does not show that it is possible for wealthy countries to decrease GDP with maintained happiness levels: we also need to know if there is a feasible way for rich nations to reduce overall consumption while maintaining present happiness levels. It is not unlikely that the next generation will be as happy as we are even if they consume less, but what about the present generation? To get clearer about this, we have to move to the individual level.

2. The connection between income, consumption, and happiness on the individual level

As a general rule, higher incomes lead to more consumption, which in turn leads to larger ecological footprints. According to Nässén (2014), '[s]everal cross-sectional studies have shown that energy demand and GHG emissions calculated from the consumption side are strongly dependent on income levels although the relationship is typically somewhat lower than 1:1.' For example, it has been shown that 'direct and indirect energy use of households increase sharply with income also in affluent countries' (ibid.).

As far as happiness research is concerned, there are many more studies on income and happiness than on consumption and happiness. It has been shown repeatedly that income is significantly related to happiness, and that the relation is much stronger for lower incomes than for higher incomes (Argyle, 2001; Cummins, 2000; Layard, 2005). We also know that income has a stronger effect on life satisfaction than on affective well-being (Kahneman & Deaton, 2010). The effect of income on happiness is partly mediated by private consumption, but there are also other mediating factors.

The relation between total consumption and happiness has also been studied directly, e.g. by Brülde and Fors (2012). In this study, a significant connection was found between happiness and how much money Swedes spend on goods like food and drink, clothes and shoes, electronics, and furniture. People who consume more are both more satisfied with their lives and effectively happier. The most avid spenders are 2.7 units higher on an 11-unit life satisfaction scale than those who consume the least, whereas the difference in affective well-being is 2.2 units.[9] The connection between material consumption and happiness gets somewhat weaker when income is controlled for, which suggests that the effect of income on happiness is also mediated by e.g. a sense of security or a sense of being successful. When other determinants were controlled for, the difference between 'high' and 'low' spenders gets even smaller, namely 1 unit in the case of life satisfaction and 0.8 units in the case of affective well-being. Regarding the overall effect of income and consumption on happiness, it can be noted that these two factors jointly explain 3–4 per cent of the differences in happiness in a country like Sweden.

The fact that the relation between income and happiness is weak for higher incomes is sometimes taken to suggest that the relation between consumption and happiness is also weak for these incomes, which in turn is taken to suggest that additional consumption has rather small effects on the happiness of the relatively wealthy, and that their happiness would not decrease with reduced consumption. However, some studies suggest that consumption can have positive happiness effects for higher incomes too, e.g. if it satisfies social or psychological needs (Patterson & Biswas-Diener, 2012), if money is spent on 'experiential purchases' or 'purchases that engage the consumer in enjoyable activities', or if one spends one's money on others rather than on oneself (Dunn et al., 2008). This is rather bad news from an environmental perspective, since there is no reason to believe that pro-social spending or 'experiential purchases' are more sustainable than other forms of consumption. Moreover, even if a further increase in consumption would not increase our happiness, a *decrease* in consumption may well have negative effects on happiness, especially if involuntary.

Before we ask ourselves how a decrease in consumption would affect our happiness *in the long run*, let us first move from the probable to the possible, to question (2). We can first note that it seems possible to consume very little and still be reasonably happy. If we ask ourselves how much consumption is really necessary for a decent level of happiness, we would probably conclude (mainly on theoretical grounds) that little would suffice, and we also know (on empirical grounds) that it is possible for *some* to consume little and still be happy. This might not be very relevant, however, since it is far more important to ask whether it is possible for sufficiently many of the global rich to *reduce* their high level of consumption radically and still be equally happy (or even happier than before). Recall the family in the 'One tonne life' project, who had to make substantial sacrifices to reduce their emissions from 2.8 to 1.5 tonnes per person. If their life satisfaction and affective well-being would have been measured we would probably see a significant decrease in happiness.[10]

A note on hedonic adaptation

But what if we take a longer view? Suppose that we (the global rich) decided to make a substantial reduction in our consumption. If we ignore the indirect effects (e.g. on employment) how would this affect our happiness in five or ten years? It can be assumed on theoretical grounds that we may well adapt hedonically to this change, i.e. that we might eventually return to our former happiness levels. Hedonic adaptation is a rather common phenomenon. When we experience positive or negative *events*, our happiness can be strongly affected in the short run, but for most events we tend to return to our former levels relatively soon. We also adapt to many positive *changes*, like moving to a new house, getting a higher salary, or having children (Clark et al., 2007), and to negative changes like being sent to prison or becoming disabled (Frederick & Loewenstein, 1999). But we do not adapt fully to all changes, and it sometimes takes a long time before we return to our former happiness levels. For example, it can take many years to adapt hedonically to the loss of a loved one (ibid.) or the loss of one's job (Clark et al., 2007), and getting married can have a permanent positive effect on people's happiness (Frey, 2008). Given these findings, it would be rather surprising if we would not adapt fully to a substantially lower level of consumption after a few years. However, it is not clear to what extent this information might make people more willing to support radical environmental policies.

3. Materialism, general consumption patterns, and happiness

It is sometimes pointed out in this context that people with a materialist value orientation are less happy than 'idealists'. Moreover, the more 'idealistic' and the less materialistic people are, the happier they are (see Hellevik's chapter in this volume). Materialists value material possessions, consumption, shopping, status, income, and economic growth. They put themselves before others, are more conformist, and less concerned about the environment (Hellevik, 2003; see also Hellevik's chapter in this volume). 'Idealists' give more importance to spirituality, religion, personal development, creativity, intimate relationships, and health. They spend more time in nature, contribute more to society, care more about the environment, and are more willing to support policy change (ibid.). Idealists are also more experientially oriented, less self-centred, and more generous (Tatzel, 2003).[11]

The finding that materialists are less happy can be related to a certain critique of *consumerism*, a phenomenon that is intimately connected to materialism. The term 'consumerism' often refers to a lifestyle or culture which is preoccupied with the acquisition of consumer goods, or to a social and economic system that encourages the purchase of such goods (in amounts far beyond what is necessary to satisfy basic needs). Consumerism has not just been criticized from an environmentalist perspective, but also from the perspective of well-being, e.g. it has been argued that a consumerist lifestyle jeopardizes some objective value, like freedom or personal development. It has also been argued that we would be happier if we were less preoccupied with consumer goods, and if we consumed less. The finding about materialism supports the former claim, but this does not imply that we would be happier if we consumed less (cf. above).

The finding that idealists are happier than materialists can only be relevant in this context if the two value orientations give rise to different consumption patterns *and* if one of these patterns is associated with higher GHG emissions. We know that idealists support sustainable policies and practices to a higher degree, but all we know about the differences in lifestyle is that idealists use public transportation more often for environmental reasons (see Hellevik's chapter in this volume). However, we can assume that materialists consume more material goods, while idealists tend to make more 'experiential purchases' (like travel and education) and spend more on others. This difference in consumption patterns can probably explain part of the difference in happiness between the two groups, e.g. it has been shown that experiential consumption has stronger and more lasting effects on happiness than consumption of most material goods (Van Boven & Gilovich, 2003). This is consistent with the finding that the three types of spending most conducive to happiness are travelling abroad (experiential consumption), giving to charity (pro-social spending), and consumption of food (often both experiential and pro-social) (Brülde & Fors, 2012).

This does not show that idealists leave smaller ecological footprints than materialists, however, in spite of their environmental concern. We have already seen that there is a strong relation between income and ecological footprint, and there is little or no difference in income between idealists and materialists.[12] It has also been suggested (by Wilson et al., 2013) that income trumps environmental attitudes in this context. Moreover, we cannot assume that 'experiential consumption' and 'pro-social spending' are more sustainable than material consumption, e.g. 'experientalists' may well travel more by air. It is also worth noting that many enjoyable activities require quite a lot of material possessions, but according to Brown and Kasser (2005), happier people attach more value to activities that require less material goods. However, it is still possible that happy idealists fly and drive more to engage in e.g. stimulating outdoor activities.

But even if there is little difference between idealists and materialists at present, we have to consider that idealists are both more environmentally aware and more willing to support sustainable policies, like environmental taxes and fees (see Hellevik's chapter in this volume). Idealists are also more willing to make a personal effort to protect the environment, and the more idealistic the more willing (ibid.). All this suggests that idealists are more disposed to adopt a sustainable lifestyle, and that they would experience e.g. a life without meat as less unpleasant than materialists would. So it might be possible to change the behaviour of idealists by e.g. political means, but it is probably rather difficult to turn materialists into idealists. In any case, we need to learn more about why people become idealists (or materialists), and whether people's value orientation can be influenced by e.g. political means.

4. The relation between the 'energy intensity' of our specific activities and living conditions on the one hand, and happiness on the other

The consumption patterns described above (e.g. experiential consumption) are quite general, and only vaguely related to emissions, and it might be argued that we need to take a more direct approach. One such approach is to focus on specific activities or living conditions, to see if there is any systematic relation between their 'energy intensity' and how they affect happiness. For example, are people who fly more often happier than people who fly less, if we control for other variables? But it is also possible to take a holistic approach and focus on the energy intensity of people's leisure as a whole, since this would take all the relevant factors (including transport and heating) into account.

From a practical perspective, it is probably more useful to focus on specific activities, but it is worth noting that there are studies that have taken a more holistic approach. Using this approach, Wilson et al. (2013) found that there was no connection between happiness and GHG emissions in an urban setting, whereas Andersson et al. (2013) found a weak (0.14) but significant positive relationship between subjective well-being and total GHG emissions. They also found that the correlation is caused by emissions from transportation, aviation, and other consumption, rather than emissions from residential energy or food consumption.[13]

As far as specific activities are concerned, it is well documented that a physically and socially active leisure time makes us happier, and there are many happiness-inducing activities that require little use of energy, like spending time with friends, dancing, or exercising (Argyle, 2001). Examples of other activities that seem beneficial both from a climate perspective and from a happiness perspective are gardening, outdoor activities, and spending time in nature (Brülde & Fors, 2013). Regarding commuting and transportation, it was found that people who bike more often and travel more by train are somewhat happier. This is consistent with earlier research, which has shown that the most sustainable forms of 'commuting' (walking and biking) are conducive to happiness (Holmberg et al., 2011). This supports the idea that cities should be dense and services within cities decentralized.

Other 'activities' are beneficial from a climate perspective but *not* conducive to happiness, e.g. people who use public transportation more often are somewhat less happy. There are also activities and conditions that might be beneficial from a happiness perspective but not from a climate perspective. For example, Brülde and Fors (2013) found that people who drive or eat meat at least once a week are somewhat happier than others, as are those who fly at least twice a year. However, Andersson et al. (2013) found no significant correlation between happiness and the amount of car use, flying, or red meat consumption when they used more precise measures (kilometres per year, flights per year, and meals per week). But even if car driving (etc.) has no positive happiness effects, this does not imply that people would be equally happy if they stopped driving, since the loss of something that is taken for granted may have negative effects. But again, it is possible that we would adapt to driving less over time.

Certain living conditions are also conducive to happiness but harmful from a climate perspective. People who live in the countryside feel better than people living in cities, and people who live in houses are somewhat happier than people who live in apartments (Fors & Brülde, 2011). But living in the country (etc.) is less sustainable, e.g. because it requires more energy to heat or cool a house, and because it leads to longer commuting times (Holmberg et al., 2011). It is worth noting that people living in the country are happier even though more commuting is detrimental to happiness.

A factor that is harmful from a climate perspective but *neutral* from a happiness perspective is having dogs, cats, and other pets (Veenhoven, 2013a). The same thing holds for having children. Every child that is born can be expected to emit a lot of GHGs, but having children has little or no effect on people's happiness (Veenhoven, 2013b). I doubt that this information would have any effect on people's desire to have children, however. It is also worth noting that the alternative theories of well-being tend to imply that having children is conducive to well-being: many people strongly desire to have children, and it can also be regarded as objectively valuable.

To conclude, some activities and conditions that are conducive to happiness require little or no use of energy, whereas others are quite energy-intensive. In fact, the least sustainable activities and conditions (e.g. flying, living in a house, and driving) might all be happiness-inducing (statistically speaking). But if we move our attention to question (2), there is some cause for optimism, since the fact that there are many happiness-inducing activities that require little use of energy suggests that it is *possible* to live a life that is both happy and sustainable. However, it might be hard for many to maintain their present happiness if they can no longer drive or fly as much, but on the other hand, many of us may well adapt to a low GHG emission lifestyle over time.

5. The relation between working hours and happiness

It has been proposed that shorter working hours would be a good way to cut emissions, i.e. that such a reform might be beneficial from a sustainability perspective. The most interesting policy proposal in this context is not that individuals shorten their working hours voluntarily, but a *general* shortening of our working hours, a reform that might lead to less consumption and less commuting (Holmberg et al., 2011).

It is well documented that unemployment is detrimental to happiness (Frey, 2008), but less clear how many working hours are optimal from a happiness perspective. Some tend to believe we would be happier if we worked somewhat less, e.g. because we would experience less time pressure and have more time to socialize and engage in leisure activities (Kasser & Sheldon, 2009). Shorter working hours might not benefit people with attractive jobs and a less attractive leisure, however (Holmberg et al., 2011). In a recent Swedish study, it was shown that people who work somewhat more than 40 hours a week are most satisfied with their lives, whereas people who work 35–40 hours are higher in affective well-being (Fors & Brülde, 2011).[14] However, these numbers might be irrelevant if we want to assess how a general shortening of working hours would affect happiness, and they might change considerably if the '40 hour norm' would weaken its grip on us. It is also worth noting that the alternative theories of well-being may well imply that shorter working hours would improve the lives of many, e.g. because working less would have positive effects on intimate relationships, personal development, or other objective values.

Moreover, when assessing such a proposal from a happiness perspective, there are many things that need to be taken into account besides the direct effects, i.e. how those who work less would be affected (given that everyone works less). We also need to ask what effects it would have on society as a whole, e.g. whether it would lead to less unemployment through job sharing, how it would affect gender relations, and whether it would jeopardize our publicly funded welfare services.

If we move our attention to question (2), we can argue that it may well be *possible* for many of us to work somewhat less and yet maintain our present happiness, even if working less means consuming less.

6. Health, sustainability, and happiness

Health has positive effects on happiness (especially over time), and it might be argued that an environmentally responsible lifestyle has positive long-term effects on happiness because it is healthier than an energy-intensive lifestyle. However, some claims about the relation between health and sustainability are highly speculative and of dubious value, e.g. that the factors that are detrimental to health (like stress) also have negative environmental effects (because stress leads to overconsumption).

There are some factors that seem detrimental to our health and the environment alike, however, as in the case of red meat. For example, Pan et al. (2012) have shown that a high consumption of red or processed meat increases the risk of premature death through e.g. cancer or heart disease. It is also worth noting that local policies may have good effects on both health and climate, e.g. decisions to decrease traffic in big cities. And even if the relation between health and sustainability is not very strong, it seems desirable to synchronize the project to promote health with the project to reduce emissions.

7. 'Nature relatedness' and environmental awareness

We already know that 'green' activities are conducive to happiness (see also Nisbet et al., 2011). It has also been shown that people who feel more strongly related to nature are both somewhat happier than others (ibid.) and more engaged in environmental issues (Nisbet et al., 2009). This is consistent with the finding that people who are environmentally motivated are somewhat more satisfied with their lives (Brülde & Fors, 2013). They do not feel better than others, however.

The fact that people who are high in 'nature relatedness' are more environmentally conscious does not entail that their lives are more sustainable, however, e.g. nature lovers might live closer to nature (which means emissions from heating and commuting) and fly long distances to experience awe-inspiring nature on different continents. In fact, it has been found that 'eco-efficient attitudes are not associated with environmental impact' (Wilson et al., 2013, p. 11). But as in the case of idealists, it might be easier for people with pro-environmental attitudes to live lives that are both sustainable and happy. After all, environmentally aware nature lovers are probably more disposed than others to adopt a sustainable lifestyle, and it might be easier to change their behaviour by e.g. political means. But it is probably quite difficult to make people feel more related to nature by political means (if not in kindergarten or in school). In any case, we need to learn more about why some develop a stronger relation to nature than others, and how people's connection to nature can be strengthened.

Conclusions

The first question of this chapter is how a more sustainable lifestyle would affect our well-being (happiness), and the tentative answer is that most people would most probably be *less* happy than today if they changed their behaviour, at least in the short run. But if we take a longer view this might not be the case, since we may well adapt to these changes over time.

In any case, it seems possible for some of us to live lives that are both sustainable and happy, at least if we can afford the latest technologies and are willing to simplify our lives considerably. After all, there are several factors that are beneficial both from a climate perspective and from a happiness perspective – like spending time with others, exercise, and outdoor activities – and the weak connection between total emissions and happiness suggests that our well-being would not suffer very much if we adopted a lower emission lifestyle (at least within certain limits). It is also worth noting that pleasure is not identical to happiness, and that it might not be detrimental to happiness to refrain from e.g. the pleasures of eating red meat.

However, the fact that it is possible for *some* to live lives that are both happy and sustainable does not imply that it is possible for *many*, and it is even more unlikely that it is possible for each or for sufficiently many. After all, the car gives us great freedom if we avoid traffic jams, air travel is associated with pleasant holidays and novel experiences, and many forms of consumption are conducive to happiness. However, it is worth emphasizing that we know very little about the relation between sustainability and happiness, even on the individual level and in the short run. We know even less about how our long-term happiness would be affected if more sustainable policies were introduced, e.g. if we *all* had strong incentives to fly or drive less. This suggests that even if a more sustainable lifestyle would have negative short-term effects on happiness, the long-term effects might be less negative than most people think, especially if everyone is forced to make similar changes.

Our third question is even more difficult to answer, but a few points can be made about when (if ever) considerations of well-being can make people more willing to e.g. accept more radical environmental policies. First, these considerations can only have the desired effect if people endorse some traditional philosophical theory of well-being, like the happiness theory or objectivist pluralism, or if they endorse some specific 'vision' of well-being, like 'the simple life'. It is hard to tell whether people can be influenced in this direction, however, e.g. whether it is possible to convince people that happiness is more important than a high standard of living. Second, considerations of well-being (or happiness) will probably make more of a difference if people would learn more about hedonic adaptation, and if they would realize that radical environmental policies would most probably not give rise to any permanent loss in happiness. But even if considerations of well-being can make people somewhat more willing to accept more radical environmental policies under these conditions, such considerations can never be sufficient. If we want to influence people in an environmental direction, we should not appeal to their self-interest. Instead, we should use moral arguments, and try to convince them that we should all be prepared to make sacrifices if this can benefit future generations and the world's poor.

Notes

1 In this chapter, the term 'well-being' is defined as the value of a life for the person who lives it, i.e. to have a high degree of well-being is the same as having a good life (see below). The reason why I mostly use the term 'well-being' rather than the phrase 'the good life' is partly that the notion of well-being is more accepted in philosophy, and partly that it is a dimensional concept that allows for degrees. I could also have used the phrase 'the value of a life for the person who lives it', but this would have been rather clumsy.

2 In this chapter the focus is on the climate problem, but it is worth noting that there are also other environmental problems, and that environmental responsibility includes more than living and acting in a 'climate-friendly' manner.

3 At least if we restrict ourselves to private consumption and disregard all emissions from our shared public consumption, which amounts to 1.8 tonnes per person in a country like Sweden.

4 There are also other affective conceptions of happiness besides the hedonistic view, e.g. happiness can also be regarded as euphoria or as peace of mind. The latter conception is most common in spiritual contexts, and it can be argued that it is the most 'sustainable' form of happiness (cf. Brülde, 2009).

5 It is worth noting that the first and the third theories had advocates already in classical Greece, whereas the desire theory can be traced back to nineteenth-century economics. It is also worth noting that Parfit's (1984) classification is not the only possible one. An alternative classification has been proposed by Kagan (1992), who suggests that theories of the good life can be classified as subjective versus objective on the one hand, and as internalist versus externalist on the other. There is also a distinction between formal and substantive theories of well-being (Griffin, 1986; Brülde, 2007a).

6 It is worth noting that this is a hybrid theory which incorporates elements from all the theories above, e.g. (a) is a preferentialist idea, whereas (b) is objectivist.

7 There are other limitations as well. On the national level, it is not just difficult to determine how average levels of happiness would be affected, but also how politically induced changes would affect the distribution of happiness, e.g. whether environmental taxes would affect the poor significantly more than the rich. It is also difficult to assess how the 'key players' – e.g. influential people or those who are most likely to resist change – would be affected.

8 One should not be confused by the Happy Planet Index here, or by the fact that wealthy nations do badly on this index. The index (created by New Economics Foundation) does not just include happiness and life expectancy, but also ecological footprint (in the denominator). This explains why the perhaps happiest nation on the planet (Denmark) ranks as number 99, while we find countries like Colombia, Costa Rica, and Cuba at the top. In my view, the index is worthless even as a measure of sustainable happiness, since it ignores how animals are treated and how countries affect other countries.

9 These differences are higher than the corresponding differences in the case of income: the life satisfaction in the highest income group is 1.8 units higher than in the lowest, whereas the difference in affective well-being is 1.5 units.

10 We might also ask how a decrease in consumption would affect other prudential values besides happiness, e.g. our relationships. My guess is that reduced consumption can only have a positive effect on these values if combined with shorter working hours.

11 Regarding *why* materialists are less happy, see Hellevik, 2003; Hellevik's chapter in this volume; Patterson & Biswas-Diener, 2012.

12 According to Hellevik (see his chapter in this volume), extreme idealists earn 7 per cent more than extreme materialists.

13 It is not clear what we can conclude from this, however, since most respondents are probably well within the 'comfort zone'.

14 This finding was confirmed by Larsson et al. (2013), who also found that people who work less experience less time pressure and a better work/life balance, and that they have more time to exercise and socialize.

Bibliography

Andersson, D., Nässén, J., Holmberg, J. and Larsson, J. (2013) 'Would lower greenhouse gas emissions imply lower subjective wellbeing? A study of Swedish households'. Paper presented at the *SCORAI conference*. Worcester, MA: Clark University.

Argyle, M. (2001) *The Psychology of Happiness*. London: Routledge.

Beavan, C. (2009) *No Impact Man*. New York: Farrar.

Brown, K.W. and Kasser, T. (2005) 'Are psychological and ecological well-being compatible? The role of values, mindfulness, and lifestyle' in *Social Indicators Research*, Vol. 74, pp. 349–368.

Brülde, B. (1998) *The Human Good*. Gothenburg: Acta Universitatis Gothoburgensis.

Brülde, B. (2007a) 'Happiness and the good life: Introduction and conceptual framework' in *Journal of Happiness Studies*, Vol. 8, pp. 1–14.

Brülde, B. (2007b) 'Happiness theories of the good life' in *Journal of Happiness Studies*, Vol. 8, pp. 15–49.

Brülde, B. (2009) *Lyckans och lidandets etik* [The Ethics of Happiness and Suffering], Stockholm: Thales.

Brülde, B. and Fors, F. (2012) 'Kan man köpa lycka för pengar? Om konsumtion och lycka' ['Can one buy happiness for money? On consumption and happiness'], *Konsumtionsrapporten 2012*, Handelshögskolan, Göteborgs universitet.

Brülde, B. and Fors, F. (2013) 'Är lyckan grön?' ['Is happiness green?'] in *Ekonomisk debatt*, Vol. 41, pp. 1–9.

Clark, A.E., Diener, E., Georgellis, Y. and Lucas, R.E. (2007) 'Lags and leads in life satisfaction: A test of the baseline hypothesis' in *CEP Discussion Paper* 836. London: London School of Economics and Political Science.

Cummins, R.A. (2000) 'Personal income and subjective well-being: A review' in *Journal of Happiness Studies*, Vol. 1, pp. 133–158.

Dunn, E.W., Aknin, L.B. and Norton, M.I. (2008) 'Spending money on others promotes happiness' in *Science*, Vol. 319, pp. 1687–1688.

Easterlin, R.A. (1974) 'Does economic growth improve the human lot? Some empirical evidence' in *Nations and Households in Economic Growth: Essays in Honor of Moses Abramowitz*, David, P.A. and Reder, M.W. (eds) New York: Academic Press, pp. 89–125.

Fors, F. and Brülde, B. (2011) 'Välbefinnande och livstillfredsställelse i dagens Sverige' ['Well-being and life satisfaction in contemporary Sweden'] in *Lycksalighetens ö*, Holmberg, S., Weibull, L. and Oscarsson, H. (eds) Göteborgs universitet: SOM-institutet, pp. 349–364.

Frederick, S. and Loewenstein, G. (1999) 'Hedonic adaptation' in *Well-being: The Foundations of Hedonic Psychology*, Kahneman, D. Diener, E. and Schwarz, N. (eds) New York: Russell Sage, pp. 302–329.

Frey, B.S. (2008) *Happiness. A Revolution in Economics*. Cambridge, MA: MIT Press.

Griffin, J. (1986) *Well-Being: Its Meaning, Measurement and Moral Importance*, Oxford: Clarendon.

Hedenus, F. and Björck, A. (2011) *One Tonne Life Final Report*. Available from: http://onetonnelife.com/files/2011/07/OTL_final-report_eng_screen_0630_.pdf [accessed 10 October 2013].

Hellevik, O. (2003) 'Economy, values and happiness in Norway' in *Journal of Happiness Studies*, Vol. 4, pp. 243–283.

Holmberg, J., Larsson, J., Nässén, J., Svenberg, S. and Andersson, D. (2011) *Klimatomställningen och det goda livet* [Climate policy and the good life]. rapport 6458. Stockholm: Naturvårdsverket.

Kagan, S. (1992) 'The limits of well-being' in *The Good Life and the Human Good*, Paul, E. F. Miller, F. D., Jr. and Paul, J. (eds) Cambridge: Cambridge University Press, pp. 169–189.

Kahneman, D. and Deaton, A. (2010) 'High income improves evaluation of life but not emotional well-being' in *Proceedings of the National Academy of Sciences of the USA*, Vol. 107, pp. 16489–16493.

Kasser, T. and Sheldon, K. (2009) 'Time affluence as a path toward personal happiness and ethical business practice: Empirical evidence from four studies' in *Journal of Business Ethics*, Vol. 84, pp. 243–255.

Larsson, J., Andersson, D., Holmberg, J. and Nässén, J. (2013) 'Temporal well-being: A central dimension of sustainable lifestyles?' Paper presented at the *SCORAI conference*, Worcester, MA: Clark University.

Layard, R. (2005) *Happiness: Lessons from a New Science*. London: Allen Lane.

Nässén, J. (2014) 'Determinants of greenhouse gas emissions from Swedish private consumption: Time-series and cross-sectional analyses', in *Energy*, Vol. 66, pp. 98–106.

Nisbet, E.K., Zelenski, J.M. and Murphy, S.A. (2009) 'The nature relatedness scale: Linking individuals' connection with nature to environmental concern and behavior' in *Environment and Behavior*, Vol. 41, pp. 715–740.

Nisbet, E.K., Zelenski, J.M. and Murphy, S.A. (2011) 'Happiness is in our nature: Exploring nature relatedness as a contributor to subjective well-being' in *Journal of Happiness Studies*, Vol. 12, pp. 303–322.

Pan, A., Sun, Q., Bernstein, A.M., Schulze, M.B., Manson, J.E., Stampfer, M.J., Willett, W.C. and Hu, F.B. (2012) 'Red meat consumption and mortality: Results from 2 prospective cohort studies' in *Archives of Internal Medicine*, Vol. 172, pp. 555–563.

Parfit, D. (1984) *Reasons and Persons*. New York: Oxford University Press.

Patterson, L. and Biswas-Diener, R. (2012) 'Consuming happiness' in *The Good Life in a Technological Age*, Brey, P., Briggle, A. and Spence, E. (eds) New York: Routledge, pp. 147–156.

Rogelj, J., Hare, W., Lowe, J., van Vuuren, D.P., Riahi, K., Matthews, B., Hanaoka, T., Jiang, K. and Meinshausen, M. (2011) 'Emission pathways consistent with a 2°C global temperature limit' in *Nature Climate Change*, Vol. 1, pp. 413–518.

Stevenson, B. and Wolfers, J. (2008) 'Economic growth and happiness: Reassessing the Easterlin Paradox' in *Brookings Papers on Economic Activity*.

Sumner, L.W. (1996) *Welfare, Happiness, and Ethics*. Oxford: Clarendon Press.

Tatzel, M. (2003) 'The art of buying: Coming to terms with money and materialism' in *Journal of Happiness Studies*, Vol. 4, pp. 405–435.

Van Boven, L. and Gilovich, T. (2003) 'To do or to have? That is the question' in *Journal of Personality and Social Psychology*, Vol. 85, pp. 1193–1202.

Veenhoven, R. (2013a) 'Findings on happiness and current parental status' in *World Database of Happiness*. Collection Correlational Findings, subject section C3.2. Available from: http://worlddatabaseofhappiness.eur.nl/ [accessed 25 January 2013].

Veenhoven, R. (2013b) 'Findings on happiness and pets' in *World Database of Happiness*. Collection Correlational Findings, subject section P14. Available from: http://world databaseofhappiness.eur.nl/ [accessed 25 January 2013].

Wilson, J., Tyedmers, P. and Spinney, J.E.L. (2013) 'An exploration of the relationship between socioeconomic and well-being variables and household greenhouse gas emissions' in *Journal of Industrial Ecology*. Article published online 30 September 2013: DOI: 10.1111/jiec.12057.

World Bank (2012) *Turn Down the Heat: Why a 4°C Warmer World Must be Avoided.*

6 The problem of habits for a sustainable transformation

Harold Wilhite

Introduction

In the rich countries of North America, Europe and Asia, ideas about the good life and the steps needed to achieve it are inexorably linked to consumption. Being successful, having fun, establishing a comfortable home, dressing well and keeping clean are examples of activities that involve consumption of things and energy, resulting in pollution and climate emissions. From an environmental sustainability perspective, the consumption of the things that use energy and the amount of energy that they use both need to be radically reduced. In this chapter I explore the theories and policies associated with sustainable energy consumption, contending that mainstream theory has not delivered a robust enough policy platform to engender significant reductions in the environmental impacts of consumption. Mainstream theories are characterized by reductionist assumptions about consumers and their choices. The imaginary consumer is reflexive, rational and divested of experience. A significant contributor to the ways we consume and use energy is ignored, namely habits formed through lived experience. Cultural learning, repetitive actions and purposive training all contribute to the formation of habits. There is an urgent need for a robust theory of consumption that addresses how habits form, how they change and how policy can contribute to the formation of new habits that are less environmentally intrusive.

This examination of consumption in a collection of articles on the good life calls for a few words justifying the relationship between consumption and the good life. To begin with, as the contributions to this book indicate, there are unresolved debates within the domains of research that traditionally focus on the 'good life' as to what it means and what sets it off as a set of either ideals or practices. For example, is the good life associated with a 'drop out' from everyday demands as advocated by Timothy Leary and the 'hippies' of the 1960s and 1970s, or does it mean a periodic retreat to nature or some other idyllic environment as suggested by Greek thinkers and philosophers such as Thoreau in the United States or Rousseau in France? Or is it a way of expressing what we in the rich, developed countries of the world seek in our everyday lives, involving the pursuit of social acceptance, fun, shelter, comfort, efficient time management and so on?

This latter understanding of the 'good life' is common to research on consumption and particularly in research focused on achieving environmentally sustainable consumption. Important questions are being raised in sociological and anthropological research on how high impact consumption has become normalized as an aspect of the good life and how to transform this relationship (for a representative collection of perspectives see Southerton 2011 and Lockie, Sonnenfeld and Fisher 2013).

In this chapter, I argue that at the level of household, energy intensive habits have formed and their environmental consequences accelerated over the course of the twentieth century. In the United States and many other OECD countries, this has led to the formation of what Robbins (2004) has characterized as the culture of capitalism. Robbins relates how this culture departed significantly from a culture of moderation, thrift and frugality that characterized nineteenth-century consumers. Well into the early twentieth century, home interiors were sparsely decorated, with few household items and appliances to aid housework. It was common for people to make their own clothes and to have vegetable gardens. Post World War 1 manufacturers:

> had to figure out how to transform the wartime ethic of thrift and reuse – darning socks, keeping odd pieces of string, using tea leaves to clean carpets, and sewing rags into rugs – into a culture that embraced "throwaway habits" and the willingness to spend money on new 'stuff'.
>
> (Botsman and Rogers 2010:9)

From the mid-twentieth century, the sizes of homes and the quantity of furnishings have steadily increased. This is related to an increasing demand for more entertainment technologies, more efficient time management, greater demands on thermal comfort (indoor temperatures), the use of more water and cleaning products to achieve cleanliness and so on (Shove 2003). The expansion of commercial energy production has provided the heat and/or refrigerated air for bigger houses, electricity for the increasing kinds and uses of appliances and for accelerating use of fossil fuels in transport practices that have expanded in step with the expanding geography of everyday lives. After several generations of lived experience in this growth culture, 'dispositions' (Bourdieu 1977) have formed for a never-ending treadmill of expansive consumption practices, whether they be measured in terms of money, goods or resource inputs. Expansive consumption has become a habit, and the resulting practices will be difficult to break and reform at lower levels of environmental impact. In this chapter I articulate a theory of habit and point to potential policy levers for breaking and reforming consumption-intensive habits.

A theory of habit

Pierre Bourdieu (1977; 1998) and Marcel Mauss (1973) both contributed to a theory of *habitus*, conceived as a domain of dispositions for action, created and perpetuated through performance of a practice in a given social-cultural space. These dispositions constitute a form of knowledge, which influences or pre-disposes new performances of a given practice. The *habitus* engages with the 'presence of the past' (Bourdieu 1997:304) in forming and embodying knowledge. *Habitus* can therefore be seen as embodied history; in the words of anthropologist Sherry Ortner: 'a theory of practice is a theory of history' (2006:192). Mauss proposed that lived experience embodies practices related to the ways we dress, eat, clean, organize space and use time. Many forms for body-centred practices develop deeply agentive dispositions and many of these are relevant to the performance of home practices: for example, the ways we cool and heat our homes, prepare and consume foods, wash and clothe our bodies, and how we transport ourselves from one place to another. In the face of the urgency for a low-energy transformation, habits are stubborn and thus problematic; however, they have positive effects in daily lives as well. A day in which one had to make reflexive decisions about everything would be exhausting. Habits free our minds to day-dream, plan and fantasize; all essential to a healthy, pleasurable existence. Habits will always be integrated to one extent or another in negotiating everyday tasks. The challenge from a sustainability perspective is to reduce their energy intensity.

In mainstream social theory, *habitus* and embodiment were set aside as con-tributors to human action in the post-modernist turn of the 1980s and replaced with a view of sovereign individuals whose beliefs and economic interests were fully agentive in practices (Crossly 2007; Warde 2011). Recent work revives interest in the *habitus* and what Lahire (2003:353) refers to as the interaction between (or relations between) forces that are internal and external to indi-viduals, 'between dispositions that are more or less strongly established during past socialization and . . . between external forces, i.e., between elements of the context'. Lives lived in big houses filled with lots of furnishings and electrical appliances set the stage for high-energy habits. Habits extend to encompass urban infrastructures including transport, sidewalks and distribution of shops and shopping centres.

These material adjuncts influence habit formation in important ways that have been under-theorized in the domains of social science concerned with consumption and sustainability. We can look to actor network theory (ANT), archaeology and material culture for inspiration on material agency in practices. Anthropologist Madeleine Akrich, working within the ANT tradition, theorized that the knowledge embedded by designers of technologies has a scripting effect on the actions of users. Designers embed 'their vision of (or prediction about) the world in the technical content of the new object'. She called this a 'script' or a 'scenario' . . . 'a framework of action together with the actors and the space in which they are supposed to act' (2000:208). Material agency is also important to archaeological theory, where an important thrust of inquiry is the inter-relationship between human action and material worlds. Archaeologists con-struct the actions of past societies through an analysis of artifactual remains. Archaeologist and material culturist Marci Dobres writes that the material underpinnings of the social world should be conceived 'as a verb of action and interaction, rather than a noun of possession' (2000:3). Anthropologists Appadurai (1986) and Kopytoff (1986), both working in the material culture tradition, theorize that things have social and cultural biographies, taking on different uses and assuming different meanings in the differing socio-cultural settings they pass through during their life cycles, and thereby influence actions differently in their different social incarnations. Anthropologist and material culturist Alfred Gell (1998) wrote that works of art are material objects that, once created, embody complex 'intentionalities' which act on observers.

Drawing on these conceptualizations of material agency, it can be said that habits are formed through the repetitions of particular patterns of interactions between people (with their embodied and cognitive knowledge) and things (with their enscripted knowledge) in a social context (norms, cultural practices and ideals). Cultural learning (what Mauss referred to as enculturation) is important to the formation of many forms for bodily habits, but habits can also be formed through purposive training (examples are marching, swimming and typing). An action performed infrequently is unlikely to result in strong habits. An infrequent bicycle commute, the preparation of a certain meal a few times a year, or the use of a perfume or cream on rare occasions will not likely lead to the formation of practical knowledge nor to habituation. Habits which involve few objects and are performed in uniform environments tend to be strong habits. For example, typing involves a standard keyboard. Once typing is mastered, it would take a significant disruption, such as a coffee spill, to disturb the movement of fingers on the keyboard and to invoke a cognitive response. Attaining competence in certain individual sports relies on habituation. For example, in a swimming pool with protected lanes, lap after lap can be accomplished without a conscious thought by the swimmer as to how to negotiate movements. The skilled swimmer is one whose movements flow efficiently without cognitive steering.

A theory of habit must account for social, cultural and spatial variability, not only the regularity of action but also the dimensions of the physical space in which the habit is performed. Harvey (2010) argues that tight spaces bring with them tighter scripts for action. The bounded space of the home contributes to the strength of many home consumption habits. Showering and bathing are examples of habits which are performed frequently in small spaces and which involve few material accessories. In the bath or shower cabinet, everything is close at hand, including flowing water, clothes, soaps and shampoos. In the absence of interruption, daily showering becomes strong habit. Warnier (2001) describes the home as a 'domesticated environment', from which uncertainty of many routines has been removed. Household activities such as cleaning clothes, preparing food, attending to the comfort levels in the house (heating and cooling) are practices which are preformed frequently within the bounded space of the home and can become strong habits.

How do habits change?

Social learning theory provides a source of theoretical inspiration on how habits change. Jean Lave (1991; 1993) proposed that learning new practices involves engaging both mind and body. Exposure to logical, deductive arguments for a change is seldom sufficient to unlock strong habits, especially those encompassing complex technologies such as household appliances and cars. Changing beliefs, attitudes and motivations are important catalysts for change, but it is fallacious to assume that changing beliefs are always antecedent to changes in practice. For instance, there are numerous empirical studies that show that greening of attitudes alone does not lead to the greening of consumption practices (see Brülde's contribution to this volume). From a habit perspective, the exposure of practitioners to new ways of doing things can be a more powerful change agent than cognitive explanations of the benefits of change. In the exposure to a new action or practice, the participant learns by engaging their minds and bodies with new objects in new contexts. Dispositions for action embedded in past practices get reassessed and adjusted. Future actions are then refreshed with new possibilities. As Wilhite and Wallenborn (2013:8) expressed this dynamic,

> The process by which experiences are explicitly and voluntarily transformed in new habits can be called an *experiment*. To balance the mind-centred, body-absent theoretical approach on which public policies are mainly based, an experimental approach is required. We are not referring to laboratory experiments in which the conditions of everyday life are approximated and reduced, nor are we referring to models in which bodies are replaced by numbers. We refer to experiences in real life in which there is a measure of the outcome and an associated learning process.

In the absence of the opportunity for direct experience, people often rely more on the experiences of family members or colleagues than they do on sales pitches or product information. This was confirmed in a recent study in Norway on how and why people decide to buy and install heat pumps in their homes, a heating technology that has the potential to significantly reduce heating energy. Findings show that an important source of information for potential purchasers is family members, colleagues, neighbours or friends who have made, or looked into, similar purchases. People take advantage of the experiences of others in comparing prices, exploring the choice of entrepreneur, assessing the quality of the product and the performance. The project findings show that this form for learning was more important than the advice of experts in the ways people consider the investment in a heat pump (Winther and Wilhite 2013).

In Western societies, many human-material interactions centre on ownership and control of the material objects associated with a practice. Individual ownership contributes to binding habits at high levels of environmental impacts. Unbinding them is one of the keys to transforming consumption in a sustainable direction. Individual ownership has been celebrated as one of the ultimate aims of economic development and is championed by national governments, commercial businesses and household consumers in North America and Europe. It is seen as a prerequisite for achieving the qualities associated with the good life, including individual agency, freedom and convenience. There are good reasons for questioning whether lives weighted down by things and accelerated by a drive for productivity, efficiency and overfilled agendas actually do lead to more satisfying lives (Guillen and Wilhite, *in press*).

We take for granted sharing and collaboration in a number of activities services including libraries, roads, trains, airplanes, rental cars, hotel rooms and time share apartments. A growing set of new initiatives expand on the principle of collaboration in the form of gifting, reusing, car sharing and in many other domains of consumption. This is facilitated by the growth and reach of the internet's capacity for hosting virtual collaboration, but is also growing in many neighbourhood and community initiatives around the world (Sahakian and Wilhite 2014). An optimistic interpretation of these initiatives is that a new set of ideas about the good life are being put into practice (and reinforced through the performance of practices) that include sociality, health of the environment, self-determination and deceleration.

Botsman and Rogers have reviewed these new collaborative efforts and summarized them under the headings of time, space, skills and money. They provide a comprehensive list of the specific designations for emerging collaborative consumption systems:

> swap trading, time banks, local exchange trading systems (LETS), bartering, social lending, peer-to-peer currencies, tool exchanges, land share, clothing swaps, toy sharing, shared workspaces, co-housing, co-working, CouchSurfing, car sharing, crowdfunding, bike sharing, ride sharing, food co-ops, walking school buses, shared microcreche, peer-to-peer rental.
>
> (2010:71)

These initiatives have the potential to erode the association between consumption and private ownership. Taking digital media as an example, Botsman and Rogers show how it is rapidly transforming the way that music and films are consumed. Companies like Apple (ITunes), Spotify and Netflix eliminate the need for producing and consuming hardware such as CDs or DVDs, as well as the need for transport to and from retail outlets. Collaborative consumption has significant positive environmental effects. As an example, Botsman and Rogers site a study by Intell and Microsoft which shows that music delivered by way of the internet reduces carbon emissions by 40 to 80 per cent compared to conventional music provision and consumption (2010:98).

The internet has also facilitated car sharing, allowing for convenient car reservation, driving, parking and payment. The convenience aspect is critical to this and other new forms for consumption (Shove 2003). Studies around the world reconfirm time and again that car-sharing participants have joined because they are interested in reducing costs, parking hassles, insurance fees, services and repairs (Attali and Wilhite 2001). I agree with the assessment of Botsman and Rogers that: '[f]or consumers to overcome the culturally entrenched cult of possessions, we have to get to a point where sharing is convenient, secure and more cost-effective than ownership' (2010:107). The environmental benefits are not necessarily the primary motive for joining car-sharing organizations, but are a derivative of collaboration.

Bringing the discussion back to habits and social learning, the internet facilitates experimentation with new ways of doing things and this is important to unlocking habits. Zipcar tested this theory by inviting car owners to engage in what they called a 'Low-Car Diet Challenge'. There were 250 participants who agreed to not use their car for a period of two weeks. The company collected and held their car keys. After the experiment, 100 of the 250 had found the alternatives to driving satisfactory and did not want their car keys back (Botsman and Rogers 2010:74).

Policy engagement with habits

These insights on habits can be important sources of inspiration for sustainable energy policy. Through the articulation of a theory of habit, levers for change can be identified. An important lever is related to the knowledge associated with experience and the role of experimentation with new practices in engendering change. Command and control types of policies that legislate changes in the material landscapes and frameworks for domestic consumption and transport are relevant because they encourage or enable changes in habit. For example, the banning of cigarette smoking in public spaces, restaurants and bars has been crucial to breaking the smoking habits of large segments of the smoking population. Concerning automobility, closing off certain city spaces to cars either permanently or at certain times of the day, or even restricting parking, encourages people who are habituated to car commuting to experiment with new forms of transport, such as buses, bicycles and walking (Kaufmann 2000). Evidence from cities located in many parts of the world indicates that on the whole, these reductions in car habits are regarded as positive due to improved fitness, reduced congestion and lower pollution (both noise and air) (Topp and Pharoah 1994; Bulkeley et al. 2011). When coupled with provision of infrastructure for alternative practices, the combination has the potential to enable a rapid growth in less resource intensive habits. One of the most rapidly growing alternative transport systems in Europe today is bicycling and bicycle commuting. The provision of space for bicycle lanes – coupled with efficient bicycle rental systems in cities such as Paris, Amsterdam and Copenhagen – is contributing to a revision of commuting habits among large segments of the population. It is estimated that in Copenhagen, 40 per cent of all commuting within the city is done by bicycle.

These changes in transport infrastructures provide the opportunity for experimentation with new practices and thus enable change. Demonstrations of new forms for household technologies also enable experimentation by providing an opportunity for people to visit and experience low-energy practices. In Davis, California, in the 1970s and 1980s, great strides were made in home weatherization after demonstration homes were set up in neighbourhoods around the city. People were able to observe and experience first-hand how life in a low-energy house could be more comfortable and cosy, yet use much less energy than their own house.

Experimentation occurs naturally in family transitions such as moving to a new house, getting married, having a child or getting divorced. Lahire writes that in situations like these 'it seems that the new situation induces people to feel that their habits have become strange to them' (2003:340). These transitions provide a lucrative policy opportunity. Families in transition are open to information, demonstrations and incentives for energy-saving opportunities for home and transport, providing opportunities the introducing low-energy practices.

There are a growing number of community-based efforts around the world that regularly engage in experimentation with new policies and practices for reducing energy use (Bulkeley et al. 2011). Practice changes embedded in initiatives such as the 'covenant of mayors'[1] involving over 4,000 cities worldwide, aim at significantly deeper reductions in energy use than those discussed in international negotiations or in national energy plans. These deserve wide exposure, as do other examples of participatory-driven social transformations that yield energy reductions and life-quality improvements. A transition in food and dietary habits is often the early focus of these transition communities. In a recent study in Europe, it was found that when the various forms of food consumption were consolidated (meat products, milk, cheese, bread, bottled drinks), the domain of food consumption had a greater environmental impact than all other categories of consumption, including automobile driving and maintenance (Huppes et al., 2006). As Brown and Garver (2009:64) write:

> Even a simple act like walking to the corner store to buy a carton of milk depends on a whole series of uses of material and energy. The food you ate to enable you to walk, the clothes you wear, the sidewalk, the building the store is in, the cow that produced the milk, the packing and transporting of the milk to the store, the paper money or coins used to pay for the milk and so on.

Since food, energy and fitness are deeply linked, an effort to either change food or energy habits can have both health and environmental benefits. Sahakian and Wilhite (2014) review community efforts to transform food and energy practices, giving attention to several cases, including a community project in Oklahoma City, in the state of Oklahoma, US. This is a noteworthy example because Oklahoma is in America's conservative heartland, where beef is viewed as essential to daily dining, fast food consumption is high and where the automobile reigns supreme. Oklahoma City is at the top of US rankings of obesity and general unhealthiness. The community food and sedentary transport habits can be said to be a local example of what Chopra et al. (2002) refer to as a twentieth-century global epidemic of obesity, diabetes and cardiovascular diseases. In 2007, partly motivated by his own weight problems, the Mayor of Oklahoma City decided to launch a campaign called 'City on a Diet', with the goal of getting the population of the City as a whole to lose one million pounds (450,000 kg). The campaign encouraged healthy food choices and supplemented this by enabling walking and bicycling. Financed by a one-cent sales tax, the City began revitalizing the downtown area. Sahakian and Wilhite (2014) relate that:

> Today, plans are underway for designing and constructing a new central park linking downtown with the Oklahoma River; a rail-based streetcar system; new sidewalks; over fifty miles of new bicycling and walking trails throughout the city; a public white-water kayaking facility on the Oklahoma River; and state-of-the-art senior wellness centres throughout the city.

These changes have led to more biking and walking and have measurably positive impacts on health and fitness. The one million pound reduction target was achieved in early 2012 for the City as a whole, with the Mayor himself losing 38 pounds. In all, more than 47,000 people recorded their weight-loss efforts on a website set up online as part of this campaign. Experimentation with new forms for body-active transport and healthier diets is leading to the formation of new low-energy habits.

Conclusion

A theory of habits offers new insights on stability and change in consumption. It acknowledges the co-presence of subjects and objects in the world and gives attention to the field of opportunities and obstacles that are formed in their interrelationship. It offers new directions for energy-saving policies that are lucrative yet at the same time challenging. It is one thing to acknowledge the power of habits and yet another to find ways to influence and move them. It implies a much more robust and costly policy framework as well as the necessity for a longer perspective. It implies supplementing market signals and the provision of deductive information with policies that acknowledge the role of experiential knowledge. It implies infrastructural changes aimed at allowing people to experiment with new low energy practices in the domains of home energy use, transport and food provision.

Many communities around the world have decided not to wait for a change of national policy, but are moving forward to change their own practices. The inhabitants of these communities are asking fundamental questions about how they want to live and whether the ways they live will be sustainable for future generations. The key elements in this change are participatory goal forming and decision processes, and planning for the long term. This opens for investments in infrastructural changes at the community level in areas such as transportation, food provision and low-energy housing. As Weltzer (2011:37) writes, '[t]hese projects are shaping the future – not as mere proposals, but as living examples. For the time being, the political problem of this lived-in future is its particularity, its smallness, which makes it appear insignificant as a social counterforce'. Greater exposure through best-practice type marketing, in situ workshops and supporting grants would provide non-participants with the opportunity to experience and experiment with low-energy practices, demystifying low-energy living and showing how it can be accomplished without degrading – and in fact improving – practitioners' wellbeing.

Notes

1   www.covenantofmayors.eu (accessed 2 August 2014).

Bibliography

Akrich, M. (2000) 'The De-scription of Technical Objects' in Bijker, W. and Law, J. (eds) *Shaping Technology/Building Society*. Cambridge, MA: The MIT Press, pp. 205–224.

Appadurai, A. (1986) 'Introduction: Commodities and the Politics of Value' in Appadurai, A. (ed.) *The Social Life of Things: Commodities in a Cultural Perspective*. Cambridge: Cambridge University Press, pp. 3–63.

Attali, S. and Wilhite, H. (2001) 'Assessing variables supporing and impeding the development of car sharing' in *Proceedings of the ECEEE 2001 Summer Study*. Paris: European Council for an Energy Efficient Economy.

Botsman, R. and Rogers, R. (2010) *What's Mine is Yours: How Collaborative Consumption is Changing the Way We Live*. London: Collins.

Bourdieu, P. (1977) *Outline of a Theory of Practice*. Cambridge: Cambridge University Press.

Bourdieu, P. (1998) *Practical Reason*. Cambridge: Polity Press.

Brown, P. and Garver, G. (2009) *Right Relationship: Building a Whole Earth Economy*. San Francisco, CA: Berrett-Koehler Publishers.

Bulkeley, H., Castán Broto, V., Hodson, M. and Marvin, S. (eds) (2011) *Cities and Low Carbon Transitions*. London: Routledge.

Chopra, M., Galbraith, S. and Darnton-Hill, I. (2002) 'A global response to a global problem: The epidemic of overnutrition' in *Bulletin of the World Health Organization*, 8(12), pp. 952–958.

Crossly, N. (2007) 'Researching embodiment by way of "body techniques"' in Shilling, C. (ed.) *Embodying Sociology: Retrospect, Progress and Prospects*. Malden, MA: Blackwell, pp 80–94.

Dobres, M. (2000) *Technology and Social Agency*. Oxford: Blackwell Publishers.

Gell, A. (1998) *Art and Agency: An Anthropological Theory*. Oxford: Oxford University Press.

Guillen Royo, M. and Wilhite, H. (*in press*). 'Wellbeing and sustainable consumption' in Glatzer, W. (ed.) *Global Handbook of Well-being and Quality of Life*. Frankfurt: Springer.

Harvey, D. C. (2010) 'The space for culture and cognition' in *Poetics*, 38, pp. 184–203.

Huppes G., Koning, A. and Suh, S. (2006) 'Environmental impacts of consumption in the European Union: High-resolution input-output tables with detailed environmental extensions' in *Journal of Industrial Ecology*, 10, pp. 129–146.

Kaufmann, V. (2000) *Mobilité quotidienne et dynamiques urbaines: la question du report modal*. Lausanne: Presses polytechniques et universitaires romandes.

Kopytoff, I. (1986) 'The cultural biography of things: Commoditization as process' in Appadurai, A. (ed.) *The Social Life of Things: Commodities in a Cultural Perspective*. Cambridge: Cambridge University Press, pp. 64–91.

Lahire, B. (2003) 'From the habitus to an individual heritage of dispositions. Towards a sociology at the level of the individual' in *Poetics*, 31, pp. 329–355.

Lave, J. (1991) 'Situated learning in communities of practice' in Resnick, L. B., Levine, J. M. and Teasley, S. D. (eds) *Perspectives on Socially Shared Cognition*. Washington, D.C.: American Psychological Association, pp. 63–82.

Lave, J. (1993) 'The practice of learning' in Chaiklin, S. and Lave, J. (eds) *Understanding Practice: Perspectives on Activity and Context*. Cambridge: Cambridge University Press, pp. 3–35.

Lockie, S., Sonnenfeld, D. and Fisher, D. R. (2013) *Routledge International Handbook of Social and Environmental Change*. London and New York: Routledge.

Mauss, M. (1973) 'Techniques of the body' in *Economy and Society*, 2, pp. 70–89.

Ortner, S. (2006) 'Power and projects: Reflections on agency' in Ortner, S. (ed.) *Anthropology and Cultural Theory: Culture, Power and the Acting Subject*. Durham and London: Duke University Press, pp. 129–154.

Robbins, R. (2004) *Global Problems and the Culture of Capitalism*. Boston, MA: Allyn & Bacon.

Sahakian, M. and Wilhite, H. (2014) 'Making practice theory practicable: towards more sustainable forms of consumption' in *Journal of Consumer Culture*, 14(1), pp. 25–44.

Shove, E. (2003) *Comfort, Cleanliness & Convenience: The Social Organization of Normality*. Oxford and New York: Berg.

Southerton, D. (ed) (2011) *The Encyclopedia of Consumer Culture*. Los Angeles and London: Sage.

Topp, H. and Pharoah, T. (1994) 'Car-free city centres' in *Transportation*, 31, pp. 231–247.

Warde, A. (2011) 'Social science and sustainable consumption: Symposium prospectus'. Paper presented at the symposium *Social science and sustainable consumption*, Helsinki Collegium for Advanced Studies, Helsinki, Finland, January.

Warnier, J. P. (2001) 'A praxeological approach to subjectivation in a material world' in *Journal of Material Culture*, 6(1), pp. 5–24.

Weltzer, H. (2011) 'Mental infrastructures: How growth entered the world and our souls' in *Heinrich Boll Stiftung Publication Series on Ecology*. Volume 14, Berlin: Heinrich-Boll-Stiftung.

Wilhite, H. and Wallenborn, G. (2013) 'Articulating the body in the theorizing of consumption' in *Proceedings from the ECEEE 1999 Summer Study on Energy Efficiency in Buildings*. Stockholm: European Council for an Energy Efficient Economy.

Winther, T. and Wilhite, H. (2013) 'Rebound from a practice perspective: Towards a better understanding of people's interactions with heat pumps in Norway'. Paper presented at the CREE conference, Lysebu, Oslo, September.

7 Well-being in sustainability transitions

Making use of needs

Felix Rauschmayer and Ines Omann

Happiness is not a place, but a direction

Sogyal Rinpoche

Introduction

Let us start with the basic definition of sustainable development given by the Brundtland commission: 'Sustainable development is a development that meets the needs of the present without compromising the ability of future generations to meet their own needs' (WCED 1987). This definition is familiar to us, but have we really reflected on what is meant by 'needs' in the Brundtland report? The Brundtland report uses 'needs' in very different ways: they speak of a need for food, clothing, shelter, water supply, sanitation, and health care, but also for employment, a high rate of growth of protein availability, or energy. What remains completely unclear when reading the Brundtland report is the link of needs to well-being, to capabilities, to values, or to quality of life. But at least well-being and quality of life are currently linked to the discussion on sustainability (Eurostat 2009). So, this chapter aims to use the concept of needs to strengthen such links and to clarify a potentially fruitful understanding of needs.

It is clear that current societies are far from sustainable development: poverty (understood as not meeting the needs) exists throughout the globe as well as resource depletion, biodiversity extinction, emission of greenhouse gases, etc. that make it impossible for future generations to meet their own needs. It is difficult or even impossible to individually live sustainably within these societies – at least within industrialised societies that have a high structural resource consumption. Furthermore, if one wants to be an active citizen within these societies, it is very difficult to lower one's ecological footprint to a sustainable size. Therefore, transitions to sustainable development are necessary – on the individual as well as on collective levels, from local to global.

Currently, discussions on sustainability transitions link the development of small-scale niches of a more sustainable consumption of production to their mainstreaming throughout society (Grin, Rotmans et al. 2010), but rarely include the level of individual needs, emotions, or values.[1]

Our chapter focuses on how to use this inner-individual level for sustainability transitions. It cannot, though, do more than indicate some of the difficulties that an inclusion of this level would generate for processes of sustainability governance. But realising that sustainability transitions can be achieved with high quality of life takes away one of the main reasons for resistance to sustainability: the fear that sustainability ultimately means to live in caves or up in the trees.

Linking sustainable development, needs, well-being, capabilities, and strategies

Quality of life has recently been used several times as being the central or at least one central aim of sustainable development (European Commission 2007; Eurostat 2009). Lane (1996:259) defines quality of life 'as subjective well-being and personal growth in a healthy and prosperous environment'. Here we can distinguish between two determinants of quality of life: an objective one relating to the environment and a subjective one relating to well-being and personal growth. As we will discuss below, we understand the objective side of quality of life as the capabilities a person has to fulfil his or her needs. The subjective side of quality of life can be understood as the perception of the fulfilment of the needs.

But what do we exactly mean with the concept of needs? The philosopher Finnis (Grisez, Boyle et al. 1987) has defined needs as the most fundamental dimension of human flourishing.[2] In practice this means that actions to fulfil needs require no further reasoning, or, put in other words, one could use the why-laddering (Wittmayer, Steenbergen et al. 2011): when asked why you have done such and such action, you cannot answer it any more but with a term that fundamentally refers to your flourishing, then you are at the level of needs. An example: asked, why you're reading this book chapter, you might respond: "because I'm interested in it." Yes, but why are you interested in it? "Because I want to understand better how sustainable development is important to the quality of life." Why do you want to understand this? "Because I hope to better contribute to a better world through this understanding." Why do you want to contribute? "My life would be meaningless if I couldn't contribute to a better world." So now, you are at the level of fundamental needs: contributing to a better world is, according to some (e.g. Rosenberg 2001), a fundamental human need, essential for human flourishing.

In this understanding, needs are an important internal driving force. In their essence, they are non-negotiable, as they are indispensable for the health and the well-being of people. Of course you can negotiate when and how to meet these fundamental needs, but not their fundamental importance for human well-being. Needs in this sense are universal in type, and therefore abstract. The list of needs, given in Table 7.1, exemplifies this. Examples for such needs are subsistence, participation, or freedom. Therefore, needs are neither sustainable nor unsustainable; they just are.[3] The strategies to meet the needs, though, can be sustainable or unsustainable. The selection of the strategies depends on the values, the culture, the preferences, the resources and technologies available, the chances for

Table 7.1 Matrix of needs including examples of corresponding strategies in four categories

Existential categories Fundamental human needs	Being (qualities)	Having (things)	Doing (actions)	Interacting (settings)
subsistence	physical and mental health	food, shelter, work	feed, clothes, rest, work	living environment, social setting
protection	care, adaptability, autonomy	social security, health systems, work	co-operate, plan, take care of, help	social environment, dwelling
affection	respect, sense of humour, generosity, sensuality	friendships, family, relationships with nature	share, take care of, make love, express emotions	privacy, intimate spaces of togetherness
understanding	critical capacity, curiosity, intuition	literature, teachers, policies, educational	analyse, study, meditate, investigate,	schools, families, universities, communities
participation	receptiveness, dedication, sense of humour	responsibilities, duties, work, rights	co-operate, dissent, express opinions	associations, parties, churches, neighbourhoods
idleness	imagination, tranquillity, spontaneity	games, parties, peace of mind	day-dream, remember, relax, have fun	landscapes, intimate spaces, places to be alone
creation	imagination, boldness, inventiveness, curiosity	abilities, skills, work, techniques	invent, build, design, work, compose, interpret	spaces for expression, workshops, audiences
identity	sense of belonging, self-esteem, consistency	language, religions, work, customs, values, norms	get to know oneself, grow, commit oneself	places one belongs to, everyday settings
freedom	autonomy, passion, self-esteem, open-mindedness	equal rights	dissent, choose, run risks, develop awareness	anywhere
transcendence	inner-centeredness, presence	religions, rites	pray, meditate, develop awareness	places for worship

Source: adapted from Max-Neef 1991:32–33

realising the strategies, etc. An example may help to see the (un)sustainability of strategies as well as their dependence on many factors: some people realise their need for freedom through driving in a Porsche on a German motorway without speed limit; others decide to live in a monastery to be free of mundane temptations.

The set of strategies herewith determines the lifestyle. These strategies can be related to the criterion of sustainability e.g. through the material consumption required to their implementation. Here, it is clear that the fundamental human need for subsistence requires material-rich strategies whereas other needs, such as freedom or identity, could be realised with strategies that require much less material than a SUV, a luxurious villa, or the newest I-thing. In this sense the choice of strategies and lifestyles with heavy ecological rucksacks has led to unsustainable development. But as strategies are negotiable (contrary to needs), other more sustainable choices are possible.

Table 7.1, based on the seminal work of Manfred Max-Neef (1991), presents the list of needs in the first column, and different strategies to meet these needs in the following four columns. Max-Neef differentiates the strategies along their axiological status: dependent on whether they relate to being (qualities), having (things), doing (actions), or to interacting (settings).

Let us clarify by an example how this could be meant: for both authors, behaving sustainably is often motivated by need for protection, not in the sense that we need protection but rather in the sense that it is our need to contribute to protecting other people. We can meet this need for protection by being, i.e. through our qualities, by having, i.e. through our things, by doing, i.e. through our actions, or through interacting, i.e. through the settings. More concretely, we could aim at being caring persons, we could aim at buying environmentally friendly things, we could engage with others in an environmental NGO, or we could contribute to creating decision procedures in which future generations have a say as well. This broad distinction between these four different fields of strategies to meet our need for contribution opens up new ideas on how to contribute to protect other people.

The differentiation between abstract needs that are common to all humans – unborn or born – and strategies that depend on the societal, cultural, gender, etc. context can help in two ways: on the one hand, one can see that there are many strategies to meet a need, some more and some less sustainable. We will return to this first way later on. On the other hand, adepts of sustainable development cannot really care about future generation's strategies, as the context in which future people develop their strategies is largely unknown. What we can care about, though, is that future generations have enough possibilities to meet their needs. Substantively, we do not know which strategies will be available to future generations to meet their needs: we do not know how the culture will evolve; how the social, economic, and ecological systems will evolve; and to which worldviews future generations will adhere. Normatively, we should leave people the autonomy about the way in which they want to meet their needs; independently of whether these people are already born or not. Here, the concept of capabilities, developed by Amartya Sen, is particularly helpful (Rauschmayer and Lessmann 2013; Sen 2013).

Capabilities, in Sen's approach, designate the freedoms people have to lead a life they have reason to value. There are substantive and normative reasons why it is the capabilities of future generations that count and not specific resources that enable them to meet their needs, such as a certain amount of carbon fuels, or income (Lessmann and Rauschmayer 2013). Capabilities are more than resources: to constitute real freedoms to lead a valuable life; resources have to be converted through personal, social, or environmental factors. The bike does only offer freedom to me when I am able to ride, when I am allowed to ride, and when the environment is favourable as well. A bike does neither offer freedom to a blind person, nor to a woman in Saudi Arabia, nor to someone in winter in Northern Russia. By using the capability approach, one focuses on what people are able to do or to be, on their quality of life, and removing obstacles in their life. Or, in other words, it is about conditions for human flourishing.

Figure 7.1 designs a circle of human flourishing: we assume that capabilities, strategies, needs, and well-being are all in relationship with regard to the aim of human flourishing. Human flourishing, or happiness, as called by Sogyal Rinpoche in the quote at the beginning of this chapter, is then again a precondition for discovering and establishing new capabilities. We have already dealt with three elements of the inner circle, capabilities, strategies, and needs: from the set of capabilities, i.e. the substantive freedoms to lead a good life, we select strategies, i.e. concrete courses of action, to meet our needs. Capabilities, and therefore strategies, depend on the availability of resources and they depend on the cultural context with its values, sustainable development being one of them. Even though freedom is one of the needs which we want to realise through our strategies, it has a special role in our concept: in our liberal society, expressed for example through

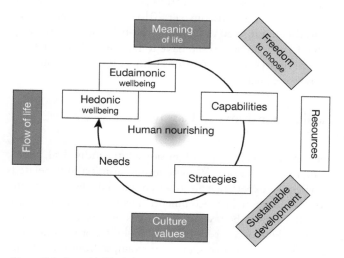

Figure 7.1 Sustainable human flourishing (source: Rauschmayer, Omann et al. 2011)

the creation of the capability approach, freedom plays a most prominent role. Now let's turn to the last element of the inner circle: well-being.

Well-being results from needs being met. Along with some philosophers and psychologists (e.g. O'Neill 2011; Spillemaeckers, van Ootegem et al. 2011), we think that it makes sense to distinguish between hedonic and eudaimonic well-being. Hedonic well-being reflects the pleasure experienced and linked to emotional well-being. Eudaimonic well-being, on the other hand, reflects the striving to realise one's personal and social potential – it is linked to the meaning of life. Both aspects of well-being are subjective experiences of one's fulfilment of needs. If we forget the eudaimonic part of well-being (and business marketing pushes us in this way), then we might end up in what is called the hedonic treadmill (Binswanger 2006): immediately after having consumed, we feel well, but – as this fades rapidly – we need more or different strategies (and usually also resources) to maintain this level of well-being. With other words, omitting eudaimonic well-being leaves the circle illustrated in Figure 7.1 open and targets for a rapidly fading place of happiness. Eudaimonic well-being, on the other hand, allows us to achieve new capabilities through intrinsic empowerment (Pick and Sirkin 2010; Schäpke and Rauschmayer 2014). Eudaimonic well-being does not fade that rapidly, gives a direction of happiness, and, we think, opens up new ways for dematerialisation. New examples for strategies aiming at eudaimonic well-being may be found in complementary currencies (Mock, Omann et al. 2013), urban gardening (Müller 2011), solidarity economy (Voß 2010), or other movements where people try to achieve well-being not through increased levels of resource consumption, but by producing in different ways (Schor 2010).

We assume that it is a challenge to flourish in a sustainable way. The value of sustainability, i.e. the importance given to the capabilities of future people, restricts and orientates the selection of strategies. Only those strategies remain valuable that allow future generations and the world's poor to find strategies for realising their needs (Lessmann and Rauschmayer 2013). As indicated above, aiming for eudaimonic well-being instead of hedonic well-being might be a way to more sustainability, but in general one would have to look at various practices in one's life. This change in lifestyle creates tensions with which anyone moving towards sustainability has to deal with.

Tensions in sustainability transitions and a way to their resolution

We differentiate between three different types of tensions: intra-individual, intra-societal, and inter-generational tensions. We encounter sustainability-related *intra-individual tensions* when we experience an inner conflict between a strategy (or a set of strategies) that is prescribed or recommended by sustainable development and our usual (or alternative) behaviour. Examples of this are the inner conflicts on whether to use a bike or a car for personal mobility, or the question of whether to fly to a conference, vacations, etc. An example from one of the authors who was asked to lecture in a PhD course in Oslo: In the case of flying rather than using video-conferencing devices, he would have realised his needs for participation, understanding, and affection by meeting the conference participants in person. Going to the conference by train instead of flying would have stopped him from being a reliable partner for other activities that he'd promised to be a part of due to the days necessary for the travel – seeing himself as a reliable person, this would have done harm to his need for identity. Flying to Oslo, on the other hand, would not have been in line with his value of sustainable development and would, therefore, not meet his needs for protection, affection, and identity. So, he experienced an intra-individual tension.

Intra-societal tensions occur when needs of an individual or societal group that wants to pursue sustainable strategies in our society are affected by the strategies of other individuals or groups. An example could be the introduction of a 'veggie day' in a specific organisation. The strategy of the group that proposes days with only vegetarian meals in a canteen affects the needs for identity and leisure of those who want to pursue eating meat. Another example is given by parents who would like to use their bikes to bring their kids to school, but do not dare to do so because of the danger brought about, e.g. by those parents who use cars for the same purpose.

Inter-generational tensions, finally, come about through certain societal strategies that, by caring for next generations, inhibit the realisation of current needs or, rather, vice versa. Examples of this include the societal practice of flying to holidays, conferences, business meetings, etc., or the practice of using resource intensive goods such as IT facilities – it is rather difficult in our societies to meet needs without the use of computers, mobile phones, or other IT devices. Especially this last type of tension demonstrates that the distinction between these three types is somewhat artificial. Inter-generational tensions are uppermost intra-individual tensions as the next generations are not present yet. It is only through the intra-individual or intra-societal representation that the next generations get a voice and become heard.

We will now present to you a four-step process that first aims to acknowledge these tensions, second helps the participant to reflect upon the internal reasons for the tensions, third supports the communication of the reflection results to others, and fourth, introduces a process of creativity to find ways of dealing with or even overcoming the tension(s). This process aims for thriving through awareness for non-conflicting strategies and is therefore called 'THANCS'. While we include a small example of one of the authors in the presentation of the process, an exemplary group process is described afterwards.

1) When selecting or implementing a strategy, attachments to unsustainable practices can be perceived as feelings of uneasiness related to the value of sustainability. It is the aim of the first step to acknowledge these tensions. Cognitively, their perception may be facilitated by trying to communicate them to others such as close persons or to persons who chose the same or a similar strategy. Another possibility to become aware of these tensions is to recognise the resistance from others against one's own strategy. The active acknowledgement of everyday life tensions, e.g. between the comfort procured by using a car to drive

to the office and the wish to protect the environment, includes the analysis of strategies that are selected to realise one's needs. This acknowledgement may lead to a momentary decrease in well-being.

This first step of recognising and acknowledging the tensions therefore addresses feelings and reflections. The ability to perceive tensions can be strengthened, e.g. by interventions of parents with their kids or of therapists or personality trainers. Administration can support such acknowledgement by informing citizens via media or educational programmes about such tensions between selected strategies and sustainability oriented strategies. On an individual level, meditations can increase the capability to perceive and acknowledge these tensions.

> Flying to conferences often gave me a feeling of uneasiness, but for a long time I preferred not to pay attention to it or to rationalise my behaviour, e.g. by telling myself: "everyone does it – if you don't fly, this does not change anything".

2) In the next step, participants reflect on the reasons for the tension: Why has the tension been triggered? Often, the cause is a conflict with several dimensions: habits, belief systems and convictions, values, and need prioritisations. As for the first step, no regulation or law can induce this inner reflection. But again, close persons, media, educational programmes, and professional training such as coaching can support this step. This second step requires a deeper reflection than the first one which focused on the strategies and the perception of tensions caused by their selection or implementation. Whenever the tensions appear within social decision processes, then reflections should not only comprehend the decision makers' dimensions, but also the needs, values, and convictions of those persons who are represented by this decision maker. An interpersonal exchange on these dimensions can increase the acceptance of decisions and lead to mutual understanding.

> Here, I ask myself: "Why do I want to fly to conferences? And why do I feel bad about it?" Answers to the first question relate to the social practice of flying to international conferences, comfort, some joy in flying, etc. Answers to the second question relate to the discomfort in the stop-and-go way of travelling by air, and to my conviction that flying emits more greenhouse gases than other traffic modes which is unjust to future generations.

3) In this third step, the participant, being aware of the tension and of its causes, is starting to communicate with other persons about common tensions and strategies. Ideally, those are people concerned by the strategy and its implementation. In the case of an intra-individual conflict, communication can consist of writing down the results of the reflection in steps 1 and 2, or by talking about these results with a close person. It is important to look for a dialogue with concrete persons and to find a common language. Methods that can support such dialogue are for example public discourse (Dryzek 1997), social learning

(Siebenhüner 2005; Tabara and Pahl-Wostl 2007; Cundill and Rodela 2012), or the intersubjective dialogue (Buber 1995).

> Being an inter-generational/intra-individual conflict, my communication about the flying issue only helps me to clarify my reasoning and to take into account values, needs, or convictions that I have left out in the first and second step. I become aware, for example, that not flying anymore might impede my family relations as my brother lives in Latin America.

4) The first three steps serve to acknowledge, reflect, and communicate the tensions in order to create awareness that there is far more than one strategy to meet a certain need. The fourth step helps to develop alternative strategies that had not been considered before. Through the first three steps, we can more easily leave the narrow-mindedness of habitual behaviour. Implementing and experiencing new strategies requires a process of creativity (herewith, by the way, meeting the need for creativity) that can be organised on a personal as well as on a societal level. Agents in polity and administration can support such processes by putting in place appropriate frame conditions, e.g. by implementing novel participatory processes such as Dynamic Facilitation (Rough 2002).[4] Facilitators who host these processes can actively stimulate the participants and use creativity techniques so that participants create such new strategies. Experiencing those new strategies (if possible with all senses) allows participants to holistically judge their efficacy in meeting needs and surpassing tensions. Using scenario-based techniques, such as back-casting, should further increase the chances that the new strategies get implemented in 'real life', also involving further actors than the participants of the THANCS-process.

The fourth step hence aims that individuals effectively change their behaviour by implementing new strategies, ideally supported through political change and backed up by knowledge on how this newly elaborated strategy can contribute to sustainability transitions. Individuals who would like to reduce tensions can do so by increasing their capability set by thinking over and changing their lifestyle, e.g. through a change in values or habitual behaviour. Supporting such possibility for change increases individual autonomy (cf. Schäpke and Rauschmayer 2014) and has the potential to increase the coherence between one's own identity and action. This is one of the reasons why new strategies may lead to an increase in well-being. New strategies might also lead to more well-being when they create synergies between the realisation of several needs instead of realising one and frustrating the other. Through a new strategy one can also implement values related to sustainable development, such as intra- or inter-generational justice or environmental justice, that had not been realised in the ancient situation; new strategies created through a THANCS process therefore have the potential not only to increase well-being, but also sustainable development.[5]

> First, I decided to adopt a 24h-rule, combined with a soft self-regulation on intercontinental flights: only destinations that can't be reached within a 24h

train ride are open for flying, and I limited intercontinental flights as much as possible. This eased my tensions, but not enough. Second, I decided not to fly anymore and – at the same time – being attentive to what this meant to my needs fulfilment. I am not completely at ease with this decision, but more than before.

The following methods, amongst others, can be used for framing the THANCS-process: needs-oriented multicriteria methods (Rauschmayer 2005; Cruz, Stahel et al. 2009; Guillen-Royo 2010; Jolibert, Paavola et al. 2014), participatory scenario workshops in transition arena settings (Wittmayer, Steenbergen et al. 2011), dynamic facilitation and wisdom councils (Rough 2002), systemic constellations (Sparrer 2007), dialogues, sociocratic, or holacratic facilitation (Charest 2009)) or further forms of process work (Mindell 1995).[6] The important feature is that the methods integrate the inner individual perspective, i.e. how individuals feel and think, what they value, and how they experience the fulfilment of their needs.

An exemplary group process: day-to-day car use

One of the authors had the possibility to apply THANCS within the inter-disciplinary course "Science and Citizens meet Challenges of Sustainability" at the University of Luxemburg in May 2011 and 2012. Approximately 20 students from different disciplines and backgrounds took part in this lecture – some of them with work experience, e.g. in NGOs, as teachers or environmental psychologists. Prior to the lecture, the students had been asked to consider an own conflict, write down the tensions, and put them down for discussion at a specific web-based platform (step 1). Those conflicts were then presented during the lecture. Finally, the students decided to work with the case 'day-to-day car use'.

In Luxemburg it is quite cumbersome to use public transport once living outside the city centre. Using public transport is particularly laborious when children are part of one's living. That is why most participants own a car which they use on a daily basis. This made all but one participant unhappy and their day-to-day car use created tensions. Using a car triggers intra-individual and inter-generational tensions. Using a car allows meeting specific needs (e.g. freedom, subsistence when used for commuting) but also prevents the protection of future generations through resource depletion and CO_2 emissions. Using a car therefore creates an inter-generational tension which is an intra-individual tension when inter-generational justice is a personal value. At the same time, car use creates intra-societal tensions, as cars endanger the security of others (pedestrians, cyclists), emit pollutants, and use space (roads, parking lots), which is then not available to the public anymore.

Having reflected on their own needs fulfilment (step 2), most participants came up with at most five needs that were either met or harmed. Those needs were not the same among the group, but finally all needs from Max-Neef's list (see Table 7.1) were named. Hearing others (step 3) made some participants complete their lists of needs. It was visible that one need can be met through the same strategy that inhibits its fulfilment, e.g.:

- Protection: Using a car offers protection in particular for children and older people, but it endangers other traffic participants and also future generations.
- Subsistence: Owning a car sometimes enables one to take up employment. At the same time, the costs for petrol, the car itself, and its repairs are so high that individual subsistence may be endangered.

For quite a few participants, the strategy 'car use' endangered as well as met the same need, and they decided which part of the need (in our case, protection of oneself and one's family or protection of other people) was more important and looked for an appropriate strategy for expressing this part of the need without endangering the other one.

The participants then selected the needs with the highest priority to develop alternative strategies to meet them (step 4). Some new and quite interesting ideas were born: 'half cars' (two families share a car during a week: each one for 3.5 days), usual car-sharing, or an initiative for creating school buses.

The feedback from the group on the process was very positive: reflecting, writing down, and communicating their own needs was new for most participants and created awareness as well as constructive group dynamics. Finding such a common basis can help any group to deal with a conflicting issue and is therefore a good starting point for discussions. Participants particularly highlighted that THANCS does not require scientific knowledge or a specialist's input, but that it can be used by anyone.

Conclusion and outlook

Weaver and Jordan (2008) argue that political decision makers require support from their constituency when they are going to take the risk of initiating a fundamental change. Such support can be based on new forms of integrating different groups into public policy making for sustainability (Robinson, Carmichael et al. 2006). This support is wider when processes are employed that aim at sustainability transitions that do not lower well-being.

Needs-based processes are a suitable means to support sustainability transitions as they are based on a universalist conception of humans (all people have the same needs, and meeting needs enhance their well-being); necessarily involve processes of individual reflection (why select strategy A to meet my needs rather than strategy B?); use a language that can be used by anyone to talk about strategies, needs, convictions etc.; and can also acknowledge the importance of those values that are building the norm of sustainable development.

Convenient starting points to initiate such transitions towards well-being and sustainable development could be: (1) a sufficiently large set of options, so that people feel free in their choice, (2) stimulation of creativity, so that alternative strategies can be found when the original strategies are not sustainable, (3) the creation of suitable frame conditions that motivate citizens, facilitators, and decision makers to go deeper into conflicts, i.e. to acknowledge and talk about needs, values, convictions, and feelings that are at the base of conflicting behaviour.

In this chapter, we argued why a transition towards sustainability necessarily creates different kinds of tensions. These tensions may impede the change or they can, when facilitated accordingly, have the potential to support sustainability transitions without decreasing well-being. This potential can only be realised when the intra-individual dimension of conflicts is acknowledged, and when there is space to start a dialogue about such conflicts and their roots.

A high quality of life is, as we all know, not necessarily realised with the help of sustainable strategies. THANCS has been introduced as a four-step process to deal with tensions that appear when realising strategies, and particularly when changing behaviour, mind-sets, culture, or the systems in which people act. Combining THANCS and political actions would mean to start any intervention with reflecting on possible tensions, i.e. to acknowledge and deal with feelings, convictions, and needs that are involved when people try to increase their quality of life.

We do not think that THANCS and the methods proposed can be tested immediately in a wide range of interventions. First, methods have to be tested and adapted according to the context of the interventions (e.g. governmental level, economic, or cultural context). Neither do we assume that the majority of current citizens currently are open and prepared for such a process. As always, transition starts with processes and actors in niches (Loorbach 2007).

We believe, though, that there already are quite a few of such niche actors who have reflected their life and work in such a holistic way or who are open to start such processes – if they are conducted in a safe environment. Much has to be better understood and, first and foremost, be done to succeed a sustainability transition. The biggest challenge lies in the practical implementation of changing the atmosphere of mistrust and socio-economic competition, generated by uncertainty and fear in society and polity.

Therefore, we are aware that our endeavour can only be a small part of such transition; at the same time, we continue our endeavour as we consider it a better strategy for meeting our needs than to resign, become cynical, or to focus our engagement on an increase in hedonic well-being for the rich parts of the world.

Notes

1   The German Advisory Council on Global Change WBGU has a chapter on values in its 2011 report on sustainability transformations, but does neither link it to societal developments nor to inner-individual conflicts (WBGU – German Advisory Council on Global Change 2011).

2   On the role of needs in philosophy, see also Braybrooke 2005; Reader 2005; Wiggins 2005; O'Neill 2011.

3   Of course, they still remain an epistemic category that has been introduced by humanist psychologists to better understand human behaviour.

4   Dynamic Facilitation is an open, chaired group discussion with a variable number of participants, ideally between eight and 20. The method relies on the participants' creativity in finding a solution, and deliberately avoids conventional, linear facilitation structures. Dynamic Facilitation is particularly suitable for issues such that the definition of the problem, the solutions tabled, and the objections to these solutions arouse emotions in the participants. The method is used extensively in organisational and management consulting, but can be transferred to other areas. It was originally developed by Jim Rough in the USA. (See www.partizipation.at/dynamic_facilitation_en.html, accessed 15 May 2013.)

5   Individuals could nevertheless decide for a different way by accepting the tensions without a further change in values or tension-triggering behaviour: perhaps self-awareness or meditation can then lead to a vanishing of the tensions. How these techniques then lead to behavioural change is beyond the scope of this chapter.

6   In June 2011 the authors organised a workshop, funded by the European Science Foundation, where more than 20 researchers applied the named and additional methods to find out whether and how those are suitable for facilitating sustainability transitions (see Omann, Bohunovsky et al. 2011).

Bibliography

Binswanger, M. (2006) 'Why does income growth fail to make us happier? Searching for the treadmills behind the paradox of happiness' in *The Journal of Socio-Economics* 35(2). pp. 366–381.

Braybrooke, D. (2005) 'Where does the moral force of the concept of needs reside and when?' in Reader, S. (ed.) (2005) *The Philosophy of Needs*. Cambridge: Cambridge University Press. pp. 209–228.

Buber, M. (1995) *Ich und Du*. Stuttgart: Reclam.

Charest, G. (2009) *Vivere in sociocrazia! Un modo di governare che riconcilia potere & cooperazione*. Italy: Esserci.

Cruz, I., Stahel, A., Max-Neef, M. (2009) 'Towards a systemic development approach: Building on the Human-Scale Development paradigm' in *Ecological Economics* 68. pp. 2021–2030.

Cundill, G. and Rodela, R. (2012) 'A review of assertions about the processes and outcomes of social learning in natural resource management' in *Journal of Environmental Management* 113. pp. 7–14.

Dryzek, J. S. (1997) *The Politics of the Earth*. Oxford: Oxford University Press.

European Commission (2007) *Progress Report on the Sustainable Development Strategy 2007*. Brussels. COM(2007) 642 final.

Eurostat (2009) *Sustainable development in the European Union – 2009 monitoring report of the EU sustainable development strategy*. Luxembourg: Statistical books.

Grin, J., Rotmans, J., Schot, J. (2010) *Transitions to Sustainable Development*. London: Routledge.

Grisez, G., Boyle, J., Finnis, J.M. (1987) 'Practical principles, moral truth and ultimate ends' in *American Journal of Jurisprudence* 32. pp. 99–151.

Guillen-Royo, M. (2010) 'Realising the "wellbeing dividend": An exploratory study using the Human Scale Development approach' in *Ecological Economics* 70(2). pp. 384–393.

Jolibert, C., Paavlola, J., Rauschmayer, F. (2014) 'Addressing needs in the search for sustainable development: A proposal for needs-based scenario building' in *Environmental Values* 23(1). pp. 29–50.

Lane, R. E. (1996) 'Quality of life and quality of persons: A new role for government' in Offer, I. A. (ed.) *In Pursuit of the Quality of Life*. New York: Oxford University Press. pp. 256–293.

Lessmann, O. and Rauschmayer, F. (2013) 'Re-conceptualising sustainable development on the basis of the capability approach: A model and its difficulties' in *Journal of Human Development and Capabilities* 14(1). pp. 95–114.

Loorbach, D. (2007) *Transition Management – New Mode of Governance for Sustainable Consumption*. Utrecht: International Books.

Max-Neef, M. (1991) *Human Scale Development: Conception, Application and Further Reflections*. London, New York: The Apex Press.

Mindell, A. (1995) *Sitting in the Fire: Large Group Transformation using Conflict and Diversity*. Portland, OR: Lao Tse Press.

Mock, M., Rauschmayer, F., Omann, I., Fuchs, D. (2013) *Do community currencies enhance sustainable quality of life?* UFZ Discussion Papers. Leipzig, UFZ – Helmholtz Centre for Environmental Research. 16/2013 GeNECA 9, www.ufz.de/index.php?de=14487 (accessed 20 October 2014).

Müller, C. (ed.) (2011) *Urban Gardening – Über die Rückkehr der Gärten in die Stadt*. München: Oekom.

O'Neill, J. (2011) 'The overshadowing of needs' in Rauschmayer, F., Omann, I. and Frühmann, J. (eds) *Sustainable Development: Capabilities, Needs, and Well-Being*. London: Routledge. pp. 25–42.

Omann, I., Bohunovsky, L., Rauschmayer, F. (2011) *Below the Waterline. How to Integrate Needs, Values, Emotions into Societal Processes Towards Sustainable Development*. ESF Exploratory Workshop Report, ESF – European Science Foundation. www.ufz.de/index.php?en=1660 (accessed 20 October 2014).

Pick, S. and Sirkin, J. (2010) *Breaking the Poverty Cycle: The Human Basis for Sustainable Development*. Oxford: Oxford University Press.

Rauschmayer, F. (2005) 'Linking emotions to needs. A comment to Fred Wenstøp's article "Mindsets, rationality and emotion in multi-criteria decision analysis"' in *Journal of Multi-Criteria Decision Analysis* 13. pp. 187–190.

Rauschmayer, F. and Lessmann, O. (2013) 'Editorial: The capability approach and sustainability' in *Journal of Human Development and Capabilities* 14(1). pp. 1–5.

Rauschmayer, F., Omann, I., Frühmann, J. (2011) 'Needs, capabilities, and quality of life. Re-focusing sustainable development' in Rauschmayer, F. Omann, I. and Frühmann, J. (eds) *Sustainable Development: Capabilities, Needs, and Well-Being*. London: Routledge. pp. 1–24.

Reader, S. (2005) 'Introduction to "The Philosophy of Needs"' in Reader, S. (ed.) *The Philosophy of Needs*. Cambridge: Cambridge University Press. pp. 1–24.

Robinson, J., Carmichael, J., VanWynsberghe, R., Journeay, M., Rogers, L. (2006) 'Sustainability as a problem of design: Interactive science in the Georgia Basin' in *The Integrated Assessment Journal Bridging Sciences and Policy* 6(4). pp. 165–192.

Rosenberg, M. (2001) *Nonviolent Communication: A Language of Life*. Encinitas, CA: Puddle Dancer Press.

Rough, J. (2002) *Society's Breakthrough!: Releasing Essential Wisdom and Virtue in all the People*. Bloomington, IN: AuthorHouse.

Schäpke, N. and Rauschmayer, F. (2014) 'Going beyond efficiency: including altruistic motives in behavioral models for sustainability transitions to address sufficiency' in *Sustainability: Science Practice and Policy* 10(1). pp. 29–44.

Schor, J. (2010) *Plenitude: The New Economics of True Wealth*. New York: Penguin Press.

Sen, A. K. (2013) 'The ends and means of sustainability' in *Journal of Human Development and Capabilities* 14(1). pp. 6–20.

Siebenhüner, B. (2005) 'Can assessments learn, and if so how? A study of the IPCC' in Farrell, A. and Jäger, J. (eds) *Assessments of Regional and Global Risks*. Washington, DC: Resources for the Future. pp. 166–186.

Sparrer, I. (2007) *Miracle, Solution and System – Solution-focused Systemic Structural Constellations for Therapy and Organisational Change*. Cheltenham: SolutionsBooks.

Spillemaeckers, S., van Ootegem, L., Westerhof, G.J. (2011) 'From individual well-being to sustainable development: A path where psychologists and economists meet' in Rauschmayer, F., Omann, I. and Frühmann, J. (eds) *Sustainable Development: Capabilities, Needs, and Well-Being*. London: Routledge. pp. 62–82.

Tabara, P. D. and Pahl-Wostl, C. (2007) 'Sustainability learning in natural resource use and management' in *Ecology and Society* 12(2). 3. [online] www.ecologyandsociety.org/vol12/iss2/art3/ (accessed 2 August 2014).

Voß, E. (2010) *Wegweiser Solidarische Ökonomie. Anders Wirtschaften ist möglich*. Dortmund: NETZ für Selbstverwaltung und Selbstorganisation e. V.

WBGU – German Advisory Council on Global Change (2011) *World in Transition – A Social Contract for Sustainability*. Berlin: WBGU.

WCED (1987) *Our Common Future, Report by the United Nations World Commission on Environment and Development*. www.un-documents.net/wced-ocf.htm (accessed, 3 April 2010).

Weaver, P. M. and Jordan, A. (2008) 'What roles are there for sustainability assessment in the policy process?' in *International Journal of Innovation and Sustainable Development* 3(1). pp. 9–32.

Wiggins, D. (2005) 'An idea we cannot do without: What difference will it make (eg. to moral, political and environmental philosophy) to recognize and put to use a substantial conception of need?' in Reader, S. (ed.) *The Philosophy of Needs*. Cambridge: Cambridge University Press. pp. 25–50.

Wittmayer, J., Van Steenbergen, F., Quist, J., Loorbach, D., Hoogland, C. (2011) *The Community Arena: A Co-creation Tool for Sustainable Behaviour by Local Communities*. Berlin: InContext. http://incontext-fp7.eu/sites/default/files/Methodological%20guidelines_final.pdf (accessed 10 September 2014).

8 Human needs and the environment reconciled

Participatory action-research for sustainable development in Peru

Mònica Guillen-Royo

Introduction

This chapter presents the processes and outcomes of a participatory action-research project for sustainable development in Acostambo, a rural municipality in the Peruvian Andes. Sustainable development was defined by the World Commission on Environment and Development (WCED 1987) as the type of development that allows the present generation to meet their needs without impairing future generations' capacity to meet theirs. At the national level, meeting needs has traditionally been associated with encouraging GDP growth, as increases in a country's wealth should improve the material standards of its populations and thus the satisfaction of needs. However, research suggests that in rich, middle-income and low-income countries, increases in income are not linked to higher levels of life satisfaction or happiness (Easterlin 2013). Other personal and societal aspects such as family relationships, physical and psychological health, employment, levels of corruption and institutional transparency seem to matter more for wellbeing than material pursuits alone (Easterlin 2003; Layard 2005; Helliwell et al. 2012). Thus, besides proving unsustainable, GDP growth or increased personal income are not the most important determinant of wellbeing, suggesting that it is possible to increase human needs satisfaction by reallocating resources towards the factors that make life good (Jackson 2008).

In order to identify and act upon the factors that improve human need satisfaction in an ecologically sustainable way, the UN calls for 'holistic and integrated approaches to sustainable development which will guide humanity to live in harmony with nature' (United Nations 2012: 6). One such holistic approach has been available to development planners and academics for over 20 years. This is Manfred Max-Neef's (et al. 1989; 1991) Human Scale Development (HSD) approach, designed as a tool for development practitioners based on a systemic view of society and used to address a wide array of development and environmental problems around the world (Cruz et al. 2009; Jorge 2010; Nangombe and Ackermann 2013). The HSD framework provides a methodology for societies, communities or groups to engage in their own sustainable development path by mobilising endogenous potentials and encouraging self-reliance. It has inspired initiatives such as the 'transition town' movement in the UK[1], but it has not been systematically drawn on to engage people in sustainable development projects (Guillen-Royo 2010; 2012).

This chapter seeks to contribute to the debate about the operationalisation of sustainable development by presenting a participatory action-research (PAR) project based on the HSD approach. The goal is to provide empirical evidence about the usefulness of the HSD perspective to engage people in sustainable development transitions and to identify the interconnected factors around which human needs and environmental conservation are articulated. The PAR project was set in Acostambo, a rural municipality in Huancavelica, one of the poorest regions of Peru. Following the HSD methodology (Max-Neef 1991) people in Acostambo were invited to analyse the factors or *satisfiers* that impeded and promoted the satisfaction of human needs in their society. Then, they identified strategies to improve satisfaction of human needs and ecological sustainability, which were later implemented during a ten-month PAR project from April 2012 to January 2013.

The chapter starts by introducing the HSD approach as a tool for sustainable development through its focus on human needs satisfaction, self-reliance and balance interdependence of people, nature and technologies. It then goes on to address the characteristics of the PAR study in Acostambo focussing on the HSD methodology and the research design. Next, the chapter presents the processes and outcomes of the PAR study illustrated by the organic vegetable gardens strategy, the one prioritised by participants as having potentially greater effects on human needs. Finally, the outcomes of the PAR project are discussed with regards to the achievement of higher levels of human needs satisfaction and environmental conservation, and conclusions are drawn.

The HSD approach: human needs and the environment reconciled

The concept of sustainable development as defined in the Brundtland Report (WCED 1987) concerns the capacity of present and future generations to satisfy their needs. This concern is based on the environmental degradation that production and consumption systems impinge on the Earth's eco-systems and the threats for quality of life derived from anthropogenic climate change (Jackson 2008). Although sometimes argued otherwise (Qizilbash 2001), recent evidence suggests that both human needs satisfaction and environmental protection are achievable at different levels of economic development (Marks et al. 2006; Abdallah et al. 2012). Resource-intensive development paths are no longer justifiable in terms of their positive effects on the quality of life. This is illustrated by the Happy Planet Index (HPI), for example, a measure used to rank 151 countries with regards to their capacity to generate long and satisfactory lives per unit of environmental input. Results for 2011 indicate that Costa Rica, the top ranked country, achieved the same life expectancy and level of satisfaction as the US with only one-third of its ecological footprint (Abdallah et al. 2012).

Linking with the above is the 'threshold hypothesis' postulated by Max-Neef already in the late 1980s. Max-Neef and his collaborators carried out a study in

19 rich and poor countries addressing the factors that were hampering wellbeing at the personal and collective level. They found that in rich countries people felt they were part of a deteriorating system, which led the authors to hypothesise the existence of a 'threshold' beyond which the socio-economic system is no longer able to provide increased welfare and the environment beings to deteriorate (Max-Neef 1995). This hypothesis was later confirmed by Daly and Cobb (1989) when they published the results for their Index of Sustainable Economic Welfare (ISEW) for the US, which was later derived for many other rich countries (Stockhammer et al. 1997; Jackson et al. 1997; Hamilton and Saddler 1997). The failure of economic growth to increase wellbeing and preserve the environment in rich countries and the failure of Latin American countries to spread welfare to their citizens following export-led development models constituted the context in which Max-Neef envisaged the HSD approach.

HSD depends on people's active participation and thus demands the prior identification of the appropriate operational scale. Once this is identified, the three interdependent pillars that sustain HSD can be put in place. These are: actualisation of fundamental human needs, increasing levels of self-reliance and the balanced interdependence of people with nature and technologies, of global and local processes, of personal and social goals, of planning and autonomy, and of civil society and the state (Max-Neef 1991: 8; Jolibert et al. 2011).

Actualisation of fundamental human needs

HSD is based on a taxonomy of fundamental human needs derived, among others, from Maslow's theory of needs[2] (1970) but without considering needs as hierarchically related except for the requirement to be alive (subsistence). Following HSD, needs are connected in a systemic way, they are interlinked and interdependent and can be categorised in two ways: the first draws on nine valued or axiological categories: subsistence, protection, affection, understanding, participation, idleness, creation, identity and freedom. The second follows the characteristics of existence as in being, having, doing and interacting. The nine axiological needs are referred to as fundamental human needs and have a socio-universal character; they do not vary with culture and history. In opposition, satisfiers, the social practices, values, attitudes, forms of organisation and political models are used to actualise needs, change with history and vary across cultures (Max-Neef et al. 1989; Cruz et al. 2009). There is no two-way correspondence between needs and satisfiers; they are related in a systemic way and people's subjective experience of satisfiers is what makes them positive or negative contributors to human needs.

The HSD approach was designed with the view to provide a tool for development practitioners. To enable its operationalisation, Max-Neef proposed a representation of needs and satisfiers through a matrix reflecting the intersection between the four existential needs (top row) and the nine fundamental human needs (first column) (see Table 8.1). The resulting empty grids are to be filled by people with the *satisfiers* that represent how needs are pursued in their society.

Table 8.1 Matrix of fundamental human needs

	Being	*Having*	*Doing*	*Interacting*
Subsistence				
Protection				
Affection				
Understanding				
Participation				
Idleness				
Creation				
Identity				
Freedom				

Source: Max-Neef et al. 1989

Given the many social, economic and environmental pathologies that rich and poor societies suffer from, it is clear that not all satisfiers will be equally successful in their contribution to the actualisation of needs.

Max-Neef (1991: 31–36) classified satisfiers into five categories based on their success in actualising needs: *synergic satisfiers* simultaneously satisfy different kinds of needs; *singular satisfiers* satisfy one specific need; *inhibiting satisfiers* over-satisfy a given need and limit the possibility of satisfying other needs; *pseudo-satisfiers* give a false sense of satisfaction of a given need; and finally, *violators or destroyers* annihilate the satisfaction over time of a particular need and impair the satisfaction of other needs. When societies are mainly articulated around violators, inhibiting- or pseudo-satisfiers, sustainable development is threatened. For example, if in a society commuting to work is satisfied with private transportation, the satisfaction of the needs for subsistence, protection, leisure and freedom might be threatened as roads, noise and pollution invade public and private spaces. This negative effect on the current generations' potential to satisfy needs might be augmented by the detrimental effects on future generations of increased CO_2 emissions from commuting.

Increasing levels of self-reliance

HSD is based on self-reliance understood as the centrality of people as leaders of their own development processes. Self-reliance does not contemplate traditional hierarchical or unidirectional relationships between actors operating at the local, regional, national and international levels. It is ideally developed at the local or community levels, as this is the more human-scale space, but it does not imply isolation or autarchy. For a self-reliant or endogenous development to be in place, local initiatives at the grassroots level have to be supported. Thus, the role of the public administration would be to look for these emergent initiatives and provide the financial or technical support for them to flourish (Max-Neef 1991). Public or private development agents would also encourage such local initiatives by, for example, organising workshops where the matrix of human needs is used as a tool to identify endogenous potentials, thus helping local groups progressing towards a self-reliant development path (Guillen-Royo 2012).

In the HSD framework, self-reliance is related to the belief that people are able to analyse their realities and design the strategies to transform the way human needs are met. This has been questioned in the development literature as there are many examples of bad investments decided by locals in bottom-up participatory processes (da Cunha and Junho 1997; Ruggeri 2001). However, self-reliance as understood in the HSD framework does not imply that strategies or their associated processes have to be designed and executed only with local resources. People and communities are meant to collaborate with experts, politicians, planners and even local elites as long as the relationships established are not of dependence but of interdependence.

Balanced interdependence of people with nature and technologies

A self-reliant development revolving around the satisfaction of human needs at the personal and socio-ecological levels involves a different articulation of the relationship between people, nature and technologies than the one we have today. As Max-Neef (1991: 59) puts it, 'since HSD is concerned mainly with the fulfilment of fundamental human needs of present as well as future generations, it advocates a concept of development that is essentially ecological'. Thus, it escapes from an anthropocentric approach to development and sees it as an eco-humanist process in which technologies are designed and used to maintain or improve the quality of the natural environment, thus serving human needs in the short and long run.

In societies where satisfiers do not result in a balanced interdependence between people, nature and technologies, human needs are poorly satisfied. For example, the intensive use of chemical fertilisers in many Andean regions has resulted in an increase in the acidification of the land and the pollution of many water sources (Corcoran et al. 2010). In the short run, chemical fertilisers might have increased the production of poorly paid traditional staples but it has also made farmers more dependent on chemical inputs, has degraded the natural environment and increased health hazards in the local community. Following the HSD, this is an example of a pseudo-satisfier or even violator, as it might have supported farmers meeting their need for subsistence in the short run but in the long run it might be detrimental for subsistence and might even reduce the possibilities of satisfying the need for protection, participation, idleness and identity. The expansion of chemical fertilisers as satisfiers in the Andes and around the world could be said to have arisen from a lack of consideration for a balanced relationship between the different components of the socio-ecological system.

PAR in Acostambo: methodology and research strategy

Acostambo is a municipality in the district of the same name in Huancavelica; one of the poorest regions in Peru with 67 per cent of the population below the national poverty line. The district spreads through a mountainous area at an average altitude of 3,500 m above sea level. Its total population in 2007 was 4,537, dispersed among 18 annexes, two populated centres, seven hamlets and six neighbourhoods. Most households in the district are smallholders depending on farming of traditional crops such as barley, potatoes, wheat, peas, beans and maize (Copestake 2008). Acostambo is well connected by road to Huancayo and Huancavelica, important administrative centres in the highlands, and is the recipient of many state and NGO-led development projects addressing pro-ductive, health-related and governance issues, among others. The state is also present through an array of social programmes targeting poverty in old age, child malnutrition, extreme poverty and illiteracy. Despite efforts to lift the population out of poverty through a range of interventions, outmigration to Lima, Huancayo and the central jungle is common, and the district experiences a constant population decline.

Three locations in the district, including the municipality of Acostambo, were investigated by the Wellbeing in Developing (WeD) countries ESRC research

Table 8.2 Research strategy in Acostambo

	Activity	*Dates*	*Description*
Phase 1			
HSD workshops	3 HSD workshops with a total of 22 participants from the municipality	November 2011	Three 3-hour workshops to identify problems and opportunities to satisfy human needs
Survey	Survey to 100 people from the district	November 2011	Questionnaire on values, subjective wellbeing and environmental attitudes (more information in Guillen-Royo and Kasser 2014)
Phase 2			
Participatory action-research (PAR) project	Implementation of the two top strategies	April 2012– January 2013	16 workshops linked to the organic vegetable gardens and adults' school strategies
Interviews	Semi-structured interviews to residents in Acostambo	April 2012– January 2013	21 interviews on people's experiences with development projects
Post-PAR survey	Survey to 21 PAR participants and 21 non-participants	January 2013	Questionnaire on values, subjective wellbeing and organic vegetable gardens to PAR participants and a matched sample of non-participants

group at the University of Bath from 2003 to 2007 with the participation of the author and one of the fieldwork assistants. Thus, the research team in this project had a previous knowledge of the site and of the factors that determined residents' wellbeing (Copestake 2008). Informed by the findings from the WeD research, we carried out a study in two phases. The first phase was undertaken in November 2011 by the author and two field assistants from the *Universidad Nacional del Centro de Peru*. It consisted of a survey on personal values and HSD workshops. The goal was to identify the *satisfiers* that could promote the actualisation of human needs in Acostambo and had synergic effects on the environment. Three workshops were held in the municipal centre involving a total of 22 people who had been invited after expressing their willingness to participate when filling in the survey questionnaire (Guillen-Royo and Kasser 2014). Workshops were facilitated by the research team and lasted from 2.5 to 3 hours with a 15-minute break halfway through. After getting participants' consent, workshops were audio-recorded and notes taken.

The second phase of the project started in April 2012 after an initial analysis of the data from the HSD exercise (Guillen-Royo 2012). The aim of this phase was twofold: to investigate whether the strategies devised by participants in Acostambo using the HSD framework a) were feasible and b) could place participants on a sustainable development path. In order to do this, the study used a PAR design defined as an 'inquiry that is done by or with insiders to an organisation or community, but never to or on them' (Herr and Anderson 2005: 3). This implied that researchers left their traditional position as complete outsiders to start collaborating with participants at the different stages of the project (design, execution, evaluation).

The PAR project was structured around periodical participatory workshops and in-depth interviews. In total, 16 participatory workshops of around 2.5 hours were held from April 2012 to January 2013, attended by an average of 18 people, and a maximum of 33. During these meetings two of the four strategies identified by participants were organised and implemented, starting with the organic vegetable gardens (OVG) and followed by the parents' school; the two top ranked strategies in terms of their positive effects on human needs. Parallel to the workshops and related activities, 21 in-depth interviews were conducted, recorded and transcribed with PAR participants and non-participants alike. Interviews revolved about the functioning, contribution and limitations of previous NGO's or state-led projects known to the interviewee.

In January 2013, PAR participants were invited to fill in a questionnaire on personal values, subjective wellbeing and the contributions of the OVG strategy. Questions on the latter were derived after analysing the data from a workshop held in November 2012 where participants had discussed how the OVG had contributed to social cohesion and the economic and education levels of participants, the three main synergic satisfiers identified in Phase 1. A total of 21 participants answered the questionnaire that was subsequently applied to another 21 residents in Acostambo. The non-participant sample was matched by age and gender with the participant sample in order to get an adequate comparison group.

HSD workshops: identifying synergic strategies for sustainable development

The two first workshops carried out in November 2011 used the HSD matrix as a basis to discuss human needs actualisation in Acostambo (a detailed description of the methodology can be found in Max-Neef 1991: 30–42). Participants in the first workshop filled the empty cells of the HSD matrix with the *negative satisfiers* that made it difficult for them to meet needs (negative matrix). In the second workshop, participants filled another empty matrix with the *synergic satisfiers* considered to enable optimal actualisation of needs (utopian matrix). In order to avoid the utopian matrix being filled with the opposite satisfiers of the negative matrix, none of the participants in the first workshop was invited to attend the second one. However, everybody was invited to the third workshop discussing *synergic strategies*.

The third workshop did not use the HSD matrix. In order to frame the discussion, participants were given a copy of the completed negative and utopian matrices discussed in the first two workshops. They were also presented with three categories of *synergic satisfiers* (unity or social cohesion, quality education and higher economic level) derived from the researcher's analysis of the utopian matrix. The discussion was articulated around the ways of being, having, doing and interacting that would facilitate the emergence of the envisaged *synergic satisfiers*. People were also asked to reflect on the extent to which the ways of being, having, doing and interacting (*synergic strategies*) could be developed endogenously or required the support of external institutions.

Figure 8.1 presents a simplified summary of the themes under which satisfiers discussed in the three workshops can be grouped (a more detailed analysis of the full matrices can be found in Guillen-Royo 2012).

Fragmentation, lack of communication and material poverty summarise a set of *negative satisfiers* that are detrimental for human needs in Acostambo.

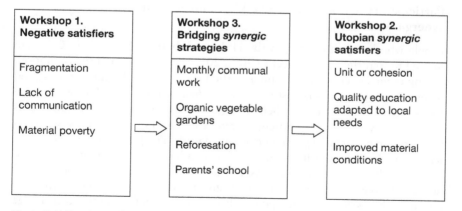

Workshop 1. Negative satisfiers	Workshop 3. Bridging *synergic* strategies	Workshop 2. Utopian *synergic* satisfiers
Fragmentation Lack of communication Material poverty	Monthly communal work Organic vegetable gardens Reforesation Parents' school	Unit or cohesion Quality education adapted to local needs Improved material conditions

Figure 8.1 Summary of negative, utopian and synergic strategies in Acostambo (source: adapted from Guillen-Royo 2012)

Fragmentation was characteristic of families, communities and district-level institutions. It manifested as despise for others' opinions, particularly women and young people, and lack of cooperation between the different local institutions. The latter was linked to a general lack of communication which was aggravated by the marginalisation of Quechua language and culture in schools, health care centres and other public places. Material poverty captured negative satisfiers associated with the low prices of agricultural products, bad housing standards, land erosion due to the intensive use of chemicals and deforestation, lack of safe drinking water and people's experiences of physical exhaustion, alienation and dependence.

The participants' utopia was composed by attributes such as cooperation, reciprocity, respect, understanding, care for water springs and soil, patience and openness. Linked with the above were specific forms of organisation, infrastructures and cultural practices that I summarised as *family and community unity/social cohesion, quality education adapted to local needs* and *improved material conditions* (see Figure 8.1). The latter did not only concern households but encompassed the financial resources needed for the municipality to improve water and housing infrastructures, maintain communal areas and provide waste management services.

After long discussions on the attitudes, values, actions, structures and environments that would contribute to the satisfiers characterising the utopian matrix, four *synergic strategies* emerged during the third workshop. These were *faenas* or communal work, organic vegetable gardens (OVG), reforestation and a parents' school. Participants considered that these strategies would positively contribute to greater unity, quality education and improved material conditions in the municipality. Most strategies were endogenous as the efforts to organise and execute them depended on participants and the community. However, people agreed on the need for support from NGOs and public institutions for most initiatives to be successful.

Participatory action-research (PAR): implementing synergic strategies

People who had participated in the HSD workshops in November 2011 were invited to join the PAR project in April 2012. Fifteen accepted the invitation, among them students and a lecturer of the local vocational school, farmers and several employees of local institutions. The first meeting aimed at ranking the four strategies with regards to their synergic effects on human needs. Participants chose the OVG as the top synergic strategy followed by the parents' school, a reforestation project and *faenas* or communal work. The latter was considered the least synergic strategy as it was more prone to failure due to what people referred to as the *culture of asistencialismo*. *Asistencialismo* relates to the paternalistic social and development assistance traditionally given to the poor based on donations or gifts in exchange for political support (clientelism) or, more recently, in exchange for participation in health or education schemes (Copestake 2008; Francke 2006). It also relates to recent development projects that have demanded people's active participation and initiative but have not delivered as expected. As a consequence, people have become reluctant to support new initiatives if food handouts or other immediate benefits are not offered (Vincent 2004).

It is quite likely that the culture of *asistencialismo* influenced the early stages of the PAR project as already in the third workshop participation fell significantly. At this point, one participant suggested moving the project from its location in the municipal centre to the neighbourhood of Vista Alegre where there was a group of 36 farmers who had expressed their willingness to work on organic gardening. The group had been engaged in a reforestation project by Agro Rural (a nation-wide programme for productive agrarian rural development from the Ministry of Agriculture) since 2006 and were used to meet once a week to discuss project-related issues. They belonged to a *comunidad campesina* (peasant community) that is a traditional local structure with a democratically elected board and voluntary membership. Members of the *comunidad* did not differ much from other residents in Acostambo with regards to values, satisfaction with life and levels of education although they were significantly poorer.[3] Given the *comunidad*'s explicit interest in participating, we decided to move the project to the neighbourhood of Vista Alegre in May 2012.

Top synergic strategy: organic vegetable gardens (OVG)

In Acostambo, farmers are used to buying industrial fertiliser for their commercial production of potatoes, barley and other cereals. Vegetables are also produced using fertilisers, although some participants declare to follow organic farming practices when growing for their own consumption. Modern organic farming is relatively new. It was introduced (or re-introduced, if traditional farming techniques are taken into account) in the region by NGOs such as ADECAP (Association for the defence and development of Andean Communities in Peru), Caritas (Development organisation of the Catholic Church) and by a former local nurse. In general, participants in earlier organic farming projects declared to be satisfied with the results. They explained that the training associated with the projects increased their knowledge about different farming practices and their effects on the environment and their health. However, people were critical of the project's long-term viability; when they no longer received food, tools or seeds they usually gave up organic farming.

The OVG strategy, as designed in collaboration with participants, was articulated around three main activities: a training session on organic farming, arrangements to get the seeds and workshops to organise and distribute tasks. The training session was led by one teacher from the local vocational school who had participated in our earlier workshops. He volunteered to give a presentation on the techniques of growing organic vegetables highlighting their economic, nutritional and environmental value. Participants engaged in the session by posing several questions about specific crops and practices before starting discussions on the preparation of the communal seedbeds where seeds would be planted at a later stage.

Seeds were donated by the municipality mayor who had offered to support the OVG strategy from the beginning of the project in April 2012. The research team had kept the mayor informed about the progress of the study and at his request prepared a prospective budget listing types of seeds, prices and quantities as agreed with participants. After making sure that the OVG strategy included a fair amount of people from the municipality the mayor took the budget to the council meeting where it was approved. Seeds were bought by a municipal agent and delivered to the researchers. We were requested to inform participants that the seeds were a contribution from the municipal council, probably for *clientelistic* purposes, as at the time the mayor was not popular in Vista Alegre.[4]

The distribution of tasks was organised by participants during their usual weekly meetings and the PAR project workshops. Chard, onion, lettuce and cabbage seeds were planted in communal seedbeds and carrot, beetroot and radish seeds were kept by the group leaders to be planted in the family gardens at a later stage. Communal seedbeds were placed by the greenhouses where they were growing eucalyptus and quinoa trees for the Agro Rural project. This way they had access to water, which facilitated taking care of the seedlings. Once seedlings grew in larger new plants, they were transplanted to private gardens according to the amount of land prepared by each farmer. In general, the arrangement and implementation of the project ran smoothly and participants followed their traditional way of organising communal agricultural activities and resolving conflicts. In January 2013, most participants had an organic vegetable garden. This became a distinctive feature of the Vista Alegre group, confirmed by the analysis of survey data showing that more PAR participants than non-participants had an OVG at the end of the PAR project (20 out of 21 versus 13 out of 21, differences significant at $p<0.01$).

Halfway through the OVG process, the PAR project turned to the implementation of the parents' school, envisaged as regular sessions addressing topics of interest for the adults in the community. Participants decided to focus the school on the following topics: ethics and values, domestic violence, citizens' rights and duties, and family planning. Sessions were organised by the research team around short presentations and participatory exercises where real life examples were discussed in small groups.[5] At the researchers' request, the local health care centre supported the initiative by sending the general practitioner, the psychologist, the nurse and the obstetrician to give presentations. The municipality governor and the manager of the municipal office of the disabled also contributed with presentations. In general, parents' school sessions were well attended and were also used to follow the OVG project, discuss organisational issues and reflect on the benefits and challenges of the processes participants were engaged in.

A sustainable development path in Acostambo?

This section discusses the outcomes of the OVG project in terms of the three pillars of the HSD approach to sustainable development: actualisation of human needs, balanced interdependence and self-reliance.

Actualisation of human needs

Organic vegetable gardens were considered a strategy that would contribute to the synergic satisfiers that characterised an optimal actualisation of needs in Acostambo. Whether these goals were achieved or not was discussed in a workshop in October 2012 and inquired through nine statements included in the post-PAR survey. The statements addressed the contribution of the OVG project to the three categories of synergic satisfiers characterising the utopian matrix.[6] Results indicate that by and large participants appraised the contribution of the OVG strategy to synergic satisfiers as positive. Table 8.3 summarises the responses to the nine statements.

Although there was only one formal training session, participants said that they became more knowledgeable from their involvement in the OVG strategy, which they did not always distinguish from the activities of the parents' school. In the workshops they stressed the importance of collective work and of learning from each other and their team leaders, highlighting the interdependence of unity/social cohesion and knowledge at the local level. However, women did not always feel capable to appraise the project. As one female participant said: 'since we do not know much, we cannot give you an evaluation'. This perceived lack of knowledge did not reflect on education levels, as by and large they were equal to those of men. It did, however, reveal the usual disregard for women's opinions in public meetings that seems to have progressively undermined their self-confidence. In addition, middle-aged and older women usually speak Quechua, and although they declared themselves proficient in Spanish (the language of workshops and presentations) they admitted that they would rather express themselves in their own language.

Regarding unity and social cohesion, most participants stressed the fact that work on the seedbeds and participation in workshops was a group endeavour. They explained that organic farming as they had devised it was a collaborative work and made them think in collective rather than individual terms. Participants

Table 8.3 Ranking of perceived contribution of the OVG strategy by mean score

Item	Synergic satisfier	Mean
General knowledge	Quality education	3,96
Household unity	Unity/cohesion	3,88
Collaboration in the community	Unity/cohesion	3,67
Savings	Improved material conditions	3,67
Household economy	Improved material conditions	3,50
Knowledge on organic faming	Quality education	3,42
Learning from neighbours	Quality education	3,42
Unity/social cohesion in Acostambo	Unity/cohesion	3,29
Earnings from sales of organic vegetables	Improved material conditions	2,25
Total sample (number)		21

Note: answers to the nine statements were coded as follows: completely false (1), not quite true (2), somewhat true (3), largely true (4) and extremely true (5)

did not touch upon the fact that workshops had often been joined by other people from the municipality. They did not refer to the donations of seeds by the mayor and did not talk about the contribution to training sessions and the parents' school of non-residents in Vista Alegre. This was reflected in answers to the survey, as participants appraised as more positive the contributions of the project to family and community than to social cohesion in the municipality.

Items concerning the contribution of the OVG strategy to the economic level of participants received lower scores than the ones related to the other two categories of synergic satisfiers. In the workshops, there was a general agreement about the positive effect on the household income of the OVG strategy but more stress was put on savings from buying fewer vegetables in the town's market than on the potential for additional income. This was further confirmed in the survey, as only three out of 21 respondents declared that it was 'largely true' that they had earned money from the sales of their organic produce, against 12 saying the same with regards to improvements in household economy, and 15 regarding savings.

The natural environment was only addressed in the workshops through the direct positive effects on health that organic agriculture provided according to participants. However, farmers had reduced their use of chemical fertilisers and were committed to continuing with organic farming after the closure of the PAR project, which suggested a positive direct effect on the environment in the long run. In addition, during the last workshop, participants agreed on asking the municipality to organise a system of garbage collection and sorting, and they discussed how to achieve cleaner streets, streams and irrigation ditches, as they were concerned about the effects of pollution on their families and crops. The increased demand for *patatas nativas* (native potatoes) from Lima and international customers was also leaning them towards the expansion of organic farming.

Balanced interdependence

Balanced interdependence between people, nature and technologies is a pillar of the HSD approach. It can be visualised through models capturing the complexity of relationships such as the ones underlying structural equations or agent-base simulations (Axelrod 1997). And while our small sample does not allow the use of these techniques, we can attempt an initial exploration of the interdependence between satisfiers and personal and environmental goals through the information extracted from a correlation matrix.

The post-PAR survey asked participants about the extent to which it was true that the project had contributed to instil into them a greater respect for the environment. Most agreed that the statement was 'somewhat true' (8) or 'largely true' (10). Table 8.4 presents the correlation matrix between a variable identifying synergic satisfiers (average score of the nine statements about the OVG project), the three categories of synergic satisfiers (mean scores of their three constituting items), answers to the question on respect for the environment and a vitality index capturing participants' wellbeing.[7]

Table 8.4 Correlation coefficients between synergic satisfiers, wellbeing and sustainability

	Synergic satisfiers	Unity/ cohesion	Quality education	Improved economy	Vitality	Respect environment
Synergic satisfiers	1					
Unity/cohesion	0.735**	1				
Quality education	0.690**	0.158	1			
Improved economy	0.549**	0.113	0.434*	1		
Vitality	0.694**	0.654**	0.362	0.256	1	
Respect environment	0.730**	0.633**	0.400+	0.255	0.630**	1

Note: Spearman correlation coefficients, **significant at the 0.01 level, *significant at the 0.05 level, + significant at the 0.1 level

Results presented in Table 8.4 suggest that the positive effects of the OVG on synergic satisfiers are associated with higher vitality (r^S=0.694, p<0.01) and respect for the environment (r^S=0.730, p<0.01). Since causality is not explored here, it could well be that people who feel more vital are also those who appraise more positively the effects of the OVG on synergic satisfiers and on their attitudes towards the environment. As happiness researchers suggest, the relationship between subjective wellbeing indicators like vitality and other socio-economic and psychological variables is likely to be bidirectional or even multi-directional (Frey and Stutzer 2002) in line with the systemic relationships predicted by the HSD approach.

It is interesting to note that the three categories of synergic satisfiers, although positively correlated among them, are not associated to the same extent. The effects of the project on knowledge were closely related to the effects on participants' economic level (r^S=0.434, p<0.05), which makes sense since Peruvians value education and information as the main way out of poverty and marginalisation (Guillen-Royo 2007). However, the contribution of the OVG to education and the household economy did not seem to be connected to the contributions to unity or social cohesion. The latter appears to be independent from the effects of the project on education (r^S=0.158, p>0.1) and economic level (r^S=0.113, p>0.1) but tightly connected with wellbeing (r^S=0.654, p<0.01) and a deepened respect for the environment (r^S=0.633, p<0.01). This suggests that the positive influence of the PAR project on wellbeing and the environment would have been lower if unity and social cohesion had not been taken into account in the processes people engaged with during the project.

Self-reliance

A self-reliant development demands that local communities remain at the centre of the development process. As the PAR project was articulated around local participation, both the processes and their content were co-defined by researchers and participants. However, participants did not envisage the realisation of future projects without external backing. They stressed that the *apoyo* (support) they got through training, workshops and seeds was an important part of the success of the OVG initiative. They also expressed their intention to participate in the future in the *papas nativas* initiative from *Agro Rural* but they would like to do it on their own terms. They believed that *Agro Rural* should analyse their soil to assess its state before engaging in any major change of crops, and agreed on writing a letter to the programme leaders asking for a soil test. These are examples of self-reliance as understood in the HSD, not as self-sufficiency but as organic articulation of strategies co-generated with the local community.

Despite the increased ownership of the project by local participants, the risk of associating the PAR project to previous NGO and state-led initiatives permeated the study as researchers were the initiators, the formal organisers and the ones deciding the duration of the project. Donations or presents, a clear characteristic of previous development projects, were kept to a minimum and only seeds and light coffee breaks were handed out to participants during the ten months of the study. In order to assess the extent to which the culture of *asistencialismo* had permeated the PAR project, the questionnaire asked participants about the meaning of *asistencialismo*, and whether they considered the OVG strategy to be an example of it. Those who defined the concept in terms such as 'giving things in exchange for doing something' or 'relying on the government for economic support' said that it was either 'completely false' or 'not quite true' that the OVG project was an example of *asistencialismo*. This might be an indication that HSD-based PAR projects – by focussing on self-reliance – have the potential to reverse deeply entrenched traditions of dependence.

Concluding remarks

This chapter has presented the processes and outcomes of a participatory action-research study based on the Human Scale Development approach in Acostambo, Peru. The goals of the study were first to provide empirical evidence about the usefulness of the HSD perspective to engage people in a sustainable development path and second to reach a better understanding of the interconnected factors that at the local level promote human wellbeing and ecological sustainability.

The HSD framework promotes engagement by bringing out a different perspective on sustainable development and by empowering participants. Workshops based on the matrix of human needs reveal that sustainable development is not only about economic resources but about other factors such as social cohesion, unity and a respect for local realities which require participants to act at the personal and communal level. In addition, the fact that synergic strategies are identified and implemented by participants has positive effects on individual and community agency that last beyond the duration of the project. This empowering effect is not common to all participatory approaches. Participation has often been used to legitimise top-down programmes designed by NGOs or government bodies with minimal involvement of the population in the design and evaluation phases (Platteau and Abraham 2002; Green 2010). For example, the recent decentralisation of the health care system in Peru was initially designed to enable citizen participation by involving local women as educators, and by being receptive to people's suggestions and demands. However, as Georgieva and colleagues (2009) claim, public involvement is still minimal and usually discouraged by local authorities or health care centres.

Even if the HSD-based PAR project relied on people's engagement from the outset, this did not happen right away. A culture of *asistencialismo* or dependence, established through years of *clientelistic* social assistance and development programmes based on donations, had the potential to threaten the study. The fact that the PAR project was initiated and facilitated by researchers could have reminded people of recent interventions by NGOs like Caritas or national programmes like Agro Rural, associating researchers with donors and participants with recipients (Vincent 2004; Green 2010). The PAR project was not based on exchanging gifts for participation, which might have explained the loss of interest of the initial group of participants. When the project moved to Vista Alegre at the request of one community member, the dynamics of the project were made explicit from the outset and participation fluctuated only with regards to the farming season. Both the participants' willingness to be involved and the characteristics of a HSD-based project might have contributed to a relatively high level of engagement.

In addition to potentially engaging communities, the HSD approach unveils a complex picture of the interlinked satisfiers that contribute to sustainable development at the local, regional or national levels. In Peru, the wellbeing of the poor has commonly been addressed through social assistance programmes now under the Ministry of Development and Social Inclusion (Ministerio de Desarrollo e Inclusion Social – MIDIS), and environmental issues have been tackled separately by the Ministry of the Environment, the Ministry of Energy or the Ministry of Agriculture, with limited institutional coordination. The MIDIS was created in 2011 in order to ensure that previously dispersed social assistance programmes worked in a coordinated manner. The goal of MIDIS is to guarantee access to universal public services and opportunities through five social assistance programmes ranging from conditional cash transfers (*Juntos*) to subsidies for people over 65 who live under conditions of extreme poverty (*Pension 65*). Some programmes work on the basis of a system of obligations concerning health checks and school attendance in exchange for monetary incentives, while others incorporate gifts or materials as a part of the process, probably reinforcing the feeling of dependence experienced by poor people. None of the interventions have an environmental dimension and the association between poverty and environmental degradation is not often made explicit.

Interventions addressing environmental issues have a more holistic approach than those addressing poverty or marginalisation in Peru. The PAR project benefited greatly from the structure set by the reforestation project of Agro Rural, for example. Under this programme, the community in Vista Alegre met weekly, worked together and were used to attend workshops and on-site training. This addressed two of the categories of satisfiers identified by participants, as it increased their economic level through the sales of trees and their knowledge through on-site training and presentations. However, the project did not contribute to social cohesion in the municipality as it did not engage actors in other neighbourhoods or from other institutions. In addition, training focussed only on technical questions and participation was not encouraged at the level of design or evaluation. As our PAR project came to a close, participants decided to write a petition to Agro Rural to analyse their soil before starting a new project on the cultivation of native potatoes (*papas nativas*). This procedure was not contemplated in the guidelines of the programme and was never implemented, illustrating the programme's lack of openness to bottom-up initiatives.

Current social assistance and environmental programmes in Peru lack the holistic approach to development characteristic of the HSD. They are articulated through a system of exchange that reinforces dependence and discourages critical participation. It could be argued that universal entitlements to quality health care, education, unemployment benefits and pension would result in a better allocation of public resources and would have a greater potential to break with the culture of *asistencialismo* than current targeted programmes. However, in Peru universal entitlements are difficult to implement due to the lack of support for redistributive policies of the wealthier population (Peru21 2012, Cardenas et al. 2011). Thus, if progress towards sustainable development must remain project-based, governmental and non-governmental organisations would do well to draw on the HSD approach. Its theoretical foundations and methodology offer the holistic perspective required to engage the population in social transformation towards sustainable development and wellbeing.

Notes

1   www.transitionnetwork.org/ (accessed 30 July 2014).
2   Psychologist Abraham Maslow (1970) developed a theory of needs based on a natural hierarchy where physiological needs (hunger, thirst) were at the bottom of human motivation and as these were satisfied, higher needs such as safety, belongingness, love and esteem would emerge. The pursuit of self-actualisation (the need to live to one's unique potential) was considered the highest motivation for action and was only felt after lower needs had been met.
3   Average household income was 311 Nuevos Soles for participants (n=21) and 468 Nuevos Soles for non-participants (n=21); differences were significant at a 90 per cent level of confidence.
4   In June 2013 the mayor was forced to quit his position through a recall referendum. Many of his opponents were residents of Vista Alegre. The donation of the seeds might have been an attempt to regain the trust of the population.
5   In order to increase women's participation, people were separated by gender until women felt more confident to intervene in mixed-groups.
6   The post-PAR questionnaire presented participants in the project with three statements on the contribution of the organic gardens concerning the three synergic satisfiers: unity, quality training and improving material conditions. Answers were on a five-point verbal scale with optional answers being: *completely false, not quite true, somewhat true, largely true, extremely true*. The nine statements were (in Spanish in the original): 'the OVG project has contributed to the union of people in Acostambo', ' I have saved money by consuming the vegetables from my OVG', 'through the OVG

project I have learnt from my neighbours', 'the OVG project has contributed to the union in my household', 'my knowledge has improved thanks to the OVG project', 'the OVG project has improved my family's economy', 'the OVG has improved collaboration among people in my community', 'I have learnt on organic agriculture through the OVG project', 'I have earned money by selling products from my OVG'.

7 Subjective wellbeing was assessed through the subjective vitality scale developed by Ryan and Frederick (1997), using the six-item version suggested by Bostic and colleagues (2000). Participants rated on a five-point scale (from 'totally false' to 'extremely true') six items concerning their levels of energy and alertness.

Bibliography

Abdallah, S., Michaelson, J., Shah, S., Stoll, L. and Marks, N. (2012) *The Happy Planet Index. 2012 Report*. London: New Economics Foundation.

Axelrod, R. (1997) *The Complexity of Co-operation: Agent-Based Models of Competition and Collaboration*. Princeton: Princeton University Press.

Bostic, T. J., Rubio, D. M. and Hood, M. (2000) 'A validation of the subjective vitality scale using structural equation modelling' in *Social Indicators Research*, 52. pp. 313–324.

Cardenas, M., Kharas, H. and Henao, C. (2011) *Latin America's global middle class*. www.brookings.edu/research/papers/2011/04/27-global-middle-class-cardenas-kharas (accessed 30 July 2014).

Copestake, J. (2008) *Wellbeing and Development in Peru: Local and Universal Views Confronted*. New York: Palgrave MacMillan.

Corcoran, E., Nellemann, C., Baker, E., Bos, R., Osborn, D. and Savelli, H. (eds) (2010) *Sick Water? The Central Role of Wastewater Management in Sustainable Development: A Rapid Response Assessment*. Norway: United Nations Environment Programme.

Cruz, I., Stahel, A. and Max-Neef, M. (2009) 'Towards a systemic development approach: building on the Human-Scale Development paradigm' in *Ecological Economics*, 68. pp. 2021–2030.

da Cunha, P. V. and Junho, M. V. (1997) *The Limits and Merits of Participation*. Policy Research Working Papers, World Bank.

Daly, H. and Cobb, J. (1989) *For the Common Good*. Boston: Beacon Press.

Easterlin, R. A. (2003) 'Explaining happiness' in *PNAS*, 100(19). pp. 11176–11183.

Easterlin, R. A. (2013) 'Happiness and economic growth: the evidence' in *IZA DP No. 7187*. (January).

Francke, P. (2006) 'Institutional change and social programmes' in Crabtree, J. (ed.) *Making Institutions Work in Peru*. London: Institute for the Study of the Americas, pp. 89–112.

Frey, B. S. and Stutzer, A. (2002) *Happiness and Economics*. Princeton, NJ: Princeton University Press.

Georgieva, S., Vasquez, E., Barja, G., García F. and Larrea, R. (2009) 'Establishing social equity: Bolivia, Ecuador and Peru' in Gacitua-Mario, E., Norton, A. and Georgieva, S. (eds) *Building Equality and Opportunity Through Social Guarantee*. Washington, DC: World Bank, pp. 143–174.

Green, M. (2010) 'Making development agents: participation as boundary object in international development' in *Journal of Development Studies*, 46(7). pp. 1240–1263.

Guillen-Royo, M. (2007) *Consumption and Wellbeing: Motives for Consumption and Needs Satisfiers in Peru*. PhD dissertation. Bath, UK: University of Bath.

Guillen-Royo, M. (2010) 'Realising the "wellbeing dividend": an exploratory study using the Human Scale Development approach' in *Ecological Economics*, 70(2). pp. 384–393.

Guillen-Royo, M. (2012) 'The challenge of transforming consumption patterns: a proposal using the Human Scale Development Approach' in Bjørkdhal K. and Nielsen K. B. (eds) *Development and the Environment. Practices, Theories, Policies*. Oslo: Akademika Publishing. pp. 99–118.

Guillen-Royo, M. and Kasser, T. (2014) 'Personal goals, happiness and socio-economic context: studying a diverse sample in Peru' in *Journal of Happiness Studies* (Forthcoming).

Hamilton, C. and Saddler, H. (1997) 'The genuine progress indicator: a new index of changes in well-being in Australia' discussion paper No. 14, Canberra: Australia Institute.

Helliwell, J., Layard, R. and Sachs J. (eds) (2012) *World Happiness Report*. New York: Earth Institute, Columbia University.

Herr, K. and Anderson, G. L. (2005) *The Action Research Dissertation*. London: Sage.

Jackson, T. (2008) *Prosperity Without Growth*. London: Sustainable Development Commission.

Jackson, T., Laing, F., MacGillivray, A., Marks, N., Ralls, J. and Styme, S. (1997) 'An Index of Sustainable Economic Welfare for the UK, 1950–1996'. Guilford: University of Surrey Centre for Environmental Strategy.

Jolibert, C., Rauschmayer, F. and Paavola, J. (2011) 'Should we care about the needs of non-humans? Needs assessment: a tool for environmental conflict resolution and sustainable organization of living beings' in *Environmental Policy and Governance*, 21(4). pp. 259–269.

Jorge, M. (2010) 'Patients' needs and satisfiers: applying human scale development theory on end-of-life care' in *Current Opinion in Supportive and Palliative Care*, 4(3). pp. 163–169.

Layard, R. (2005) *Happiness. Lessons From a New Science*. London: Penguin Books.

Marks, N., Abdallah, S., Simms, A. and Thompson, S. (2006) *The (Un)Happy Planet Index. An Index of Human Wellbeing and Environmental Impact*. London: New Economics Foundation.

Maslow, A. (1970[1957]) *Motivation and Personality*, 2nd edn. London: Harper & Row.

Max-Neef, M. (ed.) (1991) *Human-scale Development: Conception, Application and Further Reflection*. London: Apex Press.

Max-Neef, M. (1995) 'Economic growth and quality of life: a threshold hypothesis' in *Ecological Economics*, 15. 115–118.

Max-Neef, M., Elizalde, A. and Hopenhayn, M. (1989) 'Human Scale Development: An option for the future' in *Development Dialogue*, 1, pp. 17–47.

Nangombe, H. and Ackermann, L. (2013) 'Subsistence and protection needs of the elderly living in Katutura, Windhoek (Namibia)' in *Research on Aging*, 35(2). pp. 182–200.

Peru21 (2012) *Kuczynski: Pongan impuesstos a lo que quieran pero no al trabajo*. http://peru 21.pe/2012/05/11/economia/kuczynski-pongan-impuestos-lo-que-quieran-no-al-trabajo-2023861 (accessed 30 July 2014).

Platteau, J. P. and Abraham, A. (2002) 'Participatory development in the presence of endogenous community imperfections' in *Journal of Development Studies*, 39(2). pp. 104–136.

Qizilbash, M. (2001) 'Sustainable development: concepts and rankings' in *Journal of Development Studies*, 37(3). pp. 134–161.

Ruggeri, C. (2001) 'Participatory methods in the analysis of poverty: a critical review' in *QEH Working Paper Series*, 62.

Ryan, R. M. and Frederick, C. M. (1997) 'On energy, personality and health: subjective vitality as a dynamic reflection of well-being' in *Journal of Personality*, 65. pp. 529–565.

Stockhammer, E., Hochreiter, H., Obermayr, B. S. and Steiner, K. (1997) 'The index of sustainable economic welfare (ISEW) as an alternative to GDP in measuring economic welfare. The results of the Austrian (revised) ISEW calculation 1955–1992' in *Ecological Economics*, 21. pp. 19–34.

United Nations (2012) *Report of the United Nations Conference on Sustainable Development.* Rio de Janeiro, Brazil (20–22 June 2012) New York : United Nations.

Vincent, S. (2004) 'Participation, resistance and problems with the 'local' in Peru: towards a new political contract.' in Hickey, S. and Mohan, G. (eds) *Participation: From Tyranny to Transformation.* London: Zed Books, pp. 111–124.

WCED (World Commission on Environment and Development) (1987) *Our Common Future.* Oxford: Oxford University Press.

9   On the good life and rising electricity consumption in rural Zanzibar

Tanja Winther

1. Introduction

When people in Uroa explained how electricity had ended up in the village, a strikingly high number brought up a particular meal that had been consumed ahead of electrification in 1990. Uroa is a fishing village on the East Coast of Unguja Island, Zanzibar, and had not been included in the original plans for electricity.[1] Rather, it was the village administration that initiated the idea, organised meetings, wrote letters and did a whole range of activities to attract the electricity grid to the village. Although people would also mention the meetings and letters when accounting for how electricity arrived in the village, my acquaintances tended to highlight a particular meal that had been prepared for the Norwegian project manager (Swahili: *kwa ajili yake*, 'for his sake'). The food was said to be typically Uroan and consisted of locally obtainable food-stuffs: octopus cooked in coconut milk, rice and various fruits. The utterances and body languages accompanying the descriptions of this meal expressed their perceptions of Zanzibari food being something superior, irresistible and even seductive. People in Uroa regarded this initiative as having been a significant step in the process of obtaining electricity.

Electricity also matters in rural Zanzibar. During the rural electrification programme which lasted from 1986 to 2006, the grid reached most of the villages in Unguja and Pemba. The quality of public services improved significantly through the provision of pumped water and electrified health clinics, schools and mosques. For private consumption, people had to cover the expenses themselves. The cost of obtaining a connection was considerable[2] and represented four to six months of income to a fisherman. Nonetheless, by 2006, as many as 20 per cent of the households in rural Unguja – and more than half of the families in Uroa – had obtained electricity at home.[3] This speaks of electricity's importance as perceived by people themselves.

Based on ethnographic work, this chapter accounts for the driving forces for the rising electricity consumption in rural Zanzibar and discusses the uses – and non-uses – of electricity in the light of people's perceptions of the good life. Two areas of consumption, television and food, will be examined in particular. Both types of consumption are highly cherished, and the comparison of television and food provides an interesting case in terms of examining how electricity affected everyday life. Whereas people's access to electricity conditioned and propelled the new habit of watching television, rural Zanzibaris tended to keep their food at a distance from electricity. I seek to account for why this was so. I will show the cultural-specific ways in which new technologies become adopted (or rejected) and affect consumption patterns through processes of normalisation (Shove 2003, Pantzar 1997). I will also examine Zanzibari perceptions of the good life (*maisha mazuri*) in relation to the selected realms of consumption as well as people's general conditions for living.

The adopted approach regards the driving forces for increased consumption as twofold, as captured in the notion '*co-evolution*' of choice (Shove 2003). On the one hand, there is the provision and promotion of new technologies and commodities, which provide external drives for change. On the other hand, there are (potential) buyers, consumers and users of the new objects and the social dynamics that drive consumption. In the present discussion I primarily focus on the user side. The adaptation of electricity and adhering appliances may be considered as 'domestication processes' (Pantzar 1997:54) through which commodities and new patterns of consumption are introduced, negotiated, institutionalised and transformed. Mika Pantzar (1997) observes three steps in the process towards an object's normalisation. First, they are objects of sensation, toy or pleasure perceived as luxury. Second, the object achieves a stage when its acquisition does not need to be justified but may be explained in functional terms. In the third phase the object has become part of daily routines. I also adhere to Mary Douglas' general contention that '[p]eople need goods to commit other people in their projects' (1982:23). After ensuring basic subsistence, social needs constitute a crucial drive for consumption. This implies that individuals who lack access to certain objects face the threat of social exclusion. Douglas denotes such a state as poverty, which is characterised by a feeling of lack of dignity (ibid.:16).

Similarly, Daniel Miller's (1994, 1998) work on the social drives for consumption informs the analysis in important ways. Miller highlights the way people – through consumption and their ways of using objects – both mirror and produce the values that guide them (Miller 1994:54 f.n.). I will draw on Miller's (1994) work in Trinidad in which he contrasts the realms of Christmas and the Carnival when accounting for various value systems and references for identity construction. Henrietta Moore's (1994) concept of multiple identities also informs the analysis. Moore suggests that the subject occupies a specific position at each moment of interaction. Thus identities are played out contextually and the degree of social reward influences the degree of investment in a given position (ibid.). Finally, a note on the relationship between *consumption* and *practice* is in order. We are dealing with new and established realms of consumption in which aspects of continuity and change may be expected. In order to allow for a perspective on consumption that grasps the totality of the material and socio-cultural structures and agents that interplay over time, Alan Warde (2005) suggests conceiving consumption as a series of discrete, repeated instances which in sum make up practices in Bourdieu's terms. Following practice theory it is also essential to maintain a combined focus, on the one hand, on the way material objects provide 'scripts for usage' (Akrich 1994). On the other hand, there are crucial socio-cultural aspects to consider such as social relationships, values and norms including gender ideology and practices.

In the following, section 2 briefly accounts for the methods. Section 3 presents the results from a survey where people were asked what they needed to live the good life. Section 4 accounts for the main drives for electricity consumption in the rural areas and provides an overview of electricity's uses in people's homes. Section 5 treats people's acquisition and uses of television sets and accounts for the rapid normalisation of both television and electricity in general. Section 6 focuses on food and drinks. Section 7 provides a summary and relates the Zanzibari material to Miller's study of consumption in a different context.

2. Fieldwork, Uroa Village

I draw on a total of 15 months of fieldwork conducted in rural Zanzibar over a time span of 15 years (1991, 2000–2001, 2004, 2005 and 2006). When I first arrived in Uroa in 1991, one year after electrification, the village fascinated me for the manner in which it had become connected to the grid. In contrast to most electrified villages, the place had not initially been included as a target for electrification, and men in Uroa signed up as customers at an exceptionally high speed. Thus Uroa was a place where I expected electricity to be widely in use a decade later. I had observed glimpses of daily life and obtained some data on people's expectations for electricity's further uses. For example, after first obtaining electric light and a radio, men highlighted the importance of getting a freezer for storing fish so as to have the possibility to sell their products in the market when the prices were favourable. Also, the benefit of acquiring an electric stove was highlighted by approximately half of the women I talked to, and ranged second by men. I thus expected stoves to be in use a decade later and generally wished to study the changes caused by electricity over time. The main fieldwork was conducted in Uroa in 2000–2001 (over ten months) and I later returned for shorter stays. If not otherwise stated, the presented material refers to the time of the main fieldwork. I lived in a rented guest house together with my husband and our daughter, aged two years, engaging in everyday activities with my neighbours. The methods included participant observation, interviews and informal talks conducted in English and Swahili (approximately 5 per cent of the men spoke English and women rarely did). In addition, I conducted an extended survey covering 23 per cent of the 480 households in the village. I interviewed both spouses in each household. One-third of the men were married to more than one woman, which implied that these men belonged to several households, eating and sleeping in their various homes on a two-day cycle.[4] The survey covered questions on consumption, electricity, cooking and food, and I asked specifically what people need to life a good life. Finally, the electricity company in Zanzibar and its staff were also important sources.

3. What you need for living the good life in rural Zanzibar

'Today, it is a good life here (*sasa, maisha mazuri*)', an old man said when accounting for the changes in the village over the last decade. 'Today there is more money. . . . Also there are small businesses. Before it was only fishing and farming, but you got less money from doing these activities.' In the coastal village of Uroa, people used to make a living from fishing (men) and subsistence farming (women and men). The arrival of electricity coincided with the arrival of commercial seaweed production (performed by women), and the physical access to electric light and appliances triggered a growing number of shops and guest houses in the village. These changes provided some groups within this relatively poor population[5] with a certain level of money which allowed for investments in electricity at home. With the desire for appliances and the need to regularly service the arrears to the electricity company, access to cash became of increasing concern. People evaluated this trend positively, including the services electricity provides. When the man I talked to was invited to reflect on the effects of television on young people, he determinedly said: 'Yes, television is fine (*TV nzuri*). They get to see different things (*mambo mbalimbali*), they can see what the president looks like. This was not possible before, you know. They have enough money. It is development (*maendeleo*).'

The man's association between the good life and development was shared by many people in the village. During the census interviews, I asked in an open manner what people needed to live a good life. Table 9.1 provides an overview of the issues people considered to be most important.

Table 9.1 Responses to the question 'What do you need to live a good life?'. Figures are given in percent of the 106 women and 80 men who responded (Survey Uroa 2000–2001)

	Women	Men	All
Money, business	27%	34%	30%
Improve/own house	11%	19%	14%
Electricity at home	6%	5%	6%
Electric appliance	1%	1%	1%
Enough food/good food	15%	9%	12%
Other material needs	2%	4%	3%
Health, water, development, education	24%	15%	20%
Peace and social relations	11%	8%	10%
To live, happiness, religion	2%	1%	2%
Don't know	1%	4%	2%
	100%	100%	100%

People's focus on money, the house, food and other material needs amounted to 73 per cent of men's responses and 62 per cent of women's. In the group 'Health, water, development and education', health alone was the most common response; mentioned by 14 per cent of the women and 10 per cent of the men. Education was generally highly emphasised in speech and practice (nearly all the girls and boys up to the age of 17 attended school), but only mentioned by two women and three men as a priority for living the good life.

Overall, the results show that to many of my Zanzibari respondents, who were striving to make a living, their needs for living a good life were first of all associated with having income, generating activities and possessing a nice house. Houses tend to be owned by men and are the most important enduring assets in this place (land is communally owned). The stated links between the good life and food, health and water also expressed a concern for having essential needs fulfilled. Moreover, to some extent people's answers reflected their respective interests and positions within the established gender roles as provider (men) and caretaker (women). More men than women associated the good life with income and the house, whereas more women than men mentioned food/good food and water which are perceived to be women's responsibilities. Although quite a few women were also concerned about having enough money and living in a good house, none of them mentioned that the good life implies to own a house as an individual or shared aspirations for opposing the gender ideology and division of wealth. Only one person said that she associated the good life with a type of object (a phone) that had not yet become common in the village.

If we go behind the gender aspect and look closer at the position of respondents, a striking observation is that people tended to mention objects and issues which were common in the village but which they did no not possess or experience themselves. Ten people said that the good life means to have electricity at home, and nine of these did not have such connection at that time. All the six women who associated the good life with access to water were living farther away from the village taps than what is common.

Also, responses grouped in the category 'Peace and social relations' reflect the position of the respondents in significant ways. Three of the women in this group mentioned the importance of having a husband, and two of them were widows or divorced. One person said that the good life is to have children. She was a childless woman.

The tense political situation in Zanzibar also influenced some of the responses. Nearly all the people in the village supported CCM,[6] the ruling political party in Zanzibar at that time, but everybody experienced the tense situation. Five women and two men said they associated the good life with 'peace', which probably reflected their concern for the political circumstances which were felt and feared in the village. Similarly, the two men who said that 'good relations' were the most important thing for living a good life both came from Pemba Island, which means that they and their families were likely to be socially excluded in the village. The few individuals in Uroa who sympathised with the opposing party CUF[7] or simply had their origin or relatives living on the island of Pemba (whom in the public discourse are associated with CUF) were facing severe difficulties in everyday life. For example, one of my acquaintances from Pemba who openly supported CUF was excluded from going fishing with men in the village. Because it is impossible to navigate a dhow (*ngalawa*) on your own, the man was obliged to go diving, which is a physically demanding and inefficient way of catching fish. Similarly, there was a situation in the village at one point in which a man from Pemba (not included in the survey) was imprisoned for ten days because he had been uttering critical remarks about the government. I met his wife in this period, and she was frustrated and afraid and had to seek protection from hostile neighbours by moving to another part of the village. Towards the end of our conversation she mentioned the good life and I asked her to specify what she meant by the term, whereupon she noted: 'To get along with people' (*kufahamiana na watu*, lit. 'that people understand each other').

Thus quite a few people focused on what they felt they lacked in relation to other people when stating what they needed for living a good life. This feeling partly derived from not possessing normalised objects (to be treated below) such as electricity connection or not having access to common services such as water taps in one's own neighbourhood. This points to the respondents' marginalised feeling of being in a state of poverty which Douglas (1982:16) conceives in social terms in contrast to 'destitution' which is related to subsistence problems. In other cases, the respondents experienced a mismatch between their own social status and what was considered as ideals such as a woman having a husband and children. Finally, the political antagonism produced processes of social exclusion, and individuals who experienced the unfortunate consequence of such exclusion were focused on getting on good terms with other people for living the good life.

In sum, the articulated, prioritised needs for living the good life in rural Zanzibar were centred on having access to income, basic goods and services, and being able to otherwise consume and enjoy the same kind of social relationships as other people in one's social surroundings. The respondents did not bring up a desire for novelties. Neither did they mention what they would do in their leisure time, which was a central finding in a Norwegian context when people were asked about their perceptions of the good life.[8] Rural Zanzibaris highlighted work, income and fulfillment of basics needs, and individuals who experienced having limited access to normalised goods or were otherwise living with social distress associated the good life with fulfilling such needs.

4. Electrical appliances and the overall driving forces for increasing consumption

The driving forces for the increased consumption of electricity in rural Zanzibar may be understood through Shove's (2003) notion, co-evolution of choice. This implies that demand is considered to be jointly produced by the development and marketing of the system of provision on the one hand, and the internal social dynamics on the other. During fieldwork I regularly asked people why they used electricity for various purposes, whereupon a school teacher simply said:

'electricity is there'. Availability is the first condition for use, and this is far from a trivial fact. It also mattered how the system was shaped, such as electricity tariffs, availability of appliances in second-hand shops, how the new items fitted with existing material structures such as housing construction, and how the new objects were presented and marketed. Electrified governmental institutions and hotels in the area constituted showrooms for electricity's potential uses, and people were also influenced through television programmes and their frequenting to town.

Approaching people's homes, Figure 9.1 provides an overview of the types of lamps and appliances kept in Uroan electrified homes in 2000 when one-third of the village was connected. The figures show the frequencies (percentage) with which these items were observed among the 131 accessible homes that were visited. The families often kept more than one item, but the number of lamps and appliances in each home are not shown.

Following Pantzar (1997), the appliances have been divided into two main categories: objects that *replaced* existing objects and objects that *served a new kind of service or purpose.*[9] In our case, electric light (incandescent bulbs and fluorescent lamps) replaced kerosene, and electricity substituted batteries for running radios which were kept by 88 per cent of the homes, often including a tape recording

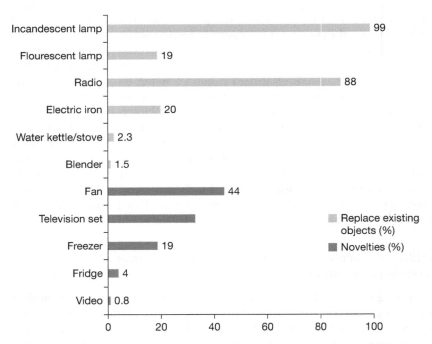

Figure 9.1 Electric lamps and appliances observed in Uroan homes in 2000. The figures show the frequencies (percentage) with which the appliances were kept in 131 electrified homes (Survey Uroa 2000–2001)

function. None of these services were new but men and women appreciated the increased convenience and comfort involved. Also, the quality of the bright, radiating electric light fixed in the ceiling was highly cherished (*mazingira yake!*, lit. 'its environment!'). The materiality of the light also had social effects in terms of affecting evening activities (e.g. enhancing domestic work, home tutoring and night classes at school), changing patterns for socialising through television watching and modifying people's perceptions of purity (Winther 2013).

Financial aspects also accounted for people's rationale for wanting to change to electricity. In the long run, kerosene and batteries were considered to be more expensive than electricity, and estimations of people's expenses on the two types of energy sources confirm this picture.

Irons heated with coal were said to have been used sporadically in the past, but this practice, particularly popular among school teachers (male and female), became more common with electric irons and were kept by 20 per cent of the homes. In terms of new cooking technology and food utensils, Figure 9.1 shows that such items were nearly absent in the village. Water kettles and stoves which in theory could have replaced the three-stone hearth were only kept by three families (2.3 per cent) and blenders, which partly replaced the mortar, were kept in two homes.

As to the objects referred to as novelties, Pantzar (1997:54) argues that these 'enter into the life of consumers as objects with almost no practical function'. According to the history of artefacts that Pantzar reviewed, new products with novel applications are always introduced as luxuries. They are objects of desire, pleasure or 'toys', and not perceived as necessities (Pantzar 1997). At the time of their introduction in rural Zanzibar, the meaning of freezers and television sets (see section 5 'Television: when novelties turn normal' and section 6 'Food: keeping electricity at a distance') resonated with the category 'objects of desire'. Also fans were constituted as novelties and were kept by 44 per cent in the sample. These objects were serving a new type of function (cooling) and were possibly perceived as luxuries in the years after their introduction. Several changes caused by electricity and new types of consumption notably contributed to producing a perceived need for cooling. Electricity is not compatible with water, and the traditional palm roofs easily lead to water leakages. The electricity company therefore required customers to have types of constructions other than palm roofs. As a result, building constructions were changing towards using bricks and corrugated iron roofs, which resulted in concealed houses with limited natural ventilation. Moreover, the increasing use of heat-producing appliances contributed to increasing the indoor temperature, as did the tendency to closing the windows (made of wood) to avoid having groups of children standing on the outside every evening watching television. The resulting drive towards a need for cooling in this relatively hot and humid climate reflected a pattern of spiralling consumption which might have been avoided given that access to sustainable and affordable building techniques had been provided together with electricity.

It is interesting to note the discrepancy between what people said they wanted the most (e.g. stoves for cooking) and the types of appliances that were actually kept in people's homes a decade later. People's answers to hypothetic questions may obviously reflect what they hope to achieve or wish to express in the interview context. As I elaborate below, such answers may nevertheless be methodologically valuable.

In sum, electricity and adhering lights and appliances partly became domesti-cated and integrated in people's homes because they replaced former energy sources by providing financial advantages and more comfort and convenience compared to existing ones. In addition, quite a few families introduced appliances that served new purposes. Such introductions were not made by individuals positioned in a social vacuum longing for the new objects in themselves. Rather, this is where the social analysis can start.

5. Television: when novelties turn normal

In 1998, Khamis had saved money in a bank account for some time and decided to buy a television set. None of his brothers possessed such an item at that time. He went to town and bought the object with his own money (200 USD). Three months later he started to feel an ache in his arms and legs. He felt he had needles in his skin and went to see a healer who diagnosed his state. The doctor told him that a bad person had become upset with Khamis's latest acquisition. By the use of evil magic (*kijicho*) he had succeeded in harming Khamis. From the doctor's description of the person and where he lived, Khamis deduced the bad person's identity. A male relative living in another ward was doing him harm.

When Khamis later returned to the doctor's place for treatment, he brought a chicken, paid a modest amount of money and did not bring relatives or in-laws, which is otherwise common in rituals involving spirits. During the ritual the doctor came in a state of possession and pulled out Khamis's pain by literally sucking the evil out of his skin. This was manifested as snails. Towards the end the doctor used a feather with which he touched Khamis's tongue. Out of his mouth came a kernel and the healing was over. The objects used were a ceramic basin for burning incense, a plastic bowl with water in it (into which the snails and the kernel were thrown) and the chicken feather. Khamis was cured and balance was restored.[10]

To Khamis this incident confirmed that television sets were dangerous to acquire. His problems were solved because the evilness had been removed.[11] However, it is significant that the dangerous aspect experienced in 1998 did not cause any reactions only three years later. At this time, when television sets had become relatively common in the village (Figure 9.1), none of the men in Khamis's network were said to experience social sanctions when acquiring such objects. Moreover, when I eventually met Khamis again in 2004 and asked if possessing a television set might cause someone harm, he said with a smile that 'today there is no problem; everybody owns a television set these days'. He said that the device had become 'an everyday thing' (*kitu cha kawaida*). Now half of the electrified homes kept a television set. It had also become common to have a television set installed at the same time as the electricity connection, whereas earlier, people had tended to first obtain light and a radio and then gradually expand the range of appliances.

The symbolic trajectory of television sets in Uroa matches Pantzar's (1997) analysis of normalisation processes in which he identifies three steps. In the first phase the object is an item of desire and the model emphasises 'difference' when explaining how novelties are introduced. Similarly, Shove (2003:49) argues that the drive for 'revaluation of difference' is what leads to innovation. In 1998, Khamis wanted this item which was closely associated with a modern way of living, and the acquisition also served to mark his levelled position vis-à-vis his friends and social observers. Generally, people's acquisitions of objects of desire might be socially dangerous (Shove 2003:50) and this was clearly the case with television sets in Uroa in 1998 when Khamis felt the ache in his body and went to receive treatment. Similarly, people said that back in the 1980s, the installation of corrugated iron roofs could jeopardise the wellbeing of individuals who first acquired them; thus at that time they had the status of being dangerous acquisitions.

Pantzar's second phase concerns the moment in time when the object's acquisition can be legitimised in rational and functional terms. As observed in Uroa in 2001, new television sets were not sanctioned any more, and people were rather concerned with what to watch, when and with whom. As I show below, this was the phase when television sets became social magnets in the neighbourhoods and when conversations in the fields often centred on the social dilemmas presented in yesterday's Swahili drama episode. Third, reflecting the object's final stage towards normalisation, television sets had in 2004 become so ordinary that their acquisition needed no justification at all. Indicative of this stage is Khamis's comment that 'everybody owns a television set these days'. At this point, when an object has become routinised, individuals may even receive sanctions for *not* possessing the item. This was the case with electricity connection already at the time of fieldwork (2001). For example, older men without electricity at home who married or considered marrying a second (or third) wife, would sometimes be criticised by younger men who found it imperative that husbands first provide 'satisfactorily' for their current wife (i.e. providing electricity) before marrying another wife. It is paramount in rural Zanzibar to treat several wives equally. The critique indicated that electricity was regarded as something a husband *should* provide his family. In Uroa, household access was achieved through a joint, participatory project, and men who installed electricity at home in the early phase did not provoke sanctions from mates and relatives. Having electricity at home soon became a norm and one may say that the status of 'household connection' in Uroa went through all the three phases towards normalisation approximately at the same time.

Of relevance for explaining the drive towards more household connections and television sets in Uroa is also Shove's (2003) notion of *coherence*. Captured as 'the packaging of expectation and practice' (2003:53), she refers to coherence as the tendency that people regard several, apparently isolated, objects and actions as belonging together in clusters, resulting in some kind of meta order. Thus if a person possesses one item, she or he will also be inclined to acquire other objects. In Uroa, such associations were reflected in the mentioned critique of older men which in effect linked electricity with the house and the ideal of being a good provider. Moreover, young men who were preparing their house before starting a family life by getting married sometimes referred to their house as not being 'finished' (*tayari*) because electricity was still lacking. We also noted that 6 per cent of respondents said that they needed electricity for living a good life and that almost all of them did not have such access. As a step towards coherence, a house in Uroa was not 'complete' without electricity. Similarly, the change in sequence of obtaining appliances (obtaining television at the same time as a connection) speaks of television as becoming considered as an integrated part of what a house should contain.

Generally, commodities fulfill social purposes (Douglas 1982) and studies of their historical trajectories in a given social context may reveal their shifting status from innovation towards normalisation and mass consumption. On a micro level, the Zanzibari case on television is illustrative in that the distinct steps towards normalisation were clearly observable, though it only took six years for these objects as dangerous novelties of desire to become everyday commodities. The Zanzibari case is also telling because the introduction of new objects involved a high degree of social negotiations which were openly articulated through moral discourse including people's expressed fear of sanctions. Socially dangerous acquisitions are markers of difference and therefore morally ambiguous, particularly in a cultural context where frugality and an egalitarian ideology (still) reigns. Here, the strongest reactions are likely to be triggered among one's equals, that is, one's own kin.

Family relations also form a crucial part of the domestication process in terms of how the objects became integrated and put to use in everyday life. First of all, Zanzibaris desired television programmes. Watching television comprised the idea of 'moving forward'; an ideal of modern life, and people repeatedly emphasised the role of television in providing them and their children with new ideas and education and also time to relax in a new way (Winther 2008). When being asked why they had obtained a television set, some explicitly referred to 'development' as the rationale. Such acquisitions suit men's role as modern providers.

Second, arrival of television sets soon attracted neighbours and extended family members in the evenings. A similar configuration of people would appear during the month of Ramadhan when family members gather outdoors after sunset to break the fast and jointly consume the cherished meal, *futari*. In 2001, when 9 per cent of the whole village possessed a television set, more than 80 per cent of the adults watched television at least once a week. Socially, the hosting spouses providing view-time enjoyed an elevated status when displaying their success as a modern couple during the evening shows (Winther 2013). The communal viewing is linked to the importance of showing material modesty and solidarity. Indicative of Khamis's duty to serve the needs of the guests, it would have been unthinkable for him to ask them to leave in the case that he became tired and wanted to go to bed (wives normally go to sleep earlier in the evening). Instead he would close the screen at midnight when the last guest was satisfied and returned home. Therefore, in relation to the way Khamis had felt vulnerable to social sanctions at the time of when the appliance was acquired, he could be regarded as compensating for his investment every time he turned on the television set for the extended group to watch. Watching the news and television shows became a social event and was expected to be so. The extended family network had a claim on taking part in the consumption of programmes.

Third, the idea that each home should provide view-time was also expressed. Some men told me that they wanted their own television set so that they would not have to go to other people's houses to watch television. In some cases this spoke of relational friction, which was the situation of one of my acquaintances who opposed the government. In other cases it might simply mean that people felt more comfortable being the owner and host on such occasions, which brings social prestige in an accepted manner to the protagonist. In sum, the rapid rise in the occurrence of televisions sets in the village, the packed homes attracting neighbours and extended family members who have a claim on taking part in the consumption of programmes, and the indications of a growing wish to withdraw to one's own living room to relax in this particular way demonstrate that watching television formed part of living a good, modern life in rural Zanzibar.

6. Food: keeping electricity at a distance

At a first glance, the absence of electric stoves in the village points to food processing and eating as a more static realm of life compared to how people spent their leisure time. Television sets were embraced, electric cookers were not. In this section, I seek to point to factors that account for why women in Uroa continued to cook with firewood on the three-stone hearth and why freezers were not used for storing cooked food.

In Zanzibar, food is an important marker of identity vis-à-vis the outside world. This was illustrated in the opening passage where we saw the strong emphasis put on a particular meal that was served to the project management ahead of electrification. Counihan (1999:6) holds that '[f]oodways influence the shaping of community, personality and family', thus food and adhering to cooking practices are dynamic and closely linked with identity formation. The celebration of Zanzibari identity through food is important and could constitute some degree of resistance against introducing stoves, but other factors were also important as I show below. It should be noted that in contrast to the social significance of who provided television view-time in the evening, consumption of food was never used as a reference for internal differentiation in the village. For example, it seemed close to a taboo to comment on a particular dish or compare the skills of different cooks (elaborated in Winther 2008).

Tastes in food (*ladha la vyakula*) were often brought up in conversations about electric cookers (a discourse that I might have initiated myself when inviting people to reflect on the issue). Men tended to stress their preference for food cooked with firewood: 'It is better to cook with firewood because the food gets better than when you cook with electricity. With firewood you cook slowly, slowly, no hurry.' Some would compare today's foods with those of the past and complain that the quality has declined, negatively affecting people's health. One man linked this trend to a shift in cooking technologies from boiling in water to frying in oil:

> people in the past ate food with strength (*chakula cha nguvu*). They ate vegetables which they boiled for a little while only. They ate fish, also boiled for a little while, not fried in oil for a long period of time as we do today. They ate maize, as we do now, but maybe the whole piece boiled in water, or grained. They did not eat much flour, rice and sugar. In this way they got more vitamins and better health than we do today.

Although cooking practices and preference for food are sometimes said to be conservative aspects of human life (Douglas 1999, Bourdieu 1984), important transformative aspects have also been noted (Goody 1982, Lien 1987, Mintz and Du Bois 2002). Eating habits and preferences in food are not static, thus we cannot simply ascribe the absence of stoves in the village to the conservative nature of such practices and preferences. As indicated in the quote above, people acknowledged that the culinary repertoire of today differs from that of the past, and men seemed particularly concerned about the way food affects the human body. In Zanzibar, having bodily strength goes beyond physiological aspects such as getting enough vitamins as it also implies being protected against evil magic and spirits. Some men even suggested that when particular kinds of trees are used as fuel on the fire, the smoke entering the food may have a favourable health effect. Magic medicine is always prepared on the fire. Such expressions linking the fire and the quality of food to obtaining bodily strength provided support for keeping cooking technologies the way they were.

Seen from the cooks' perspective, however, the issue of food, taste and health tended to look different. First of all, women were less concerned with potential differences in the tastes associated with the distinct technologies. Instead, they highlighted the (potential) benefits of electricity in terms of the positive health effects (no smoke), the time saved on not having to fetch firewood and the reduced time spent on preparing meals. Interestingly, women in Uroa used to cook three times per day, but due to their concern for time management (earning money on seaweed and watching television in the evening) they only prepared two meals per day after electricity's arrival and instead served leftovers for the third meal. This shift was the most significant change in women's cooking practices due to electricity. Most of them continued using the former technology.

Men and women's different attitudes to electric stoves were clearly related to their respective positions in the household as overall provider and cook, respectively. Electric cooking would be costly, and electricity was paid by men in contrast to firewood which was available for 'free' (women spent 12 hours weekly collecting fuel-wood). Men, as seen, also expressed a preference for the taste of food cooked with firewood. Given women's interest in stoves when being asked on the matter, I have argued (Winther 2012) that the lack of uptake partly reflected that these items fell in-between men's responsibility and control of electricity and women's responsibilities and interests as cooks.

Another barrier to people's acquisition and uses of new cooking technologies had to do with their awareness that a shift from fireplace to electric stove would touch on a whole range of practical challenges. Cooking technologies tend to form part of integrated practices with many different socio-material elements linked in chains (cf. Akrich 1994 and the concept of 'scripts'). The type of electric stove available in the village at the time of fieldwork, thus the item that most people had in mind when responding to my questions, was a coil type of plate which did not have the possibility for regulating the temperature, thus the risk of burning food was high. Moreover, this item which has a flat surface would be incompatible with the traditional clay pot (bowl-shaped bottom surface). Also, the coil stove would effectively limit the types of dishes that could be made. For example, rice cooked in coconut milk (*wali*) and pilaff (*pilau*, Zanzibar's national dish) need heating from above and beneath, which the coil stove did not allow for. When using the fire, the need for baking is solved by putting burning coal/wood/copra under the pot and also on the clay lid on top of the pot. Moreover, maize porridge (*ugari*) needs heavy beating, which would be difficult to practice on an unstable stove which was also considered to be dangerous to touch due to the risk of electric shocks. The most likely type of dish that could be made with electricity, apart from heating water for tea, was the soup that often accompanies rice in a Zanzibari meal. The incompatibility of stoves with existing cooking vessels and common techniques for making particular dishes constituted a barrier to the uptake of such stoves, as did many women's deep fear of getting electric shocks.

Women in rural Zanzibar nonetheless tended to show a keen interest in stoves. True, they expressed such attitudes in meetings with a Western, female anthropologist whom they knew was familiar with electric cooking, and this is likely to have influenced their responses. However, although they might more have been playing with the idea of electric cooking rather than expressing what they would do tomorrow if they had the money to purchase a stove, their detailed explanations and stress on issues such as time savings seemed to reflect their genuine positive attitude to electric stoves. Sometimes they explicitly referred to such potential acquisitions as a step towards development, indicating that the item would signal their modern, female identities (cf. Moore 1994). Cooking is a female task and responsibility, and men did not correspondingly link the potential uses of stoves with their (or their wives') modern identities.

The freezers in Uroa could in theory be used for storing food, a common practice in many places, but again people avoided mixing food and electricity. Freezers were uniquely used for producing sweet ice and cold drinks. The sweet ice was sold to children in the neighbourhood. Cold drinks were also highly valued, particularly during Ramadan when the distribution took on a particular significance. Similarly to the shared consumption of television programmes, the extended family members frequently borrowed cooling capacity in their relatives' houses during the fasting month. Breaking the fast with something cold was cherished, but people were also concerned about the potential, detrimental health effects. For example, cold liquids were avoided in the case that somebody was having a cold.

When accounting for why cooked food was never put in the freezer, both men and women pointed to what this would do with the quality of the food. In contrast to remains of cooked food (e.g. a stew) which were sometimes reheated on the fire without any perceived problem, putting eatables in a freezer was considered to jeopardise the taste. Some said it would not be favourable to put rice in a freezer, because 'it would be cold and that is not good' (*itakuwa baridi, sio nzuri*), as if the cooked staple had 'health' in a similar was as human beings. Other people said that such rice would obtain a watery quality (*maji-maji*). Soups were considered possible to freeze but would lose their taste (*ladha itapotea*). Finally, some pointed to the difficulty of reheating frozen food on the fire in contrast to the way this may be achieved with big electric ovens, which points to limitations caused by the objects' scripts for use (Akrich 1994). In sum, cold storage of cooked food was avoided as it was perceived to affect the quality and taste. The discussion has underlined how cautiously Zanzibaris guarded the quality of their cherished food and the multiple concerns and factors that entered the picture when new, potential food-processing technologies were considered.

7. Summary: the good life, television and food

This chapter has sought to account for the driving forces behind the increasing use of electricity in rural Zanzibar and discuss this in relation to perceptions of the good life. The construction of an electricity grid did not alone explain the fact that many people became connected and started using electricity in daily life. The lower cost of electricity in the long run, as compared to existing energy sources such as kerosene and batteries, partly accounted for the increasing demand. Moreover, the Zanzibari development discourse voiced the benefits of modern living and electricity's role within this scheme. Commercial forces displaying appliances encouraged people to change their energy use in ways that resembles life in town. These kinds of influences effectively reached people in the villages through television and radio broadcasting and people's frequenting to town. As a result, one could say that electricity became a means for marketing its own services.

Furthermore, the social drives for more consumption through the signalling of difference and social standing was relevant when accounting for the way novelties were introduced. Individuals involved in such acquisitions notably experienced the social risks involved. By scrutinising the way the status of television sets changed over a period of six years in one man's circles, we came closer to understanding some of the general dynamics embedded in normalisation processes. In an early phase, television sets were exclusive objects of desire and socially dangerous, then they were legitimised in functional terms (get education and new ideas), and finally they became 'everyday items'. The high frequency of watching and the association between progress and the good life led me to conclude that television was regarded as a prerequisite for living the good life in terms of development and progress.

People's responses to the question what they need most for living the good life tended to signal their vulnerable position. Many said they would give highest priority to items or relationships which they did not possess and/or enjoy themselves such as electricity connection. Such statements confirm the thesis that the incapacity to possess normalised goods may lead to social exclusion and a lack of dignity. Moreover, the general poverty in rural Zanzibar should be taken into account for understanding why the majority of respondents highlighted basic, material needs such as a house, work and money, when expressing what they needed most for living a good life. To them, sustainable living means moving out of a materially deprived situation. This contrasts the findings from another context where the good life tended to be associated with what people do in their leisure time.

Rural Zanzibaris generally enjoyed socialising and consuming goods beyond what they considered as basic needs. They cautiously selected and negotiated what technologies to adopt and domesticise. There was a striking contrast between the rapid uptake of television sets and freezers used for cooling drinks and sweet ice on the one hand and the enduring, former technologies used for preparing (and storing) food on the other. The absence of stoves was partly explained by the high cost of usage, the gender difference in terms of domestic responsibilities and control of appliances and by electricity's materiality in that electric stoves were not compatible with other adhering technologies and utensils, making it difficult – and dangerous – to prepare a range of dishes with electricity. Another closely related explanation for why Zanzibaris tended to keep their food at a distance from electricity was the concern for the quality of the food, which was most commonly expressed by men, in some cases linking food to health. The celebration of Zanzibari food as a marker of people's common identity was noted.

In contrast to the way stoves fell in-between men and women's responsibilities, the purchasing of television sets in rural Zanzibar fitted with practices and objects that underlined men's identity and success as modern providers. A similar image was created when freezers were obtained for producing cold drinks and sweet ice. People did not mention television sets and freezers when asked what they needed most for living a good life, which reflects that they did not consider possessing such objects as their most essential need. However, a majority of the population took part in the actual consumption of television shows and cold drinks. Such services were largely shared amongst neighbours and extended family groups who seemed to have a claim on the services provided by these items. In contrast to the individualised (male) acquisition of and ownership to appliances, in use, these objects served to strengthen family ties and other social relations.

In a treatment of modernity and consumption in Trinidad, Miller (1994) observed two different patterns for socialising and identity construction which were most purely played out during the festivals of Christmas and the Carnival, respectively. Christmas was marked by continuity, emphasising a sense of roots and traditions, celebrating decent and family relations. Miller hence captured Christmas as the lasting, transcendent realm in Trinidad. In contrast, the Carnival represented a radically different form of sociality and existence, expressing a temporal/transient rather than continuous consciousness. The Carnival was marked by loudness, dancing, drinking and the exploitation of sexual relations based on simple mutual acquaintances. The Carnival represented a sense of time and a sense of freedom where the possibility of all sociability was denied (Miller 1994:126–133). If we regard the dualism in Trinidad as containing two opposing sets of values and focus on how people shifted between various value systems, there are important elements of resemblance with Zanzibar. At the time when Khamis went to purchase the television set, this incident, if interpreted in isolation, could be understood as an act in which he operated as a free individual pursuing a project that underlined his modern identity. Similarly, a man who had purchased a freezer to enjoy a cold drink when breaking the fast could be considered as celebrating the ephemeral present through a new form of cherished consumption. In both cases, they related to a Zanzibari modern realm in which the value of progress and change were highlighted. However, as soon as Khamis displayed the television set in the village, or the freezer was installed and connected to electricity in somebody's house, the objects and their owners immediately became subject to social control. The justification for initially acquiring the television set was made through acts of shared consumption and there is good reason to expect that Khamis had the family's greater network in mind when he purchased the appliance. In sum, from the time novelties were acquired to them becoming domesticated and integrated in daily life, consumption in Zanzibar had aspects of belonging both to the transient realm as well as to the transcendent lasting realm in which the individual became submissive to the interests of the family. As Miller also acknowledges for Trinidad, it is significant that people continuously shifted between distinct value systems which sometimes produced tension but also provided space for interpretation and negotiations. In order 'to get along with people', what socially excluded individuals in Zanzibar captured as the most important thing for living a good life, many of my acquaintances strived to balance between pursuing novelties of desire and at the same time adhering to expectations embedded in the duty of showing modesty and confirming family relationships. Ultimately, in the same way as meals during Ramadhan were consumed jointly by extended family members, the pattern of shared consumption allowed most people in the village, but not all, to take part in the new types of consumption.

Notes

1 Zanzibar is a semi-autonomous state that forms part of Tanzania and consists of two main islands: Unguja and Pemba. At the time of fieldwork the population of Zanzibar was about 1 million. The electricity is imported through submarine cables from the Tanzanian mainland.
2 The connection rate including wiring was approximately 2–300 USD.

3 This is an exceptionally high connection rate compared to the Tanzanian mainland where only 3 per cent of the population have electricity at home. (See http://blogs.worldbank.org/africacan/only-14-of-tanzanians-have-electricity-what-can-be-done [accessed 30 July 2014].)
4 According to Islamic law, men are entitled to marry up to four women. Usually each wife lived in a separate house, which was treated as a household unit in the survey. Men's affiliation with more than one household accounts for why the number of men interviewed (80) was lower than the number of women (106).
5 At the time of fieldwork, a typical income for a fisherman was 30–60 USD per month. Women earned about one-third of this amount from farming seaweed.
6 Chama Cha Mapinduzi (The Revolutionary Party).
7 Civic United Front.
8 It should be noted that in the Norwegian context (Finnmark county), people were asked what the good life means to them, whereas in Zanzibar the question included 'what you need' for living the good life. I nevertheless find the difference in responses to these open questions interesting: Norwegians focused on their leisure time (going to the cabin, spending time with family and friends, and often mentioning nature) whereas Zanzibaris focused on ensuring basic needs and having what other people in their social context tend to have. The Norwegian study formed part of the project 'Do customer information programs influence electricity consumption' (Norwegian Research Council, project no 190769/S60).
9 Pantzar's model does not include a separate category for objects acquired with the purpose of generating income or other productive activities at home.
10 The main part of this account was first published in Winther 2008.
11 When I came to know Khamis three years later, his ache returned, and this time it was apparently his success with fishing that triggered the problem. A similar healing procedure was organised and this was when I observed it.

Bibliography

Akrich, M. (1994) 'The de-scription of technical objects' in Bijker, W. and Law, J. (eds) *Shaping Technology/Building Society. Studies in Sociotechnical Change*, pp. 205–224. Cambridge, MA: The MIT Press.
Bourdieu, P. (1984) *Distinction. A Social Critique of the Judgement of Taste*. Cambridge, MA: Harvard University Press.
Counihan, C. M. (1999) *The Anthropology of Food and Body. Gender, Meaning, and Power*. New York: Routledge.
Douglas, M. (1982) *In the Active Voice*. London – Boston – Henley: Routledge & Kegan Paul.
Douglas, M. (1999[1972]) 'Deciphering a meal' in Douglas, M. *Implicit Meanings: Selected Essays in Anthropology*, pp. 231–251. London: Routledge.
Goody, J. (1982) *Cooking, Cuisine and Class. A Study in Comparative Sociology*. Cambridge: Cambridge University Press.
Lien, M. E. (1987) 'Fra boknafesk til pizza. Sosiokulturelle perspektiver på mat og endring av spisevaner i Båtsfjord, Finnmark' in *Occasional papers No. 18*, Oslo: Department of Social Anthropology, University of Oslo.
Miller, D. (1994) *Modernity. An Ethnographic Approach. Dualism and Mass Consumption in Trinidad*. Oxford and New York: Berg Publishers.
Miller, D. (1998) 'Why some things matter', in Miller, D. (ed.) *Material Cultures. Why Some Things Matter*, pp. 3–23. Chicago: The University of Chicago Press.
Mintz, S. W. and Du Bois, C. M. (2002) 'The anthropology of food and eating' in *Annual Review Anthropology*. 31. pp. 99–119.

Moore, H. L. (1994) *A Passion for Difference. Essays in Anthropology and Gender.* Cambridge, UK: Polity Press.

Pantzar, M. (1997) 'Domestication of everyday life technology: Dynamic views on the social histories of artefacts' in *Design Issues.* 13(3). pp. 52–65.

Shove, E. (2003) *Comfort, Cleanliness and Convenience: The Social Organization of Normality.* Oxford, UK: Berg.

Warde, A. (2005) 'Consumption and theories of practice' in *Journal of Consumer Culture.* 5(2). pp. 131–153.

Winther, T. (2008) *The Impact of Electricity. Development, Desires and Dilemmas.* Oxford: Berghahn Books. Published as paperback in 2010.

Winther, T. (2012) 'Negotiating energy and gender: Ethnographic illustrations from Zanzibar and Sweden' in Bjørkdahl, K. and Nielsen, K. B. (eds) *Development and Environment. Practices, Theories, Policies,* pp. 191–208. Oslo: Akademika Publishing.

Winther, T. (2013) 'Space, time and socio-material relationships: Moral aspects of the arrival of electricity in rural Zanzibar' in Strauss, S., Rupp, S. and Love, T. (eds) *Cultures of Energy. Power, Practices, Technologies,* pp. 154–176. Walnut Creek, CA: Left Coast Press.

10 Celebrity chefs, ethical food consumption and the good life

Karen Lykke Syse

Introduction

November 5th was the day Guy Fawkes tried to blow up the British Parliament back in 1605 – maybe it is a date worth being associated with for attempts to make major public changes? On the 5th November 2013 the British celebrity chef Jamie Oliver was awarded an Honorary Fellowship by the Royal College of General Practitioners for his work in tackling childhood obesity – he was given credit for his attempt to improve the nutritional value of school dinners. Jamie Oliver has become a celebrity due to his strong wish to influence the way people in Britain (and elsewhere in the world) relate to food. Of course Guy Fawkes was a villain and Jamie Oliver has already been named a national hero many times over. In 2005, Queen Elizabeth II awarded him an MBE; he became a Member of the Order of the British Empire – an order that is awarded for a significant achievement or outstanding service to the community, or for local 'hands-on' services which stand out as examples to other people. Jamie Oliver – celebrity TV-chef – was given the Queen's stamp of approval for his ongoing campaigning for good food. Jamie Oliver isn't alone in his quest. Other campaigners, on and off national and international TV-screens, have similar agendas. Hugh Fearnley-Whittingstall is another British TV personality and chef with a scheme. Through the UK Channel 4 series *Hugh's Fish Fight*, Fearnley-Whittingstall uncovered unsustainable fishing around the world and instigated a campaign called The Fish Fight campaign. Through his own website and with the use of social networking sites like Facebook and Twitter, the campaign has received over 700,000 signatures to ban fish discards in the UK and elsewhere. A new food ideology is conveyed from the pulpit of celebrity chefs on TV. The ideology calls for food ethics, is critical to industrial food production and is often coupled with ideals of self-sufficiency. One can go as far as to say that the ideology has become main-stream among the chattering classes in wealthy western societies. Slow Food, cuisine de terroir, heritage breeds and a strong focus on organic food that is sourced, prepared and consumed within a short distance of where it was produced or eaten is also part of this new movement.

According to Professor of Journalism Michael Pollan, the complexities of living in a global economy obscure the connection between everyday life and actions and their consequences in the real world (2013:20). As both environmental issues and animal welfare problems are the result of the small choices we make every day, we need to address these ethical choices through what we eat and how we eat. Although a multitude of moral concerns can influence what people consider to be good food, for the purpose of this chapter, we can cluster the idea of good food into three categories: local provenance and seasonality, organics and sustainability, and animal welfare. These food attributes are often presented as the antidote to industrial farming.

By analysing TV-series, cookbooks and websites from a selection of celebrity chefs from the UK and Scandinavia, this chapter will explore how celebrity chefs project ethical food consumption as part of the quest for the good life. In which ways are consumers encouraged to feed on notions of self-sufficiency by growing their own food and even to retreat to the countryside as a means to find good food? If home-grown seems like a tall order, then these same consumers are at least encouraged to take an active part in re-establishing the connection to the food and its producer. Why has "green" food of a special home-grown kind become the trait of class, identity and values? I will, in the course of this chapter, describe a shift that has taken place in gastronomy. Even if food, as will be discussed below, always has been associated with a complex set of meanings like, for instance, class and identity, now food encapsulates a series of new values: not only should it taste good, the foodstuffs should be sustainably harvested, caught, grown or raised, taking animal welfare issues into consideration as well. In addition, the food should be local, and if it isn't local, then at least it should be fair-trade. By following these criteria, we might eat our way to the good life. This may perhaps seem like a difficult task, yet according to Janet Cramer,

> as a manifestation of culture, food is one of the most potent media for conveying meanings related to identity, ethnicity, nationhood, gender, class, sexuality, and religion – in short, all those aspects of social, political and relational life that convey who and what we are and what matters to us.
>
> (Cramer et al. 2011:317)

Maybe one of the reasons why food is becoming ever more socially evident is because we are bombarded with what *The Guardian* columnist Stephen Poole calls gastro culture (2012). According to Poole (and easily detected in any book shop), shelves are heaving under the weight of cookery books on every imaginable food topic and written by the new heroes of our time – chefs (2012:7). The idolisation does not only include celebrity chefs with a strong agenda like the Honorary Jamie Oliver, but also chefs whose main claim to fame is that they procure and produce delicious food. Chefs are the new opinion makers. An example: in 2004, a group of esteemed Nordic chefs gathered to write a manifesto. The manifesto was already sketched out as a first draft by the Danish food-business brain, chef and restaurateur Claus Meyer – partner in NOMA, named the world's best restaurant in 2010, 2011, 2012 and 2014. Using the Ten Commandments from Scandinavian dogma-film as an inspiration, Claus Meyer's rough draft of a manifesto was slightly edited and signed by 12 chefs representing the Nordic countries. Pure, light and simple became the three core adjectives and values of The New Nordic Kitchen which became a true concept in 2004, – the 'New Kitchen Manifesto'. One could argue that chefs may write manifestos without this having any true influence on the world at large, however, in connection with the UN Commission on Sustainable Development (CSD19) in 2011, the Nordic Council of Ministers (NCM) (the official body of cooperation of the Nordic countries) decided to promote the concept of New Nordic Food. Something that has been on the backburner for a while is cooking on full flame, and this chapter will, in the essayistic tradition, try to question and capture both the content and fuel of these flames.

Food is good to think with

Malinowski wrote no less than four books with the word sex in the title, yet the first sentence that his student Audrey Richards wrote in her doctoral thesis (1932) was 'Food is more important than sex'. By reading the classics in anthropology it is easy to see why and how food has been used as a starting point to understand the social and cultural patterns of any given society; not only is it a primary need, but it also governs how we relate to one another socially and culturally. Through fieldwork among the Southern Bantu, Richards explained that both food and its consumption had to be studied in their institutional setting and through their manifestations in other aspects of culture. Richards was regarded as the founder of nutritional anthropology, and her important publications to the field were followed by other central studies. In fact, one could argue that some of the greatest anthropological contributions during the last five decades have been drawn from food studies (Farquhar 2006), with Lévi-Strauss *The Raw and the Cooked* (1964) and *The Origin of Table Manners* (Lévi-Strauss et al. 1969) being perhaps the most central to the field. Mary Douglas also showed how food, culinary forms, food taboos and rituals were the key to understanding symbolic boundary maintenance (Douglas 1966).

People consume food in a multitude of ways – they look at its preparation; listen to it being spoken of by celebrity chefs; read about it in books, lifestyle magazines, on blogs and on webpages; people admire or criticise it, or even criticise people who admire it. Finally the food is cooked and consumed. What is the impact of this food? Is it sustainable? Is it nutritious? Does it contain residue toxins? Has its production had a negative impact on the livelihood of its producers?

Thinking in dichotomies, if food can be good, then food can be bad. But rather than trying to classify food as one or the other, perhaps it is more fruitful to dissolve the dichotomy and discuss the gliding scale between two extremes; along this scale, food can be more or less nutritious, it can be more or less healthy, and its production, transport and processing can be more or less destructive to the environment and the people living within this environment. If the food is wild its harvesting or hunting can be carried out without depletion of a particular species or ecosystem – or not. From an animal welfare point of view, the animals used for food can live decent lives in a natural environment protected from stress and pain, or they can be treated as a commodity without respecting them as sentient beings. Food is transformation, transforming a raw material into something edible. Various factors along this transformatory scale may influence how we may evaluate food: 'who carried out this transformation, how was it conducted, and where did the transformation take place?' Answering these questions brings us to the many dilemmas associated with global food systems, and it is becoming increasingly difficult to navigate among these dilemmas today. Eating has become a complex ethical act. A general – albeit short – definition of ethical consumption is: 'people purchasing and using products and resources according not only to the personal pleasures and values they provide, but also to ideas of what is right and good versus wrong and bad, in a moral sense' (Starr 2009:916). If we expand our focus to include food ethics, the sociologist Unni Kjærnes explains the recent turn in food ethics as a 'slowly changing morality of eating, mostly normalized, but sometimes with explicit moral and practical dilemmas' (Kjærnes 2012:151).

The present discourse concerning ethical eating is most often geared towards topics that have been aired publicly, and often through media channels. For instance, organic certification, local provenance and animal welfare are flagged as important. These concepts are comprehensible and tangible to most consumers, yet they are constantly renegotiated within the global food systems, as organic becomes increasingly industrial organic, and as locally produced food might be packaged far afield. A poignant question regarding local food is whether it operates in conflict with social justice campaigns to support fair trade food (Lyson 2007). People might feel incapable of action in such a complex situation, and examples like the ones given above are daily dilemmas for conscientious consumers. While food on the one hand can connect us to nature as we devour the elements of nature's bounty, food might just as well distance us from the same nature through the physical distance and lack of translucence or comprehension of global food systems, food politics and sustainability issues. A short yet useful definition of sustainability is: 'the ability to sustain right relationships between humans and earth in a manner conductive to both' (Cramer et al. 2011:320), and a question worth posing is whether good food is the same as sustainable food. When we apply the classical dimensions of sustainability – the social, the economic and the environmental issues – to the concepts of organic foods and seasonal foods, is the food good both on a collective and global scale as well as an individual and local scale? These questions become so intricate and so difficult to address that when celebrity chefs try to do so, they (and their fans) become easy targets for critique. Perhaps it is easy to criticise the new foodie-focus. What is perhaps less self-explanatory is why people are so receptive to this new take on food, something which I will explore below – following the anthropologist Marianne Lien's statement that what at first might seem to be debates about food might in fact be debates about something else (Lien and Nerlich 2004:8).

Nutrition and reproduction are considered primary needs; nevertheless, the most basic need of all is nutrition. In a cross section of societies people have always had to satisfy this basic need before attending to any other. In the overfed affluent west, food as a basic need is taken for granted and most of the practical issues related to procuring it have been thoroughly simplified for the consumer. This simplification has been driven by a series of agro-technological, industrial and commercial transformations that have been instrumental and preconditioning for the development of modern societies. Had it not been for these changes in how our society produces its food, most of the other societal developments of the twentieth century could not have taken place. The technological, sociological, commercial and cultural aspects of this process have contributed to create a success story in terms of the accessibility and ease in which we can find food: most people will simply go to a supermarket, fill a shopping trolley and pay for their food at the till. However, following classical Marxist theory or thinkers such as Raymond Williams and John Berger, one could claim that the distance or disconnection between the production and procurement of what we eat has created a sense of alienation – a problem the aforementioned Michael Pollan has also explored thoroughly through his writing. Pollan claims that Americans suffer from a national eating disorder (Pollan 2006:1) and questions why and how this has happened. One answer to this is offered by the historian Warren Belasco who argues that the food industry itself has deliberately[1] tried to obscure the links between farms and dinner tables. In the 1970s, livestock journals advised their readers to forget the pig as an animal and treat it like a machine in a factory (Belasco 2008:4). As a response to this, some people are trying to reconnect themselves to the food chain by seeking to understand and relate to agricultural issues, animal welfare and fossil fuels involved in transport. Reconnection thus both means understanding where and how the food was produced, and maybe even shortening the chain between field and food. But reconnection isn't the only driver. According to the sociologist Mara Miele, increased affluence in modern capitalist countries has created a new class of discerning food consumers who call for food commodities that are diverse (Murdoch and Miele 1999:469). They represent a new Vebleian order of consumers, demanding food to be healthy, small scale, sustainably sourced and ethically produced. In short, they demand good food and many of them have been told why they ought to demand it and what its consumption involves in the comfort of their armchair, through the gospel of celebrity chefs. Calling it a gospel might be considered a slight exaggeration, but the subtitle of the *Official Foodie Handbook* is after all *Be Modern, Worship Food* (Barr et al. 1985).

Although being inspired by a celebrity chef might seem like a passive action – and food consumption without being involved in any kind of food production is in itself in many ways a passive action – people in affluent societies do invest in civic, ethical and social concerns through their choices and practices. Accordingly, the food we consume is both part of choice and practice. When we choose a certain kind of food, and choose a certain way of eating this food, we embody our choices. As the food runs through our digestive tracts and becomes part of us, our choices become physical, shaping us or influencing us in concrete ways. But these same choices shape our identity, our social belonging and our cultural standing, something Bourdieu (1984) has explored thoroughly. And anyone who has read – or even read about – Proust will recall how the taste of madeleines dipped in linden tisane triggers Mr Swan's memory, and most of us have encountered the sensory experience of food memories ourselves. Food can carry our thoughts through temporal spheres. In short, food interweaves us both physically and mentally. According to Marianne Lien,

> Food may be followed through its various entanglements, across boundaries both legal and moral, beyond and between nations, bodies, persons and nutrients. If we do that, we will find that what appears as controversies about food often turns out to be controversies about something else.
>
> (Lien and Nerlich 2004:8)

Untangling these all-encompassing questions is beyond the scope of this chapter; nevertheless, I will use the platform of food studies to explore the concept of "good food". With this as a starting point, I will explore the role celebrity chefs have in transmitting cultural, social and ethical values. Our food-choices have the power to critique, support and label various ways of producing food actively.

From green food to growing food

Ordinary people in modern western societies invest in civic, ethical and social concerns through their choices and practices (Lewis 2008). Citizenship involves making choices about sustainable living, and even if most of us do not live sustainably, we can dream of sustainable lifestyles through what we watch and what we read. Green issues have been incorporated into mainstream lifestyle formats on TV – maybe due to the stresses and limitations of modern lifestyles. How do the celebrity chefs trigger people to behave in a particular way, and how is a georgic retreat to the countryside presented as the key to the good life? In this section, I will first present the empirical material showing how some celebrity chefs convey a certain green ethic, and move on to explore how the countryside and self-sufficiency ideals are presented as an antidote to alienation and decadence.

Although Hugh Fearnley-Whittingstall had been exposed to TV audiences before, it was the UK Channel 4 *Escape to River Cottage, Return to River Cottage* and *River Cottage Forever* that gave him real celebrity status. In the series, he produced everything himself, almost mimicking the humorous 1970s BBC series *The Good Life*. Most of Fearnley-Whittingstall's TV-series have been accompanied by books, and the same is true for the *River Cottage* series. The cookbooks that are published with the TV-series aim more or less explicitly to reacquaint the consumer with the food source. In the UK, *River Cottage* has become a bestselling manifesto and guidebook for choosing and storing food grown in the garden, butchered from prize animals and foraged or caught locally. Moreover, Fearnley-Whittingstall is an ardent defender of organic food production, and his books are not only containers for recipes. In the original introduction to the *River Cottage Cookbook*, the British TV-celebrity Hugh Fearnley-Whittingstall writes:

This book is written with a strong awareness that our current food production system leaves a great deal to be desired. Most of the meat we eat comes from industrially farmed animals that lead miserable lives and are fed on inappropriate diets. It is neither as tasty nor as healthy as it should be. Many of the fruit and vegetables that we consume are the products of intensive agriculture that pollutes the land that we live on and leaves unnecessary residues on and in the produce. I don't like that, and I know more and more people who feel the same way. This book is therefore also aimed at helping those who care about such issues make more informed choices. It's political, because if there are enough of us we can start to change the way things are done.

(Fearnley-Whittingstall 2001:48)

The quote above is taken from the first edition of *River Cottage* which was published in 2001, and Hugh Fearnley-Whittingstall labels it his most significant piece of work. In the introduction to the second edition, he writes that the book *River Cottage* was:

key in defining what I suppose you could call my mission in life. This was the first time I set out in print some of my most cherished beliefs and the first time I stuck my neck out on various issues.

(2011:11)

River Cottage explains and chronicles the pursuit of a more sustainable lifestyle through the recipes presented. In the second edition of the book, Hugh Fearnley-Whittingstall reflects on the many changes that took place in the decade between the first edition (2001) and the second edition (2011) of the book, particularly on issues of ethical consumerism and self-sufficiency.

Both Hugh Fearnley-Whittingstall and Jamie Oliver are British, but focussing on green issues is not limited to the UK. The Norwegian TV-celebrity and food writer Andreas Viestad is also trying to reconnect to the food chain, increase awareness of environmental damage and address animal welfare issues that are associated with industrial food production. Viestad wrote a book called *Ekte Mat* (Real Food) in 2010. Here he explains how he believes real food is about two things: the pleasure of eating good, wonderful and delicious food that not only satisfies our stomachs when we are hungry, but also provides wellbeing and happiness. He argues that real food is about meaning – if not the meaning of life, then the meaning of food (Viestad and Randem 2010:7). He is also the author of the book *Bærekraft til Bords* (Sustainability on the Table) (2011). In 2003, Viestad hosted the public TV-series, *New Scandinavian Cooking*. With 5 million US viewers per episode at the time, it was regarded as the greatest ever exposure of Norwegian culture, second only to the 1994 Lillehammer Olympics.[2] However, celebrity chefs have stretched the boundaries of their interest beyond the food itself. Interestingly, issues of sustainability are very often presented in a particular setting; namely on a farm, smallholding or in a kitchen garden. TV-viewers and readers are encouraged to take a baby step or giant leap towards the good life in a rural setting to live sustainably, and including a chicken or two is also encouraged:

> I find this flourishing of domestic poultry-keeping enormously encouraging. On the simplest level, it signifies that lots of people are producing a little more of their own food. And once you have a few chickens, you find yourself, almost without trying, living in a slightly more sustainable way: you give your kitchen scraps to the birds, they provide you with eggs of course but also manure, which is great on the compost heap and if you've got a compost heap, you're a step closer to growing even more of your own lovely fruit and vegetables.
>
> (Fearnley-Whittingstall 2011:22)

Hugh Fearnley-Whittingstall also claimed that his book *River Cottage*:

> really did mark a turning point for lots of people; it was a catalyst that encouraged them to do things a little differently. For some, that meant abandoning an urban life and launching into full-scale small-holding. For others, it was the growing of a few vegetables or the raising of a flock of chickens and ducks.
>
> (2011:13)

Although *River Cottage* might have been a turning point for ordinary people, it was also a trigger for many other chefs to follow suit. Six years after Hugh Fearnley-Whittingstall's *River Cottage* was first published, Jamie Oliver published *Jamie at Home: Cook Your Way to the Good Life* to accompany the TV-series with the same name. This TV-series was mainly about his vegetable plot and meat sourced locally and from shooting parties with his friends. Jamie Oliver explains the title to his book in this way:

> I grew up watching that TV programme "The Good Life" about Barbara and Tom, the couple who didn't have much but grew everything themselves. [. . .] My view is that we are all pretty spoilt now, as far as luxuries are concerned, but I reckon that the best luxury in life comes from experience and knowledge, and I think food and cooking are among the most important things out there for us to learn about.
>
> (2007:6)

Celebrity chefs convey variation over a rural theme, and this theme isn't limited to an Anglophone audience – Scandinavian chefs also promote the ideals of living the life in the countryside to reconnect to nature. Like Hugh Fearnley-Whittingstall, the Norwegian celebrity chef and food writer Andreas Viestad refers to a massive change in both his life and lifestyle when he decided to take on his uncle's old smallholding four hours south of Oslo. He now feels rooted, he feels anchored to the place and he has found meaning in life. In the TV-series

New Scandinavian Cooking, Andreas Viestad serves up – among other things – weeds and beef. The weeds are foraged by Miles Irving (described on the series' webpage as the world's foremost forager). The beef is locally sourced from neighbouring farms, and with this as a starting point Viestad creates Wild Norwegian Carpaccio, Grilled Sirloin with Forest Salad and Sunday Roast with Oxtail Sauce. Nature is omnipresent in the series, and this particular programme is both shot and presented from Viestad's country retreat – his idyllic farm south of Oslo.[3] In his book *Ekte Mat* (Real Food) he rhetorically asks his readers:

> I don't know whether you've tasted milk straight from the cow – squirted into your mouth from the cows' teat, or had a glass of fresh milk, still warm from the udder. Most people find this – the most natural thing in the world and not so different from the first thousand meals we had – a bit nasty. This is an example of how unnatural we sometimes find the natural.
>
> (Viestad and Randem 2010:125)

Another Scandinavian worth mentioning is Camilla Plum; a Danish good-lifer and celebrity chef with a strong no-nonsense approach British TV audiences might associate with the UK celebrity chef Clarissa Dickson Wright – if not for her size (Clarissa Dickson Wright's programme was called *Two Fat Ladies*) then for her presence. 'Today's program is about beef,' Camilla Plum says in episode 7 of *Den Sorte Gryde* (the Black Cauldron), as she leads a heifer alongside the steadings of her organic farm, which is also the venue of her cooking programmes. 'It's difficult looking into her big brown eyes and thinking about how delicious she would taste in a casserole, but this is actually what it's about' she says. The next episode in the series begins with the sound of a bleating black lamb, softly cradled in Camilla Plum's arms. She explains that:

> this lamb was born last night and will end up as lamb-chops and leg of lamb, something that might be a bit difficult to accept right now. All in all, we have a complicated relationship with the fact that we kill animals.

She then goes on to quote Gertrude Stein: 'Before every good meal, murder must *be done*.' A similar rural focus can be found in Camilla Plum's programme series *Fra Muld til Guld* (from Soil to Gold). The introduction to the first episode shows Camilla Plum in her kitchen garden, and it is practically impossible to hear her voice over the deafening sound of birdsong.[4]

Animals are an important presence in Andreas Viestad's food prose too. He explains to his readers that whenever he meets a chicken or pig that doesn't want to die, he is reminded that someone has to die for him to consume animal flesh, and he contemplates this every time he eats meat (Viestad and Randem 2010:10). Viestad states that every meal has a beginning. The beginning of a piece of meat is a living breathing animal that might have been treated well or might not have been treated so well. The beginning of mashed potatoes is a farmer and a field and an industrial or organic approach to farming. Whether the potato ends up as mash and leaves a trail of pesticides and insecticides in its wake or not, the actions leading up to this potato mash has significance and an environmental impact.

Another claim celebrity chefs make is that sustainable eating involves devouring the whole animal, including its offal. According to Hugh Fearnley-Whittingstall, 'Offal offers us a chance to pay our respect, in a full and holistic manner, to the animals we've raised for meat'. This he refers to as the hallmarks of 'animals more in tune with their environments, and farmers more fully and mutually engaged with their livestock' (2011:182). He explains how his first experience of taking home-reared animals to slaughter had made him feel not guilty, but anxious that everything should go according to plan, which it did:

> I went home that day with a bag of offal, a bucket of blood and a clear conscience. Back at River Cottage I made black pudding and fried a sliver of liver for my supper. The next time I saw my two pigs they were hanging in a butcher's cold room four days later. By that time I had really forgotten all about their charming personalities; they were nothing more nor less than the raw materials for a very exciting culinary challenge. I couldn't wait to get cracking. And, indeed, crackling.
>
> (2011:183)

Concluding the empirical part of this chapter, it might be worth asking whether the present zeitgeist reflects an excessive preoccupation with food and the cultural meanings we assign to food. The following section will discuss these matters.

Campaigning for green domestic happiness

Celebrity chefs argue that people ought to reconnect with food, and they advocate the choice to do so through the double helix of another choice: the good life. This may not be a surprising choice – according to the anthropologists Lien and Nerlich (2004:8) 'the controversies and ideologies of food are really controversies about how to live a good life'. By cooking on a gas burner in natural surroundings or in a kitchen suitably close to a vegetable plot, celebrity chefs both convey the dream of the good life and show us how to get there. They encourage their viewers to cook, which according to Pollan gives us the power to convert grains, vegetables and meat in a way that transforms us from simple consumers to creative producers (Pollan 2013). However, the food production that viewers are encouraged to take part in does not solely involve cooking, but also growing their own food. The turn back to nature via the vegetable plot is becoming increasingly popular, and is even catching on in urban areas – rooftop farming and guerrilla gardeners are appearing in towns and cities in both affluent and less affluent societies. People are encouraged both to re-establish the links from the vegetable plot to the dinner table and re-establishing the links between animals and meat. This recent turn back to nature, back to the farm, towards the good old days when life was simpler and food chains shorter can be understood as part of a tradition of self-sufficiency writing and practice. Ideals of self-sufficiency and country life have moved from being ridiculed (as a concern for people with a special, green "hippie-like" interest) to becoming part of mainstream concerns for an overheating planet. Parallel critical movements abound, like the Italian Slow Food (Miele and Murdoch 2002), the French cuisine de terroir, and a strong focus on meat that is sourced, prepared and consumed within local communities and regions. Often posed as critiques of industrially mass-produced food, these contributions argue that we need to reintroduce the idea of the vegetable plot, small-scale farming and edible animals into our cultural consciousness (see, for instance, Fearnley-Whittingstall 2001; 2004; Oliver 2007; Oliver et al. 2005; Viestad and Randem 2010; Plum 2010).

Growing one's own vegetables, keeping chickens and "going organic" has become an accepted, if not commonplace, ideology, and so has the idea of living an environmentally sustainable life. Nature's value as a retreat is thoroughly emphasised. According to the sociologist Klaus Eder (1996), environmentalism and the social construction of nature is a key index of social order and structure in modern society. Building on Keith Thomas, he claims that modern views of nature fall into two main camps: nature as the source of ultimate goodness, and nature as a source for human exploitation:

> The double symbolization of nature enters into the antagonism between cultivated land and wilderness. It produces the antagonism between dominance and protection of nature, and it produces the peculiar relationship to animals that is torn back and forth between meat and mercy. It is seen in housing, recreation, and, above all, food.

> (Eder 1996:147)

Thus nature can be seen as exploited through industrial agriculture, or protected as a retreat for people eager to get their fingernails dirty. The recent turn towards "food nostalgia" – portrayed by celebrity chefs and writers like Hugh Fearnley-Whittingstall or Jamie Oliver in Great Britain, Camilla Plum in Denmark and Andreas Viestad in Norway – might offer a compromise; a re-negotiation of domination and protection, a post-modern interpretation of self-sufficiency writing and practice. According to T. Lewis, the TV-shows 'all emphasise the links between locality and food, often demonstrating a nostalgia for traditions of cooking that have become "endangered" by the rise of industrial and globalised food practises' (Lewis 2008:232).

However, the concern runs deeper than Hugh Fearnley-Whittingstall's first TV-series, and one can easily trace the ideas of the good life as a rural retreat far back to antiquity and the georgic genre. But celebrity chefs are undoubtedly inspired by the writing and thinking of John Seymour.[5] Seymour (1914–2004) was a writer, broadcaster, environmentalist, smallholder and activist. In his best-known book, *The Complete Book of Self-Sufficiency* (1976), he tried to show how living in harmony with nature was a simpler and more satisfying way of life, and believed that industrial food production not only alienated consumers, but also compromised the food's quality:

Because the sources of our food are getting further away from our tables and the food goes through more and more industrial processing, the only quality now deemed important is shelf life. Such food is dead food: all the life has been taken out of it.

(Seymour and Sutherland 2002:13)

The TV-shows and cookbooks convey a yearning for the past, which might be in tune with how many people feel about the impersonal scale of the global food systems and the lack of sustainability and animal welfare that might be associated with these systems. Warren Belasco (2006) claims that the food movement we see today has emerged from the food counterculture evident in the late 1960s and early 1970. Seymour was a strong voice in the British version of this counter-culture. During the years that have passed since Seymour referred to "dead" food, the industrialisation, globalisation and "big-food" power of food production has escalated far beyond the situation in the 1970s. As increased urbanisation has enlarged the divide between food production and consumption, the sources of food are even harder to track. The distance which has been created is amplified, as fewer people know how to actually prepare food unless it is ready sliced or chopped for the pot and wrapped in Styrofoam containers. Media scholar Tania Lewis explains that lifestyle TV shows focussing on food are often 'demonstrating a nostalgia for tradition of cooking that have become "endangered" by the rise of industrialized and globalized food practices' (Lewis 2008:232.) This is particularly evident in the case of meat.

Focussing on sustainable meat from grazing animals rather than the environ-mentally more problematic industrial beef production is also a recuperation of (seemingly) pre-industrial animal relations. Under the industrial agricultural regime, awareness of where our meat actually comes from has become nebulous. Perhaps this isn't so surprising, as – according to Belasco – the meat packing industry's main concern during the last 150 years 'has been to insulate consumers from any contact with the disassembly of warm-blooded mammals into refrigerated, plastic-wrapped chops and patties' (2008:4). The French anthropologist and philosopher Noelie Vialles explains how industrial agricultural systems demand a certain compartmentalisation that conceals the connection between animals and meat. In her book *Animal to Edible* (1994) she explores how the act of killing an animal is divided into several operations, each performed by a designated worker, so that, in the end, one cannot really tell who actually does the killing. Accordingly, the human alienation towards nature touched upon above becomes complete. Animals are 'treated as raw material' and 'processed like manufactured commodities' (Berger 1980:11) in the industrial food systems.[6] Animals have even disappeared from traditional cookbooks in Norway (Syse and Bjørkdahl 2012), but they have been reintroduced with full force in the TV-celebrities cookbooks (see for instance Fearnley-Whittingstall 2001; 2004; Oliver 2007; Oliver et al. 2005; Viestad 2011; Viestad and Randem 2010; Plum 2010). Again, it might be interesting to link these attempts at reconnection to the animal source of meat to what Belasco coined as the food counterculture. The animal studies scholar Jovian

Parry, has coined this particular kind of reconnection to the animal source of our food "meat nostalgia". He argues that taking part in slaughter is a rejection of trivial urban sentimentalism and is part of a sentimental and nostalgic yearning for a pre-industrial pastoral utopia. Parry also analyses the role celebrity chefs like Jamie Oliver and Hugh Fearnley-Whittingstall play in the propagation of these ideologies (Parry 2009). Like Andreas Viestad and Camilla Plum, they encourage eating the whole animal rather than just the best cuts and explain that this is a sustainable choice, thus cementing green ideals with the ideal of returning to the countryside, where finding these whole animals is tangible.

Moving to the countryside is not a possible choice for the vast majority of people, and it is even practically impossible for everyone to have their own urban vegetable garden or allotment. So is good food for all or just for a financial elite? Although economic privilege facilitates access to organic or fair trade food, cultural capital gives access to food decision making (Bourdieu 1984). According to Johnston et al. (2011:293): 'Ethical eating constitutes a cultural repertoire shaped by factors such as class and ethno-cultural background, and symbolic boundaries are drawn through eating practices'. Hugh Fearnley-Whittingstall does not believe this critique is justified: 'Some people think that this local, seasonal, organic approach to food is just for the privileged few; but I think it's relevant to everybody and I am ready to put my passion and principles to the test'.[7]

Hugh Fearnley-Whittingstall's goal is to encourage his readers and viewers to become less dependent on industrially produced food, to support farmers' markets and other local food initiatives, and to harvest their own wild food from hedgerows and forests. Naturally he doesn't make his living as a smallholder but as a TV presenter and writer and can afford to indulge in various luxuries. Nevertheless, he claims that his sense of what true luxury is has changed:

> Picking blackberries in the hedgerow in high summer, and trampling the wild garlic in early spring, buying a huge cod from Jack's boat in West Bay for just a few quid; netting eels in the River Brit; committing infanticide on my own baby broad beans; picking elderflower; bartering eggs for cider; these are my new luxuries.
>
> (Fearnley-Whittingstall 2011:51)

They are luxuries that just about everyone can afford; an alternative form of hedonism – as Kate Soper has so aptly coined these pleasures.

You aren't what you eat

Is there a danger of overemphasising the individual choices of a small affluent segment in society by applauding their sustainable choices? In Britain, maybe the crassest critique stems from *The Guardian*'s columnist Steven Poole. He argues that foodies – or foodists as he prefers to call them – bask in a 'private warm glow of moral righteousness' and claims that small-scale ethical food consumption diverts emphasis away from collective action in a global world and offers nothing in its place (Poole 2012:123). He also argues that 'The mission to save the planet comes at the expense of a lot less fortunate people struggling right now to live on it' (ibid.:119). By eating food grown locally one does not contribute to global trade, nor does one help farmers in the global south find a market for their produce. A similar critique is posed by the scholars Johnston and Bauman, who claim that 'the North American food discourse focusses a lot on environmental issues while mainly ignoring questions about hunger, social justice or agricultural labor' (Johnston and Bauman 2010:139–140). However, the critique that seems to be most prevalent, or at least obvious, is that the new trend in food consumption is not available for all and that the ability to cook at leisure depends on both a physical and cultural distance from both economic and temporal constraints. Steven Poole indicates that food nostalgia and organically sourced food is a snobbish idea hipsters indulge in (Poole 2012). Poole's polemic echoes scholars who point to similar problems in academic terms, such as Johnston et al. who argue that:

> Many so-called ethical products – organic produce, grass-fed meat, fair trade coffee, free-range eggs – are more expensive than their conventional counterparts. In addition, many of the shopping and eating spaces articulating a discourse of ethical consumption, such as Whole Food Market, are positioned to serve economic elites.
>
> (2011:294)

One may question whether this elite wants to save the world without really trying. According to Poole, eating for change is an idea embraced by organic-loving yuppy locavores with no connection to reality (Poole 2012:119). Critics are most probably right when they say it is utopic to believe that everyone can retreat to houses or second homes in the countryside, and for most people this idea might be a pleasant daydream rather than a realistic alternative to everyday life (Cramer et al. 2011:85). Watching or reading about celebrity chefs procure and cook food in rural surroundings might indeed embrace a certain kind of escapism. Do the TV celebrities actions in any way represent tangible ideals for the public to follow? According to Steven Poole, TV-chefs seem to live in a different world. They never visit supermarkets but farmers markets, farms or food stalls. Purchasing food directly from the farm or food stall is presented as interactive social exchanges, with banter and cordiality on both sides of these exchanges. The social exchanges on the one hand emphasise the links between locality and food, and on the other hand they, in a naïve way, demonstrate a nostalgia for the past before the accelerating force of modernity dissolved time and space (Giddens 1990) and alienated us all from nature (Williams 1973).

When Hugh Fearnley-Whittingstall encourages his audience and readers to eat more organically grown vegetables and sustainably sourced food, refers to "endangered meat traditions" and encourages consumers in general to reconnect with the food source, is this an honest agenda or candid entertainment? Ironically, there has never been so much information and talking about cooking on TV and people spend an amazing amount of time watching foodie-TV, yet few people actually spend time cooking. According to an OECD report from 2011, the average American spends as little as 30 minutes per day cooking (this includes cleaning up). Other OECD countries spend 52 minutes doing the same, which still isn't a lot compared to the time it takes to watch an episode of Jamie Oliver or Camilla Plum prepare a meal on TV. Another poignant question is whether the focus on eating locally produced food is selective. Air miles might be easier to swallow if people are not asked to give up everyday indulgences like chocolate, coffee, tea and wine. Maybe the focus on ethical food is a new kind of luxury, an interest or activity pursued at leisure, when it is convenient, in the comfort of the armchair. The celebrity chefs can be accused of producing comfort porn, providing readers and viewers with a dream of domestic self-sufficiency in a well-equipped home insulated from the terror and "austerity" of the world outside (Poole 2012:122). One could also question whether the kind of foraging TV-celebrities encourage – be it in farm shops or in the larder of nature – is simply a day trip escape, providing escapism and entertainment both as one watches and as one forages. Ironically, while the TV-celebrities themselves criticise super-markets, global food chains and modern consumption practices, they are also part and parcel of the consumption through their own commercial activity. For instance, Jamie Oliver has his own brand of "Food and home" products, his own food-line sold in supermarkets, his own seeds and his own glossy magazine called, poignantly, *Jamie Magazine* (publishing ten editions per year). Hugh Fearnley-Whittingstall's *River Cottage* and Camilla Plum's organic seeds service are also commercial ventures at the end of the day. But is there more at stake?

Baby greens out with the bathwater

Although some of the critique presented above is just and important to discuss, it is important not to throw the baby out with the bathwater. Focussing on values that oppose pollutants, that minimise fossil fuels by reducing food miles, and that maintain the social values of local food markets, creates both awareness to what food production is and makes us more resilient and demanding towards prevailing global food systems. Facing the environmental problems of the twenty-first century, curbing our urge to increase consumption is necessary. Alternative lifestyles, de-growth rather than growth and a focus on environmental values undoubtedly benefit an overheating planet. As mentioned above, Kate Soper has introduced the term "alternative hedonism", advocating the simple joys of life. Chasing the good life in the country is another form of alternative hedonism, spending one's extra time and money on home-grown or organic local food rather than expensive cars, for instance. This does not excuse the commercial apparatus that some of the celebrity chefs create, yet if you scale up the good and the bad associated with their message, the good seems to weigh heavier on the scale. Claiming that the focus on ethical food consumption is only for the well-off is also questionable – indeed stating that belonging to a lower social class automatically indicates that one does not know about, care about or engage with moral issues about eating. People who are not well-off can gain "green" cultural capital in other ways, for instance, by eating less meat and less ready-made food. Johnston et al. call this approach creative adaptation to dominant ethical eating repertoires (2011:312). Marte Giæver's thesis (2014) studying sustainable food consumption in London also supports the claim that motivations for choosing to eat sustainably sourced food goes beyond the classical class boundaries.

Through TV-shows and cookbooks, celebrity chefs present both modern society as broken and the earth as damaged through industrial food systems, with need for political and social healing. That they succeed in conveying their message can be confirmed by the number of people signing up to campaigns like Hugh's Fish Fight and the fact that Jamie Oliver was awarded an MBE. Cramer's (et al. 2011:320) definition of sustainability – an ability to sustain right relationships between humans and the earth in a manner conductive to both – is what celebrity chefs point their audiences in the direction of by focussing on the good life. Many people yearn for a time when people had both the physical and social connection to food production, farmers and their livestock, and promoting a reconnection to this creates a culture of awareness. People might feel paralysed trying to respond to global food issues, yet focussing on ethical eating gives people a chance to support an environmental agenda. A challenge in this respect might be to find a balance between reconnecting to the chain of food and disconnecting from society at large.

People like Jamie Oliver, Hugh Fearnley-Whittingstall, Andreas Viestad and Camilla Plum play an important role in making green issues mainstream. They create awareness of animal welfare, organic produce and even the joys of growing your own vegetables, fishing your own fish or eating the whole animal without wasting any part of it. They convey the bonus of being outdoors and spending time and effort cooking for friends and family rather than purchasing processed food which might have had a negative environmental impact. This awareness can extend beyond one's own back yard, and in turn can affect things like pesticide use, animal ethics and sustainable food production. It can even create social meeting places and better lives. Gardening is both a social, contemplative and healthy activity. In this way, the celebrity chefs convey both a way of life and a reconnection with the natural process of food production that may benefit both the environment and the psyche. Hugh Fearnley-Whittingstall claims that 'the way we choose to feed ourselves can make a huge difference – to ourselves, to our families, friends and neighbours, and to the world around us' (Fearnley-Whittingstall 2011:13). After all, chasing a rural idyll and coupling it with ethical food consumption – even conspicuous ethical food consumption – is a form of alternative hedonism which if not totally harmless, is less harmful than other types of conspicuous consumption. The celebrity chefs point us in the direction of other values, which echo John Seymour's words first written in 1961, but are all the more urgent facing the serious environmental issues we need to deal with today: 'It is time to cut out what we do not need so we can live more simply and happily. Good food, comfortable clothes, serviceable housing and true culture – those are the things that matter' (Seymour and Sutherland 2002:9).

Notes

1   www.norden.org/en/news-and-events/news/new-nordic-food-at-the-un-cooking-for-a-sustainable-future (accessed 9 June 2014).
2   www.dn.no/vinguiden/2004/09/18/norsk-tvserie-verden-rundt (accessed 9 June 2014).
3   www.newscancook.com/tv-series-guide/episode-3-close-to-home/ (accessed 9 June 2014).
4   Both series are available online at www.dr.dk/DR2/camillaplum/og-den-sorte-gryde/Udsendelser/udsendelser-oversigt.htm#/7792 and www.dr.dk/DR2/camillaplum/fra-muld-til-guld/#/46603 (accessed 9 June 2014).
5   John Seymour's *The Complete Book of Self-Sufficiency* is in the reading list of Hugh Fearnley-Whittingstall's *River Cottage*, as well as in Andreas Viestad's *Ekte Mat*.
6   John Berger is, along with John Seymour, listed in Andreas Viestad's bibliography – and so is Vergil's *Georgics*.
7   "River Cottage Treatment EP01 PRT1" (Video upload). YouTube. Google, Inc. (Retrieved 6 January 2013.)

Bibliography

Barr, A., Levy, P. and Dale, D. (1985) *The Official Foodie Handbook: Be Modern, Worship Food*. London: Doubleday.
Belasco, W. (2006) *Appetite for Change: How the Counterculture Took on the Food Industry*. Ithaca, NY: Cornell University Press.
Belasco, W. (2008) *Food: The Key Concepts*. Oxford, New York: Berg.
Berger, J. (1980) *About Looking*. New York: Pantheon Books.
Bourdieu, P. (1984) *Distinction: A Social Critique of the Judgement of Taste*. London: Routledge and Kegan Paul.
Cramer, J.M., Greene, C.P. and Walter, L.M. (eds) (2011) *Food as Communication: Communication as Food*. New York: Peter Lang Incorporated.
Douglas, M. (1966) *Purity and Danger: An Analysis of Concepts of Pollution and Taboo*. London: Routledge and Kegan Paul.
Eder, K. (1996) *The Social Construction of Nature: A Sociology of Ecological Enlightenment*. London: Sage.
Farquhar, J. (2006) 'Food, Eating and the Good Life' in Tilley, C., Keane, W., Kuechler, S., Rowlands, M. and Spyer, P. (ed) *Handbook of Material Culture*. London – Thousand Oaks – New Delhi: Sage Publications. pp. 145–160.
Fearnley-Whittingstall, H. (2004) *The River Cottage Meat Book*. London: Hodder & Stoughton.
Fearnley-Whittingstall, H. (2001) *The River Cottage Cookbook*, 1st edn. London: Harper Collins Publishers Limited.
Fearnley-Whittingstall, H. (2011) *The River Cottage Cookbook*, 2nd edn. London: Harper Collins Publishers Limited.
Giæver, M.E. (2014) *Eating for the Planet: Exploring Sustainable Food Consumption in London*. Oslo: University of Oslo.
Giddens, A. (1990) *The Consequences of Modernity*. Cambridge: Polity Press.
Johnston, J. and Baumann, S. (2010) *Foodies: Democracy and Distinction in the Gourmet Foodscape*. New York and London: Routledge.
Johnston, J., Szabo, M. and Rodney, A. (2011) 'Good Food, Good People: Understanding the Cultural Repertoire of Ethical Eating' in *Journal of Consumer Culture*, 11. pp. 293–318.
Kjærnes, U. (2012) 'Ethics and Action: A Relational Perspective on Consumer Choice in the European Politics of Food' in *Journal of Agricultural and Environmental Ethics*, 25. pp. 145–162.

Lévi-Strauss, C. (1964/1969) *The Raw and the Cooked*. Chicago: University of Chicago Press.

Lévi-Strauss, C., Weightman, J. and Weightman, D. (1969/1990) *The Origin of Table Manners*. Chicago: University Of Chicago Press.

Lewis, T. (2008) 'Transforming Citizens? Green Politics and Ethical Consumption on Lifestyle Television' in *Continuum*, 22. pp. 227–240.

Lien, M.E. and Nerlich, B. (2004) *The Politics of Food*. Oxford: Berg.

Lyson, T.A. (2007) 'Civic Agriculture and the North American Food System' in Hinrichs, C.C. and Lyson, T.A. (eds) *Remaking the North American Food System: Strategies for Sustainability*. Lincoln and London: University of Nebraska Press. pp. 19–32.

Miele, M. and Murdoch, J. (2002) 'The Practical Aesthetics of Traditional Cuisines: Slow Food in Tuscany' in *Sociologia Ruralis*, 42. pp. 312–328.

Murdoch, J. and Miele, M. (1999) '"Back to Nature": Changing "Worlds of Production" in the Food Sector' in *Sociologia Ruralis*, 39. pp. 465–483.

OECD (2011) *Society at a Glance 2011: OECD Social Indicators*, OECD Publishing. doi: 10.1787/soc_glance-2011-en

Oliver, J., Loftus, D. and Terry, C. (2005) *Jamie's Italy*. London: Michael Joseph.

Oliver, J. (2007) *Jamie at Home: Cook Your Way to the Good Life*. London: Penguin Group.

Parry, J. (2009) 'Oryx and Crake and the New Nostalgia for Meat' in *Society and Animals*, 17. pp. 241–256.

Plum, C. (2010) *The Scandinavian Kitchen*. London: Kyle Books.

Pollan, M. (2006) *The Omnivore's Dilemma: The Search for a Perfect Meal in a Fast-Food World*. London: Bloomsbury.

Pollan, M. (2013) *Cooked: A Natural History of Transformation*. London: Allen Lane, Penguin Group.

Poole, S. (2012) *You Aren't What You Eat: Fed up with Gastroculture*. London: Scribe Publications.

Richards, A. (1932/2004) *Hunger and Work in a Savage Tribe: A Functional Study of Nutrition Among the Southern Bantu*. London and New York: Routledge.

Seymour, J. (1976) *The Complete Book of Self-Sufficiency*. London: Faber & Faber.

Seymour, J. and Sutherland, W. (2002) *The New Complete Book of Self-Sufficiency*. London: Dorling Kindersley.

Starr, M. (2009) 'The Social Economics of Ethical Consumption: Theoretical Considerations and Empirical Evidence' in *The Journal Of Socio-Economics*, 38. pp. 916–925.

Syse, K.V.L. and Bjørkdahl, K. (2012) 'Dyret i Kogebogen' in Gjerris, M. (ed.) *Kød*. Copenhagen: Tiderne Skifter. pp. 93–106.

Vialles, N. (1994) *Animal to Edible*. Cambridge: Cambridge University Press.

Viestad, A. (2011) *Bærekraft til Bords*. Oslo: Wittusen og Jensen.

Viestad, A. and Randem, M. (2010) *Ekte Mat*. Oslo: Cappelen Damm.

Williams, R. (1973) *The Country and the City*. London: Chatto and Windus.

11 Follow the food

How eating and drinking shape our cities

Jesper Pagh

Introduction

During the last decade, food has moved centre stage in urban design and planning. Not in the sense that we shape our cities to secure or ease food distribution or that regional planning ensuring sufficient agricultural land for future sustainable food production gets much attention. These matters are often brought forward and discussed in academia and in books such as *Hungry City* (Steel 2009) or exhibitions such as the world traveller *Hungry Planet* (Menzel and d'Aluisio 2007) but hardly have any influence on the daily debate. Rather, the pivotal point is the way we consume and experience food and how this encourages spending, stimulating the economic growth we take for granted as indispensable.

To be more accurate, instead of food as such, one might say it is the eating and drinking of it that has moved centre stage. With 'hungry', the titles of the above-mentioned works explicitly refer to the fundamental and vital need for food to survive, which in our part of the world has long been superseded by abundance and gluttony. Eating and drinking plays an important part in fulfilling both our physiological needs and our need for self-actualization – and as such is no longer a private matter achieved through daily struggle, but a part of our performance in public space.

Combined with a need for authenticity and a turn towards the local and seasonal in some of the world's finest restaurants specifically and in the global gourmet discourse in general, this leads to several paradoxes and contradictions. The examples are legion – one recent and obvious example is the food tourism trend, which gets this dry and precise comment in a blog by a master student at the University of Oslo:

> The most pervasive trends in fine dining right now is local, seasonal and sustainable – so isn't it ironic that people will travel halfway around the world to taste what's on offer? The food may be local, but the diners are not.
>
> (Medaas 2013)

Uncommented and with no critique or tongue-in-cheek, the lifestyle magazine *Monocle* is perhaps one of the best places to follow the somewhat odd combination of fashion, food, luxury consumption, globalization, authenticity, tradition, politics, design and business – all wrapped up in glossy images of the young, the rich and the beautiful living the good life in the womb of Mother Earth – blissfully emancipated from lies, power and corruption.

Food and the city

In the urban fabric this can be observed in several ways: Local corner shops are taken over by city-, country- or worldwide chains of luxury burger bars, coffee shops, juice joints, bakeries and the like. Instead of offering their own personal, local specialties, these new businesses market 'quality' in terms of standardized, painstakingly odd-named products – often just replacing traditional names for the exact same thing. Or they take over products like the traditional Danish open sandwich smørrebrød (which was previously a standard product available in a cafeteria on every other street corner to eat in or take out – the working man's preferred and cheap lunch) and turn them into a luxury product for the urban upper middle class. If one thought that irony and distance was so 1990s, this hipsterization of random commodities and phenomena goes to prove otherwise. This can make the regular and trivial hard to track down and lead to awkward situations if you just preferred a traditional and regular commodity, as here observed by the Danish daily *Politiken*'s satirical columnist Listen (literally: 'The List') under the headline 'Old School Delicious':

"A cup of black coffee, please."

"You mean an americano, right?"

"No, we don't you barista amoeba. We mean black, ample and bitter like a neglected housewife".

(*Politiken* 2013, own translation)

Much could be said about this – about experience economy, gentrification, displacement and much more. In this chapter, however, it is the field of urban planning and spatial design, which too has been influenced by these developments, that is in focus. Special attention will be given to the design and use of spaces and places for food trade and consumption.

One thing is that a privately run bakery today is no longer just a place you go to pick up a loaf of bread, but to a great extent is (also) a place to eat the produce – a boutique carefully designed with large windows facing the street, prompting you to exhibit your business as you consume their goods. Another thing is when private and public affairs are mixed together, and the combination of commercial needs, a profound longing for the good life, and an unspecified need for a sense of authenticity and community perhaps long lost, meet contemporary urban planning's agendas for public life, sustainability and experiences, leading to a slippery slope of privatization and segregation – intended or not – under cover of urban regeneration and thoughtful planning for the common good. With Torvehallerne Market in Copenhagen as the main example, this is what this chapter tries to shed a light on, by taking a closer look at the design, its intentions and conditions.

The structure of the chapter

The chapter is organized around the example of Torvehallerne Market in Copenhagen, which opened in 2011 after almost 15 years of preceding work by the Food Market Guild, initiated by the architect Hans Peter Hagens, owner of the architectural office Arkitekturværkstedet (literally: The Architecture Workshop). To provide some context and perspective for this example, two other examples are introduced: Koncerthuset (the Danish Broadcasting Corporation's Concert Hall) and the town of Frederikssund, some 40 km outside of Copenhagen. These two examples are not analysed individually, but serve to illustrate how the circumstances concerning Torvehallerne Market are not unique but can be seen elsewhere in planning too – and vice versa, to illustrate how consequences of planning observed elsewhere can provide a better understanding of what is going on in and around Torvehallerne Market. Moreover, the three examples represent an urban space, a single building and a whole town.

Following this, I will give a brief introduction to the history and theory of architecture since the early twentieth century. This serves to deepen the understanding of the role of the architect before moving forward to analyse the example of Torvehallerne Market through three different lenses. These analytical lenses I have called 'Experiences, Public Space and Economic Growth', 'Vagabond Capitalism and Tourist Urbanism' and 'Ethics, Responsibility and Apparent Objectivity'. This leads to a concluding discussion about the increasing capitalization of public space and the role of the architect herein.

However, as it is very much the architect and architecture that are in focus in this chapter, I would like to briefly introduce what I consider a very central theme in this discussion, namely *the market turn* within architecture as it has appeared during the past 30 years or so.

Architecture and the role of the architect

Scandinavian architecture in the twentieth century is inextricably linked with the development of the welfare state. The welfare state developed in the post-war years – a period often referred to as a golden age in Scandinavian architecture – and its landmarks are still standing today: The housing projects, schools, libraries, town halls, sports halls, etc. from this period are a substantial part of our cultural heritage. As pointed out by Gøsta Esping-Andersen (1990), the Scandinavian welfare model is characterized by a high degree of state intervention in daily life requiring a comprehensive institutionalization – both in the structural and material sense. Realizing the Scandinavian model thus would not have been possible without the engagement of architects, and the contributions from the profession to society have often been pointed out (Faber 1963; Jørgensen 2004; Dirckinck-Holmfeld et al. 2007; Creagh et al. 2008; Mattsson and Wallenstein 2010; Pagh 2013b).

Today, however, architects in general have turned their attention from the social to the financial aspects of housing and planning – from the community to the market (Vindum 2010; Kvorning 2010). The first and foremost question today is not how the architect can contribute to improving society, but how he can contribute to improving the client's profit. 'We live, after all, in a world in which the rights of private property and the profit rate trump all other notions of rights' as David Harvey puts it (2008:23). Though the architecture, I will argue, has suffered from this turn, the architects have survived and during the 2000s even prospered as perhaps never before. But for what, and for how long?

> The position of the European Architect is less exceptional than it used to be, and is fast becoming as marginal as in the rest of the world. Because more and more in Europe, as in for example China, all that is expected from an architect is a sketch or a preliminary design, which can act as a lever or springboard to get the project off the ground, a project in which both the architect and the architecture are soon regarded as quantités négligeables. This marginal position is incompatible with the self-image of the architect as all-rounder whose activities will, if not deliver a better world, make the world a better place.
>
> (Ibelings 2012:54)

Ibelings is a Dutch art historian and architecture critic, and in his recent book, co-authored with the architecture studio Powerhouse Company, he paints a dystopian picture of the future of the architectural profession by pointing out that it may actually be architects alone who would not be able to imagine a world without architecture, as we know it.

We shape our buildings . . .

At this point it might be relevant to ask why architecture should mean anything to anyone else but architects in the first place. First of all, we must recognize architecture as a discipline within the arts, directly related to design, which is often considered a sub-discipline of architecture – or vice versa.

In an oft-cited article, Buchanan describes how extensively design affects contemporary life and describes 'the four broad areas in which design is explored throughout the world by professional designers and many others who may not regard themselves as designers' (1992:9) as symbolic and visual communication, material objects, activities and organized services, and complex systems or environments for living, working, playing and learning. To put it short, design shapes our physical environment in a broad context.

As any planning effort in society – be it within politics or economy – is sooner or later reflected in our physical environment, the quality of the design hereof is of course of utmost importance. Moreover, not only are political and economic prioritizations reflected in the physical environment, the physical environment in turn has a great impact on the practices of our everyday lives and what thereof follows. Winston Churchill said as much at the occasion of an award ceremony for the Architectural Association in London in 1924: 'There is no doubt whatever about the influence of architecture and structure upon human character and action. We make our buildings and afterwards they make us. They regulate the course of our lives' (Brand 1995:3).

A modern architectonic art

From this understanding of architecture and design we see that although its main activity is shaping things, its scope and impact is much wider than this. In an essay written at the time of his accession at the Harvard Graduate School of Design in 1937, Walter Gropius – one of the founders of the German Bauhaus who had a significant influence on the development of European and international modernism – argues for an understanding of design as a liberal art:

> The Bauhaus was inaugurated in 1919 with the specific object of realizing a modern architectonic art, which like human nature was meant to be all-embracing in its scope. [. . .] Our guiding principle was that design is neither an intellectual nor a material affair, but simply an integral part of the stuff of life, necessary for everyone in a civilized society.
>
> (Gropius 1962[1937]:9)

This modern architectonic art is nowadays often referred to as design thinking, covering the application of 'designerly ways of knowing' (Cross 2006), addressing what Rittel and Webber (1973) described as wicked problems. Rittel and Webber's description of wicked problems can be compared to the formulation of an equation with an indefinite number of unknowns: Wicked problems are indeterminate and therefore 'there is no definitive formulation of a wicked problem' (ibid.:161). Trying to solve a wicked problem by reducing it to a clear and specific formulation is cheating, just like reducing the unknowns in the equation by guessing would be. Architects have the programme, the site and the building technology to relate to and restrain their work, but that can never lead to one and only one solution.

Architects and designers, interestingly, often point out that it is the restraints that enable them to come up with creative, innovative and disruptive solutions. If there are no restraints, anything is possible, and when anything is possible, often nothing is accomplished.

From Rittel and Webber's description of the wicked problems also follows that 'there is always more than one explanation, with explanations depending on the Weltanschauung of the designer', as Buchanan puts it (1992:16), which for a start offers a perhaps very banal explanation of the turn of attention from the social to the financial aspects of housing and planning: Does it simply have to do with the preceding decades' neoliberalization? Neoliberalization, which according to David Harvey (2009:33), 'has meant, in short, the financialization of everything', and has 'deepened the hold of finance over all other areas of the economy, as well as over the state apparatus and [. . .] daily life'.

This financialization of everything is central for understanding the Torvehallerne Market, and the ways in which this financialization materializes – not only through bricks and mortar, but significantly through the meaning and function of architecture – will be the main target for the following analysis. Let us first, however, take a closer look at the examples up for discussion.

Examples

The example of the Torvehallerne Market is – like Koncerthuset and Frederikssund – not a unique one. Rather all three examples are more or less generic; a vast number of similar cases can be found all over the world. They are significant by being – I will argue – examples of the consequences of an increased focus on experiences and consumption in urban planning, and of the architects' orientation towards the market in favour of the community, and as such serve to understand the nature of this turn.

Torvehallerne Market

> The keywords are quality, freshness and availability for the pleasure and benefit of everyone – from producer to consumer. A regular destination for the city dwellers and visitors from near and far.
>
> (Torvehallerne 2012; own translation)

Torvehallerne is a food market in the centre of Copenhagen, inaugurated on 2 September 2011. It is a result of a citizen-led initiative introduced by the architect Hans Peter Hagens through the Food Market Guild set up to provide the foundation for the market. Torvehallerne Market started as an idea put forward by Hagens in *Politiken* in 1997, and the aim was to create a public market like the ones known from Barcelona, London and even Stockholm, which were not – and had never been – present in Copenhagen. The original idea was to create:

> a compelling jumble of indoor and outdoor stalls with regional fruit and vegetables, all kinds of Danish apples, pears, plums and cherries, vegetables, Nordic mushrooms, berries from the forest, the fields and the shore, honey from all corners of the country, eggs and lots more.
>
> (Hagens 2012; own translation)

The food market was erected on the public square, Israels Plads, in the centre of Copenhagen which until the 1950s had held an open air vegetable market and is directly connected with the most busy train station in the city – a prime spot for attracting customers. After years of dispute in 2002, the City of Copenhagen passed a district plan for the project. In accordance with a decision made two years earlier, however, the municipality refused to put any money into it but required that funding and operating the market should be handled by a private party. After years of struggle to find a private investor, in October 2009 the municipality announced that the property developer Jeudan was granted the concession to develop and run Torvehallerne Market and in turn a 50-year lease on half of Israels Plads, designated for its construction. It was the municipality who turned to Jeudan and invited them to partake in the project. The company's role as owner of several buildings around Israels Plads obviously made them interested in the future upgrading and regeneration of the area.

In a concept document from 2006, the architect describes the vision of the market as a place where everybody can do their shopping. The concept document thoroughly describes how the everyday life will unfold in the realized Torvehallerne Market. It covers everything from the daily rhythm and the atmosphere in the covered market, location of the cold store, the type, mix and individual location of stall-keepers and their opening hours to a very detailed description of the design of the individual stalls in the market.

> A series of smaller invigorating eateries are planned: a tapas place, a sushi place, a soup and salad place, an oyster and wine place, a coffee and chocolate place, and a café open during day and evening – in tune with the operation hours of the Metro, just like the bakery and the coffee stalls will open up early in the morning when the trains start running.
>
> (Hagens 2006:2; own translation)

The concept document further describes how the market in itself will be an alternative to supermarkets and health campaigns through 'brisk business generated by local stall-keepers downgrading the additives [. . .] and substituting it with their own produce' (ibid.:3), which leads to the conclusion that Torvehallerne Market in its totality should be considered a Gesamtkunstwerk (a project where one architect has been responsible for the entirety of the design – from the urban context to the actual building, landscape, furniture, etc.). In the concept document, strong regulation with the market is applied, guaranteeing a large degree of day-to-day flexibility, taking for granted that there will always be an excess of stalls, opening it for:

> the beekeeper from Western Jutland, the potato farmer from Samsø, the plantation owner from Fejø and Mrs. Hansen who was in the forest in May to collect 100 bunches of windflowers [who] will all have the possibility to rent an outdoor stall and sell their goods directly to the consumer.
>
> (ibid.:5)

The document emphasizes the importance of dubbing the tenants 'stall-keepers' in favour of 'shop-keepers', as this is more in line with the overall concept for Torvehallerne Market, and it emphasizes the need for the tenants to primarily be smaller businesses, staffed by the owners themselves to create the right atmosphere of a market.

The concept document is based on research into European market halls carried out by the Food Market Guild, but apart from a reference to the price level in Stockholm's and Göteborg's Saluhaller, the direct use of this research material is scarce and unreferenced.

The realized food market is mainly indoors, divided into separate shops, housing primarily high-end food stores, franchises of major brands and expensive take-away cafés. These alterations were made from the district plan, describing the market as a covered but open space, which was passed in 2002 until the building permission was issued in 2010. In the original building permission and several later revisions hereof, several exemptions from the intentions in the district plan are made, allowing Jeudan to enclose the market halls, erect a two-storey café building, not to plant the trees originally described, etc. – exemptions strengthening the privatization of the space and easing the possibilities for further expansions of the rented out sales areas from which Jeudan make their profit.

Though today, a couple of years later, the outdoor stalls seem to be gaining momentum, the contrast between what the architect describes in the concept document and the realized project is quite obvious. Few stalls can be said to be mom-and-pop stores as originally described, and the majority of outdoor seating is clearly marked as being for paying customers only. Rather than guaranteeing day-to-day flexibility as originally described, Jeudan's regulation of stall-keepers is applied to prevent internal competition and optimize the value of presence at Torvehallerne Market for each stall-keeper.

People have compared Torvehallerne Market with the food department of the high-end department store Magasin in Copenhagen, and the market halls have been exposed to a wave of heavy critique of its exclusivity, price level, offerings and design passing through the press (*Politiken* 2011a; 2011b). The architect, whose vision is the reason for the Torvehallerne Market's existence in the first place, has had to listen to stall-keepers likening him with 'a hysterical pregnant bitch [sic]' (*Politiken* 2012b) in a dispute over the function and design of the apparently inadequate sunlight protection in the revised design of the market halls.

All this aside, however, Torvehallerne Market is widely popular and as such a huge success for its stall-keepers and investors. The forecast at the opening was 2–2.5 million annual visitors while the actual figures were 4.7 million in the second year from September 2012–2013 (*Berlingske* 2013). Claiming the fundamental problems with this way of engaging in public–private partnerships – as I will do in the following – is therefore often problematic and silenced with the argument that the project as a whole is of benefit to the city and its citizens.

Koncerthuset

With its new DR Concert Hall, Copenhagen has gained a prominent position on the world map of grand concert halls.

(Danish Architecture Center 2012)

In the northern part of Ørestad – a new town just outside the centre of Copenhagen – towers the Danish Broadcasting Corporation (DR)'s new concert building Koncerthuset. It is designed by Ateliers Jean Nouvel, who won an international design competition in 2002 and built on what used to be a part of Amager Commons – a major recreational area in Copenhagen. Construction began in 2004, and Koncerthuset was inaugurated in 2009. One of the main requirements in the competition programme was to create a concert hall with acoustics at an international top level. The final result, however, has been heavily criticized by the artists performing in Koncerthuset and even after a re-design, experts still claim its shortcomings (*Politiken* 2009; 2012a). The logistics inside Koncerthuset are far from ideal and the exterior, which in the winning design proposal was visualized as coming alive through projections of artwork – a highly important architectural element – is only rarely used. The cost of the concert building tripled the original budget (from DKK 550 million to 1.6 bio in 1999 figures) (*Berlingske* 2008; KPMG and Grant Thornton 2012), leading to following cuts in DR's budget with predictable consequences for public service broadcasting. Thus, instead of improving the conditions for DR's production, erecting Koncerthuset has led to a distribution of funds from function to form – from content to the container.

Frederikssund

> Frederikssund is one of the capital region's fine old merchant towns, set in a beautiful area between Roskilde Fjord and Isefjord which features idyllic villages and rolling countryside . . .
>
> (Frederikssund Kommune 2009)

As one of five towns representing the fingertips of the Finger Plan – a strategic plan from 1947 for development of the Copenhagen metropolitan area – Frederikssund is placed in the outskirts of the capital region. Due to the electrified S-train line, however, the town is closely connected to Copenhagen. After World War II, Frederikssund, which served as the main town for a large surrounding area of mainly farm land, developed into an active commercial and industrial city comprising a dairy, a slaughterhouse, a metal works and machinery manufacturer, commercial harbour and shipyards (Frederikssund Kommune 2009; Dansk Center for Byhistorie n.d.). All these activities have closed down today and with the dairy buildings as the only exception, all traces of this previous activity have been removed. As a result of eager and successful marketing of the city, in 1958 the town succeeded in convincing the chemical engineer and industrial entrepreneur Haldor Topsøe to first erect production facilities for his catalyst company and later a silicon wafer production plant on the city's north-facing salt meadows. Other companies followed and situated themselves in a newly planned industrial area placed on the town's highest slope with unhindered vista over (and from) the fjord (Christoffersen 1986). More than half of the town's building stock has been built after 1970, primarily as detached housing (Dansk Center for Byhistorie n.d.).

Following the discontinuance of the original harbour activities, the harbour areas have been developed into an area of mainly private housing, breaking the connection from the town's historical centre and place of origin to the fjord. In 2009 the 29.000 sqm shopping centre Sillebroen opened, directly attached to the S-train station but outside the original town centre in which the shop premises are now increasingly emptied.

Contradictions and consequences

Before moving on, it might be a good idea to clarify why these three small examples are interesting at all, and what the role of the architect is in each of the examples. Contradictions between the intended, described and realized design are obvious, but the resulting consequences should perhaps be scrutinized more closely.

Torvehallerne Market is the most complex and thus intriguing of the three. It is actually the architect who drove the project forward based on a personal engagement and a normative view on the use of his profession as a lever in creating a city with a more lively and diverse public life – in this example through richer and cheaper offerings of fresh food.

The average share of the disposable income spent on food in Denmark is 11.5 per cent, compared to the 29.8 per cent spent on housing (Danmarks Statistik 2012) – approximately the opposite of the situation in Southern Europe – and the need for competition and new offerings of food is widely recognized in Denmark and in Copenhagen. This was a driving force through the long years in which the Food Market Guild tried to convince the municipality and possible investors to take part in realizing the project. However, it is not for the architect to decide what target group of customers the private developer finds most suiting in order to optimize his return on investment, and neither can he force the kind of merchants he thinks would be the right ones to rent stalls at the food market.

The concept document thoroughly describes how the windows will open, what the aquariums in the corners of the fishmonger's stall will look like and how the season's fresh local apples should be advertised, but says only very little about the harsh realities of the market forces that came to drive the development of the market as it was realized.

What is left then of the architect's vision is the physical structure of the food market and the story about bringing fresh, cheap and local food to the people as a central message in advertising. The actual result and the benefits from it are completely different, and a decade's work to realize a food market that should serve everyday purposes for the average Copenhagener now serves as a pleasant backdrop in the private investor's advertising.

Koncerthuset is perhaps the most obvious of the examples. Koncerthuset was built from public money, and as the Danish Architecture Center stated: Rather than a concert hall benefiting the local musical environment or the tax payers that provided the funding for the building, its function is to put Copenhagen on the world map of great concert halls. Koncerthuset serves to benefit the Danish capital in a global competition between networked cities (cf.

Sassen 2001). In this respect, Koncerthuset serves as a global landmark, and the architect therefore cannot be anyone. As Ibelings (1998) and Kvorning (2010) point out, architects in this contexts are brands, and there is a small elite that has been dubbed 'starchitects', whose personal or company brand supersedes all other aspects of their practice, including the artistic value and level of their work. Like the red tab on a pair of Levi's jeans, Jean Nouvel's signature on Koncerthuset adds a surplus value to the building that goes far beyond land, materials and labour involved in the construction process. The basic requirements need to be in order, but the value of having a Jean Nouvel building in Copenhagen and as a part of Ørestad, where development is still going on, trumps the value of having a concert hall with a top-level performance on less 'rock'n'roll' characteristics such as acoustics, logistics and whether the proposed design is actually feasible in terms of construction and economy.

This role of the architect is of course in stark contrast to the role played by the architect behind Torvehallerne Market, whose normativity and visions of the future drove him – however unsuccessfully – to use his architectural skills not only to design a spectacular vision, but to put forward a utopian dream of a better world where good, cheap and sustainable food play a central role in people's pursuit for the good life. The result, in terms of marketing the final project, however, shares a remarkable resemblance, and Torvehallerne Market often mentions the architectural design and the story behind it side-by-side with the matter-of-factly ascertainment that they serve to improve tourism in Copenhagen.

In Frederikssund, the architect perhaps seems invisible or absent, but is not, which might exactly be the core of the example. What the town markets itself with is its proximity to nature, the surrounding villages and its history as a merchant town. What has happened through the last 20–25 years is a focused eradication of the town's connection to the part of the fjord from where it originates, together with buildings and structures related to its past as an industrial and merchant town. On the harbour where the town was established, warehouses, silos, the shipyard and the nearby metal works and machinery manufacturer have all been demolished. Instead the harbour now boasts private housing and a supermarket. Where the harbour was formerly a central part of town with a clear vista to the fjord and public access to the vast industrial areas with large-scale structures, there is now small-scale terraced housing with private gardens and courtyards. Though the architecture of these new buildings is not of a quality that would ever be featured in an architecture magazine, the participation of the architects involved has been absolutely crucial to provide arguments for local planners to pass the needed district plans: 'It is a professional who suggest this to be built.'

Though the architect has been much more in focus in the case of Torvehallerne Market, from the investor's point of view, the role of the architect as a purveyor of a feasible project should not be neglected. It is not very likely that a project like Torvehallerne Market by a private investor with no record of engaging in public affairs would have been granted the same possibilities as was the case for the owner of Torvehallerne Market who had the architect's vision to put forward.

194 *Jesper Pagh*

Theory and history

To better understand how these contradictions can occur and have developed, it might be useful to move back in time and take a look at some of the historical developments in the relation between architecture and society.

Dreaming of a just distribution of the goods

Apart from being a peak in the architectural history – at least in Denmark and Scandinavia – the architecture from the post-war period is a material mani-festation of the vision of a more socially just society. The architects of that time, however, did not just participate with their practical and professional skills to realize the visions of others. To many it was an idealistic and explicitly normative project, in which they participated actively themselves by encouraging peers to add an ethical dimension to the aesthetic and practical ones of their practice. Especially in the inter-war period this can be seen in writings like *Acceptera* (Asplund et al. 1931) and *2 Værelser Straks* (Heiberg 1935). Both are very explicit in their call for architects to engage in social development through their pro-fession instead of either visualizing utopian but unrealizable proposals, or discarding the architectural career as a whole in favour of a political one.

Creating a worthless vacuum

The societal focus shifted – as in many other areas of society – during the 1970s when ideology, 'grand theories', utopianism, the youth revolt, the modernist mind set and the welfare project gradually lost attention (Langkilde et al. 1998; Vindum 2010). From the late 1970s and through the 1980s the need for new construction stagnated and the crisis in Europe brought the building industry to a halt. The architectural profession turned inwards and to a greater extent started theorizing on the nature of architecture rather than the utility of architecture (Nygaard 1995; SKALA 1999). Modernism was gradually replaced by postmodernism which is really not one thing but rather a conglomerate of -isms like neo-rationalism, deconstructivism and the 'candy-colored classicist style' as Ibelings (2012:14) calls what became the result of *Learning from Las Vegas* (Venturi et al. 1977[1972]) – famously urging architects to be more receptive to the taste of 'common people' and discover 'The forgotten symbolism of architectural form' as the subtitle of the book says. Ibelings discards postmodernism as a whole as 'the cultural relativism of anything goes [. . .] a complex form of stagnation, the creation of a worthless vacuum' (Ibelings 2012:14).

Today modernism is often heavily criticized for its seeming inhumanity and is largely held responsible for suburban ghettoization in Western Europe and the US. Le Corbusier's infamous quote about the house as 'a machine for living in', from his manifesto *Towards a New Architecture* (1931), is often referred to as the true, evil spirit of modernism, and modernist critics like the Danish urban design specialist Jan Gehl have built their career as 'humanist architects' on condemnation of modernism. This is a very long and complex discussion that deserves its own place, but it is important to point out that while it is true that many of the period's great efforts in urban planning failed to deliver on their promises of the good life, this is not only due to the architecture or the architects but as much to structural issues in the period of heavy economic growth after World War II at large.

> We need to be very careful not to throw the baby out with the bath water. Just because a number of architects got it wrong doesn't mean that architecture or physical design – spatial design – is not essential. I think it absolutely is.
>
> (Burdett in Pagh 2013a:28)

The critique of the modernists' efforts is as much based on a normative view on what makes a good city that differs from the one that was the dominant at the time, as it is based on actual insight in the background and contemporary intentions. Though good intentions can never make up for a disastrous result, it seems unethical and unproductive to judge the past on the basis of our present knowledge.

Quietness, cleanliness and regularity

It is important, though, to mention that not all Danish or Scandinavian architects were a part of this social movement within architecture, and that it is not solely a Danish or a Scandinavian phenomenon. In Denmark, some of the period's finest architects – including Arne Jacobsen, Vilhelm Lauritzen and Halldor Gunnløgsson – were not at all interested in this notion of architecture and design, but to a larger extent preoccupied with the project of creating order in the messy and dirty realm of people's everyday lives through spatial and formal discipline.

If we want to understand some of the contradictions that appear between the conceptualization and realization of the Torvehallerne Market, a part of the explanation lies in this deeply felt urge for architects to prefer quietness, cleanliness and regularity, and to be deeply convinced that all this can be taken care of through design. It is a line of thought that can be followed all the way through the modern period, and is omnipresent in architects' interventions in the urban from the renaissance until today. Though the architect has taken an outset in a dream of a compelling jumble, the nitty gritty detailing of every detail in the market halls is in stark contrast to the rough, intermediate and spontaneous character found in many of the markets referred to as role models in Rome, Venice and Barcelona.

Theory was fun – now we have work

In the midst of the shift away from a societal focus, and while the building industry stagnated, the theoretical basis for meaning in architecture changed as well.

Whereas in the 1960s and 1970s the architects read sociology, in the 1980s and partly during the 1990s, philosophy was the backdrop for developing architectural theory. Compared to the actual practice of building houses, this resulted in a somewhat abstract and detached approach to theory, which divided the profession into a theorizing and a practicing wing, which no longer inspired and cross-pollinated but rather fought one another (Speaks 2002). Around the time when I went to architecture school myself, in the late 1990s, architects apparently ceased reading at all. The economy and with it the building industry resurrected; the demand for architecture for almost all other purposes than that of the common good skyrocketed, and so architects began, once more, to build. Michael Speaks (2002:209) sums this up elegantly: 'Theory was interesting, or at least not harmful when there was no work; but now that we have work we must leave thinking for later'.

Since the beginning of the financial crisis in 2009, the pace of the building industry has slowed down, and what could be more appropriate than to take advantage of the extra time gained by not working with a concrete mixer breathing down your neck all day, but to catch up on thinking? I will try to suggest what kind of thinking could be useful.

Analysis

There may very well be several others, but here I aim to suggest three areas of interest which in the example of Torvehallerne Market could be relevant to discuss in greater detail, and in general perhaps could lead to a better understanding of the externalities affecting architecture and in turn our society in general.

Experiences, public space and economic growth

Although unique and peculiar, all three examples share the use of architects and architecture to create economic growth through experiences in the urban realm.

At a public debate on 'Public Life as a Resource' at the inauguration of the Danish Pavilion at the International Architecture Exhibition at The Biennale in Venice 2012, the city architect of Copenhagen explained how one of the most important things for a city like Copenhagen is to create economic growth, and how a high quality of urban life with green areas for recreation, infrastructure for bicycles and a wide array of experiences is one of the key levers to attract investors and keep people staying in the city even when they have finished their education, started a career and had children (Weiss 2012). In a recent documentary on the work of Jan Gehl, the Commissioner for the New York City Department of Transportation, Janette Sadik-Khan further explains how PlaNYC – mayor Michael Bloomberg's strategy to transform NYC into a greener city and reduce its carbon footprint – was spawned from an understanding of how a city's livability enhanced its international competitiveness (Dalsgaard 2012).

Attracting investors and creating economic growth through making a better city for people seems like an obvious example of the pragmatic 'you can have both' approach that has been appreciated through the 2000s (Ingels 2010; Vindum and Weiss 2012). In all the three examples, however, creating economic growth through what on the surface seems to be a better city for people, actually occurs through an optimization of the existing resources on the market's terms and includes transfer of values from the public to the private realm.

Torvehallerne Market was funded by private money but realized through a planning practice that allowed what was previously public space – a centrally located square in the capital – to be effectively transformed into a private, commercial space. Instead of access for the citizens of Copenhagen in general, the space now offers an exclusive experience with access for paying consumers. You can go there of course, but now as a consumer – no longer as a citizen. The surplus belongs to the private developer who invested in the realization of the project. A striking example of this is the difference between the architects' description of access to outdoor stalls on a day-to-day basis even for Mrs Hansen and her windflowers, as mentioned earlier, and the actual practised procedure, where you have to apply online with a business plan, and the investor behind Torvehallerne Market will decide whether you fit into the concept.

Parallel to this, Koncerthuset was funded by public money and now works as an engine to attract tourists to Copenhagen for the benefit of trade and the private cultural and experience-based economy in the city. In its neighbourhood, Koncerthuset serves to brand the new town Ørestad, which it is a part of, hence making it more attractive for future investors and developers, raising the price on land.

In Frederikssund, public accessible areas with a great recreative value – and the value of a shared right to access – have been turned into private property. Though the areas may also beforehand have been privately owned, in effect they provided qualities for the common good. Connections from the city to the fjord and a bond to history have not been preserved, but the private investors taking over the areas herein have capitalized the values.

Vagabond capitalism and tourist urbanism

> The phrase vagabond capitalism puts the vagrancy and dereliction where it belongs – on capitalism, that unsettled, dissolute, irresponsible stalker of the world.
>
> (Katz 2001:709)

With this, Katz aims to frame the notion that in this age of globalization, capital is seemingly free to pursue no other interests than its own.

The privatization and capitalization of the common good may perhaps not be visible to the naked eye, when standing in front of Torvehallerne Market on a sunny day. And even though you may not feel part of globalization yourself living in, say Sundbyvester – a traditional working class neighbourhood a few blocks away from Koncerthuset – in both examples global capital turns up and gets the best out of what used to be the shared qualities and walks on with the surplus; just like on the harbour front in Frederikssund. Though architects are not the investors gaining the surplus, they do play an important role in the creation of it.

Katz's vagabond is not the one that Bauman (2000) describes as the counterpart to the tourist, who surfs the globalized world without friction. In Katz's article, vagabond capitalism rather is the travel companion of the touring capitalists, who like flocks of grasshoppers violently graze one field just to fly off to the next.

Tourist urbanism, on the other hand, is a notion used by architect and professor in urban planning, Jens Kvorning, to question the nature of the production of architecture in globalization. Kvorning's notion relates directly to Bauman:

> One could ask if what we as a profession are involved in could be called the production of tourist urbanism? In other words, the production of images and urban projects that produce a world tailor-made to create a comfortable setting for the activities of the global middle class.
>
> (Kvorning 2010:87)

Kvorning argues that with this as an outset, architects create a frictionless system of corridors where we see variety and diversity as something which 'alone should be a question of [. . .] form in the middle-class and investor world – and forgetting the social and cultural diversities and the contradictions and conflict zones they create' (ibid.:88). In this sense, what architects have turned to instead of the project of creating a more just society, is to create separate places and spaces for different classes created by globalization – the tourist excluding the vagabond.

We see it in the three examples with starchitecture on what used to be Amager Commons, private housing on what used to be a part of a common good, a common identity and memory of a city's origin. And perhaps most visible in Torvehallerne Market – a high-end food market on what used to be a public square and now to a great extent only welcomes the upper middle class; not only due to the prices and the offerings, but as much due to the exclusive atmosphere created through design.

Ethics, responsibilities and apparent objectivity

Ibelings (2012:55) points out the self-image of the architect as an 'all-rounder whose activities will, if not deliver a better world, make the world a better place'.

This stance is supported through recent conversations with leading architects from the post-war period (Pagh 2013b; 2013c), so how come they end up being caught up in this mess? One of the reasons, I argue based on these conversations, is the apparent objectivity of the architect's practice. Practicing architects to a great extent will argue that there is no subjectivity or normativity in their approach to their work – only the mere objective production of architecture to fulfil someone else's (the client's) requirements. In various ways, they would like to point to the client's responsibility to address these matters and emphasize that architecture is not a political project.

But what is it then? How is it possible to participate in – or even initiate – a project to create a building or change a public space or a city into something else, without any subjective notions of why? Facing the ethics and responsibilities of these actions is absolutely mandatory, if change is not just something that happens coincidently or by the intervention of something or someone else who might have another agenda. Again the contrast between the dream world of the architects' concept description of Torvehallerne Market and the realized project tells a story about good will but little realization of the consequences of entering into a world where "power defines, and creates, concrete physical, economic, ecological and social realities", as Bent Flyvbjerg (1998: 227) has shown. That the good intentions of creating a food market could be used to privatize public space was clearly not calculated, but goes to show the power – intended or not – embedded in the architectural practice. If it is not used cleverly and strategically by the architects, it will be by someone else.

'Design is the transformation of existing situations into preferred ones' is an often (mis-)used quote on the nature of design from Herbert Simon (1969:55). Simon implies that the transformation is good. It is changing things for the better. Why else would we do it? But still – as the practice of architects have changed from addressing societal issues into being consultants on a global market of private property – architects increasingly define their practice as a non-political, objective one. 'What if Architecture can Change the World?' was the tagline of an exhibition at the Danish Architecture Center some years ago. It can, and it already is. The question is: Into what do we want to change it? And what are the architect's means to this end?

The architect always survives

Whatever happens, there are no signs that the architect will not survive the coming decades. The recent acquisition of the Danish architectural firm Witraz by the engineering company Rambøll (by Witraz dubbed 'a friendly take-over') indicates a shift in the hierarchy between these two professions though, and the question of the future role of the architect remains an open one.

In the example of Torvehallerne Market, the importance of this role has clearly been realized too late. In the other two examples we have been looking at, it is fair to say that the role of the architect has been too big (DR Koncerthuset) or too little (Frederikssund). While Hagens is still stuck in struggling for his dream of Torvehallerne Market – realizing he has spawned a monster – in the other two examples, the architects have now moved on to something else, somewhere else, accompanying the vagabond capitalism:

> Architecture follows the money. No money, no buildings (let alone details). Money does not always and everywhere lead to architecture. But architecture is like an index fossil of capital: Where there is a lot of architecture there is also a lot of money and the economy grows.
>
> (Ibelings 2012:40)

If architecture is again going to mean something to others than architects and the capitalist developers they support, then architects need to be able to put forward new visions of what a better and more just society might look like and face the power it takes to realize them instead of just acting as levers for the creation of surplus value in an ever-globalized economy. The problems around us are vast: climate weirdness, credit crunch and peak everything within reach. And though architects may reasonably enough not be able to solve everything by themselves, just like in the earlier years of modernism, they might be able to point to solutions and use their profession as architects to make the necessary change feasible:

> We're on a slider bar between the Unthinkable and the Unimaginable. Sustainability is a mighty effort to haul that slider bar toward general survival as the smouldering planet groans at the seams. The Unthinkable is a global Somalia, Baghdad as the world's model city. The Unimaginable is a set of awesome interventions, we scarcely have words for yet: new design, new manufacturing, new culture, new cities, new infrastructure, new factories.
>
> (Sterling 2007:135)

In this article in *Dwell*, the American science fiction writer and design theorist Bruce Sterling sets out to embrace design and urge designers (including architects and urban planners) to leave unsustainable business where 'dumb money is losing wars, losing office and losing lives' (ibid.), and instead take on the challenge of visualizing what a sustainable future might look like. This might be a way out if they want to not only survive but also survive for a reason. Sterling's way out is not a way out of the limitations and contradictions of capitalism as such, but it may serve as a starting point and provide a breakaway from the path tread by following the money and into a normative and explicitly ethical way of practicing, where utopias for a better and more just society are once again on the forefront of architectural theory and practice as a way to – paraphrasing Sterling – imagine the unimaginable.

The basic structures of society as such are not within reach of the architects to change. But by keeping on rephrasing the questions addressed, insisting on the wickedness of the problems, however, we might be able to find little cracks in the slippery surface of global capitalism, cracks that enable us to hold on and steadily widen them to create in-between spaces of hope, as David Harvey (2000) has dubbed it, where new notions of a good life based on a framework of the common good can evolve.

Ironically, this is exactly what Hagens is trying to do in his dreamy vision of how the Torvehallerne Market will be. Reading the descriptions carefully you get a clear image of how Hagens longs for a sense of community which has since long been eroded and superseded by something else which may be harder to get a hold of.

In this way, as we have seen, the architecture is pushed in front of the project to clear the path – the architect has made himself and his architecture quantités négligeables, just as Ibelings points out (2012). Architecture serves the purpose of paving the way for the project, but afterwards, any visions put forward by the architect are refused and he must even take being called names.

Architecture follows the money, and money for architecture and urban planning tends to follow the political agendas that indicate where the soundest investment can be made. Public life is high on the agenda because it is an important factor in the global competition between cities. And as we in our daily lives try to cope with the alienation brought forward by globalization – longing for an unspecified sense of authenticity and community as a foundation for the good life – we find it around a need as basic as food, which in turn becomes pivotal in the planning of public life. Therefore, to follow the money, you have to follow the food.

Bibliography

Asplund, E. G., Gahn, W., Markelius, S., Paulsson, G. and Åhrén, U. (1931) *Acceptera*. Stockholm: Tidens Förlag.

Bauman, Z. (2000) *Globalization: The Human Consequences*. New York, Chichester: Columbia University Press.

Berlingske (2008) 'Koncerthusets Arkitekt: Blev det virkelig så dyrt?' in *Berlingske*. www. b.dk/danmark/koncerthusets-arkitekt-blev-det-virkelig-saa-dyrt (retrieved 16 August 2012).

Berlingske (2013) 'Torvehallerne overgår ejerens forventninger' in *Berlingske*. www.business. dk/vaekst/torvehallerne-overgaar-ejerens-forventninge (retrieved 30 September 2013).

Brand, S. (1995) *How Buildings Learn: What Happens After They're Built*. New York: Penguin Books.

Buchanan, R. (1992) 'Wicked Problems in Design Thinking' in *Design Issues*, 8(2). pp. 5–21.

Christoffersen, K. B. (1986) *Købstaden Frederikssunds historie 1801–1970*. Frederikssund: Thorsgaard i samarbejde med Frederikssunds Historiske Forening.

Corbusier, L. (1931) *Towards a New Architecture*. London: J. Rodker.

Creagh, L., Kåberg, H., Frampton, K. and Lane, B. M. (2008) *Modern Swedish Design: Three Founding Texts*. New York: The Museum of Modern Art.

Cross, N. (2006) *Designerly Ways of Knowing*. London: Springer.

Dalsgaard, A. M. (2012) *The Human Scale*. [Documentary]. Copenhagen: Final Cut for Real.

Danish Architecture Center (2012) *Dr Concert Hall*. www.dac.dk/en/dac-life/copenhagen-x-gallery/realized-projects/dr-concert-hall/ (retrieved 20 August 2012).

Danmarks Statistik (2012) *Statistisk Årbog: 2012*. Danmarks Statistik: Copenhagen.

Dansk Center for Byhistorie (n.d.) *Danmarks Købstæder: Frederikssund*. http://dendigitaleby port.byhistorie.dk/koebstaeder/by.aspx?koebstadID=6 (retrieved 20 August 2012).

Dirckinck-Holmfeld, K., Keiding, M., Amundsen, M. and Smidt, C. M. (2007) *Danish Architecture Since 1754*. Copenhagen: Danish Architectural Press.

Esping-Andersen, G. (1990) *The Three Worlds of Welfare Capitalism*. Cambridge, UK: Polity Press.

Faber, T. (1963) *A History of Danish Architecture*. Copenhagen: Det Danske Selskab.

Flyvberg, B. (1998) *Rationality and Power: Democracy in Practice*. Chicago: University of Chicago Press.

Frederikssund Kommune (2009) *Historien – 200-års jubilæum Frederikssund*. www.200aar. frederikssund.dk/content/dk/kultur_fritid/200-ars_jubilaum_frederikssund/historien (retrieved 20 August 2012).

Gropius, W. (1962[1937]) *Scope of Total Architecture*. New York: Collier Books.

Hagens, H. P. (2006) *Torvehallerne på israels plads. 1.0 Konceptbeskrivelse*. Copenhagen: Arkitekturværkstedet.

Hagens, H. P. (2012) *Torvehallerne handler ikke om en elitær arkitekt*. http://politiken.dk/ debat/ECE1601646/torvehallerne-handler-ikke-om-en-elitaer-arkitekt/ (retrieved 2 September 2012).

Harvey, D. (2000) *Spaces of Hope*. Edinburgh: Edinburgh University Press.

Harvey, D. (2008) 'The Right to the City' in *New Left Review*, 53(5). pp. 23–40.

Harvey, D. (2009) *A Brief History of Neoliberalism*. Oxford: Oxford University Press.

Heiberg, E. (1935) *2 Værelser Straks*. København: Socialistisk Arkitektgruppe.

Ibelings, H. (1998) *Supermodernism: Architecture in the Age of Globalization*. Rotterdam: NAi.

Ibelings, H. (2012) *Shifts. Architecture After the 20th Century*. Amsterdam: The Architecture Observer.

Ingels, B. (2010) *Yes is More: An Archicomic on Architectural Evolution*. Cologne: Evergreen.

Jørgensen, L. B. (2004) *Den sidste guldalder: Danmark i 1950'erne*. Copenhagen: The Danish Architectural Press.

Katz, C. (2001) 'Vagabond Capitalism and the Necessity of Social Reproduction' in *Antipode*, 33(4). pp. 709–728.

KPMG and Grant Thornton (2012) *Revisorundersøgelse af DR's byggeprojekt i Ørestaden*. København: Kulturministeriet.

Kvorning, J. (2010) 'Tourist Urbanism – The Peaceful Path to Real Reform?' in *Arkitektur DK*, 54(2). pp. 87–89.

Langkilde, H. E., Dirckinck-Holmfeld, K. and Hegner Christiansen, J. (1998) *Arkitekten 100 år*. Copenhagen: Arkitektens Forlag.

Mattsson, H. and Wallenstein, S. O. (2010) *Swedish Modernism: Architecture, Consumption, and the Welfare State*. London: Black Dog Publishing.

Medaas, A. E. (2013) *Taste Trekkers*. Oslo: University of Oslo. http://blogg.uio.no/sum/ matlaere/content/taste-trekkers (retrieved 29 April 2013).

Menzel, P. and d'Aluisio, F. (2007) *Hungry Planet: What the World Eats*. Napa, CA: Material World.

Nygaard, E. (1995) *Arkitektur i en forvirret tid: internationale strømninger 1968–1994*. Copenhagen: Christian Ejlers' Forlag.

Pagh, J. (2013a) 'If Technology is the Answer, What is the Question' in Pagh, J. (ed.) *Conversations on Housing and Planning*. Arkitektur DK 2013 (1). Copenhagen: The Danish Architectural Press.

Pagh, J. (2013b) 'Introduction' in Pagh, J. (ed.) *The Architecture of the Welfare Society 1957–1982*. Arkitektur DK 2013 (2). Copenhagen: The Danish Architectural Press.

Pagh, J. (2013c) *The Architecture of the Welfare Society 1983–2012*. Arkitektur DK 2013 (3). Copenhagen: The Danish Architectural Press.

Politiken (2009) 'DR erkender koks med akustikken i koncerthuset' in *Politiken*. http:// politiken.dk/kultur/ECE767936/dr-erkender-koks-med-akustikken-i-koncerthuset (retrieved 16 August 2012).

Politiken (2011a) 'Læserne: Torvehallerne er et lille stykke Gentofte'. http://ibyen. dk/restauranter/ECE1384396/laeserne-torvehallerne-er-et-lille-stykke-gentofte/ (retrieved 2 September 2012).

Politiken (2011b) 'Manden bag Torvehallerne: Hvor er alle de billige boder?'. http://ibyen. dk/gadeplan/ECE1403614/manden-bag-torvehallerne-hvor-er-alle-de-billige-boder/ (retrieved 2 September 2012).

Politiken (2012a) 'Akustikere: Lyden dør i DR's koncerthus'. http://politiken.dk/kultur/ musik/ECE1672523/akustikere-lyden-doer-i-drs-koncerthus/ (retrieved 16 August 2012).

Politiken (2012b) 'I Torvehallerne er de glade for de grimme presenninger'. http://ibyen.dk/ gadeplan/ECE1598955/i-torvehallerne-er-de-glade-for-de-grimme-presenninger/ (retrieved 2 September 2012).

Politiken (2013) http://politiken.dk/ibyen/ (retrieved 26 April 2013).

Rittel, H. W. J. and Webber, M. M. (1973) 'Dilemmas in a General Theory of Planning' in *Policy Sciences*, 4(2). pp. 155–169.

Sassen, S. (2001) *The Global City*. New York – London – Tokyo: Princeton University Press.

Simon, H. A. (1969) *The Sciences of the Artificial*. Boston, MA: MIT Press.

SKALA (1999) 'Udvalgte artikler fra SKALA' in Rivad, K. (ed.) *Nordisk Magasin for Arkitektur og Kunst, 1985–1994*. Copenhagen: Henning Larsens Tegnestue.

Speaks, M. (2002) 'Theory was Interesting . . . But Now we have Work' in *Architectural Research Quarterly*, 6(03). pp. 209–212.

Steel, C. (2009) *Hungry City: How Food Shapes Our Lives*. London: Vintage Books.

Sterling, B. (2007) 'Another Green World' in *Dwell*, November 2007. pp. 134–135.

Torvehallerne (2012) *Om Torvehallerne*. http://torvehallernekbh.dk/historie (retrieved 16 August 2012).

Venturi, R., Scott Brown, D. and Izenour, S. (1977[1972]) *Learning from Las Vegas: The Forgotten Symbolism of Architectural Form*. Cambridge, MA: MIT Press.

Vindum, K (2010) 'Hvem tegner arkitekterne for?' in *ArkitekturTV*. http://arkitekturtv. 23video.com/video/1030681/hvem-tegner-arkitekterne-for (retrieved 22 August 2012).

Vindum, K. and Weiss, K. L. (2012) *The New Wave in Danish Architecture*. Copenhagen: The Danish Architectural Press.

Weiss, K. L. (2012) *Urban Life as a Resource*. www.ifhp.org/ifhp-blog/urban-life-resource (retrieved 2 September 2012).

12 Caged welfare

Evading the good life for egg-laying hens

Kristian Bjørkdahl

The term *oxymoron* comes from Greek and is composed of its words for 'sharp' and 'dull'. The function of this rhetorical figure is the function of the word itself, namely to bring together what does not belong together. William Shakespeare was a master of this trope. Here is Juliet, caught in an extended moment of fascinated frustration with her beloved and despised Romeo:

> O serpent heart, hid with a flowering face.
> Did ever dragon keep so fair a cave?
> Beautiful tyrant, fiend angelical,
> Dove-feather'd raven, wolvish-ravening lamb!
> Despised substance of divinest show!
> Just opposite to what thou justly seem'st!
> A damned saint, an honourable villain!
>
> William Shakespeare, Romeo and Juliet,
> 3.2 (lines 73–79), pp. 1025–1026

Shakespeare, of course, was a master of every trope, including the *euphemism*. This too is a word from Greek and it means 'to speak auspiciously'. It is a species of the *periphrasis*, which means 'to speak around', and the point of this figure is to make something offensive appear more acceptable. Here is Agrippa, realizing that Caesar and Cleopatra had been doing the horizontal mambo – and with tangible results, to boot:

> Royal wench!
> She made great Caesar lay his sword to bed.
> He plowed her, and she cropped.
>
> William Shakespeare, Antony and Cleopatra,
> 2.2 (lines 237–239), p. 131

In this chapter, I tell the story of the public debate about egg-laying hens in Norway, from the introduction of the battery cage in the 1960s to the EU ban in 2012. The question at stake is what constitutes a good life for an egg-laying hen, and more specifically, whether the battery cage can accommodate for such a life.

My goal is not to answer *that* question, but to offer a few glimpses of how Norwegians have argued about it. Given this purpose, one might think that Shakespeare and his *fiends angelical, dove-feather'd ravens*, and *royal wenches* are evasions. That they are, but as such they are also illustrations of the case at hand. My argument is that the debate in question is one of rhetorical evasion strategies enacted, challenged, adjusted, and exposed. To be more concrete, the debate about the battery cage is a story of an oxymoron which was put under pressure until it exploded, at which point it was replaced by an easily exposed euphemism.

   To say that the debate about the battery cage resembles an oxymoron is to say that the notion of 'caged welfare' – the idea that the relevant components of a hen's happiness could be satisfied in cages – went against the grain of all established wisdom about how to keep hens.[1] Many felt that the cage was even contrary to the Animal Protection Act, which stated that animals are to be dealt with well, and that the 'instincts and natural needs of the animal should be taken into consideration, so that it does not suffer needlessly'.[2] For decades, farmers, poultry fanciers, and agricultural scientists had been telling each other that good poultry keeping was precisely the *opposite* of putting hens in cages. It was believed that hens, to be happy, required plenty of fresh air and sunlight, ample space outdoors, access to grass and to the ground, interaction with roosters, the chance to search for food, etc. In short, a happy hen was a hen living out its natural inclinations. So deeply rooted were these ideas that historians of the industry have dubbed them 'the early modern norms for poultry keeping' (Berger 1997: 92).

   With the arrival of the battery cage, a shift of focus took place, as the industry managed to subtly change the subject. Instead of talking about hens' natural needs and behavioural instincts – requirements which were only dubiously met in the case of caged hens – the emphasis was now on productivity and absence of disease. Whereas the logic had previously been, 'Hens must live out their natural inclinations to be happy and thus productive', it now became, 'Hens as productive as these cannot be unhappy'. Concern for the natural needs and inclinations of hens dropped out of the story. In this capacity, the battery cage was only one of many examples of an emerging agricultural system where animals were seen as malleable 'material' developed for maximum yield within an industrial infrastructure (see Orland 2004; Horowitz 2004; Finlay 2004). They were seen, as Ruth Harrison suggested with her famous book, as 'animal machines' (Harrison 1964).

   This shift – which was simultaneously technological and ideological – never managed to completely discredit the older notion. The idea that animals were machines had to coexist with the older idea that they were sentient creatures with needs – a notion kept alive not just by the animal movement, but by the Animal Protection Act, and probably also by common sense attitudes. Over time, the oxymoron 'caged welfare' was felt increasingly as a case of hypocrisy. When the EU ban went into effect in 2012, the industry thus enacted another evasion strategy: Instead of talking about hens' productivity, they now started talking about their 'abodes' – what they could only do because the 'bare' cages would be replaced by 'enriched' ones. Instead of the response, 'Hens can indeed have welfare in cages!', they were now saying, 'These are not cages!' – swapping one trope (oxymoron) for another (euphemism).

In presenting a few instances from this history, I apply the gaze of a rhetorical scholar, which means I look for how language use contributes to making what we – at a particular time and in a particular place – hold to be true, good, useful, sensible, interesting, or relevant about a particular subject. This overarching ambition is of course largely stunted in a short piece like this, where compromises are legion. One significant limitation is that I have used newspapers as a proxy for 'public debate', and further, that I have had to limit my material using simple key word searches in the digitized newspaper database Retriever.[3] Because I am trying to reconstruct a public debate that spans more than half a century, I can do no more than offer a few glimpses, which I hope will accumulate into a relatively coherent narrative. Finally, because I have had so much empirical ground to cover, I have had to largely neglect the standard academic requirement to position my effort in a landscape of similar research. I beg the reader to forgive these deficiencies, and hope the fact that I present new research can go some way towards compensating for them.

From eggs of whimsy to eggs of industry[4]

In preindustrial Norway, hens were hardly considered proper farm animals. They received very little attention and care, did not have designated housing, and were seldom fed anything but scraps. In general, they were considered an inessential presence on the farm – by some even a nuisance. With the establishment of the Norwegian Poultry Association, in the 1880s, this changed. Consisting largely of urban bourgeois poultry hobbyists, the organization was determined to improve the quality of the Norwegian poultry stock – among other ways, by importing animals from abroad. As a result, the prospect of making a financial venture of poultry slowly emerged. Thus began a first 'rationalization' of poultry keeping in Norway – one important component of which was the writing of manuals for effective poultry keeping.

In the system advocated by those manuals, the basic idea was that a thriving hen was good for business, 'for if the hens do not thrive', as one such manual writer stated, 'one cannot expect them to create a surplus' (in Berger 1997: 53). Several who wrote on poultry keeping were preoccupied with understanding the natural behaviours of the hen. One writer, Nilsen, explained:

> In the wild state, hens are most at ease in high grass and on the margins of forests, where they find their food (both animal and vegetable), such as worms, insects, berries and seeds, and therefore they are also better off in domestic settings if they have the greatest possible freedom to roam and to procure a significant portion of their food themselves.
>
> (op. cit.: 54)

One writer, Høie, acknowledged that poultry farmers had begun to keep their hens indoors, but concluded: 'The sun, the grass, and the movement outdoors will serve a function in the long run' (op. cit.: 90). Another, Brandt, wrote: 'In summer, the hens must be allowed outdoors in adequately large grass-covered yards, amply lit by the sun . . . Life outdoors is of great importance if the hens are to thrive' (ibid.). A third, Engnæs, wrote that one ought to 'let them have the chance to move', and added that '[t]his promotes the growth of muscle and bone' (ibid.). None of the writers on poultry in the pre-war era recommended cages. In fact, they did not recommend keeping hens indoors, and even those who mentioned this practice still pleaded that hens ought to be let out at least an hour each afternoon: 'This hour of freedom is a consolation to them – they kick around and go searching for many a delicious worm, and around 6 o'clock they often return inside of their own will' (op. cit.: 91).

Until the 1950s, the growing class of agricultural experts, as well as manual writers and many farmers, thus contributed to consolidating a particular constellation of poultry management ideas and methods where the main factors were ample sunlight, plenty of grass, fresh air, and the chance to roam freely outdoors. One historian of the industry, Kjersti Berger, calls this 'the early modern norms for poultry keeping' in Norway (Berger 1997: 92).

The fact that this notion was so deep-seated might help explain why the battery cage was so belatedly introduced to Norway, though there were also many other factors at play. But if the introduction of the cage was somewhat stalled, it could not be held back for very long. This was the 1950s, after all, and a wind of progress was blowing across the Western world, including – not least – its agricultural sector (see Fitzgerald 2003 and Almås 2002). In the late 1950s, a couple of farmers on the Western coast of Norway built their own battery cage installations and within just a few years, the system was sold commercially to Norwegian farmers. The year 1964 saw the arrival of the first Norwegian supplier of battery cage systems, catering to the Norwegian market. British cages were sold in Norway the same year.

While farmers were gradually overcoming their economic reservations against the large investment required by a battery cage system, they had also to deal with concerns about hens' welfare. As I have pointed out, the battery cage was somewhat of an oxymoron. Hens were believed to lead good lives only in environments where their natural instincts and species-specific behaviours could be expressed, but life in a cage literally closed off that possibility. According to Berger, the new system had therefore developed an attendant notion of how hens should (or *could*) be treated: 'Earlier, rational management was synonymous with sensible management, and sensibly managed was a poultry system that accounted for the natural behavioural needs of the hens. Now rational management came to be synonymous with less time-consuming management' (Berger 1997: 93). This was made possible, she argues, because one had come to realize that the productive capacity of the hens was not – at least not closely – tied to their welfare, as previously understood. It was simply not true that hens would be productive only if and when they had access to sun, grass, fresh air, and plenty of space.

If the link between a *natural* life and a *productive* life was thereby severed, that did not mean that the concern with 'natural behavioural needs' disappeared.

Indeed, the early modern norms for poultry keeping lived on, all the way up to the EU's ban on those cages – a ban which itself was motivated largely by concerns similar to those we find in the old manuals.

Bird on the wire (floor)

An appropriately ambivalent example of how the battery cage was first treated in Norwegian news media is an article from *Verdens Gang*, a leading tabloid, in 1968 – four years after the cages started coming into widespread use.[5] The article left no doubt that a new, technological era was descending upon the feathered creatures. 'He collects a million eggs a year', states one of the article headings, suggesting that poultry farming was now in the process of becoming a truly *industrial* business. As an example of the emerging industry, the article interviews an egg farmer who manages one of the largest and most modern hen houses in the country. There are 5,000 hens producing eggs on his farm – although the writer adds that the scale of production makes the label *factory* more accurate: 'In two short weeks, 3000 new hens will be inserted into these three-story apartment block buildings, so this can truly be called factory production of eggs'.

The main axis of the piece is to convey to the reader how this new system works. Obviously, with industry comes technology, and large parts of the article consists in a curious, but still somewhat nervous, infatuation with the efficiency of industrial egg farming. The facility 'is so mechanized', the article continues,

> that one man can single-handedly manage all the work. Last year, more than a million eggs passed through the hands of Egil Isumhagen, as the only thing the manager has to do is collect and sort the eggs before they are shipped to the Egg Central.

The near ubiquitous buzzword in the agricultural sector during the 1960s was of course 'rationalization', and what could be more 'rational' than having *one* man handle *millions* of eggs? Although the general tone of the article reveals a certain awe of this progress, that sentiment is coupled to nostalgic concerns for the hens and their welfare. Another heading reads, for instance, 'A Light Switch Determines the Life of a Hen'; an implicit reminder of the older notion that hens need natural light to thrive. Indeed, the whole article struggles to reconcile the new developments with a concern for the hens' needs.

> Production and effectivity, rationalization and profit, these are words that in recent years have caused large transformations in our world of animals. It is a rarity where a small hen . . . can chuckle and churn in the proximity of a rooster – or lay an egg, at her own convenience, when she needs to. According to the experts, she is just as productive, however, even if she is born in an incubator and has never been awakened by a rooster's happy morning melody.

The rhetorical effect of this paragraph is worth noting, since it turns on its head what had been a premise in poultry keeping for several decades. Previously, to ensure a 'natural' life for egg-laying hens had been seen as a prerequisite not just for their productivity, but for their overall well-being as well. Now, the experts insisted there was no such connection; hens were just as productive if they had been born in an incubator and never seen a male of their own species, and even if they were not allowed to chuckle and churn. But although the extract establishes that caged hens are just as *productive*, it does not say they are just as *happy*.

The writer thus struggles to incorporate the new, industrial way of making eggs with the established notions of good poultry keeping, as she understands that the former is 'the end of a romantic era'. Especially, she wants to know what this new system entails for the welfare of the hens. 'Do the hens not become ill from being stuck in a cage?', she asks, to which the farmer responds, 'The rate of illness is very low, but it does happen that one dies'. The journalist does not relent immediately, 'From a broken heart, perhaps?', to which the farmer now responds with emphatic rejection, 'What nonsense! You wouldn't think the wellbeing and production would be like this if the hens were lacking in anything?'. Whereas the earlier discourse focused on how hens should be kept in order to make them happy, and thus productive, now the logic is reversed: Caged hens are eminently productive, hence, they cannot be unhappy.

The campaigning 1970s

The 1970s saw a growing number of news stories about caged hens. Most of these articles had a somewhat less rosy starting point than the article from 1968. Whereas the earlier article had introduced the phenomenon of caged egg production as a technological novelty, suggesting with its rhetorical framing how impressive the whole system was, the issue was now increasingly framed as a contentious one. With headings like 'Legalized Animal Abuse', 'Demands Freedom for Caged Hens', and 'Their Lives Are Worse than the Slaughter',[6] it was dawning on Norwegians that the battery cage system was not just 'the end of a romantic era', but the start of a deeply troublesome one – one where farms were like factories and animals like machines.

Incidentally, Ruth Harrison's classic, *Animal Machines* (1964), was translated into Norwegian the year after its release in Britain, and awoke many Norwegian animal activists to the dramatic changes underway in the agricultural sector.[7] The case against caged hens was to become one of the Norwegian animal movement's main issues throughout the 1970s.[8] One of the spearheads in this battle was the *Campaign against Caged Hens*, whose associated members contributed pieces to the newspapers throughout the 1970s, creating a steady stream of protest against the changes in the egg industry. Helen Hegermann, a vocal animal activist, led the Campaign. Even before it was launched, she had been a frequent writer of letters to the newspapers, often pieces concerning the importance of considering the natural needs of hens. But if the Campaign's protests were impressively persevering, they were nevertheless consistently relegated to the readers' letters columns and other such *marginal* corners of the public sphere.

When the Campaign was launched, another representative, Ulf Gleditsch, wrote to *Aftenposten*:

> A new animal protection campaign is about to unfold and to set its course over all of Norway. The animal movement has grown tired of the conditions under which caged hens live, in spite of the Animal Protection Act's clear message to consider the instincts and natural needs of animals.[9]

Gleditsch's piece is an early example of the rhetorical strategy the Campaign would standardize and repeat during the rest of the decade. It begins with a concrete description of how a caged hen lives: 'It stands on a slanting wire floor, and lives its entire life on a space not much bigger than the size of a sheet of paper. It never sees sun or grass, but is exposed exclusively to artificial light.' Then the piece describes the consequences of this life: 'It develops deformed claws, and when a cage hen is taken out and placed on the ground, it cannot walk! Cannibalism is common, and weak animals are often picked on until they die.' Then follows a contrast with what is assumed to be requirements for the good life for egg-laying hens:

> A caged hen cannot pick in the ground for feed, stretch its wings, ruffle its feathers, sandbathe, or develop social standing in normal ways. It cannot hide in a soft place when laying its eggs, or find a place to perch and rest.

Finally, the argument closes with the suggestion that caged hens live *unnatural* lives, often with a reference to the law's requirement to the contrary: 'All of its natural needs, which the Animal Protection Act establishes, it is not allowed to experience, as long as it lives.'

This critique formed the platform for practically all protests against the battery cage system in Norwegian public debate, not just in the 1970s, but all the way up to the EU ban. Its main axis is the premise that hens need to express their natural inclinations in order to have good lives. *Happy hens are hens that are allowed to do what hens do.* What is interesting is that this closely resembles – if it is not simply identical to – what Berger called 'the early modern norms for poultry keeping'. Most of the media coverage concerning caged hens in the 1970s revolved around the same points, formulated in almost exactly the same language. Part of this could be due to the Campaign itself, which probably worked towards streamlining the message they would transport to the media. But the newspapers themselves were, at this point, quite willing to use similar descriptions.

For instance, in 1979, there was a more direct confrontation in the media between proponents and opponents of the cage. The Campaign had previously submitted a petition of 10,000 signatures to the agricultural authorities, and had told media that another was now in the works. *Aftenposten* referred to the animal movement's stance that the cages had been scientifically proven to cause stress in the hens, and added on its own accord that 'the animals are placed on slanting wire floors, do not have the space to stretch their wings properly, no roosts, and no opportunity to sandbathe.'[10] But if the newspapers seemed willing to take on the analysis offered by the Campaign, none of them were able to work up much pressure on the government. When the Ministry of Agriculture in the same story was confronted with the animal movement's challenge, the response was that they saw 'no reason to change the animal protection act and ban the cages', while the veterinary director told the newspaper that,

> We cannot see how the cages are in conflict with the Animal Protection Act. There are not weighty enough reasons to suggest a change of the act, and it is beyond doubt that a ban would have large economic consequences.

The Campaign managed to sustain debate about the issue of caged hens throughout the 1970s, with the result that *Aftenposten*, in 1981, announced it would no longer print contributions to this debate. The debate had been a 'never-ending event in Aftenposten's letters column', the editors wrote, and added that, 'At this point we cannot continue this repetitive debate. The space in the columns is too scarce, and the contributions too many.'[11]

What, then, had the Campaign achieved? In terms of altered regulation or practices, nothing at all. In terms of public sentiment, probably not much, although the newspapers overall were quite willing to convey the critics' protests verbatim. But the Campaign did manage to tease out their counterparts' main justification for the battery cage system: *Economics*. This was to become important in the coming decade, when the egg industry was challenged on principle grounds – in the courts.

Henrietta hen goes to court

When *Aftenposten* excused itself from printing any further readers' letters, this marked the transition to the 1980s. Whereas the news coverage in the 1970s had revolved around the Campaign against Caged Hens, and consisted largely of readers' letters written by representatives of the Campaign, in the 1980s, critics were to pursue a different track: *Lawsuits*. The discrepancy between the requirements of the Animal Protection Act, which emphasized the importance of the 'instincts and natural needs of the animal', and the reality of life in a battery cage, had long been felt – and occasionally expressed – by the animal movement. Now, the Norwegian Society for Protection of Animals (NSPA) intended to expose this oxymoron to the courts. This, however, was to prove more difficult than expected.

In 1982, the authorities introduced new regulations for keeping hens in commercial egg production.[12] The regulations were designed to be more humane than the ones they replaced, but the animal movement quickly jumped on the occasion to highlight what they saw as a judicial oxymoron: The regulations allowed a form of production which violated the law of which the regulations were supposed to be elaborations. After the NSPA had issued a writ of summons to the

State, its leader, veterinarian Toralf Metveit, told *Aftenposten* that, 'Our claim is that the regulations for the keeping of hens in cages are not in harmony with article 2 [of the Animal Protection Act].' The story went on to say that a similar case had been raised in Germany, where one talked about 'concentration camp eggs', suggesting rather vividly to the reader that these were facilities one could not easily square with an ambition of ensuring animal welfare.[13] Again, the message to reach the media was that our way of producing eggs – at this point about 95 per cent of Norway's egg production – was something of an oxymoron. It was a system *approved*, but not *approved of*.

In the first instance, the lawsuit was dismissed for procedural reasons, and the court held that if NSPA wanted to see the case tried, it would have to sue one or several egg producers.[14] Consequently, in 1985, the NSPA announced their decision to sue an individual farmer, and the next year it became clear that they had chosen Karl Wettre, the manager of an average Norwegian egg farm of about 2,000 hens, but – more importantly – a board member of the Norwegian Farmers' Association and also the leader of a regional Egg Central.[15] Wettre told the media that he was not worried about the case, but that he felt sad being displayed as society's animal abuser number one. He affirmed, however, that he was confident of winning the case, since his production was done in accordance with the authorities' regulations.[16] His confidence was arguably somewhat paradoxical, since these regulations were precisely what the NSPA wanted to target with its lawsuit.

An important factor in the case was the treatment the battery system had received in preparation of the new Animal Protection Act of 1974, as this was the law which the regulations were supposed to supplement. A story in 1986 brought to light how the balancing act between animal welfare and agricultural economics had been an explicit part of the discussion in 1974. In drafting the Act, the Parliament's agricultural committee referred to our 'limited knowledge about the individual animal's need for activity and unhindered expression of its instincts', and added that we should consider 'practical and economical rationalization viewpoints', before it concluded that 'if we are to have practical poultry keeping in today's society, the system of keeping hens must probably be approved.'[17] Only reluctantly accepting the fact that money ruled, the article went on to state that public opinion was thought to be strongly in opposition to battery cages, and that many veterinarians were also against it. An interesting caption added to the impression:

> It was probably nicer to be a hen in the old days, when the animals were granted what the Parliament's agricultural committee has called 'animals' need for activity and unhindered expression, which is now balanced against practical and economic rationalization concerns.

The trade-off between economics and hen welfare surfaced repeatedly during the court case. As various scientists were put on the witness stand to express their equally various views on the welfare of caged hens, NSPA began to take a somewhat firmer stance. 'We know more now about animal psychology and animals' instincts than when the Animal Protection Act was written in 1974', stated the NSPA's attorney Hjort, before he went on to elaborate how battery hens tend to develop behavioural disorders.[18] To this, the council for the other side responded firmly, though with something of a concession, in an article entitled 'Economically Necessary To Imprison Animals':

> If we were to consider the animals' interests, exclusively, we could just as well let them free. Then we would have to eat grass and plants instead of meat, eggs, and that kind of thing, said Supreme Court attorney Annæus Schjødt in [court] yesterday. The suffering imposed upon the animals has to be balanced against economy, a concern for the industry and the rural population, Schjødt said. Many farmers rely on this because they are short of land, Schjødt said, who believed that the farmers would be willing to let the hens free more if one could design a system that would yield approximately the same economic results. Does this mean that one will have to impose greater degrees of suffering on the animals to drive down the price for eggs, Supreme Court Justice Odd Jarle Pedersen, the court administrator, asked. Yes, you could say that, Schjødt replied.[19]

'[W]e are faced with economic considerations', admitted the NSPA's attorney Hjort in response, but added that 'it is facile to do what the farmers have done, to say simply that we must have the battery cages system because everything else is unprofitable.' These positions were predictable. What is interesting is that even the defence admitted it was in the hens' interest to have greater freedom of movement. In other words, even the industry had to admit that 'caged welfare' was a sort of oxymoron. Cages did not really square with the hens' natural needs, but they did satisfy certain other needs, not least the one of appeasing the industry and other representatives of rural interests.

In 1988, it was announced that the farmer, Karl Wettre, had been acquitted of the charges, and this put an end to a legal spectacle which had occupied the better half of a decade. The court's conclusion was hardly very definitive on the issue of the welfare of caged hens, however. *Aftenposten* reported that '[t]he question about whether caged hens suffer or not was not treated, since the court felt it was not competent to make such a discretionary judgment.'[20] The court added only that this production system had been considered during the preparations for the new Animal Protection Act of 1974, and in that context deemed acceptable.[21] In other words, the battery cage continued to be approved – albeit with increasing unease.

The great egg carton controversy

The case against Wettre was in reality a case against the oxymoron allowed by the agricultural authorities, that is, against the fact that the regulations for poultry keeping violated the Act of which they were supposed to be elaborations.

According to the critics, the government was saying *both* 1) animals are to express their natural behaviours *and* 2) hens can be kept in cages where they cannot express their natural behaviours. Another aspect of the oxymoronic status of caged hens was first pointed out by one of Norway's leading animal advocates, Kåre Knutsen, in his book *Dyrenes rettigheter* (1974), an indictment of current human-animal practices. In one of the book's chapters, Knutsen targeted an iconic egg carton, on which was printed an image of a small, romantic hen house, 'where hens are walking leisurely about, nibbling on grain and straw' (op. cit.: 25). Knutsen wanted to know whether the 'Egg Central does not agree that the ads on these cartons smell rotten?' considering that, 'The hen strutting about at liberty, can today be found only on these cartons and in children's ABCs.' In other words, the illustration on the egg carton was highly unreal, whereas,

> In this most modern of realities, hens never get to see the sun, but are kept their entire lives inside. There – where there is often very little light – she can exert her full efforts on laying Sun eggs.
>
> (Ibid.)

Knutsen's critique is interesting because it echoes the concerns of the early modern norms for poultry keeping, but also because it reveals that egg producers appealed to the very same notion. The Egg Central sold industrially produced eggs from battery hens, but in its advertising used images of poultry keeping as it had looked more than 50 years ago. If the idea of caged welfare was an oxymoron, this is a case in point. Not even the producers were able to square the battery system with hen welfare, but reverted instead – nostalgically – to the image of a previous, traditional system.

Knutsen's critique was left to simmer in the animal movement for more than two decades, when it surfaced in another court case. In 1996, the NSPA had decided to file a lawsuit against the Egg Central, claiming they were using misleading advertising on their egg cartons. The announcement attracted plenty of attention from the news media. Commenting from the opening day of the court case, *Aftenposten* reported:

> Central to this conflict is the well-known egg carton from Prior, which depicts a proud hen behind two giant eggs, in a rural environment, with a farm and a Norwegian flag in the background. People associate this image with the method of production, and hence, it gives a completely skewed portrait, said the NSPA's legal representative, Supreme Court Attorney Tore Sverdrup Engelschiøn, in his opening statement.[22]

At stake was the question of the consumers' awareness of how eggs were produced, and in extension, how likely they were to be misled by the image on the carton. 'Everyone knows that hens lay eggs in cages', pronounced a representative of the Egg Central in one article,[23] to which the NSPA's attorney responded, in another article, 'I don't know where the Egg Central gets this;

how can they think that consumers are aware that they are buying eggs from caged hens?' Their secretary general expressed the same point, saying, 'This is not correct. We often do informative stands, where we tell people how caged hens live. Our experience is that most people have no idea what reality is like.'[24]

Just as in the previous court case, the media proved willing to present the case in a manner congenial to NSPA's message, although in this particular instance, they did so in the midst of a steady stream of puns on the word 'egg' – suggesting perhaps at the same time that the case was somewhat marginal. One example was a story in VG – which one might translate 'An Egg-Cellent Court Meeting' – which despite the pun gave newspaper readers the gist of the conflict. 'The hens live in wire netting cages', began the writer, sounding as he continued very much like a representative of the Campaign against Caged Hens:

> [T]hey have space equal to a sheet of paper, they never see the light of day ... they stand all day on reclining wire floors, their legs are stunted, they cannot flap their wings, they are frustrated from the lack of a rooster's company, and they peck on each other.

He went on to refer the NSPA's complaint, which was that the carton 'must be deemed illegal, because it gives the consumer a false impression that he/she is buying eggs from free range, unfettered and joyful hens'. He also referred to the Egg Central's stance, which according to their attorney was that:

> this case is not about whether caged hens have a good life or not. It is about how the public sees this box of six large eggs, and whether they are buying eggs on the wrong assumptions. It is a side-track to mix into this issue the lives of hens. Also: According to our experts, caged hens do not suffer greater strains than so-called free range hens. There are pros and cons of both forms of production. So let's disregard the issue about whether the hens live agreeable lives or not, and concentrate on the issue at hand.[25]

The attorney was right to say that the court case concerned the accuracy of the advertisement. However, there would be little point to such a case if no one saw anything objectionable in the current form of egg production, and the Egg Central's attempt to redirect the public's attention can hardly be called anything but an evasion strategy. The obvious premise of the case was that the carton presented a *beautified* image of how eggs were produced.

Despite a certain level of opposition and ridicule, the NSPA won the case, and this was widely reported in the media.[26] 'Happy hens are to be removed from the egg carton', announced the tabloid *Dagbladet*, and continued, 'Yesterday, Oslo city court concluded that this is misleading advertising, because the carton actually contains eggs from caged hens.' The article went on to cite Secretary General of NSPA, Tatiana Kapstø:

This is a great victory for us . . . The carton from Norwegian Egg Central shows a drawing of a hen lying on a bed of straw in the sunshine. The drawing fools people into thinking that they are eating eggs from free range hens. But the truth is that the animals live shitty lives in their cages, Kapstø says. She thinks the cartons should have an image of suffering battery hens, so that the consumers get to see "how eggs really are made" . . . In that case, most people would make a different decision, Kapstø says . . .

About a month after the verdict, the Egg Central announced that it would not appeal, but added that, 'The Norwegian Egg Central believes this case to be so ridiculous that we do not wish to saddle the court with it any further.'[27] In the same case, however, it came to light that the demand for free-range eggs had grown considerably in the month following the verdict. The newspaper took this to mean that the Judge had been right to conclude that the advertisement had skewed demand 'in the consumer group which the Advertising Act was primarily meant to protect, namely those in between the engaged and/or enlightened and the indifferent.' Not even this caused the industry to reconsider anything much. In December that same year, a new carton design was announced, where the free-ranging hen which had previously adorned the carton had been replaced by another egg. Apart from that, the carton remained the same.

'All hens are now free!'

Things were destined not to remain the same for very long, however. From the late 1980s and into the 1990s, a more varied set of critical voices began to be heard in the debate. But this increased attention was still nothing compared to the veritable rush of news coverage that started once the news of the EU's prospective ban on the cages broke. This was to be the central axis of the debate throughout the 2000s.

The ban, which was to come into effect on 1 January 2012, was agreed in 1999, and Norwegian newspapers immediately started bringing news about the welfare of hens, about the need for farmers to invest in new equipment, about the consequences on agricultural production of the new systems, etc. Of course, farmers were facing a need to reinvest, but what was left out of much of the news coverage was the fact that they were in fact investing in *new cages*. Many of the articles left the impression that the changes to be made were substantial, and a great number even stated – what was blatantly untrue – that hens would no longer be kept in cages.

If the public debate around the issue had resembled, up to this point, an oxymoron – a situation approved but not approved of – the news of the EU's ban rather quickly turned the atmosphere of the debate around, from an oxymoron to a euphemism. This was in part the outcome of the industry's own communication strategy, but partly also an effect of the media's evident lack of sufficient research and/or accurate reporting.

One of the most telling examples of how the issue was now framed euphemistically is a small note, in the tabloid *Dagbladet*, under the heading, 'All caged hens now liberated', which did not say much more than that hens were no longer confined to cages, since the EU ban on the cage would come into effect as of 1 January 2012.[28] The short article stated that 'new EU regulations which ban caged hens have led to big changes in Norwegian egg production.' It stated further that 'previously, one used cages with three hens in each. With the new environmental interiors, seven hens are put together in an "apartment" where they have more room, perches, sandbaths, and a nest in which to lay their eggs.' This description can hardly be called anything but misleading. In reality, the new cages have only marginally more room, and although they do have perches, the 'sandbaths' and 'nests' are probably not at all what the average newspaper reader would associate with those words. The sandbath is a bit of straw, and the nest is a small compartment within the cage, with metal walls and a piece of flapping plastic as a door. What is more troublesome, perhaps, is that for someone who has not actually witnessed the new cages, this note might be completely misleading about whether hens are now to be kept in cages at all. What does an 'apartment' for egg-laying hens look like, really? Is it more like a cage or more like a hen house?

Not all the coverage was as misleading, but a surprising number of articles left the newspaper reader with more or less the same idea. In *Stavanger Aftenblad*, a regional daily, one could read, 'Half of all egg production in Norway is in caged hen systems which will be banned from 2012.' This development, the newspaper refers to as a 'transition to so-called environmental cages with furnishings.'[29] An 'environmental cage with furnishings' – what precisely does that refer to? The newspaper reader is not told. In 2009, the rural daily, *Nationen*, wrote: 'Many Norwegian caged hens need a new and improved residence. Before 2012, all laying hens will have houses with their own perch and spa section.'[30] Here, it is quite unclear for someone who is not already aware of the details what is about to happen. Hens need a new 'residence' – but is that residence a cage or not? They are to have 'their own perch', but how proprietary is this perch really? They are to live in a 'house', but do they resemble the old, often spacious, hen houses? And are they really to have their own 'spa section'? If the 'spa section' refers to the so called 'nest', then the article is certainly a case of euphemism.

More or less the same effect is left by an article in *Aftenposten*, in 2011, which uses many of the same terms. 'A new EU directive has sent Norwegian hens on the move', the article begins, and establishes further that:

> beginning next year, all laying hens must be free range or reside in hen houses with environmental interiors. The furnishing means that the hens will have more room, with access to perch and a sandbath. It also has a separate nest and the possibility to whet claws and beaks. All the old cages will thereby be banned.[31]

One has to be quite knowledgeable – indeed, more knowledgeable than the average Norwegian newspaper reader – to realize that cages are still being used.

All one hears is that hens are to be kept in 'hen houses with environmental interiors' – and 'furnished' ones, to boot.

An article in *Agderposten*, a regional daily, is perhaps the most misleading of all. It begins:

> Here, 7,500 hens are tripping about in their new luxury home. They supply eggs for those Sunday breakfast tables. Happy hens are the new trend. Just in the last three years around 40 million kroner have been infused into rebuilding or building of production facilities adapted to the new rules for hen keeping. Next year, the traditional caged hen production will be banned in this country.[32]

The article goes on to introduce an example of a farmer who has rebuilt his facility – a man, as the article states, who has 'chosen to live off happy hens.' 'The hens live freely in this house. They fly between the different platforms, bathe in straw sand, eat and drink when they wish, the newly hatched egg farmer says.' Under the heading 'Happy hens', the article adds: 'From January 2012 caged hens will be completely banned in this country.' Again, for anyone who has actually witnessed the new cages, this is obviously wrong, and the wording throughout is arguably dubious. The trouble was not just that most people had not in fact witnessed the new cages, and were largely ignorant of how they looked, but that they were also confused about the fact that they were, indeed, *cages*.

There were, however, many protests against the euphemistic way of describing the situation. Most notably, the animal protection organizations were quick to express that ordinary consumers were being fooled by sneaky rhetoric. One opinion leader on agricultural topics, the veterinarian Anne Viken, wrote in the daily *Vårt Land*, under the heading, 'You've Been Fooled':

> You might have read it in the media: Cages for laying hens are now forbidden in Norway. There is only one problem: This is not true. 'Cages are banned'. This happy news spread as fire in dry grass after New Year's, but I am sorry to say, this is a scam. Fact: The only change is that we have a new type of cage. Laying hens are no longer placed in so called traditional cages, but in environmentally furnished cages. To say that these are 'not cages' is newspeak, a rhetorical move . . . [O]ne's eyesight must be pretty impaired to say that these cages are not cages.[33]

A series of reader's letters from animal activist Tetyana Kalchenko made much the same point. She wrote to the daily newspaper *Dagsavisen*, for instance, under the heading, 'Caged Hens Are Not Forbidden', saying,

> 50 per cent of Norwegian eggs come from caged hens. Several newspapers have been fooled and have written that new EU rules ban caged hens. Unfortunately, this is not true. About half of all Norwegian hens will continue to be placed in cramped cages also with the new rules.[34]

And an editor of *Trønderbladet* stated that,

> Everyone with eyes can see that these environmental interiors are cramped, and when Dyrevernalliansen calls this a prison, it is hard to disagree. The environmental interiors are so tight that hens cannot even beat their wings. These new cages are not a great leap of progress for animal welfare.[35]

Finally, a representative of the progressive animal protection organization, *Dyrevernalliansen*, wrote a piece which would be printed in several newspapers.

> [T]he poultry industry makes it sound as if there will be no caged hens from next year. The old, bare and tight cages for laying hens are in any case soon a thing of the past. From 1 January next year, we will no longer have caged hens, but environmental hens, said director of communications for Nortura, Nina Sundqvist, to Nationen on 5 August. The industry's magazine, *Fjørfe*, also claims that caged hens are about to become history, and they often use the word environmental furnishings about cages. This is dishonest communication on the part of the poultry industry ... To call caged hens environmental hens is just as misleading as selling some caged eggs as Farm eggs. Battery cage facilities cannot be called anything but animal factories.[36]

For the egg industry – and for everyone else invested in a relative *status quo* – the prospect of banning battery cages was paramount to economic death.[37] When the news of the EU's ban first broke, farmers were therefore quick to complain about the costs it would engender. But as the industry reluctantly realized that the ban could not be stopped, it began to cling to the idea of the cage – in whatever form it could have it. The public's opposition against the very idea of caging hens had grown, however, and just as 100 years previously, people now thought that a caged hen could not be a happy hen. The industry hence reverted to the euphemism as a rhetorical evasion strategy. Where they had previously told the public, 'Hens can indeed have welfare in cages!', they were now saying, 'These are not cages!' – swapping one trope (oxymoron) for another (euphemism). But just as the Campaign of the 1970s and the court cases of the 1980s and 1990s had tried to expose our way of producing eggs as an oxymoron – as a form of production not in tune with our expressed values, as a system *approved* but not *approved of* – critical commentators were now quick to expose the euphemisms employed by the industry. The EU's ban appears to have ignited an even fiercer criticism of the very idea of putting hens in cages, and the industry's rhetorical strategy of euphemistically referring to the new cages as 'environmental interiors', 'houses', 'apartments', 'furnished cages', etc. – not to mention the impression that hens would no longer be kept in cages at all – was too easily identified and exposed by observant critics.

The (new) traditional notion of good poultry keeping

Whether a reaction towards such rhetorical evasion strategies or not, consumers have recently begun to liberate themselves from commercial egg production altogether. Newspapers tell with increasing frequency of people who are no longer merely *consumers* of eggs, but who have also become *producers*, keeping their own, small flocks of hens for a self-sufficient supply of eggs. As such, this represents a reaction against egg production both as oxymoron *and* as euphemism. In the place of approving what we do not approve of, and instead of calling things by other names, these people suggest a return to the motives and practices represented by the preindustrial form of poultry keeping described at the start of this chapter.

Aftenposten brings one such story, interviewing an Oslo architect who reveals some of the motivations of this new group of poultry hobbyists:

> It is good to know where the eggs come from, and here, they have lived nice, free lives, strolling around in the garden . . . My impression is that more people are now thinking about animal welfare. It feels better to eat eggs when you know that the animals have had good lives. There's something about being able to trace your food [to its source]. It feels natural.[38]

This new trend of self-sufficient poultry keeping has perhaps the outward appearance of the traditional way – as these hens typically occupy gardens or front yards, and have free access to the outdoors, with fresh air and sunlight and all the rest – but it is actually far removed from that context. Today, as compared to then, no one in this part of the world actually needs to produce food, either as a living or as a matter of sustenance. These people are thus hobbyists, but not as those of former times, whose interest in poultry was primarily to bring forth exemplary specimens of *gallus gallus domesticus*. Rather, the hobby is to produce food. At the same time, the hens of the new poultry hobbyist class are much more than providers of eggs; they are a special kind of pet, a neighbourhood attraction, and an invitation to the world of animals and to nature.

Most of the stories about the emerging self-sufficient poultry keeping culture emphasize that these are *happy* hens, *lucky* hens, *free* hens – and that they are all of those things because *they have escaped the cage*. These articles – and the hobbyists they describe – keep alive the idea that hens are happy only when kept in small numbers, when they are outdoors in green and spacious yards, with plenty of air and sunlight, where they can move around and search for their own food, etc. If the new trend of self-sufficient poultry keeping is nothing much besides nostalgia, it is still a testament to the latent presence in our culture of the idea that 'the instincts and natural needs of the animal should be taken into consideration, so that it does not suffer needlessly.'

Conclusion

Throughout this chapter, I have employed the rhetorical terms *oxymoron* and *euphemism* as my analytical aids. I have argued that the introduction of the battery cage to Norway was the introduction of an oxymoron – a situation where we were asked to approve what we really do not approve of. This oxymoronic situation persisted because we were never thoroughly asked to forsake our previous notion of the good life for egg-laying hens, what Berger called 'the early modern norms for poultry keeping'. Instead, the industry changed the subject, and asked us to refocus our attention on the hens' productivity and absence of disease. This situation withstood several bouts of criticism, and when it finally exploded, largely due to the EU's ban, the industry's response was to enact another evasion strategy, the euphemism, the gist of which is to call a spade something other than a spade.

I personally believe that there can be no good life for egg-laying hens where they are denied freedom of movement to the extent imposed on them by a battery cage – whether 'enriched' or not. What I have said in this chapter does not hinge on my personal opinion, however, since my point is that Norwegians *in general* appear to have remained committed to something like the early modern norms for poultry keeping, while implicitly accepting a system that belies this set of values and priorities. This is apparent not just in the fact that the criticism which the battery cage met with from its very inception was based precisely in the early modern norms for poultry keeping; it surfaces also – and not least – in the Animal Protection Act, which underlines that 'the instincts and natural needs of the animal should be taken into consideration.' But most interestingly, it surfaces in statements and decisions made by the egg industry itself. Why, for instance, did the egg industry decide to illustrate their egg cartons with such an unreal and nostalgic image? Was it not because they assumed it would be more acceptable, and have more appeal, to the regular Norwegian consumer? *Undoubtedly.* And why did they make that assumption? Well, because the way eggs were *in fact* produced in Norway was perhaps approved, but not approved of. For this reason, I believe we can tell the story of the debate about the battery cage as one of rhetorical evasion strategies enacted, challenged, adjusted, and exposed.

Notes

1 I use the phrase 'battery cage' because it is the established term in English, but I should note that there is no Norwegian equivalent; the most common designation in Norwegian is simply 'hen cage' or 'hens' cages'.
2 Animal Protection Act (1974), Article 2. http://lovdata.no/pro/#document/ROL/lov/1974-12-20-73?searchResultContext=1062 (accessed 10 June 2014). Revised in 2009, the law is now called the Animal Welfare Act. www.regjeringen.no/en/doc/laws/acts/animal-welfare-act.html?id=571188 (accessed 10 June 2014).
3 The database is also known as Mediearkivet and A-tekst. Because there is no word in Norwegian for 'battery cage' the literal translation 'batteribur' turned up no results when used as a search word. 'Burhøns' [caged hens] turned up 989 hits. 'Hønsebur' [hens' cages] turned up 92 hits. The combination 'bur' + 'høne' [cage + hen] turned up 299 hits, many – but far from all – of which overlapped with hits from the previous searches. I also used 'høne' [hen] and 'høns' [hens] to browse early cases, that is, before cages started to appear in the newspapers. The material consists largely of readers' letters and news stories. The database is quite comprehensive, but it does not hold complete volumes of all the relevant newspapers, and my reading thus slants towards its admittedly contingent selection of newspapers.

4   In this section I lean heavily on Berger (1997).
5   Kari Bay Haugen, "Han plukker 1 mill. egg pr. år", *Verdens Gang*, 14 November 1968, p. 14.
6   Harald Greftegreff, "Legalisert dyrplageri", *Aftenposten*, 27 March 1979, p. 24; Ellen Margrethe Dahl, "Krav om frihet for høns i bur", *Aftenposten*, 24 September 1979, p. 2; NN, "Livet er verre enn slaktingen", *Verdens Gang*, 17 December 1979, p. 42.
7   See Sayer (2013) for the reception of Harrison's book in Britain.
8   A comprehensive history of animal protection in Norway has yet to be written, but a summary is given in Ellefsen (2013).
9   Ulf Gleditsch, "Aksjon mot burhøns", *Aftenposten*, 2 February 1976, p. 9.
10 NN, "Burdrift med loven i ryggen: Eggprodusenter innbys til dialog med dyrevern", *Aftenposten*, 13 June 1979, p. 20.
11 NN, "Punktum for bushøns-debatt", *Aftenposten*, 8 April 1981, p. 23.
12 Svein Thoresen, "Burhøns mot Staten", *Verdens Gang*, 12 July 1982, p. 16.
13 Else Brudevold, "Dyrebeskyttelsen mot Staten: Høns lider", *Aftenposten*, 17 December 1983, p. 18.
14 NN, "Burhøns i byretten", *Aftenposten*, 23 June 1984, p. 9.
15 NN, "Rettsak om burhønsenes situasjon", *Aftenposten*, 23 April 1985, p. 64.
16 Mona Østby Beck, "Norges Dyrevernbeskyttelsesforbund [sic] vil vedtekter til livs: Burhønsholder i Nittedal saksøkes", *Aftenposten*, 8 October 1985, p. 7.
17 Per Arne Langen, "Norges Dyrebeskyttelsesforbund: Går til rettsak mot burhønshold", *Aftenposten*, 18 January 1986, p. 12.
18 NN, "Ulovlig å holde høns i bur?", *NTB*, 1 February 1988.
19 Håkon Letvik, "Økonomisk nødvendig å holde dyr i fangenskap", *Aftenposten*, 3 February 1988, p. 60.
20 Håkon Letvik, "Frikjent for å ha høns i bur", *Aftenposten*, 13 February 1988, p. 21.
21 Håkon Letvik, "Frikjent for å ha høns i bur", *Aftenposten*, 13 February 1988, p. 21.
22 Karin Bøhm-Pedersen, "Høne-kampen begynte i dag", *Aftenposten*, 16 September 1996, p. 6.
23 Kåre Hunstad Jr., "-Glansbildet må fjernes", *Dagbladet*, 17 September 1996, p. 22.
24 Karin Bøhm-Pedersen, "Dyrevenner vil forby eggemballasje", *Aftenposten*, 17 September 1996, p. 5.
25 Jan Øyvind Roar Hagen, "Et egge-rørende rettsmøte", *Verdens Gang*, 17 September 1996, pp. 30–31.
26 Anne Kristin Hjukse, "Eggende seier for hønemor", *Dagbladet*, 16 October 1996, p. 10.
27 Karin Bøhm-Pedersen, "Norske Eggsentraler anker ikke dom: Glad høne skal fjernes før jul", *Aftenposten*, 15 November 1996, p. 3.
28 NN, "Alle høner er nå fri", *Dagbladet*, 30 December 2011, p.13.
29 NN, "Ingen egg-løsning i sikte", *Stavanger Aftenblad*, 21 January 2009, p. 9.
30 NN, "Verpehøns på flyttefot", *Nationen*, 12 February 2009, p. 13.
31 NN, "Høns på flyttefot", *Aftenposten*, 5 September 2011, p. 10.
32 Liv Ekeberg, "Håper ny høneluksus lønner seg", *Agderposten*, 8 March 2011.
33 Anne Viken, "Du er lurt", *Vårt Land*, 15 June 2012, p. 3.
34 Tetyana Kalchenko, "Burhøns blir ikke forbudt", *Dagsavisen*, 3 January 2012, p. 5.
35 Liv Helen Vaagland, "Ut av glattcella", *Trønderbladet*, 15 October 2011, p. 2.
36 Hilde Valbjørn Hagelin, "Miljøhøns? ", *Klassekampen*, 17 August 2011, p. 22.
37 In retrospect, such fears appear greatly exaggerated. As of 2014, around half of Norway's egg production is free range.
38 Heidi Borud, "Ja til frittgående høner", *Aftenposten*, 11 October 2012, pp. 2–3.

Bibliography

Almås, R. (2002) *Norges Landbrukshistorie, vol. IV: Frå bondesamfunn til bioindustri*. Oslo: Samlaget.

Appleby, M. (2003) 'The European Union Ban on Conventional Cages for Laying Hens: History and Prospects' in *Journal of Applied Animal Welfare Science*, 6(2). pp. 103–121.

The Arden Shakespeare Complete Works (2001) London: Thomson Learning.

Berger, K. (1997) *Fri som fuglen?: Modernisering av hønseholdet i Norge, 1880–1975*. Oslo: University of Oslo.

Ellefsen, R. (2013) *Med lov til å pine: Om bruk og beskyttelse av dyr*. Oslo: Inspirator/Fritt forlag.

Finlay, M. (2004) 'Hogs, Antibiotics, and the Industrial Environments of Postwar Agricultures' in Schrepfer, S. and Scranton, P. (eds) *Industrializing Organisms: Introducing Evolutionary History*. New York: Routledge. pp. 237–260.

Fitzgerald, D. (2003) *Every Farm a Factory: The Industrial Ideal in American Agriculture*. New Haven: Yale University Press.

Harrison, R. (1964) *Animal Machines*. London: Vincent Stuart.

Horowitz, R. (2004) 'Making the Chicken of Tomorrow: Reworking Poultry as Commodities and as Creatures, 1945–1990' in Schrepfer, S. and Scranton, P. (eds) *Industrializing Organisms: Introducing Evolutionary History*. New York: Routledge. pp. 215–235.

Knutsen, K. (1974) *Dyrenes rettigheter: Ulovlig og lovlig dyreplageri i Norge*. Oslo: Dreyer.

Orland, B. (2004) 'Turbo-Cows: Producing a Competitive Animal in the Nineteenth and Early Twentieth Centuries' in Schrepfer, S. and Scranton, P. (eds) *Industrializing Organisms: Introducing Evolutionary History*. New York: Routledge. pp. 167–189.

Sayer, K. (2013) '*Animal Machines*: The Public Response to Intensification in Great Britain, c. 1960–1973' in *Agricultural History*, 87(4). pp. 473–501.

13 Being salmon, being human

Notes on an ecological turn in the modern narrative tradition

Martin Lee Mueller

The ongoing appeal of the anthropocentric narrative

In August 2010, Rögnvaldur Hannesson, a professor of fishery economics at the Norwegian School for Economics and Business Administration, publicly raised the question of whether or not it was time to sacrifice all of Norway's wild salmon in favour of their domesticated cousins. The Norwegian business newspaper *Dagens Næringsliv* has described Hannesson as one of the country's leading experts on fishery economics, and so his contention is not to be taken lightly. Here is what Hannesson wrote:

> We should perhaps ask ourselves what we want wild salmon for? If wild salmon get in the way of the fish farming industry, then I must say we must be ready to sacrifice wild salmon. The industry creates great values and jobs along the entire coast. It is an important business branch, one that is important to keep. We need not feel pity for the upper class that will miss a playroom; surely they will find some corresponding amusement . . .
>
> (Hannesson, 2010. Author's translation)

Hannesson's brief but plain suggestion to let wild salmon go extinct in favour of industrially farmed salmon is representative of a particularly human-centred narrative which goes on thriving in our modern minds, despite the fact that there has been a radical *ecological turn* in modern thought since the early twentieth century, a turn, as I argue here, which lets thinking such as Hannesson's appear not only dangerously self-centred and short-sighted, but indeed fully obsolete. Owing to this ecological turn, we increasingly understand the richly complex ways in which our human lives unfold within the larger and more-than-human community that is the living Earth itself. Just like aspen trees, or spiders, or wolves, or indeed salmon, so too humans are tuned for relationship, as the ecophilosopher David Abram so poignantly writes (1996; 2010). This chapter unfolds in the tension that arises between, on the one hand, a flourishing and quickly expanding fish farming industry – which carries on the vision that sees humans at the centre of it all – and, on the other hand, that ecological turn in our thought, which strives to de-centre the human and to re-narrate our story within the far older, and larger, story of the Earth.

Three further introductory remarks are in place. *First*, the question of how we understand life invites for a discussion of the metaphysical implications of ecology. For ecology is that science which studies the ways in which individual organisms, including humans, relate to the larger house that is the biosphere. To ask about the metaphysical implications of ecology is already to suspect that we have insight to gain from focusing on this *relational aspect* of life.

Second, I suggest that in line with the other chapters in this collection, this chapter too unfolds against the ultimate horizon that is the ecological crisis. My more specific angle within this larger horizon is the difficult situation that salmon face in their encounter with modern humans. Two decades ago the philosopher-pair Richard Sylvan and David Benett predicted that a successful overhauling of the anthropocentric narrative was imminent. Optimistically they wrote:

> Changing to respectful approaches to the environment and supplanting the place of humans in the world and their ethical systems may seem excessive and extreme. Yet what is now seen as unthinkable, as the voice of extremism, will in a decade or two be seen as a necessity.
>
> (1994:184; in Curry, 2011:12)

The thinking of Hannesson, as well as his social status, speaks a different language. The anthropocentric story has outlived Sylvan and Benett's confidence in its timely demise. Once more, and unsurprisingly, it is the more-than-human others whose demise we are witnessing instead, this time whooped by a remarkably bold and explicit anthropocentric cheerleader.

And yet, Sylvan and Benett were also right. The actual voice of extremism is not that which attempts, with diligence and care, to reinterpret humans radically within the larger context of the biosphere. It is rather that which seeks to go on defending the separatist notion of humans as *outside* that larger context. They were also right in that the overhaul of the anthropocentric narrative is indeed a necessity, and an urgent one at that, for despite our great (and perhaps inevitable) difficulties in predicting with some measure of accuracy the precise *details* of planetary ecocide, we have sufficient certainty that many of the changes wrought in the name of anthropocentrism already are irreversible, and harmful to the resilience of individual species as much as to the larger unfolding of life.

Bruno Latour has written that '[t]he critical mind, if it is to be relevant again, must devote itself to the cultivation of a stubborn realism, but a realism dealing with . . . matters of concern, not matters of fact' (2004:18; in Curry, 2011:26). Realism of a narrow kind would take the (factual) prevalence of the anthropocentric narrative as a given premise, as axiomatic. The *fact* is that modern humans continue to have both the perceived moral entitlement and the power of the technoscientific complex to force other members of the biotic community down the one-way lane to extinction. The fact is that according to an anthropocentric interpretation, this is not considered problematic. But the *concern* remains: that something deeply wrong is underway when a particular group of moral actors stakes their version of the good *life* on the *death* of others.

This is to say that there is vitally important cultural work yet ahead. This work is subversive, in that the explicit intention is to continue to deconstruct a story of the good life that holds enormous import not only over our own (human) lives, but also over the lives of *everyone else*. The ongoing challenge is to develop analytical tools that help us train our critical stance, and disengage the massive and massively life-denying story, one narrative strand at a time. The hope and chance is that our de-construction will help co-create an open space of imaginative creativity and liberty; a space within which tenets for other, more life-affirming narratives of the good life can germinate, and eventually flourish.

Then there is the *third* and final introductory remark. To make either of these two preceding suggestions is already to position myself ethically. For to take issues with the ecological crisis in general, and with the plight of salmon in particular, means that I *begin* from the (normative) notion that a wrong is being committed. Likewise, to look to ecological thought for remedies against the crisis is to cast a certain 'fore-structure of suppositions' (as Heidegger would have called it) onto what I expect the outcome will be, and this fore-structure is informed fundamentally by that sense of wrongness. The philosopher Patrick Curry (2011:12ff.) observes that in keeping with certain academic traditions, such normative positioning commonly remains relatively unspoken. But the point can also be turned on its head, says Curry, for our descriptions of *what is* cannot usually be disentangled neatly from our suggestions of *what ought to be*, or *what ought not to be*. The angle we choose for our inquiries already impacts the insights we are likely to gain from these inquiries. And so like Curry, I too choose to make my own position overt, in the hope that it will contribute to an open and fair, though nonetheless critical, dialogue.

An atomistic and materialistic narrative tradition

The American philosopher J. Baird Callicott has written that both ecology and physics are now emerging into a 'consolidated metaphysical consensus . . . which may at last supplant the metaphysical consensus distilled from the scientific paradigm of the seventeenth century' (1989:102). This consensus verges on the still-unfolding understanding that 'we are enfolded, involved, and engaged within the living, terrestrial environment – that is, implicated in and implied by it' (ibid.:101). In a sense, this present chapter might already end right here, with this observation. But being human, we live inside narrative, and the still-dominant narrative of anthropocentrism sees the human as essentially outside of, and above, the larger and more-than-human community of life. We are far from fully comprehending, let alone *enacting*, the import of ecological thought to our narrative tradition. A reason may be that, as Callicott has also written, the holistic thinking implied by ecology is 'virtually unprecedented in the Western intellectual canon' (1994:84), which is another way of saying that we simply have had very little training in the matter. Instead, we have a 2,500-year-old track record of cultivating a narrative tradition that is both atomistic and materialistic. It appears expedient to begin with the beginning, and to take cautious and deliberate steps from there.

First developed by the Greek thinkers Leucippus and his student Democritus in the fifth century BCE, our own ontological tradition thinks that Being can be broken down into small, immutable, indestructible units called atoms (from Greek ἄτομος *a-tomos*, 'indivisible'). These atoms are further surrounded by a void. According to Leucippus, if you take a piece of wood and cut it into half, and then you cut either half in two halves, and so on, you will eventually end up with parts that can no longer be divided, and hence these indivisibles form the ground of Being. Here is an early origin of the *reductionist thinking* that we still find in the modern narrative of anthropocentrism. There is also a budding *mechanical* aspect to this narrative tradition. It lies in the way that all causal relations are thought to be, in Callicott's words,

> reducible to the motion or translation from point to point of simple bodies or the composite bodies made up of them . . . Only a mechanical solution [to presumed causal relations such as Newton's gravitational theory] could be satisfactory, since only a mechanical solution implicated exclusively the fundamental ontology of atomic materialism.
>
> (1989:102–103)

At the dawn of modern philosophy, we find this atomistic materialism reinterpreted through Descartes' famous formula *Cogito, ergo sum*, 'I think, therefore I am'. With Descartes, a deep ontological crack began to shoot far and fast through the phenomenal world, not unlike when lake ice relieves its inert tension in a rumbling boom that reverberates through the frozen landscape, leaving behind a jagged lake surface. Here, on the one side of the Cartesian split, was *res cogitans*: creative, intelligent, self-conscious, rational, *human* mind. And there, on the far end of the split, was *res extensa* or, in simpler (but no less succinct) terms, *everything else*: our own bodies, the domesticated animal companions with whom we shared our homes, all wild creatures, mountains, rivers, primal forests, the atmosphere, the oceans, the geological forces of the planet, the whole of the planetary presence.[1] The common denominator of 'everything else' (including, once more, our own bodies) was that it was devoid of creativity, devoid of (self)consciousness, devoid of intelligence, devoid of agency. It was other. It was mere matter, dead, machinelike. With Cartesian thinking, the 'machine' became the *first* ontological metaphor, the primordial way in which the modern mind encountered the world. This was a profound ontological re-interpretation of the world, and our own place within it. Both the American writers Charlene Spretnak and Carolyn Merchant have pointed out that never before had any tradition of thought considered the world to be a machine; the most prevalent world-metaphor up until then had been that of the world as a *living organism* (Merchant, 1993; Spretnak in Mills, 1997:163ff.). Descartes' re-interpretation of the world from a living being into a machine was an unprecedented, entirely novel way of seeing the world. Coupled with earlier atomistic thought, the metaphor of the machine would become a powerful monistic lens, through which our particularly modern narrative tradition came

to know the more-than-human world, and our own place within it. Writes
Callicott:

> The terrestrial natural environment consists of a collection of bodies
> composed of molecular aggregates of atoms. A living natural body is in
> principle a very elaborate machine. That is, its generation, gestation,
> development, decay, and death can be exhaustively explained reductively
> and mechanically. Some of these natural machines are mysteriously inhabited
> by a conscious monad, a "ghost in the machine." Living natural bodies come
> into a wide variety of types or species, which are determined by a logico-
> conceptual order, and have, otherwise, no essential connection to one
> another. They are, as it were, loosed upon the landscape, each outfitted with
> its (literally God-given) Platonic-Aristotelian essence, to interact catch-as-
> catch-can.
>
> (1989:104)

Others have made similar observations. The ecologist and philosopher Paul
Shepard has written that our received ontological intuition 'presumes naively that
the landscape is a roomlike collection of animated furniture' (1999:69), into
which we embodied creatures are arbitrarily placed like cupboards and sofas and
armchairs, dwelling therein for a while but being essentially replaceable. Likewise,
Anthony Quinn writes:

> In [the Newtonian] conception . . . the world consists of an array of precisely
> demarcated individual things or substances, which preserve their identity
> through time, occupy definite positions in space, have their own essential
> natures independently of their relations to anything else, and fall into clearly
> distinct natural kinds. Such a world resembles a warehouse of automobile
> parts. Each item is standard in character, independent of all other items, in
> its own place, and ordinarily unchanging in its intrinsic nature.
>
> (in Callicott, 1989:105)

This Newtonian-Cartesian-materialistic-atomic conception still reigns
powerfully today. Take the company Billund Aquaculture, which is working on a
joint Danish–Chinese endeavour to build salmon tanks in the Mongolian desert,
one of the remotest places anywhere, from any ocean. Bjarne Hald Olsen, a
leading engineer of the project, puts it as follows:

> As long as you have access to water and electricity, you can produce salmon
> anywhere you please in the world . . . Salmon can now be produced in places
> you earlier wouldn't even have dreamed of. In principle it can be done even
> in the Sahara, but in reality we're going to see farms springing up close to the
> large salmon markets in the US and in Asia.
>
> (Langberg, 2012. Author's translation)

In Norway, the debate around moving salmon inland is characterized by heated opposition. On the one hand there are those, like then-minister of fisheries Lisbeth Berg-Hansen, who have called the trend 'unrealistic' and 'problematic' (Berg-Hansen, 2012. Author's translation). On the other hand there are those like her predecessor in the ministry, Svein Munkejord, who have talked about a 'sea change' in the industry. Munkejord himself has invested several hundred thousand kroner of private funds in an Irish project seeking to move salmon inland. He argued for his decision with a remarkable nod to ecological concern: 'By investing in land-based farming, *environmental arguments* [such as the notorious issues with escapees, lice, or eutrophication] will fall away. Such structures will, so-to-speak, *give full control*' (in Ystad, 2011. Author's translation and emphasis). What we see here are symptoms that salmon are moving ever deeper into the gravitational horizon of the atomistic-materialistic narrative, becoming, en route, redefined as *terrestrial* creatures, and becoming also increasingly alienated from the oceans and rivers into which they have evolved.

A further symptom for this trend deserves a more lengthy commentary. This concerns the so-called AquAdvantage Salmon™.[2]

Genetically modified salmon

Say that you have found a way not only to domesticate salmon, but to make these domesticates grow to market size in half the time it takes your competitors. Say that you have invested 20 years of research and $60 million to develop the technology to make that happen. The technology is complicated, and from the specific angle of practicality, it is also rather successful: First, you take the anti-freeze promoter from a creature called ocean pout. Ocean pouts are eel-like fish who live in the Northwest Atlantic, off the coast of New England and Canada. The anti-freeze proteins in their blood enable the fish to live in near-freezing waters. The proteins are made by a promoter that is basically an on–off switch, and because ocean pout live where they live, the switch is always 'on' to ensure a constant supply of anti-freeze hormones in their bodies. Now that you have extracted this on–off switch from the ocean pout, you splice it with a Chinook salmon growth hormone gene. The result is a Chinook growth hormone gene that is perpetually switched on, and that will never cease generating growth hormones. At last you take this new gene and transplant it into Atlantic salmon. You end up with a creature who outwardly resembles Atlantic salmon, but whose inward metabolism is a hyperactive, restless composition that strives unceasingly towards one overarching end – rapid growth. The creature is so novel that the company who knows how to make it, AquaBounty Technologies of Waltham, Massachusetts, has deemed it best to patent it. Enter AquAdvantage Salmon.

Say, next, that this same company has been in business long enough to understand some of the major concerns of aquaculture critics. The company is familiar with the annual numbers of escapees from open-ocean raising pens into the surrounding waters, and it knows the many hazards these escapees bring to the free-roaming, indigenous salmon populations. The company also knows the many reservations the public has towards genetically modified (GM) organisms. It is fully aware that their product is like no other; if approved to markets by the US Food and Drug Administration (FDA), AquAdvantage Salmon would be the first-ever GM animal to be mass-produced, anywhere. These salmon are a landmark case. There have been *vegetable* precedents such as GM soybeans, GM maize, and GM cotton, and their market shares in the US are astonishing.[3] But before salmon, no other *animal* has ever been genetically modified for humans to eat on a large scale. The company knows all this. And so it goes about advocating its product very cautiously. It has adopted a zero-tolerance policy for escapees. Its vision is that no GM salmon will ever be given the chance to interbreed with wild salmon. Knowing full well that there are no individual measures that can guarantee a 100 per cent escape guarantee, the company has concocted a safety net of a number of overlapping and partially redundant measures to contain the fish. There are, first, *biological* measures. All of the fish produced by the company are female fish, made possible through a breeding strategy that is considered 100 per cent effective. Further, all of these females will be treated to possess not two but three sets of chromosomes in their cells. As with other triploid creatures – creatures with three sets of chromosomes – the resulting fish will be sterile.[4] Both of these biological measures combined are meant to prevent cross-breeding between GM salmon, as well as make breeding of female GM salmon with non-GM male salmon (nearly) impossible.

Then there are *physical* measures to contain the fish. All AquAdvantage Salmon will be bred exclusively in inland sites. They will spend their juvenile phase in tanks on Prince Edward Island, Canada. Smolts will then be shipped to another inland facility in Panama, where they will grow until they are ready for slaughter. Along every step of the process, a multiplicity of tanks, screens, filters, covers, and nets will be installed to prevent their escape. The company mentions also that in the unlikely case of uncontrolled escapes, chemicals such as chlorine are available to kill the fish. Further, the company plans to implement strict security routines. The routines will include preventing unauthorized personnel from accessing the production site, surveying the movements of those who are authorized to be there, and preventing other-than-human predators from entering. To make sure that neither unwanted humans nor any other animals will be able to come anywhere near the tanks, the company plans to install fencing topped with barbed-wire around the entire facility. All in all, the company will erect 11 sequential barriers between the fish in the tanks and the nearest river.

Finally, biological and physical containment measures are complemented with measures of *geographical* containment. The grow-out site in Panama is situated in a tropical environment, and the nearby river drains into the Pacific at a latitude inhospitable to any salmon. Water temperatures in the lower reaches of the watershed are so high that even in the unlikely event that any GM salmon should ever make it this far alive, it would die from hyperthermia before it could reach the ocean (cf. AquaBounty, 2010).

The containment does not end with the living fish. It extends also to those salmon who, for one reason or another, die before they are ready to be slaughtered and shipped to markets. Those who die during their earliest phase on Prince Edward Island will be frozen, collected, and eventually all incinerated together. Those who die later on in Panama will not be burned but buried on-site. The company has laid out precise routines for how these burials are to be organized:

> Each burial pit will be excavated to an initial depth of 1.0 m (0.5–0.75 m diameter). As dead fish are deposited, they will be covered with caustic lime, followed by another layer of dead fish and caustic lime, etc. until the burial pit is ~0.5 m deep, at which point it will sealed [sic] with plastic and covered with soil.
>
> (Ibid.:47)

Say that you do all this. Say that you intercept the genetic continuity of the salmon by introducing genetic sequences of two other fish into their flesh, one of whom is not remotely related to salmon. Say that you terminate their ability to procreate independently by engineering all-female, sterile populations. Say that you remove them from the rivers and even from the sea, so that they will live their lives in contained, barbed-wired, elevenfold-secured facilities. Say you do not feed their dead to the land but incinerate them, or seal them with plastic. Say you do everything in your power to keep the salmon in, and everything and everyone else out. The question is, can you remove a salmon this far from her habitat and still have a salmon?

In the fall of 2010, AquaBounty submitted an application to the FDA to approve their new product to the US market. Their application went hand in hand with a meticulously orchestrated media campaign. Throughout the many interviews, articles, and video clips that appeared both in national and international publications during that time, a particular sentence stood out for the frequency with which it surfaced. Take for an exemplary case this following statement by Ron Stotish, the chief executive of AquaBounty Technologies: 'In every measurement and every respect, these fish are identical to Atlantic salmon' (in Poulter, 2010). The statement is peculiar for two reasons. *First*, because it stands in direct opposition to another statement, this one also by AquaBounty, and from that same fall:

> However, triploid salmon *cannot* be assumed to be identical to diploids, as some differences do occur . . .: poor performance under conditions of low oxygen availability and/or high oxygen demand; jaw abnormalities, which have been observed by a number of investigators; and, somewhat poorer performance relative to diploids, especially when grown in sea water.
>
> (AquaBounty 2010:59–60. Emphasis added)

On the one hand these fish are defined as identical in every measurement and every respect. On the other hand the same company publishes a paper that says these fish *cannot* be assumed to be identical. Such a remarkable ontological puzzle deserves commentary.

The *second* reason for why Stotish's statement is peculiar is that it is rather counter-intuitive. You take a salmon, you implant a distant cousin's growth hormone into it – a growth hormone that you have equipped with the on–off switch taken from a third fish's anti-freeze gene – and then you say, "In every measurement and every respect, these fish are identical to Atlantic salmon." Such a blatant contradiction between utterance and intuition, too, deserves commentary.

Beginning with the *second* puzzle, it will be helpful to take a brief historical excursion. The early 1990s were the time when the first GM plants were being developed, and companies with an investment in this emerging market sought profits in return for their investments. On 17 July 1991, Michael Taylor was appointed as the FDA's first Deputy Commissioner for Policy. The position had not existed before him. His job was to oversee legal concerns regarding existing genetically modified organisms (GMOs), and to develop legal guidelines for future organisms with altered genetic memories that would be introduced to the market. Taylor had worked for the FDA before, between 1976 and 1981, when he had served as the executive assistant to the FDA's Commissioner. Then, in 1981, he went into private law practice, where he founded and led his law firm's 'food and drug law' practice. One of his most important customers was Monsanto, and Taylor played a key role in legalizing Monsanto's GM bovine growth hormone (which has since been banned from use in Canada, Australia, New Zealand, Japan, Israel, as well as by all members of the European Union). He then returned to the FDA as Commissioner for Policy in 1991, and during his tenure, the FDA ratified the so-called *principle of substantial equivalence*. The principle says that any new food – genetically modified or not – must be considered *the same and as safe as conventional food if it shows the same composition and characteristics as the ordinary food*. There have been those who defended the principle as a well-designed instrument to deciding what foods are safe and what are not. Here is a quote from the article 'Substantial equivalence is a useful tool', published in *Nature*, in which Peter Kearns and Paul Mayers argue in the principle's favour:

> Substantial equivalence is not a substitute for a safety assessment. It is a guiding principle which is a useful tool for regulatory scientists engaged in safety assessments. It stresses that an assessment should show that a GM variety is as safe as its traditional counterparts. In this approach, differences may be identified for further scrutiny, which can involve nutritional, toxicological and immunological testing. The approach allows regulators to focus on the differences in a new variety and therefore on safety concerns of critical importance. Biochemical and toxicological tests are certainly not precluded.
>
> (1999:640–641)

But there have also been those who criticized the tool for being too lax and essentially useless, because there is no binding agreement as to what precisely makes one organism substantially different from another. Erik Millstone and his colleagues wrote that:

> The concept of substantial equivalence has never been properly defined; the degree of difference between a natural food and its GM alternative before its "substance" ceases to be acceptably "equivalent" is not defined anywhere, nor has an exact definition been agreed by legislators. It is exactly this vagueness which makes the concept useful to industry but unacceptable to the consumer.
>
> (1999:525–526)

The following publication by the Royal Society of Canada expresses a similar concern, though in a more straightforward tone: 'Substantial equivalence does not function as a scientific basis for the application of a safety standard, but rather as a decision procedure for facilitating the passage of new products, GE and non-GE, through the regulatory process' (2011:182). In other words, the Royal Society consider it to be the principle's foremost purpose that new products can be moved quickly towards approval without causing much regulatory stir. It allows for new products to be approved within months of being developed, whereas comparable products in other industrial sectors are required to be tested stringently at high costs and through years of testing before they are either approved to or rejected from markets. By implication, FDA policy since the beginning of the 1990s can be read as a synergetic and progressive de-regulation of the GMO market.[5]

AquaBounty's decision to brand their GM salmon as 'identical in every measurement and every respect' to other Atlantic salmon becomes clearer in relation to this. AquaBounty knows that legal as well as commercial success is most strongly implied in the principle of substantial equivalence. They know also that no case brought to the FDA has ever been declined on accounts of substantial *difference*. Writes the Alliance for Natural Health: 'In past hearings on GMOs, the FDA has *never* found that genetic engineering in itself constitutes a material difference' (cf. Alliance for Natural Health, 2012. Emphasis added). In this light, the public relations strategy appears as a simultaneous appeal to FDA guidelines and to public concern. The precise wording may change, but the message does not: 'The chinook growth hormone is the same as the Atlantic salmon growth hormone; it is simply regulated differently. Their ability to grow faster does not change the biological make-up of the fish' (cf. AquaBounty, 2012a). Or: 'Triploid eyed-eggs for *AquAdvantage* Salmon are produced in a manner that results in the culture of an all-female population of triploid fish that are otherwise substantially equivalent to farmed Atlantic salmon' (AquaBounty, 2010:10). Or:

> AquAdvantage(r) Salmon (AAS) include a gene from the Chinook salmon, which provides the fish with the potential to grow to market size in half the time of conventional salmon. In all other respects, AAS are identical to other Atlantic salmon.
>
> (cf. AquaBounty 2012b)

But of course the constant repetition of the same paradox does not make that paradox any less problematic. Genetically modified salmon are genetically modified salmon are genetically modified salmon. And having been modified, they are not identical with other Atlantic salmon. Vandana Shiva, the Right Livelihood Award laureate, has argued against the principle of substantial equivalence:

> A very convenient tool called substantial equivalence principle was cooked up to say "let's just treat genetically engineered organisms like conventional crops". Of course, they don't say that when they want to patent these things. Then, at that point, they say these are "novel", these are not natural. But when it comes to safety, they say: it's just like nature, exactly as nature made it. I sometimes call this "ontological schizophrenia".
>
> (cf. Soechtig, 2013)

Before we move on to place the discussion more squarely into the context of ecological thought, let us halt for a brief resume. We are beginning to see that the concurrent alienation of farmed salmon from their ecological communities and the demise of their wild cousins both are *implied* in the narrative structure of an atomistic, materialistic ontology. Take AquAdvantage salmon, who are in a perplexing ontological situation. They are *identical* insofar as they serve the interest of the market. They are *special* insofar as they serve the interest of the market. They are contained elevenfold, with barbed-wire lining the horizon of their lives. Their dead will be buried beneath a layer of plastic. They will be flown from Canada to Panama and then back to US markets. They are defined by economic categories and contained for the sake of profit. Like other land-locked salmon, they are fundamentally and essentially objectified by a logic which adheres to a reductionist understanding of being.

Likewise, wild salmon are increasingly at odds with this same understanding. To the degree that wild salmon cannot be accounted for 'within' reductionist, atomic, materialist thinking – to the degree that they are 'externalities' to it – they become ontologically negligible. At best they 'get in the way of the fish farming industry' (Hannesson, 2010). The next conceptual step is as logical as it is frightening: that 'we must be ready to sacrifice wild salmon' (Hannesson, 2010). In other words: Once salmon *cease to exist conceptually*, it is but a small step until they *cease to exist*. This shows the great relevance of reading narratives and the ways in which such narratives mediate between ourselves and the more-than-human world. For while they ultimately are *our* (human) narratives, they become *world* narratives in lockstep with the pace at which the actions of modern technoscience send ripple effects throughout the biosphere. In other words, as our powers to fundamentally alter the world grow proportionally to our technological leverage, so too the world we inhabit increasingly comes to resemble that which our narratives encourage us to envision.

Resurgence of an ancient world-metaphor

Interestingly, the science of ecology arose from within this same ideological horizon. Early ecological thought portrayed the biosphere as what Callicott calls a 'mechanical Leviathan', a gigantic machine which itself consists of many smaller machines. The following remark by the Swedish botanist and zoologist Carl von Linné (1707–1778) clearly shows its indebtedness to the Cartesian thought: 'Like a planet in its orbit or a gear in its box, each species exists to perform some function in the grand apparatus' (in Callicott, 1989:105). This received ontological canon was finally overhauled in the early twentieth century, when the American plant ecologist Frederic E. Clements (1874–1945) conceived of another first, or fundamental, ontological metaphor for ecological thought: that of the *superorganism*. Writes Callicott:

> From the point of view of the Clementsean ecological organicism . . . the whole Earth's living mantle might . . . be represented as a vast "comprehensive" organic being. Furthermore, each higher level of organization – from single cell to multicelled organism, from organism to local superorganism (or "ecosystem", in a terminology not yet invented in Clements' day), from ecosystem to biome and biome to biosphere – is "emergent"; thus the whole cannot be reduced to the sum of its parts.
>
> (1989:105–106)

With the theory of the whole of the 'biotic community' as one superorganism, Clements breathed coherence, affinity, and life back into what had previously been a worldwide array of atomistic, individual spare parts. And this means that with Clements' theory, the ancient, pan-cultural first ontological metaphor of the world as a living organism was revived once more, and curiously so from within the one (and only) culture which had abandoned the metaphor three centuries earlier in favour of the 'world-machine'.

In the century since, the reclaimed metaphor has been further thought through both in its ecological implications and with regards to its 'ontological overtones' (Shepard, 1999:69). In mid-century, the ecologist Aldo Leopold called 'land' the 'foundation of energy flowing through a circuit of soils, plants, and animals. Food chains are the living channels which conduct energy upward; death and decay return it to the soil' (quoted in Ross 2001:101), a circuit composed of living creatures and the soils and waters and air in which they dwell. Not long after, philosopher Paul Shepard juxtaposed the classical atomistic model of Being with the emerging field theory of Being. Nature, according to the classical model,

> is epitomized by living objects rather than the complex flow patterns of which objects are temporary formations . . . the landscape [in this atomistic model] is a room-like collection of animated furniture . . . but it should be noted that it is best describable in terms of events which constitute a field pattern. Plants and animals participate in it without questions (that is, sinlessly) in an attitude of acceptance which in human terms would be called faith.
>
> (Shepard, 1999:69; see also Callicott, 1989:108)

In the 1970s, the American biophysicist Harold Morowitz gave further support to this emerging field theory:

Viewed from the point of view of modern [ecology], each living thing is a dissipative structure, that is, it does not endure in and of itself but only as a result of the continual flow of energy in the system . . . From this point of view, the reality of individuals is problematic because they do not exist per se but only as local perturbations in this universal energy flow . . . An example might be instructive. Consider a vortex in a stream of flowing water. The vortex is a structure made of an ever-changing group of water molecules. It does not exist as an entity in the classical Western sense; it exists only because of the flow of water through the stream. If the flow ceases the vortex disappears. In the same sense the structures out of which the biological entities are made are transient, unstable entities with constantly changing molecules dependent on a constant flow of energy to maintain form and structure.

(in Callicott, 1989:108)

At about the same, the chemist and engineer James Lovelock worked with biologist Lynn Margulis on the articulation of Gaia Theory, which is perhaps the most audacious and far-reaching continuation of Clementsean thought, with vast implications for a unified field theory of life. Its key theoretical insight is that the Earth's biosphere is not so well-understood as a machine, or as a mechanical set of processes, but rather that the Earth itself – including all of the animals, all of the plants, all of the bacteria and fungi within it – acts as a single, living organism, or metabolism. The world that we are a part of is itself alive, through and through. The theory ushered in an emerging recognition that biotic life does not merely *adapt* to its so-called environment, but that it also *alters* the planet's physical and chemical conditions in turn, subtly but decisively changing the atmosphere, the climate, the mean temperature, the ocean's chemistry, creating a planet that is hospitable to life. Gaia Theory thinks the whole of the planetary presence, including, once more, the rocks, the air, and the water as a *unified*, *non-hierarchical*, *living*, and *evolving* superorganism. With Lovelock, Gaia is 'an ensemble of living and non-living components which acts as a single self-regulating system' (in Harding, 2006:64).

Also in the 1970s, the Norwegian philosopher Arne Næss marked a major turn in his own thinking, from a preoccupation with logics, semantics, and Gandhian thought towards a synthesis of all his previous work in a truly ecological philosophy. Not surprisingly, Næss' personal *ecological* turn began with an *ontological* renouncement of the classical atomistic model and an embracing of a field theory. At a conference in Bucharest in 1972, Næss publicly announced his turn, saying:

The deep ecology movement rejects the human-in-environment image *in favour of the relational, total-field image: organisms as knots in the biospherical net or field of intrinsic relations* . . . The total-field model dissolves not only the human-in-environment concept, but *every compact thing-in-milieu* concept.

(Næss, 2005:7. Emphasis added)

Seventeen years later, in his major work on ecological philosophy, *Ecology, Community, and Lifestyle*, Næss would write:

> Speaking of interaction between organisms and the milieux gives rise to the wrong associations, as an organism is interaction. Organisms and milieux are not two things – if a mouse were lifted into absolute vacuum, it would no longer be a mouse. Organisms presuppose milieux.

(Næss, 1989:56)

Callicott distils three major tenets that constitute this ecological turn towards a new and, as we saw, also very ancient field theory of the more-than-human community of life. *First*, this turn is characterized by an *organic* metaphysical foundation, which implies that:

> energy seems to be a more fundamental and primitive reality than are material objects or discrete entities – elementary particles and organisms respectively. An individual organism, like an elementary particle is, as it were, a momentary configuration, a local perturbation, in an energy flux or field.

(1989:109)

Once more, this thinking is directly compatible with the new physics:

> [I]f we combine quantum theory with ecology, as well as compare them, and resolve the erstwhile solid and immutable atoms of matter which compose the molecules, which in turn compose the cells, of organic bodies into the ephemeral, energetic quanta, then we may say quite literally and unambiguously that organisms are, in their entire structure – from subatomic microcosm to ecosystemic macrocosm – patterns, perturbations or configurations of energy.

(Ibid.)

The *second* tenet implied in this ecological turn is that ontological thought must be *holistic*:

> It is impossible to conceive of organisms – if they are, as it were, knots in the web of life, or temporary formations or perturbations in complex flow patterns – apart from the field, the matrix of which they are modes. Contrary to the object-ontology of classical physics and biology in which it was possible to conceive of an entity in isolation from its milieu . . . the conception of one thing in the New Physics or New Ecology necessarily involves the conception of others and so on, until the entire system is, in principle, implicated.

(Ibid.:110)

It is important to qualify this emphasis on holism further. The holism implied by an ecological turn is not an *undifferentiated* holism. Rather, says Callicott, the larger and unified living community 'is a *structured, differentiated* whole. The multiplicity of particles and of living organisms, at either level or organization, retain, ultimately, their peculiar, if ephemeral, characters and identities. But they are systematically integrated and mutually defining' (ibid.:111).

Then there is the *third* implication of this ecological turn. This third implication revives what was once known, during the heyday of German and English idealism in the late nineteenth and early twentieth century, as the doctrine of *internal relations*. Writes Callicott: 'The basic idea is that a thing's essence is exhaustively determined by its relationships, that it cannot be conceived apart from its relationships with other things . . . internal relations are straightforwardly implicated in ecology' (ibid.:110). And further:

> Ecology represents such a radical departure from the Western worldview because it focuses on the relationships between organisms rather than on organisms in isolation from one another and from the elemental environment. Ecology reverses the typically Western focus on the figure at the expense of the ground in the proverbial figure-ground gestalt. Relationships are ontologically upgraded, and classical entities, proportionally, ontologically downgraded. From an ecological point of view, relationships become the primary realities and entities the subordinate realities . . . From an ecological point of view, an organism has been shaped and moulded – in its size, form, viscera, sociology, and psychology – by its interaction with other species.
>
> (1994:84)

Mark the way in which the ecological turn of thought constitutes a fundamental and radical critique of classical atomistic thought (and, by extension, of business-as-usual). Rather than being entity-oriented, it stresses the importance of process. Rather than being dualistic, it thinks Being as a unified (but multi-centric, richly layered, and intricately structured) process, in which each entity is implicated by all others, in which there is a unity in opposites, and in which none can exist without the fluid context of all others. In the embodied thick of living communities, there are no discrete units. There are only relationships.

This all has implications for this cursory look at the encounter between modern humans and salmon. If you define GM salmon as being identical to free-ranging Atlantic salmon, you must ignore that each species has evolved in the context of these relationships. You must ignore that abstracting salmon from their places, and from those who inhabit these places, amounts to destroying their identity. If you treat salmon as discrete units, you annihilate them, because you cannot modify, displace, and contain salmon and still have salmon. Instead what you get is a knowledge system that can in principle be exported anywhere. You can set it up on Prince Edward Island, or in Panama, or in Mongolia, or in the outskirts of Beijing, Moscow, or Dubai. You can take it anywhere the market suggests a competitive edge. But you will not be able to bring along salmon. All you will be able to bring are more or less edible, more or less palatable, more or less healthy spare parts. Consider the following quote by maverick thinker

Thomas Berry, who lends his own eloquent voice to the ecological turn in our narrative tradition:

> To be is to be related, for relationship is the essence of existence ... relationship is discovered rather than forged ... An unborn grizzly bear sleeps in her mother's womb. Even there in the dark with her eyes closed, this bear is already related to the outside world. She will not have to develop a taste for blackberries or for Chinook salmon. When her tongue first mashes the juice of the blackberry its delight will be immediate. No prolonged period of learning will be needed for the difficult task of snaring a spawning salmon. In the very shape of her claws is the musculature, anatomy, and leap of the Chinook. The face of the bear, the size of her arms, the structure of her eyes, the thickness of her fur – these are dimensions of her temperate forest community. The bear herself is meaningless outside this enveloping web of relations.
>
> (Berry, 1992:77–78)

Consider further the following quote by the Pacific West coast writer Derrick Jensen, who has come to a similar understanding in his critique of modern zoo practices, *Thought to Exist in the Wild*. Jensen writes:

> We learn that you can remove an animal from her habitat and still have a creature. We see a sea lion in a concrete pool and believe that we're still seeing a sea lion. But we are not. That is all wrong ... A sea lion is her habitat. She is the school of fish she chases. She is the water. She is the cold wind blowing over the ocean. She is the waves that strike the rocks on which she sleeps, and she is the rocks. She is the constant calling back and forth between members of her family, this talking to each other that never seems to stop. She is the shark who eventually ends her life. She is all these things. She is that web. She is the process of being a sea lion, in place. She is her desires, which we can only learn by letting her show us, if she wants, not by encaging her ... Zoos teach us that animals are meat and bones in sacks of skin. You could put a wolverine into tinier and tinier cages, until you had a cage precisely the size of the wolverine, and you would still, according to what zoos implicitly teach, have a wolverine. Zoos teach us that animals are like machine parts: separable, replaceable, interchangeable. They teach us that there is no web of life, that you can remove one part and put it into a box and still have that part. But that is all wrong. What is this wolverine? Who is this wolverine? What is her life really like? Not her life constrained by moats and walls, but her life in the forest, surrounded by that life, doing what wolverines do?
>
> (Jensen and Tweedy-Holmes, 2007:86–87)

We can say as much about salmon. AquaBounty is trying to teach that salmon are flesh and bones in sacks of skin. You can lock up salmon into tighter and tighter containers, until you have a steel-reinforced concrete tank lined with rows of barbed-wire; you can treat these units of meat and bones into triploidy to make most of them sterile; you can rewrite their genetic memory to conform with the grammar of your own desires, and you would still, according to what AquaBounty explicitly teaches, have a salmon. But that is all wrong. A salmon is her river. She is the unique smell of that one estuary, that place where she once passed from her freshwater youth into her saltwater adulthood. She is the magnetic field that spans from pole to pole and sends waves of recognition through her sensing body on her long journey back home. She is the anticipation of riverside humans who hungrily await her return from the ocean. She is the pace with which riverside Sitka spruce metabolizes icy skin into wooden bark, and the way in which grizzly bear metabolizes her into the hair and fat that will sustain grizzly through another cold season. She is the seasonal swelling of her river's currents. She is her river's topography, its resistance, its moods. She is all that. With Callicott we could say, abstractly speaking, that salmon is 'almost, but not quite, implied by all the other foci of its matrix. If its habitat could be expressed as a set of propositions, the [salmon] would be almost, but not quite, deducible' (1994:84). Take all these essential aspects of being salmon away from salmon, and the only thing left that binds your resulting sack of flesh and bones to salmon is ambiguous and deceptive rhetoric. Take all that away from her and you will not only have destroyed salmon, but also severely diminished – perhaps irreversibly – the watershed community itself. A fundamental superstition of our modern narrative tradition is that we are skin-encapsulated egos. This is as true of ourselves as it is true of salmon. It also ignores physical reality. To define the creature away from her web of relations, and the web of relations from the creature, is to open the way to exploiting this creature, to diminishing her, violating her, abusing her, killing her, denying her. We are who we are only in relation to others. Salmon are salmon only in relation to the places they inhabit.

Concluding thoughts

In this chapter I have complemented this book's ongoing dialogue on the conditions of a *good* life with a discussion of the phenomenon that is *life*. I hope to have shown that any narrative of the good life must be fundamentally life-affirming, in the most comprehensive manner, and that means it must affirm life in its full ontological implications. I have written several times that the ecological turn implies a radical overhaul of the status quo, but, as Curry has said so succinctly, 'let us not exaggerate its radicality . . . [For after all, all that is needed is to realize the truth . . . that "We are Earthlings first, humans second"' (2011:50). This does not replace a careful conversation on the conditions of goodness, propriety, or (human) well-being, a conversation which fills many pages in this volume. But it certainly helps place that intra-human conversation more meaningfully within the larger frame of an Earth-consciousness. And so, while the understanding that we are enfolded, involved, and engaged within the larger planetary presence awaits being fully expressed in our lifeworlds, ecological literacy turns out to be an essential condition for any notion of good living.

Some say we should perhaps ask what we want wild salmon for. If we can no longer uphold a (sharp) distinction between self and other; if it becomes more prudent to speak of relational selves; if the human mind participates in, and is nourished by, the larger web of relations to the same degree as our bodies; if both human minds and bodies are but aspects, or angles, of a unified, stratified, differentiated whole;[6] if, that is, we think through the full implications of the ecological turn in our narrative tradition, then can we not conclude, with the words of the American educator David Orr, that 'it is not possible to unravel the creation without undermining human intelligence as well'? Can we not conclude, that is, that the ecological turn poses a direct challenge to those who suggest that human well-being will not be affected by the death of salmon? For, as Orr adds, 'The issue is not so much about what biodiversity can do for us as resources as it is about the survival of human intelligence cut off from its source' (Orr, 2004:51–52). If it is true that we, like salmon, are fully embedded in the living matrix, entirely therein and entirely thereof, then we can indeed say that we are only healthy to the degree that salmon are healthy. We only thrive to the degree that they do. We are only human to the degree that we give salmon the space and opportunity to be salmon.

Notes

1 Minus our own minds.
2 To-date, the Norwegian fish farming industry has no comparable practice for genetically engineering salmon. The case of AquAdvantage Salmon is specific for the North American market. Still, it remains relevant for this chapter as a conspicuous representative of the Cartesian mindset.
3 By 2009, some 85 per cent of US corn was genetically modified, as were 91 per cent of all soybeans and 88 per cent of cotton (whose oil is a widely used additive in food products).
4 Or at least most of them will; the technology is only considered 99 per cent effective.
5 After having served at the FDA a second time, and after having fortified the principle of substantial equivalence in FDA policies, Taylor returned once again to Monsanto, this time to become its vice-president. But even that was not his last walk through the infamous revolving door. In July 2009, he joined the FDA a third time, this time under the Obama administration, serving first as senior advisor to the FDA Commissioner, and then, half a year later, assuming another newly created post, that of Deputy Commissioner for Foods. This third tenure of Taylor's with the FDA coincided with the passing of the so-called *S510 Food Safety Modernization Act*. The act grants the FDA unprecedented power over the entire food production process: 'No Limit on Secretarial Authority – Nothing in this section shall be construed to limit the ability of the Secretary to review and act upon information from food testing, including determining the sufficiency of such information and testing' (S510 (111th): *FDA Food Safety Modernization Act*. www.govtrack.us/congress/bills/111/s510/text). In other words, the FDA decides if, when, where, and what types of food tests will be undertaken. It decides also what test results will be made available 'in the interest of national security'. Now it would seem that the best way to act in the interest of national security would be to publish *all* tests, and then let the public decide for themselves how they

wish to handle the results. Whose security – whose interest – are you serving when you have absolute power to withhold certain test results, and to publish others?

6   Rather than distinct 'substances', or 'essences'.

Bibliography

Abram, D. (1996) *The Spell of the Sensuous*. New York: Random House.

Abram, D. (2010) *Becoming Animal. An Earthly Cosmology*. New York: Vintage.

Alliance for Natural Health (2012) *Action Alert: Genetic Modified Salmon*. www.anh-usa.org/action-alert-genetically-modified-frankenfish/ (accessed 1 March 2014).

AquaBounty Technologies, Inc. (2010) *Environmental Assessment for AquAdvantage(r) Salmon*. www.fda.gov/downloads/AdvisoryCommittees/CommitteesMeetingMaterials/VeterinaryMedicineAdvisoryCommittee/UCM224760.pdf (accessed 1 March 2014).

AquaBounty Technologies, Inc. (2012a) www.aquabounty.com/documents/press/2010/AquaBounty%20Fact%20Sheet.pdf (accessed 1 March 2014).

AquaBounty Technologies, Inc. (2012b) *AquAdvantage Fish*. www.aquabounty.com/products/products-295.aspx (accessed 1 March 2014).

Berg-Hansen, L. (2012) 'Laks på land' in *Dagbladet*. www.dagbladet.no/2012/10/11/kultur/debatt/debattinnlegg/fiskeri/laks/23825741/ (accessed 15 February 2014).

Berry, T. (1992) *The Story of the Universe*. San Francisco, CA: Harper.

Callicott, J. B. (1989) *In Defense of the Land Ethic*. Albany, NY: State University of New York Press.

Callicott, J. B. (1994) *Earth's Insights. A Multicultural Survey of Ecological Ethics from the Mediterranean Basin to the Australian Outback*. Berkeley – Los Angeles – London: University of California Press.

Curry, P. (2011) *Ecological Ethics*. Cambridge: Polity Press.

Hannesson, R. (2010) 'Hva skal vi med villaksen?' in *Dagens Næringsliv*. p. 4.

Harding, S. (2006) *Animate Earth. Science, Intuition, and Gaia*. Totnes, Devon: Green Books Ltd.

Jensen, D. and Tweedy-Holmes, K. (2007) *Thought to Exist in the Wild*. Santa Cruz, CA: No Voice Unheard.

Kearns, P. and Mayers, P. (1999) 'Substantial equivalence is a useful tool' in *Nature*, 14 October; 401(6754).

Langberg, Ø. K. (2012) 'Kina skal produsere laks i ørkenen' in *Aftenposten*. www.aftenposten.no/okonomi/Kina-skal-produsere-laks-i-orkenen-7010054.html#.UwM1d43KxUY (accessed 20 February 2014).

Merchant, C. (1993) *The Death of Nature. Women, Ecology, and the Scientific Revolution*. San Francisco, CA: Harper Row.

Mills, S. (1997) *Turning Away from Technology. A New Vision for the 21st Century*. San Francisco, CA: Sierra Club Books.

Millstone, E. et al. (1999) 'Beyond "substantial equivalence"' in *Nature*. 7 October; 401(6753):525–526.

Næss, A. (1989) *Ecology, Community and Lifestyle. Outline of an Ecosophy*. Cambridge: Cambridge University Press.

Næss, A. (2005) *Deep Ecology of Wisdom. Selected Works of Arne Næss*. Glasser, H. and Drengson, A. (eds) Vol. X. Dordrecht: Springer.

Orr, D. (2004) *Earth in Mind. On Education, Environment, and the Human Prospect*. Washington – Covelo – London: Island Press.

Poulter, S. (2010) 'Scientists create GM "Frankenfish" which grows three times as fast as normal salmon' in *Daily Mail*. www.dailymail.co.uk/news/article-1287084/Scientists-create-GM-Frankenfish-grows-times-fast-normal-salmon.html#ixzz2tfVJ6mFH (accessed 20 February 2014).

Ross, S. D. (2001) *The Gift of Property: Having the Good – Betraying Genitivity, Economy and Ecology, an Ethic of the Earth*. Albany, NY: State University of New York Press.

The Royal Society of Canada (2011) *Elements of Precaution: Recommendations for the Regulation of Food Biotechnology in Canada, Ottawa*. http://gmoreport.blogspot.com/2011/03/substanital-equivalence-anything-bu.html (accessed 5 March 2014).

Shepard, P. (1999) *Encounters with Nature: Essays*. Washington, D.C.: Island Press.

Soechtig, S. (2013) *Fed Up. Genetic Engineering, Industrial Agriculture and Sustainable Alternatives*. Documentary Film. http://fedupmovie.com/ (accessed 1 February 2014).

Ystad, V. (2011) 'Fiskerisjefar tek laksen på land' in *Dag og Tid*. http://old.dagogtid.no/nyhet.cfm?nyhetid=2060 (accessed 10 February 2014).

14 Afterword

Beyond the paradox of the big, bad wolf

Thomas Hylland Eriksen

You and I, lucky enough to be alive at the outset of the third millennium CE, live – objectively speaking – in paradise. This particular 'you and I' does not, alas, refer to humanity *tout court*, but to the richest fifth of the global population, somewhat more than a billion people; us who constitute the global middle and upper classes; we who inhabit the leafy suburbs of the global village, who enjoy a fast internet connection and a remote control for our television set, who ask ourselves what we should have for dinner and daydream about a nice holiday. It is those 20 per cent of us who consume 80 per cent of the world's wealth, to which category everybody who reads these words, naturally, belongs. Never before in human history or prehistory have so many people had so much – so many things, so many opportunities for partaking in rewarding leisure activities, such good health, so much freedom of choice, such a high life expectancy. Entirely average people enjoy a material standard of living which in most respects surpasses that of the landed aristocracy in the mid-nineteenth century.

It must be conceded that on the whole we do have fewer thoroughbred horses and crystal chandeliers, fewer private chamber orchestras and less silverware than nineteenth-century aristocrats. But at the end of the day, that may not matter so much. In the mid-nineteenth century, statisticians estimated how thick the layer of horse droppings covering the streets of central London would be a century later, provided the current development continued. The scenario was alarming. The pessimists envisioned a future when the preferred footwear for crossing Piccadilly Circus would be wading boots or perhaps stilts. A few years later (in 1864), the Underground opened its first lines, and another few decades later, the horses had become a pure tourist attraction, analogous to the sperm whales of Lofoten (northern Norway) at the beginning of the twenty-first century. The sign had not changed its physical appearance, but suddenly it signified tourist titillation rather than economic utility.

In all earnestness, it must be conceded that we who belong to the global middle class manage pretty well without two hundred crystal glasses and pompous, dusty and impractical chandeliers. Chamber orchestras, naturally, have long since been replaced by affordable Asian stereo systems capable of reproducing music at virtually the same quality as the original, at any time of day or night.

Perfectly ordinary people who belong to the global middle class – and it includes the vast majority of West Europeans – live in spectacular luxury, regardless of the basis for comparison. We live in warm, bright, clean and not least spacious dwellings. (In 1946, a two-room unit with a kitchen and a bathroom was considered a functional European family flat.) On the whole, notwithstanding allergies and personal preferences, we can eat whatever we want to. The food is quality controlled and generally tastes good. (It is well known that the animals we sometimes eat do not necessarily lead fulfilling lives, but animals were not necessarily happy in earlier times either.) Thanks to improved methods of production, an inexpensive wine from Australia or South Africa tastes as good as, if not better than, wines imbibed by royalty a couple of centuries ago. In contrast to nineteenth-century aristocrats, we are also able to enjoy the exotic tastes of bananas, oranges and mangoes all year round, in addition to a range of foodstuffs they had never heard of.

Books, to mention another example, have become incredibly cheap. Many cost less than an average hour's salary, and the selection is unlimited. We can listen to our favourite music whenever we want to, even when the musicians are asleep or dead. When we North Europeans take our four, five or six weeks of annual vacations, millions of us can spend some of them at a pleasant hotel in a remote area. A hundred years ago, Norwegians in general had no holidays; fifty years ago, they went on a camping trip to neighbouring Sweden or Denmark; and by now, Thailand has become a standard destination for a family vacation. By 2013, more than 80 per cent of the Norwegian population went on at least one holiday trip abroad, spending on average two weeks a year in a hotel.

When members of the global middle class have a spare moment, and they often do, since the number of working hours has decreased steadily in the last hundred years, they have many options. Some engage in various leisure activities, from golf to singing in choirs, but they can also be entertained or enlightened by others at whim. Concert halls, cinemas, sports arenas and theatres sell tickets within purchasing range for most, and at home, practically everybody has one or several television sets with a varied selection of enlightening, distracting or entertaining programmes. During the last few years, the internet has also become an important source of entertainment, distraction and enlightenment.

The level of education is increasing, and the proportion of jobs which are hazardous to health or physically exhausting is being reduced (or outsourced) by the year. The number of hours spent on housework among European women has decreased steadily since the Second World War, at the same time as the size of the dwellings has increased.

Moreover, we live longer than earlier generations, including the aristocracy, which had a tendency of dying halfway through life from consumption or broken hearts. This is also the case with the materially poorer countries, except those African countries which are most affected by AIDS. Average global life expectancy in 1900 was 31; a hundred years later it was 66.8 (more than a doubling!), and in many of the richest countries it hovers around 80 (Morgan 2002). Many of you who read this will live to be a hundred. We stay healthier than earlier generations, thanks to medicines and vaccination programmes, better nutrition and changes in the world of labour. The dehumanising and dangerous jobs in agriculture, mining and industry have been humanised in our part of the world, and in the global middle class it is uncommon that people are physically exhausted at the age of 40. Today, our kind of people – the wealthiest fifth of humanity – simply do not grow old the way they used to. Some years ago, a dear colleague and friend died, and his death was especially sad because he was so young, only 62. But as late as 1928, the American demographer Louis Dublin predicted that the ceiling on life expectancy would be reached at a national average of 64.75 years. He was in fact an optimist, as expected longevity in the USA at the time was 57 years (Dublin himself lived to be 87).

We have lived in paradise for some time now. Most of the denizens of our global middle class world only know absolute scarcity and poverty through stories from mass media. If they live in countries with severe inequality, they are nevertheless intermittently exposed to glimpses of poverty on their way to work or leisure activities. One exception is immigrants from poor countries and their children. Although their social mobility has in most cases been spectacular, they have vivid memories of scarcity, which remains a fundamental reality in the country of their close relatives.

Two general aspects of life in paradise deserve mentioning. First – and this is the case with all earthly paradises – it cannot last forever. Second – and this concerns our specific paradise – we now know that objectively paradisical conditions do not necessarily make the inhabitants of paradise satisfied. Studies from the UK and the USA suggest that the subjectively experienced well-being ('SWB') has not increased noticeably since the 1950s (Offer 2006), that is a time without holidays in the sun, mobile telephones, colour television and Saturdays off. There is also influential and much-cited research that suggests that well-being is not correlated with income, at least for those who do not live in absolute poverty (see e.g. Easterbrook 2003). Researchers are not entirely agreed amongst themselves: Some claim that more money fails to make an impact only for the richest 25 per cent, while others have argued that most people in fact do not enjoy a higher level of well-being with an increase in material welfare, provided they had enough to begin with.

'We have everything, but that's all we have', said the Norwegian folk singer Ole Paus some years ago. Although this observation was later quoted by two prime ministers in their televised New Year's speeches, it has not led to perceptible shifts in politics. Even in incredibly rich Norway it would have amounted to political suicide to propose reduced consumption and a reduced material standard of living – in spite of the fact that it is now fairly widely known, and not least experienced, that increased well-being or happiness in an affluent society depends on other things than an ever higher material standard of living.

The view that it is necessary to reduce carbon emissions, and thus energy consumption, and indeed economic growth, in order to halt climate change is not universally held, but it is widespread and influential. There are few objections from politicians or editorialists whenever the IPCC (Intergovernmental Panel on

Climate Change) presents conclusions to the effect that energy consumption and lifestyles in the affluent countries have to change. The need to be serious about the threat of irreversible global warming frequently figures in public speeches; yet, next to nothing is being done about the issue, and so far, few vote for politicians who sincerely promise to contribute to developing a post-extractive or carbon-neutral society. Nearly everybody, moreover, agrees that money, power and fame do not make you happy, and yet exactly such values govern both the workplace and the economy as such. Most members of the global middle class would say, if asked, that we are a single humanity who has to find ways of living together, yet there is considerable intolerance towards culturally different groups. The most significant contradiction, or double-bind, however, is that which exists between growth and sustainability. One cannot have it both ways in the long run; through our spectacularly successful and comfortable way of life, we are simultaneously undermining the conditions for our own existence. Perhaps it is true that in the global middle class we have everything, but ultimately that's all we have.

What is missing? Perhaps the short answer is hope. That is to say, contemporary affluent societies are lacking hope. To most people belonging to the global middle class, life after death is – at the most – a vague notion. It is far too weak to provide sufficient hope to live by. Moreover, material scarcity has been left behind, at least for now, and there is little indication that it will return in our lifetimes. The satisfaction of material needs, in other words, is not a source of hope either. With a minimum of security precautions, we Europeans can move safely wherever we might wish to in our near surroundings, without having to fear attacks from wild animals or gangs of bandits. If we become ill, we may reasonably expect to recover. Throughout the history of humanity, the struggle for survival has been a major topic and a major source of hope. This is no longer the case among the privileged classes. Hope is no longer necessary to keep us going; life now runs on an autopilot.

For this condition, I propose a diagnosis I label the syndrome of the big, bad wolf. The foundational story is as follows. The voracious and always hungry Zeke Wolf, who lives in a dense forest not too far from the dwarfs' quarry and Cinderella's stepmother's mansion, has one big, overarching project in his life, namely to capture, cook and eat three delicious, pink pigs who live less than a mile away in the same forest. For this reason, he gets up every morning and lays his dastardly plans after consuming a frugal breakfast (usually oatmeal porridge). He develops original disguises (a favourite being the elderly, gangrenous woman with a stick and a basket of apples) and builds sophisticated traps, conjures up labyrinthine routes through the forest as if he were a master chess player, and lies in hiding with great patience near paths he knows the pigs often take. He subscribes to the local press in order to follow news of public events such as fancy fairs, where the pigs might be present; he becomes an actor, an engineer and an athlete, all for the sake of capturing the pigs.

Usually, the pigs are one step ahead of the wolf, but on at least one occasion, he succeeded in catching them. The details elude me, but I remember him bundling the three plump pigs together with a length of rope and dropping them in his big iron pot. The water began to warm up as Zeke Wolf chopped up onions and carrots, adding them to the water along with a few pinches of salt, and it seemed as if all hope was gone for the pigs. It was at this point that Practical Pig, the smartest of the three (the one with the blue dungarees and cap), turned towards the wolf and asked him: 'So, Zeke Wolf, what are you going to do tomorrow, then?'

The wolf was visibly shaken by the question. What on earth was he going to do tomorrow? For a moment, he pondered the issue at hand, gazing emptily in front of himself, and turning away, he released the pigs – an act he immediately regretted, but by then they had already jumped out of the window and run away.

In a rare glimpse of reflexivity, Zeke Wolf realised that his entire *raison d'être* rested on the project of catching, killing, boiling and finally eating the three little pigs. Without the pigs on his horizon, he would have no reason to rise from bed in the morning.

We the affluent are Zeke Wolf on the day of the hangover. Overfed and giddy, we lie on the couch asking ourselves what we should do tomorrow. Depending on his class identity, the wolf might have spent the rest of his life with a remote control and a six-pack in front of the television, or on a terrace in southern Spain near a golf course, with a glass of white wine. Briefly, there are strong indications that we need some new pigs to hunt.

The serpent in this earthly paradise may be called hopelessness. It is tautologically true that you may lose hope in the end if you are hopelessly poor, but you may also lose it if you are hopelessly rich. There is no surplus of excruciatingly difficult, but urgent and deeply necessary, collective projects around here for the time being. Dreams tend to be small, private and generally realistic. If you spend November evenings dreaming of an emerald lagoon on a tropical island, and you end up going there already next February, the dream is too puny and too realistic. (You end up disappointed anyway, as the island turns out to be a sleepy and uneventful place with bad food and mosquitoes.)

Being healthy with a long life expectancy helps, but it is not enough. It also helps to be able to read Dickens and listen to Mendelssohn (or, for that matter, Ludlum and Springsteen) whenever you wish, and to eat your fill of first-rate food daily, but that's not enough either. It certainly helps to live in a society where nobody needs to go hungry to bed, but after a while, we take this for granted as well, following the law of diminishing returns, and it scarcely occurs to us that we ought to be grateful for all this. The good life, and the good society, is, somehow, something else.

The planet has a poverty problem and an environmental problem that cannot be solved by one state alone, and in an important sense, we are in the same boat. We live in one world; we are one humanity. Where I sit, writing, in the extreme north-west of the Eurasian continent, we are nevertheless capable of boredom, and it is partly due to the fact that we lack a future-oriented, collective project. It is as though all problems have been solved. The Nordic countries and similar places, from the Netherlands to New Zealand, have overachieved. We have developed the most well-organised, decent, materially rich and wholesome societies seen throughout world history. However, I have already mentioned that earthly paradises do not last, and ours is fast being dethroned by its inherent contradictions. In Oslo, where I sit, there is an increasingly visible gap between Norway, the world champion in global solidarity and promoting sustainability abroad, on the one hand; and Norway, the filthy, disgusting country addicted to oil – a country responsible, through its petroleum exports, for 3 per cent of the world's CO_2 emissions although it has less than 0.1 per cent of the total population.

It is no longer easy to argue against the view that something ought to be done about the way of life predominating in the global middle class. Anything else would be short-sighted, cruel and indecent. The colonisation of the future by the present has become a colossal problem.

Research on happiness and 'subjective well-being' has not led to the formulation of a set of general laws of happiness. Yet, the chapters of this book suggest, along with a few thousand years of sustained philosophical, religious and artistic reflection on the place of humanity and the quest for the good life, that a few provisional conclusions might be pertinent:

- Human beings are simultaneously driven by a desire for equality and community (the solidarity instinct) and a desire to stand out as individuals (the competitive instinct). In a good society, the two impulses keep each other reasonably well in check; too much community deprives the individual of freedom, while too much individuality leads to accelerating inequality.
- Great discrepancies in prosperity and opportunities for self-realisation make people unhappy and discontented. In enormously unequal societies, the rich fear the poor, and the poor hate the rich. The less the differences in actual (not just formal) life opportunities, the better (Wilkinson 2005).
- A great deal of the subjective well-being or life-satisfaction experienced is partly caused by inherited tendencies, yet both our cultural surroundings and the events we go through contribute to our well-being. It is possible, as some American psychologists claim, to learn how to think positively, but this exercise may not help if you find yourself at the bottom of the ladder in a hierarchical, highly competitive society.
- Human beings, moreover, desire recognition, that is to be respected – or even admired, at least on a good day – for what they are and what they do. There are many ways of achieving recognition, from driving a boat really fast in a competition with others who also drive their boats really fast; by taking care of children in a caring and humorous way; by publishing erudite papers or cooking the world's best pasta, or in one of a thousand different ways. Although some universal tendencies are embedded in our evolved nature, culture and history decide how they can best be expressed. A century and a half ago, a man in his forties could garner great respect in the American South if he owned many slaves, had a dignified paunch and a good hand with the whip, and kept his daughters' honour intact until they married. Today,

similar ideals would scarcely gain anybody widespread respect anywhere, and certainly not in Alabama. Values, in other words, change. One day, perhaps in a not too remote future, people will obtain other people's respect and social recognition through ecologically sustainable ways of behaving.

- Finally, experience and history tell us that large-scale collective projects may satisfy both the demand for equality and solidarity, and the need individuals have to prove themselves. When involved in such projects, you do something with others, and you have the chance to display yourself at your best.

All of this is fairly uncontroversial, notwithstanding the internal disagreements among happiness researchers concerning the relative significance of genetic factors, the role of inequality and a few other things. These minor disagreements notwithstanding, recent research on well-being and life-satisfaction implies that there is no necessary connection between, for example, extensive driving and flying, uninhibited energy consumption and happiness in a society. At the same time, it is no less obvious that had we, in our neck of the woods somewhere in the affluent world, quit using fossil fuels altogether, beginning tomorrow morning, the majority of the population would have experienced a steep decline in well-being, coupled with not insignificant rage directed at the powers that be. Authoritarian measures introduced without soliciting popular opinion are never popular. Short of dictatorial measures, changes must therefore come about through a broad reassessment of the nature of the good life. The arrow of time will not change its direction on its own accord.

The easiest choice is always to continue with business as usual. Already thirty years ago, green activists were jokingly telling each other that 'we are standing at the edge of the cliff, about to take a long step forwards'. Pessimists argue that we have already taken that step (like the man jumping from a skyscraper, shouting, as he passes the fiftieth floor, that it is going rather well), and that the world as we know it will soon be gone as a result of the flooding and droughts, melting glaciers and rising seas, huge migration waves, pestilence and mass deaths caused by climate change. It is tempting to draw the connection between these contemporary prophets of doom and those who were waiting for the apocalypse in the year 1000. Yet the fact that the most spectacular predictions are likely to be mistaken does not mean that prospects are great. Global climate does change, and yes, there will be repercussions everywhere.

And yet, even if the entire scientific and public debate about climate change should be exposed as a gigantic piece of propaganda (although it is hard to guess who should be responsible for such a gargantuan conjuring trick and why), there are good reasons to address the values and way of life in our kind of society. The final stages of material welfare growth, after all, did not increase the general well-being, only the level of frustration; and simultaneously, welfare growth up here made millions less happy down there, since their relative deprivation was a constant reminder of global injustice.

Neither classic socialism nor liberalist market ideologies offer satisfactory models, even if we disregard their dismal environmental record – the former inhibits the individual's need to excel at something, while the latter is splendid as long as you experience smooth sailing, but the moment you hit a reef, there is nobody to blame but yourself.

The question is which kind of societal model is compatible with what we now know about well-being and life-satisfaction, as well as being ecologically sustainable. That question has been addressed in several of the chapters in this book, and I now propose to take it for a final spin. An annual publication, which deserves more attention than it gets, is *The Happy Planet Index*, published by the radical New Economics Foundation (2013). Intended as a supplement and a corrective to the UNDP's annual *Human Development Report*, the index takes the global conversation about happiness and the quality of life a step in an interesting direction. The people behind the report, mostly economists, calculate the relationship between SWB and life expectancy on the one hand, and ecological footprint on the other hand, that is – in brief – how much you have to pollute in order to enjoy a certain degree of life satisfaction and length. The NEF have, thus, entirely discarded GDP as a relevant criterion, which seems to be justified, as huge amounts of quantitative research now show that beyond a certain minimum level, there is no clear correlation between the average income in a country and the level of well-being. Other factors, such as the distribution of wealth (measured in gini coefficients), are far more important (Wilkinson 2005; Wilkinson and Pickett 2009), and inequality is now slowly being introduced as a fourth pillar by the Foundation.

The report usefully confirms things that most of us knew already; for example, that the rich live longer and pollute more than the poor. At the same time, it enables us to view the world in a slightly new way, with new connections and new potentials for change. For example, it documents that the inhabitants of the USA leave an ecological footprint which is 60 per cent higher than that of Germans, and yet the Germans live four years longer than, and are about as happy as, the Americans. Several Latin American countries are at or near the top of the table (the top five are Costa Rica, Vietnam, Colombia, Belize and El Salvador). The inhabitants of Costa Rica live long, pollute modestly and report – on the whole – that they are satisfied with life. Compared to a country like Finland, they naturally save a lot of energy on simpler housing and no central heating. Perhaps the kind of life quality that, in a place like Norway, requires a 300-square-metre house, a mountain cabin, HDTV and two annual vacations in warm places can be achieved in El Salvador with a 70-square-metre house with some afternoon shade on the terrace, well-behaved children and a plaza nearby with music, dance, food and drink on Saturdays. In earlier editions of the report, small island-states like Vanuatu and Dominica were near the top; in the latest versions, these countries are, for methodological reasons, not included.

Some countries vary little regarding ecological footprint, but considerably when it comes to satisfaction and longevity. Jamaicans live 27 years longer than Equatorial Guineans (figures from the 2008 report; the latter country was not included in 2012), but they pollute about as much (or little), and Jamaicans are – understandably – palpably more satisfied with life than Equatorial Guineans, who live in an exceptionally brutal and insensitive dictatorship with huge inequalities.

There are other interesting variations and correlations as well. Hondurans report a far higher quality of life than Latvians; the two nationalities have roughly the same life expectancy, and the ecological footprint of the Latvians is more than twice that of the Hondurans. This difference reflects the importance of cultural values and cultural style, network types and trust, but also intangible but real factors such as the experience of improving versus deteriorating trends in societal development. As mentioned, small, manageable island societies with relatively dense networks and short social distances, incidentally, did well in the earlier versions of the report, when they were included.

The most interesting finding is perhaps that the countries which do best in the Happy Planet Index are neither those at the top nor those at the bottom of the UNDP Human Development Index, but those in the middle. The inhabitants of the poorest countries suffer from all kinds of deprivations, while the richest countries pollute far more than others without this being compensated through increased well-being or longevity. The spiralling growth which has led to a doubling in world energy consumption since 1975 has done little to improve the quality of life among those who were already reasonably well off then.

The first OECD country on the Index is New Zealand, in 28th place, followed by Norway (the impact of petroleum exports is not included in the footprint measurement); both countries are ranked below Indonesia and the Philippines and just above India and the Dominican Republic. The first Muslim country is Bangladesh, in 11th place, while the Gulf States are near the bottom of the table due to their huge carbon footprint, with Qatar and Bahrain in 149th and 146th place, respectively (the total number of countries in the index is 151). The USA is, owing to its very high carbon footprint, ranked as number 105 and China as number 60. In spite of Western propaganda to the effect that the Chinese are now the worst polluters in the world, the average Chinese leaves a modest carbon footprint (less than a third of the Americans), lives beyond 70 years and report (possibly with some subtle indirect nudging from the Party) that he is quite content.

The report confirms the provisional conclusions made earlier and strengthens arguments developed in the other chapters of this book, namely that it is not necessary to destroy the planet's ecology or to pester one's neighbour in order to be content with life.

The opposite may indeed often be the case. Most people, one may presume, would prefer to be liked rather than feared, and now that we increasingly find ourselves in a catch-22, a double-bind (Bateson 1972) between growth and sustainability where it is being confirmed every day that you cannot have it both ways, it is far from unlikely that many members of the global middle class will change their priorities. Driving gas-guzzling cars will appear tasteless and stupid if you live in the city: the oversized SUV becomes a sign indicating that the owner is out of kilter, analogous to showing off your prestige by parading a dozen well-trained slaves in New Orleans in 1870. Flying becomes an increasingly rare necessity as long as it lasts, and will then slowly be phased out (provided solar-powered planes do not take over the market).

Science fiction? Daydreaming? Perhaps, but not necessarily. The dramatic transformation in the public attitude towards tobacco smoking shows that cultural mores and habits may change rapidly. Beginning in California in the 1980s, negative attitudes towards smoking spread like wildfire during the next decade and into the twentieth century. By 2010, smoking in public spaces had become anathema in large parts of the world, from India to South Africa, from Ireland to Colombia. When the smoking ban in restaurants and bars was introduced in Norway in 2004, pundits predicted that half of these establishments would be out of business before Christmas. Yet, it took only a few months before the absence of tobacco smoke, even in brown cafes patronised by workmen and heavy drinkers, had been naturalised and internalised. Smokers were literally left out in the cold, and today, some think wistfully, albeit with a tinge of disgust about the dim and distant past more than twenty years ago when everything smelled vaguely of tobacco smoke. This may be the ultimate fate of ecological irresponsibility as well. Now that it has been conclusively proved that it is not necessary for human beings to undermine the conditions for their continued existence in order to be happy, there are no good arguments for continuing on that particular path.

The small, mountainous country of Bhutan – east of Nepal, north of India and south of Tibet – is often mentioned in the happiness literature as a counter-example to Western 'affluenza'. In 1976, King Jigme Singye Wangchuck declared that it would be wise not to open the country to Western influence. His son, King Jigme Khesar Namgyal Wangchuck, largely follows up his father's policy, but has decided on a few reforms, such as introducing television and political elections. There is still no mass tourism in Bhutan, and it is a McDonald's-free country with little commercialisation. This is in itself far from a guarantee for a high quality of life; neither the Cambodia of Pol Pot nor Stalin's Soviet Union were particularly McDonaldised. However, Bhutanese authorities have decided on 'gross national happiness' instead of the Western standard 'gross national product' as a yardstick for measuring how well the country is doing. Unlike Pol Pot, they do not massacre people who can read, and unlike Stalin, they are not obsessed with beating the Americans in childish competitions within sport, chess or space travel. Recently, the Centre for Bhutan Studies in Thimphu has begun to operationalise criteria for national happiness. They include obvious dimensions such as health, education and good governance, but also less common criteria such as cultural vitality, ecological diversity, time use and psychological well-being. Interestingly, Bhutan is not included in the Happy Planet Index due to a lack of comparable data. The Bhutanese authorities try to learn from the mistakes of the West without having to commit them. The Bhutanese have a life expectancy about ten to 15 years shorter than that of the global middle class, so the health care system arguably leaves a bit to be desired; yet, the average lifespan in Bhutan is the same as what Louis Dublin, back in 1928, estimated to be the highest possible average for a society. In South America, the popular movements associated with the concept of *buen vivir* (living well) – based on local, often indigenous, notions of sustainability and the good life – follow a similar logic (Escobar 2013), with growing success locally in countries such as Ecuador, Colombia and Bolivia.

Much could have been different here as well. A growing proportion of the global middle class not only believe that it is necessary to reduce consumption, but positively yearn for a life bringing them into closer contact with themselves and the ecology of which they are part. Of course, consumption does have its rewards (even if short-lived). To some, buying shoes gives a form of pleasure that may be compared to the pleasure others experience when listening to jazz. Modernity can be an extraordinarily rewarding epoch in which to live; the point is that it is possible to continue leading a modern life without destroying the planet, and without reducing one's quality of life. Soon, perhaps, people who love shoes will again begin to have them repaired instead of throwing them away, and perhaps they will start buying shoes that have not been sent halfway around the planet in a shipping container. There are some intuitively understandable, liberating aspects of a slower, less consumption-intensive life. Rather than working oneself to death on the stock exchange, we can be herders in the morning and fishermen in the afternoon, and in the evening we may hold our beloved's hand as much as we wish, provided we prefer that to criticising.

A revolution is not required in order to reach this kind of a situation, which many desire. The question remains, however, as to why nothing has happened so far, after decades of increasing affluence, which has not led to a concomitant increase in life-satisfaction, but instead threatens to undermine its own conditions. A short answer, to do with path dependency, is that business as usual is always the easiest option. Both the powerful and the less powerful have invested so much in the presently hegemonic model for growth and prosperity that changing the course will require a new mentality. Since the fossil fuel revolution around the year 1800, development and increased happiness have been associated with increased energy use. What is now called for may seem tantamount to reversing the arrow of time, which seems intuitively wrong.

For this reason, it is necessary to show that an ecologically sustainable future does not amount to turning the clock back. Two main arguments have been proposed against the hegemonic world order in this regard: It did not just create wealth, but also poverty; and it destroys the environment and the life opportunities for our descendants. To this I have added a third argument: The growth model which did lead to an increased quality of life (and not just a higher standard of living) for millions in the past two centuries no longer helps make people happier. The positive effect of affluence on the quality of life decreases and eventually vanishes when basic needs are satisfied. Granted that this is the case, a new language, new models for thought and a new epistemology are needed in order to talk about development and progress, where ecological footprints and life quality, not economic growth and increased production, form the baseline. What is needed more than anything is a net growth in the domain of political imagination.

In a society with considerably lower disposable monetary income than what is typical of the rich world today, it would suddenly seem rational to begin to look after one's belongings again. Services would become cheaper; goods would become more expensive. There would again emerge a demand, in the richest countries, for tailors and furniture upholsterers. When your scanner broke down, you would have it repaired instead of buying a new one. There would be fewer meetings and less reliance on Microsoft Outlook. More poetry and live music. Fewer costly, alienating and ecologically destructive construction projects. More small-scale enterprises, fewer megacorporations. More free time and less rubbish. You might even take a boat from Portsmouth to Buenos Aires instead of a plane; the trip would do you good, and it would take 13 days rather than 13 hours.

Late in the evening, over a drink, most people, including politicians, agree with this reasoning. What is required today – following the latest reports from the IPCC about climate change, the newest research on what makes people happy and the last news stories about the proportion of Americans who take pills every day just to keep going – are politicians and community leaders who have the courage to declare, without caveats, that the spiral of growth must be reversed as from next year, that the richest should start, and that there are good reasons to rejoice in our ability to do this.

In order to shake off the syndrome of the big, bad wolf, a large, collective project is necessary. Such a project would enable us to transcend ourselves, to do something both difficult and necessary, to reap other people's recognition for it, to take part in an encompassing and encouraging community and to perform some morally defensible acts in the world. Such a project would reconnect politics and everyday life among the global middle classes with planetary needs. At the moment it may seem remote, but we have reached a historical crossroads where it is becoming visible. Details must by necessity be worked out locally, but some common elements are environmental responsibility, justice, slow time, personal challenges and a reasonable balance between rights and duties.

The time since the global turn towards neoliberalism, around 1980, has been a long period of transition. Material scarcity had been overcome in the global middle classes, and there were no plans for the future beyond the consolidation of affluence. Self-realisation became an objective in itself, an empty signifier with no ulterior goal. The treadmills were filling up, literally and figuratively speaking. Irony became the preferred mode of engagement. With the hindsight of the early twenty-first century, it is clear that ways out of this impasse are within reach. What is on the horizon is a difficult, necessary, collective project with the promise of simultaneously saving the planet and enabling the global middle classes to shake off the syndrome of the big, bad wolf.

Bibliography

Bateson, G. (1972) *Steps to an Ecology of Mind*. New York: Ballantine.

Easterbrook, G. (2003) *The Progress Paradox: How Life Gets Better While People Feel Worse*. New York: Random House.

Eriksen, T. H. (2001) *Tyranny of the Moment: Fast and Slow Time in the Information Age*. London – Sterling, VA: Pluto Press.

Escobar, A. (2013) 'Teritorios de la diferencia: La ontología política de los "derechos al territorio"'. Document prepared for the SOGIP workshop *Los pueblos indígenas y sus rerechos a la tierra*. Paris, 18–21 June 2013.

Morgan, K. (2002) 'Forecasting Long Life: How low can human mortality go?' in *Sci. SAGE KE* 2002 (19), nw62.

New Economics Foundation (2013) *The Happy Planet Index*. www.happyplanetindex.org (accessed 7 October 2013).

Offer, A. (2006) *The Challenge of Affluence*. Oxford: Oxford University Press.

Wilkinson, R. (2005) *The Impact of Inequality*. London: Routledge.

Wilkinson, R. and Pickett, K. (2009) *The Spirit Level: Why More Equal Societies Almost Always Do Better*. London: Allen Lane.

Index